IMMIGRATION

THE MACMILLAN COMPANY
NEW YORK · BOSTON · CHICAGO · DALLAS
ATLANTA · SAN FRANCISCO

MACMILLAN & CO., LIMITED
LONDON · BOMBAY · CALCUTTA
MELBOURNE

THE MACMILLAN CO. OF CANADA, LTD.
TORONTO

IMMIGRATION

A WORLD MOVEMENT AND ITS AMERICAN SIGNIFICANCE

BY

HENRY PRATT FAIRCHILD

New York
THE MACMILLAN COMPANY
1913

Set up and electrotyped. Published May, 1913.

Norwood Press
J. S. Cushing Co. — Berwick & Smith Co.
Norwood, Mass., U.S.A.

To

ALBERT GALLOWAY KELLER

INSPIRING TEACHER

CONSTANT FRIEND

PREFACE

In the preparation of this book the author has endeavored to avoid that narrowness of treatment which so easily besets the writer on such a topic as immigration. The effort has been made to regard immigration, not simply as an "American public problem," but as a sociological phenomenon of world-wide significance. While the primary viewpoint is that of a citizen of the United States, several other viewpoints are considered, and regarded as equally valid. It is pointed out that there are a number of interests to be taken into account, aside from those of the native American workman, or even of the American nation as a whole. The immigration question is set forth as a part of an inclusive conservation program for all humanity. The modern situation is placed in its appropriate historical setting. Particularly, it is demonstrated that the popular notion that a belief in restriction is inconsistent with sympathy for the immigrant is false. The restrictionist may be the truest friend of the alien.

At the same time, this book does not profess to be an exhaustive treatise on immigration. To deal with this question exhaustively, as Dr. Leopold Caro has pointed out, is too much of an undertaking for a single man in a lifetime. This is for two reasons. In the first place, the mass of data is too great, involving the intimate history of most of the civilized nations of the world for a period of from half a century to three centuries. In the second place, the subject is highly dynamic. It is a present movement, displaying aspects which are continually changing, and embodying relations which are constantly shifting. The student is prevented by his human limitations from keeping his information up-to-date in every particular.

For these reasons the purely descriptive features of such a book must necessarily be limited in scope and subject to inaccuracy. The writer is constantly constrained to qualify his general statements in the effort to avoid dogmatism or positive error. But the purely descriptive features are, after all, of secondary importance. The fundamental matters are the laws or principles which underlie the great type of population movement which we call immigration, and these are relatively constant and unchanging. It is a knowledge of these principles which fits one to understand the movement in its ever changing aspects, and to grapple with it as a problem of practical politics or sociology. To define and clarify the concepts involved, to set forth clearly the laws and principles, and to point out the opportunities and responsibilities, is the chief aim of this book.

These considerations account for the summary treatment of some topics, and the omission of others. Some aspects of the question may seem to have received more attention, others less, than their relative importance would warrant. Thus the section on crises, exhibiting as it does the intricate relationship between immigration and one of our most important economic problems, also suggests other equally detailed analytical studies which might be made; as, for instance, the relation between immigration and strikes, or child labor, or public education. The discussion of the effect of emigration on the countries of Europe, while dealing with a topic of equal importance with the effects on the United States, is manifestly only suggestive in character. Only such tables have been included as are necessary for illustration or demonstration. The statistical matter on immigration is now so voluminous that it is impracticable to include it in a treatise dealing with the general aspects of the situation in a narrative manner.

Some portions of this book have already appeared in print. The section on crises is practically a reprint of an article entitled "Immigration and Crises," which appeared in the *American Economic Review* for December, 1911. The discussion of the effects of immigration on population reproduces almost *verbatim* an article, "The Paradox of Immigration," which was printed in the *American Journal of Sociology* for September, 1911. An article entitled "Some Immigration Differences," printed in the *Yale Review* for May, 1910, contained matter which has been incorporated in different portions of this book. To the editors of these three journals the author extends his thanks for permission to use this material in the present volume.

The author wishes to acknowledge his indebtedness to Professor Albert G. Keller, Professor Roswell C. McCrea, and Professor Allen Johnson, who have read the manuscript wholly or in part, and have made many helpful suggestions.

H. P. F.

NEW HAVEN, CONNECTICUT,
April 9, 1913.

TABLE OF CONTENTS

IMMIGRATION

CHAPTER I

INTRODUCTION

THE study of immigration is a part of the study of the dispersion of the human race over the surface of the earth, but only one of the most recent parts. The most important population movements by which the habitable portions of the globe became peopled took place long before there was anything which might accurately be styled immigration. The dawn of the historical period found the principal sections of the earth's surface already inhabited by races not widely different from those now native to them.

About the early movements by which man was scattered from his original home to the four corners of the globe we have as yet little definite information. It seems safe to conclude that they must have resembled the instinctive movements of animals more closely than the rational movements of modern man. They must have been gradual, by slow stages, and in immediate response to the demands of the food supply or of the changing climate. Such movements, which may be designated by the term "wandering," were the necessary precursors of the more recent developments. They furnish the background for the historic period, and constitute the original factors in modern relations.

They may be taken for granted, and a detailed knowledge of them is not necessary for an understanding or investigation of such a historic question as immigration.

The word "immigration" is one of those terms which are in common use in everyday speech, and which convey a certain general impression to the hearer, but which need to be given a limited and specific meaning when used in a scientific study. Many vague and erroneous notions about immigration may be traced to the failure of those using the word to form an exact idea of its connotation. Particularly is it necessary to distinguish clearly between immigration and certain other forms of population movements to which the term is frequently applied.

There are three of these forms of movement. They all fall within the historical period, and consequently we have some definite information about them. They may be designated as invasion, conquest, and colonization. These, with immigration, all have this in common, that they are reasoned movements arising after man had progressed far enough in the scale of civilization to have a fixed abiding place. That is, they are definite movements from one place to another. This distinguishes them from what has been called "wandering," and justifies including them in a separate category, to which the general name "migration" may be given. In using this term for this purpose, however, we must rid our minds of the association which it has with the movements of animals and birds. When we speak of the migrations of birds we customarily refer to seasonal changes of location, occurring regularly year by year. They are not cases of a change of home, but of having two homes at the same time.

Man, too, has his seasonal movements. It is a very common practice of primitive men to move from one location to another at different times in the year in the pursuit of food, seeking a certain locality at the time that a particular fruit ripens there, or a certain bird lays its eggs. "The Haida Indians of British Columbia annually voyage as many as 500 miles southward to Puget Sound to lay in a supply of dried clams and oysters for their own consumption and for trade."[1] Many nomadic tribes follow the pasture from the lowlands to the highlands, and from south to north, as the seasons change. Even civilized man, in his highest development, has his seasonal journeyings, from his summer home to his winter home, and back. But none of these comings and goings deserve to be included as true movements of peoples, or to be called migrations in the present sense. Migration involves an actual and permanent change of residence. It thus becomes evident that migrations can occur only in the most rudimentary form among people in the hunting stage; more developed cases may occur among pastoral people, when they change their base of operation, as when the Israelites moved from Canaan into Egypt, and back after several generations; but in its most complete form, migration appears only after man has reached the agricultural stage.

Since man, when he migrates, leaves a fixed home in response to a rational impulse, there must be some definable cause for the migration. There are certain general causes which are found to underlie all migratory movements, and which are worthy of examination. In

[1] Mason, Otis T., "Migration and the Food Quest," *American Anthropologist*, 7 : 279.

the first place we find that the cause of a migratory movement must be a powerful one. Man inevitably becomes attached to the locality in which he finds himself placed. Bonds of many kinds arise to tie him to his home. Among these may be mentioned family connections, sentimental associations, familiar customs and habits of the community, political and religious attachments, business interests, property owned, superstitious veneration for graves. All of these, and others, unite to make the home ties very strong. The life of man is closely bound up with his environment, and a change of environment is a momentous event. As a result, there is a marked inertia, a resistance to pressure, among human beings, and the presumption is that people will stay where they are, unless some positive force causes them to move. And no trivial occasion will suffice.

This force, which results in movement, may be a very complex one, but in general it must present one of two aspects — it must be either attractive or repellent. Men are either drawn or driven to break the ties which bind them to their native locality. The attractive force must, of course, exist in the country which is the objective point, the repellent force, in the existing environment. This distinction is well brought out by Professor Otis T. Mason, who classifies the causes of migration into "positive" — advantages, satisfactions, etc. — and "negative" — discomforts, compulsions, etc.[1] In view of the strength of the "home ties," however, it is evident that the repellent type of forces must be much the more important. It would have to be a very alluring prospect indeed that would lead a man to leave a

[1] Mason, Otis T., "Migration and the Food Quest," *American Anthropologist*, 7 : 275.

spot where he was contented. In fact we can hardly conceive of a man deserting a spot where he was really contented. There must be some dissatisfaction with existing conditions to induce him to take the step. Attractions often operate by inducing dissatisfactions, through comparison. There is no attraction in a foreign region unless it seems superior to the home surroundings. Then the home conditions appear inferior, and there is dissatisfaction. This is what Professor Sumner called a process of idealization.

It may be well, also, to distinguish between the causes and motives of migration. Motives are subjective feelings existing within the individual which inspire his actions. They are the immediate forces which lead to movement, and may be divided into the same two general classes as causes. Causes are objective forces or conditions existing outside of the individual, which react upon him. They may exist in the physical environment or in the human environment, and operate by arousing motives, which in turn are the immediate springs of conduct. Since human nature is everywhere enough alike so that similar causes arouse similar motives, and since motives can hardly arise without some exterior cause, in our search for the origins of migratory movements it will ordinarily be sufficient to examine merely the causes. Thus in almost every case of migration we are justified in looking for some cause of a repellent nature, some dissatisfaction, disability, discontent, hardship, or other disturbing condition.[1]

These discomforts may arise in any of the various

[1] Professor A. G. Keller brings out this point in his unpublished lectures on Colonization, where the causes of emigration are classified under unsatisfactory conditions of environment, either physical or human. He also emphasizes the strength of the home tie in resisting emigration.

interests of human life, and may be classified according to almost any classification which will include those interests. Probably the most satisfactory is the familiar one of Economic, Political, Social, and Religious. The economic causes of migrations are the earliest and by far the most important. They arise in connection with man's efforts to make his living, and concern all interests which are connected with his productive efforts. They are disabilities or handicaps which affect his pursuit of food, clothing, and shelter, as well as the less necessary comforts of life. These are vital interests, and any dissatisfaction connected with them is of great weight with men.

There is a wide variety of economic causes of migration, of which the following may be noted. Permanent natural inhospitableness of soil or climate or scarcity of natural resources may make the struggle for existence a perpetually hard one. Temporary natural calamities, such as drought, famine, flood, extreme seasons, etc., may interrupt the course of an ordinarily tolerable existence. Serious underdevelopment of the industrial arts may make life difficult in a nation by limiting the productive power of its citizens or handicapping them in the struggle for trade. A common economic cause of migration is overpopulation. This means that the population of a region has increased to the point where, under the existing industrial conditions, there are too many people for the supporting power of the soil. In man's struggle with nature for a time an increase in numbers is an advantage. But there comes a point where the ratio between men and land reaches such an equilibrium that any increase in the number of men means a smaller amount of the materials of existence for each one.[1] This results in hardship and dissatisfaction. Many migratory movements, particularly in the case of primitive men, or men on a low stage of culture, may be very simply explained by overpopulation.

Political causes are those connected with the organization of government or the actions of the governing power. In this case the dissatisfaction arises from the failure of the individual or group to secure what is believed to be a rightful share in the control of the government, or in some positive repressive or persecuting measures on the part of the governing body toward some of its citizens. Hence we may look for motives of infringed liberty, lack of freedom, or the feeling of oppression. A bad government may put such handicaps on the entire body of its citizens as to make life unsatisfactory to them.

Where social causes of migration exist, the dissatisfaction arises from some fault in the social organization. Some classes or individuals are subjected to a feeling of inferiority to other classes or individuals. A caste, or aristocratic, organization of society gives certain classes an advantage over others, and makes it impossible for the lower classes to rise to a higher level. In case people living under these conditions learn of another region where advancement is possible, migration may easily ensue.

Religious causes include those cases where restrictions are placed on certain members of the body politic because of their religious beliefs or practices. There may be actual persecution, though this is coming to be some-

[1] Henry George does not appear to recognize this dividing line, but seems to regard an indefinite increase of numbers as bearing with it the possibility of improvement. The opposite view is maintained by Professor Irving Fisher, *Elementary Principles of Economics*, pp. 434 ff.

what rare in modern times. The oppression may manifest itself in various disadvantages, imposed on other interests of life, but which are primarily due to religious differences. The great historical example of this class of causes is found in the case of the Jews.

All of these kinds of causes may overlap, and almost always two or more of them exist in conjunction. Cases where social causes alone account for a migration are rare. They are frequently, however, a contributory factor. The economic causes are by far the most important and universal, though we need frequently to look for other causes back of them. Political maladjustments often express themselves through economic or social disabilities, religious differences through economic and social limitations, etc. In any actual case of migration it is probable that the motives of migration will be due to a complication of causes. This fourfold classification, however, is of great aid in isolating and understanding the underlying forces.

The effects of migratory movements, involving the transference of bodies of people from one region to another, are far-reaching and extremely diversified. They concern both the country of origin and the country of destination. They differ widely in specific cases, so much so that it is scarcely possible to lay down any general rules or conclusions which will be of value. They manifest themselves under three main heads, viz. the density of population, the physical stock, and the customs and institutions, or mores. The most obvious effect, and the one which is commonly assumed to follow any migration, is a decrease in the population of the country of source, and an increase in that of the country of destination. But even this, as will appear hereafter, is not by any means the universal rule. There is commonly some effect on the physical stock of the country receiving the migrants. This effect may vary between wide extremes. Whether the customs and institutions shall be also affected depends upon a variety of circumstances which are likely to make each instance distinctive. There is scarcely one of the vital interests of either country concerned which may not be deeply affected by an important migratory movement. But the factors concerned are so complicated, and so subject to individual variation, that movements which bear a general resemblance may have very diverse effects, and each case must be studied by itself.

As to the routes or channels of migratory movements, it may be said that in general they follow the lines of least resistance, as determined by the combination of all the forces involved. The closer the movement is to a purely natural one, the more it will follow the natural routes marked out by the configuration of the earth. River valleys, such as the Danube in Europe and the Ohio in America, have always been favorite migratory routes. If mountains have to be traversed, the easiest passes will be chosen, such as the Cumberland Gap in the United States. In general, water has been a bond and not a barrier between different lands, and the earliest routes of distant travel were undoubtedly by water. Greece became the source of numerous migratory movements partly because of her extended coast line.[1]

Having thus considered some of the essential features of migration as a whole, it will be well to distinguish further between the four great types of migrations to

[1] Cf. Bryce, James, "Migrations of the Races of Men Considered Historically," *Contemporary Review*, 62 : 128.

which reference has been made. One of the earliest, simplest, and most natural of migratory movements is the invasion. This occurs when a rude people, on a low stage of culture, but with much native physical virility, leaves its location, and overruns the territory of a more highly developed state. It is a movement *en masse*, involving the whole, or a large portion, of the tribe. The tribe acts as a unit, and the end sought is the benefit of the tribe as a tribe, not of any individuals. The forces back of it approach the unconscious and irrational, characteristic of wandering, more closely than in any other form of migration.

The power of the invasion lies in brute force and numbers. It is a case of a lower civilization temporarily overcoming a higher one — temporarily, because the rude virility which enables the invaders to maintain their own customs for a time succumbs eventually to the enervating influence of a civilization to which it is not trained. Civilization in the end proves itself more permanent than barbarism. This result is often furthered by the fact that the physical stock of the higher race is improved by the infusion of new blood from the very foreigners who are attacking it. This effect upon the physical stock may be very profound and lasting, as an invasion customarily involves large numbers of people. But while the invaders may succeed in checking the progress of civilization for a time, they seldom leave any permanent monuments of themselves, either material or institutional. They are not likely to affect the language, religion, or social customs of the invaded nation to an important degree. The mores are more enduring than the racial stock of the people who possess them.

There have been numerous instances of invasions in the history of Europe. In fact, the barbarian invasions are perhaps the most important single factor in the history of that continent during the Dark Ages. An excellent example is furnished by the Goths, particularly by the eastern division of that people. The original home of this people was in East Prussia, near the Baltic and the Vistula, where they were known in Roman days as traders in amber. There were two principal branches, the western or Visigoths, and the eastern or Ostrogoths. Their physical and mental characters were well marked and definite. In physique they were tall, blond, and athletic, in disposition brave and generous, patient under hardship, chaste and affectionate in their family relations. As to their habits of life before their migration, we have no very complete picture. In general, they seem to have been living on the pastoral-agricultural stage. They had no cities or villages, but lived in scattered dwellings upon farms, which they cultivated with the aid of slaves descended from captives. Much of the land was held in common, and upon it were pastured the vast herds of cattle which constituted their chief subsistence. The powers of government were centralized in a king, chosen by popular voice from certain great families. They had progressed far enough in learning to have an alphabet, but had not developed any written literature.

It is evident, then, that the Goths were a settled people, and while the ties which bound them to their home land were not very complex, and they were undoubtedly used to long warlike expeditions, yet there must have been some powerful motives to induce them to leave a land where they had become so well established.

As to the exact nature of these motives, and the causes which lay back of them, there is no accurate record. It is not probable that they were driven out by the pressure of stronger neighbors. "Most likely it was simply the natural increase of their population, aided perhaps by the failure of their harvests or the outbreak of a pestilence, that made them sensible of the poverty of their country, and led them to cast longing eyes towards the richer and more genial lands farther to the south, of which they had heard, and which some of them may have visited."[1] This explanation is admittedly largely based on guess. But it has every element of probability and marks the movement of the Goths as a perfectly typical example of a migration due to economic causes, natural overpopulation, augmented by temporary natural calamity, arousing motives of dissatisfaction through comparison with other seemingly more desirable regions.

Whatever the causes, the Goths determined to move. Uniting with the Gepids, Herules, and some other kindred peoples, they formed a great throng, which moved through what is now western Russia to the shores of the Black Sea and the Sea of Azov. Thence they journeyed westward to the north bank of the Danube. On the way they were joined by other groups of people, of Slavonic race. Their real history may be said to begin about 245 A.D., when they were living near the mouth of the Danube, under the rule of the Ostrogoths. For about twenty years they had been the allies of the Romans, who paid them money to defend their borders from the attacks of other would-be invaders. The

[1] Bradley, H., *The Story of the Goths*, p. 21. Cf. Von Pflugk-Harttung, J., *The Great Migrations*, p. 110.

Roman emperor, Philip the Arab, put an end to this payment, thereby arousing the anger of the Ostrogoths, who crossed the Danube and plundered the Roman provinces. This was the beginning of a long series of invasions extending down into Greece and Asia Minor. Many cities were plundered cruelly and brutally. Fortunately for civilization, however, the Goths had been converted to Christianity in the meantime, so that the army which finally entered and devastated Rome in the year 410 was not the utterly barbarous throng which had started on the journey from northern Europe. Their leader, Alaric, was himself a Christian and did what he could to restrain the natural passions of his followers. Yet in spite of all, the sack of Rome was a cruel and bloodthirsty affair.

It is characteristic of an invasion that over two centuries were consumed in the journey from the old home to Rome, so that no single individual of those who started on the undertaking lived to reach the final destination. For nearly a century and a half after the fall of Rome the Ostrogoths lived in or near Italy. Their fortunes in war fluctuated, and for a time, under Theodoric, they were the masters of the peninsula. Their kindred, the Visigoths, were in the meantime settled in Gaul and Spain. Finally, in the year 553, after repeated reverses, the Ostrogoths retired from Italy to the north, and as a people disappeared from history, leaving scarcely a trace behind. The Franks were never driven from Gaul, but eventually lost their native language and became absorbed in the people whom they had invaded. The Goths " have bequeathed to the world no treasures of literature, no masterpieces of art, no splendid buildings. They have left no conscious impress on the manners or the institutions of any modern European people."[1] Even Gothic architecture has no historic connection with the people whose name it bears.

Other barbarian tribes invaded Europe at about the same time as the Goths, and during the succeeding centuries. One of the most powerful was the Huns, a people of rude culture but great virility, belonging probably to the Mongolic or Tatar stock, who appeared about the fourth century A.D. They were followed by other races from the same general region and belonging to the same great stock, the Avars who arrived about 555, and the Magyars who put in an appearance at the close of the ninth century. The most recent explanation of the migrations of these Asiatic tribes is that their habitat suffered a change of climate from one of those great cycles about which we are beginning to have some information, which resulted in drying up the region, and furnishing a much smaller amount of subsistence than the people had been accustomed to. This is overpopulation, and furnishes another case of that great economic cause.[2] Another powerful Asiatic invader was Timur or Tamerlane, who with his Tatar hordes devastated Asia Minor during the latter part of the fourteenth century.

A conquest is almost the reverse of an invasion. In this case the people of higher culture take the aggressive. It is an overflow of civilization, of manners, of organization, of government,—not to any great extent, of population. Conquest occurs when a well-developed state, full of vigor, sends its armies over the territory of less advanced peoples, imposing its political system upon

[1] Bradley, *op. cit.*, p. 365. See this work for fuller details of the Gothic invasion. Also Von Pflugk-Harttung, *op. cit.*, and Hodgkin, Thomas, *Theodoric the Goth.*

[2] Huntington, Ellsworth, *The Pulse of Asia*, pp. 357, 373, 383.

them, and laying them under tribute, but not slaying the people or destroying their wealth any more than is necessary to secure subjection. It is an enterprise of the state, seeking its own glory and aggrandizement. The movement of population to the conquered territory may be insignificant, and in this, conquest differs from all the other forms of migratory movements. Consequently the effects on the racial stock of the conquered people may be very slight, and in most cases are. The effect on the mores, on the other hand, including the language, may be profound and lasting. Conquest differs from the other forms of migration also in the fact that the motives belong more nearly to the positive, or attractive, group than in any of the others. It is energy, ambition, etc., which lead to conquest rather than fear, cowardice, etc. Many of the individuals who change their residence under conquest are state officials, sent out in the pursuit of their duties to the sovereign, not because of any particular choice of their own.

It scarcely need be said that the great historical example of conquest is Rome. Her policy was to extend her dominion by making outlying tribes realize that it was to their advantage to acknowledge her sway and pay tribute. So long as they did this quietly and regularly, little else was required of them. As far as possible, the native governmental organization was continued, and simply grafted on to the great Roman stock, the native officials being made subordinates in the Roman organization. Roman traders came and went, carrying culture and civilization with them, and exerting a powerful influence on the mores of the provinces, but the permanent movement of people from the central state was comparatively slight. Alexander the Great was a spreader of conquest, though his early death destroyed whatever possibility there may have been of his establishing a permanent empire. The career of the British government in India has many of the characteristics of conquest. Native rajahs are, to a great extent, utilized as officials of the British government, and there is no large migration of people from England to India, save those connected in some way with the government service, or persons engaged in commercial pursuits, who maintain their permanent home in England. But the influence on the mores of the native inhabitants is great.

The third form of migratory movement, which has a particularly close connection with immigration, is colonization. This occurs when a well-established, progressive, and physically vigorous state sends out bodies of citizens, officially as a rule, to settle in certain specified localities. The regions chosen are newly discovered or thinly settled countries, where the native inhabitants are so few, or are on such an inferior stage of culture that they offer but slight resistance to the entrance of the colonists. For while the two previous forms of migration have been warlike, colonization is essentially a peaceful movement. The rivalry for certain favored localities may involve the colonizing power in war with other civilized nations who desire the same thing, but as far as the seizure of the colony itself is concerned, it requires slight military exertion. Colonization, like conquest, is a state enterprise, conducted for the benefit of the state, but differs from it in that its motive is rather the commercial advancement of the state than its military or political aggrandizement. Colonization has often been resorted to, also, when a state has believed itself to be overpopulated, and has aimed directly at improving the condition of its citizens, both those who go and those who are left, — something that is scarcely dreamed of under conquest. Several classifications of colonies have been made. The most satisfactory is that adopted by Professor A. G. Keller, which makes a twofold division into farm and plantation colonies.[1] These differ from each other so much in their essential characteristics that it will be well to examine them separately, before making any further generalizations regarding colonies as a whole.

This classification is based on the typical form of the industrial organization in the colony. As colonies are always new and undeveloped regions, the fundamental industry is always of an extractive nature, almost universally agriculture in some form, though it may be mining or fishing. Practically all important colonies in the history of the movement, however, have been agricultural, so that the above division serves every purpose. In the first place, it must be noted that practically all colonizing nations have been situated in the north temperate zone, and primarily in Europe. Outside of this continent, Phœnicia and China are the sole important representatives. These, with Greece and Rome, made up the colonizing powers of the ancient world. As far as modern colonizing nations are concerned, the question is limited to the countries of Europe.

A farm colony springs up in a region similar to that held by the colonizing state, that is to say, in the temperate zone. Colonies of this class have appeared both north and south of the equator. The requirements are that the conditions of soil and climate be such as to

[1] Keller, A. G., *Colonization*, Ch. I.

make the products of the colony similar to those of the home state, and to render acclimatization either unnecessary or very easy.

Under these conditions, a large movement of population takes place from the home state to the colony, and it is a movement of families. Men find it possible to take their wives and children with them, and a normal population is established in the new land. Agriculture may be taken up according to the methods with which the colonists are familiar in the old country. As land is abundant and cheap, each man will prefer, and will find it possible, to take up a piece of land of his own, and to cultivate it independently, rather than to hire out his services to any other cultivator. Consequently, hired agricultural labor is almost impossible to secure, and each man is compelled to rely on the labor of himself and his family to cultivate his land. As a result, the typical agricultural unit becomes the small holding, occupied and tilled by a single family. The system is further established by the fact that the products of such a region are well adapted to this form of culture. This is the typical "farm" organization which gives its name to this class of colony.

Plantation colonies, on the other hand, arise in regions different in climate from the home state, that is, in tropical or subtropical regions. Here conditions of soil and climate are such that the natural products are of a kind which cannot be raised under home conditions, and hence are luxuries rather than staples. Acclimatization is practically impossible for men, and almost wholly so for women, so that normal family life is precluded for the colonist. Furthermore, as it is impossible for natives of the temperate zone to engage in agricultural labor in the tropics, for physiological reasons, all work of that kind must be performed by the natives, or by other similar races imported for the purpose. As a rule, the natives do not wish to work, and wages are no sufficient inducement. Hence they must be made to work, and slavery, either openly or in one of its disguised forms, appears. Since a very small number of Europeans will suffice to direct the activities of a large number of natives, the movement of population from the home state is small, and we find agriculture in the tropics developing along the line of a large unit, producing a single commodity, and operated by compulsory labor, under conditions of waste and exploitation. This is the typical "plantation."

Thus we see that the social and industrial conditions are diametrically opposed in the two forms of colony. In the farm colony we have a vigorous population, similar in stock to that of the home state, each family tilling its own piece of land, and largely self-supporting. Under such conditions large families are an economic advantage, and population grows rapidly. In the plantation colony the colonists are few and mostly males, who superintend the cultivation of large estates, with the purpose of making as much money as possible and getting back to the home land at the earliest possible moment. As far as the population of the colony is affected, it is mainly by the growth of a body of half-breeds, who are always a troublesome class. Morals are low, and life unhealthy and artificial. In the political interests of the colonies similar distinctions exist. Life in a farm colony tends to develop enterprise, independence, and political and social equality. A feeling of patriotism toward the colony, as distinguished from the home state, inevitably develops. The manifest destiny of the farm colony is to become an independent state, either with a wholly separate government, or with only the most tenuous ties binding it to the home authority. In the plantation colony life develops along an aristocratic groove, with well-defined social and political classes. There is no love on the part of the colonist for the colony as such, and no body of local feeling grows up among the colonists. This development is furthered by the customary action of the central government, which regards the farm colony as of little importance because of the similarity between its products and her own, but devotes an enormous attention to the plantation colony because of the apparent importance of its unique products. Hence the farm colony is left free to develop along natural lines, while the plantation colony is subjected to all sorts of artificial restrictions and limitations which hamper its growth. As a result of all these factors, the plantation colony seldom achieves its independence, but remains subject to the home state indefinitely. Examples of farm colonies are the Thirteen Colonies, Canada, New Zealand, etc.; of plantation colonies, Java, Jamaica, Brazil under the Portuguese, etc. As will be seen, the farm colony has a peculiarly intimate relation with immigration movements.

This preliminary survey of the earlier forms of migration prepares the way for a clear understanding of the characteristic features of the fourth form. This is immigration, which in many respects differs from any other population movement. These distinctions merit emphasis.

In the first place, both of the two states concerned in an immigration movement are well established, and on approximately the same stage of civilization. Immigration can take place only over what Professor Sumner calls a single culture-area. Secondly, immigration is a distinctly individual undertaking. States may direct, control, regulate, or encourage immigration, but the motives which lead men into this form of movement are strictly individual ones, and the causes which arouse these motives are conditions which react upon the individual alone. The end sought is neither the advantage of the country of origin, nor of the country of destination, but the improvement of the condition of the individual.

The two countries concerned in an immigration movement resemble each other not only in the stage of culture but in climatic conditions and circumstances of life. There has never been any immigration between the temperate zones and the tropics, in either direction, nor have the polar regions ever figured. In fact, practically all immigration, historically speaking, has been between different countries in the temperate zone. But while there are these resemblances between the countries concerned, there must also always be some differences, otherwise there would be no motive for movement. The first and primary difference between the two countries is that the one which receives the stream of immigration is newer, and therefore much less thickly settled, than the other. Other things being equal, the chances for a comfortable living are greater in a country where the ratio between men and land is still low. This ratio between men and land is of extreme importance, and ought never to be neglected in the discussion of any sociological or economic problem.[1] It is especially vital as regards migrations, which are so directly connected with the shifting of populations.

[1] Sumner, W. G., *War and Other Essays*, "Sociology."

Other differences which may be looked for between the two countries concerned in an immigration movement are the following: the country of destination is more democratic than the other, and its people enjoy greater social and political equality; there is more of individual freedom of conduct, and fewer traditional or legal restraints; military burdens are lighter, and there is greater latitude for religious belief and practice. On the other hand, life in the new country is likely to be more arduous, industry more insistent, the demands for personal ability more urgent. These features at once suggest those typical of the farm colony, and in point of fact we find that practically all countries which receive large streams of immigrants are developed farm colonies. These are, at the present time, the United States, Canada, Argentina, Australia, South Africa, and to a certain extent parts of Asiatic Russia.

The requirements, then, for an immigration movement are the following: two well-developed countries, one old and densely populated, the other new and thinly settled, the two on friendly, or at least peaceable, terms with each other. For immigration, even more than colonization, is a phenomenon of peace. On the part of the people who are to take part in the movement a high degree of civilization is demanded. They must be trained to act on individual initiative, and must have sufficient personal enterprise to undertake a weighty venture without an official or state backing. They must have sufficient intelligence to know about the objective point, and sufficient accumulated capital to enable them to get there. There must be adequate, easy, and inexpensive means of transportation between the two countries, in order to enable any large number of people to make the journey. The immigrant is not in any sense an adventurer or explorer. On the part of the nations concerned there must be a willingness to allow individuals to come and go at their own pleasure, without any extreme restrictions or regulations. There must be nothing of the old idea of the feudal bond between the person and the land.

From the above it appears that immigration must be distinctly a modern movement. Scarcely one of the foregoing requirements — not to speak of the conjunction of all of them — is more than three or four centuries old. Consequently immigration, in the sense in which we have defined it, has existed only for a comparatively short time, practically since the Discoveries Period. Moreover, it seems likely to be a purely temporary phenomenon. With the disappearance of the conditions which differentiate the countries which are now receiving immigrants from the older European countries, it seems probable that immigration will cease, for as far as the human eye can see, there will be no new lands to be opened up for the purpose.

In addition to these four chief forms of migration, there are certain other less important forms of which mention should be made to avoid any confusion. First among these stands what may be called forced migration. This occurs when bodies of people, for any reason, without any choice of their own, are compelled to leave a certain region, and go elsewhere, either with or without a specific destination. A familiar example is that presented by the Jews, who were expelled from England in 1290, from France in 1395, and from Spain and Portugal in 1492 and 1495. The Moors were also expelled from Spain in 1609, on penalty of death. Another familiar example is that of the Huguenots, who were expelled from France at the end of the seventeenth century. Such movements as these have usually resulted in a nation's losing the most valuable elements of its population. The cause has usually been religious.

A different type of forced migration has been exemplified in the slave trade. In this case the migrants are compelled by actual force to go from one region to another specified one. The movement of the Africans to America is a familiar example. The motive is the economic one of securing a supply of labor at a minimum expense. Still another type is furnished by the penal colonies, such as have been established in Australia and elsewhere. All these forms of forced migration are evidently different in principle and in most of their characteristics from the great types of migration which have been mentioned. Their study is a subject by itself.

Still another form of migration is what is known as the internal or intra-state migration. This is manifestly going on all the time in every civilized country. It is only when it involves large masses of people, moving in certain well-defined directions, with a community of motives and purposes, that it deserves to be classed with the great population movements. Then it may become of great interest and significance, as in the case of the great westward movement of the people of the United States. It is evidently a wholly different matter from the other forms which have been emphasized.

There is, of course, also a continual passage of individuals between all the nations of the earth, in every direction. A permanent change of residence is frequently involved. These movements, obviously, may not correspond to any of the principles which have been laid down for any specific form of migration, and, if they were sufficiently numerous, would constitute exceptions to all that has been said. In point of fact, they are isolated, scattered, and occasional. They do not rank in any sense as movements of peoples, nor do they complicate the discussion of the great sociological phenomena in which we are interested.

CHAPTER II

THE UNITED STATES. COLONIAL PERIOD

In taking up the special study of immigration, it is necessary to bear in mind at the outset that the word is to be used in a limited and semitechnical sense. It is not always so used in common speech nor even in scientific writings, and much confusion and inaccuracy not infrequently result. Let us state once more exactly what is meant by immigration. Immigration is a movement of people, individually or in families, acting on their own personal initiative and responsibility, without official support or compulsion, passing from one well-developed country (usually old and thickly settled) to another well-developed[1] country (usually new and sparsely populated) with the intention of residing there permanently. The same movement may equally well be referred to as emigration. It is obviously only a question of the point of view. The two words may be used interchangeably without danger of confusion, if the point of view is regarded. There is only one movement, and one set of people, emigrating from one country and immigrating to another.[2]

[1] Well developed, of course, in the sense of culture, not in the exploitation of natural resources.

[2] There has not only been much looseness and ambiguity in the use of the word "immigration," but also an apparent feeling that immigration and emigration are two different things, as is witnessed by the title of one of the standard works on the subject. They are, in fact, only two different ways of looking at the same thing. As so often happens in the social sciences, the student of immigration is under the necessity of taking a word from the common language, and

As observed in the foregoing chapter, immigration is a movement which could not have originated before the Discoveries Period, and did not, in fact, become a matter of much importance until a century or so later. The countries which are now the objective points of large streams of immigration are, without exception, countries which have been opened up since that epoch. An exhaustive study of immigration should take up each of these countries in turn, and examine conditions in Canada, Argentina, South Africa, Australasia, and the United States. The plan of the present volume does not include so exhaustive a treatment; it is intended primarily for American readers. The specific study of immigration will be limited to the United States. This is the more justifiable, inasmuch as the United States is, beyond comparison, the foremost country in immigration movements, both in point of numbers and of world interest. All the fundamental principles of immigration are exemplified here more fully than in any other country. To the citizen of the United States it is a matter of the greatest importance and interest, for it has to do with a unique subject — the make-up of the American people itself.

The history of immigration into the United States may for convenience be divided into five periods. The first of these includes the time between the first settlement of the North American colonies and the year 1783. This date is chosen for the end of this first period because, as Professor Mayo-Smith has expressed it, "At that time the state was established, and any further additions to the population had little influence in changing its form

giving it a more restricted and inflexible meaning than either everyday usage or the etymology of the word would warrant.

or the language and customs of the people."[1] The second period, from 1783 to 1820, marks the beginning of national life. It was a period of small immigration, and closes with the year in which federal statistics were first collected in regard to the stream of immigration. The third period begins in 1820 and ends roughly about 1860. This period is marked by the beginning and culmination of the first great rise in the immigration stream, by a growing opposition to the immigrant, and by state control of the admission of aliens. The period from 1860 to 1882 begins with the Civil War agitation, witnesses the disappearance of state control, and closes with the year in which the first immigration law was passed by the federal government. The fifth, or modern, period is from 1882 to the present. Other features which distinguish and separate these periods will manifest themselves as the periods are examined more closely.

It is customary with some writers, as, for instance, Professor Mayo-Smith in the reference above quoted, to include all movements of people into the North American colonies, previous to the Revolution, under the head of colonization, and to call everything after the beginning of national life immigration. The second part of this classification accords with the definitions given above, but the first part does not. For it will be remembered that colonization refers to movements of people from a central state to its dependencies, while immigration is a movement from the territory of one nation to that of another. The fact that the receiving region is itself a colony does not alter the case. Hence, in so far as the people who came to the North American colonies in the early days came from a state to which the region

[1] Mayo-Smith, R., *Emigration and Immigration*, p. 36.

where they were going was subject, they were true colonists. They were simply going from one part of a national territory to another. But all who came from any European state to a dependency of another state — and there were a goodly number of them — were immigrants. Thus, even in colonial days, there were both colonization and immigration.

In establishing this distinction it must be noted that while the colonies were undeveloped as regards their natural resources, they were highly developed in respect to their stage of civilization and their advancement in the arts. In this respect they were the peers of the most cultivated European states of the period. The factors which gave a primitive aspect to life in the colonies were due to the newness of the settlement and the sparseness of the population. These were, in turn, just the factors which made them desirable to immigrants and colonists alike.

The truth of this position is further established by the fact that this distinction was clearly recognized by the early settlers themselves. A very different attitude was manifested in the colonies toward persons who came from the home state than toward those from any other country. The former were generally welcomed; the latter were regarded with suspicion, if not actual hostility. The history of immigration to the North American continent reaches far back toward the days of the earliest settlement, and many of the characteristic problems and arguments connected with the immigration situation were familiar long before the Revolution. A familiarity with these early aspects of the question furnishes many enlightening comparisons and parallels, and is of great value in correctly estimating the modern situation.

The peopling of the North American continent by persons of north European stock began with the formation by James I of England of two companies of settlement in the year 1606. These were known as the London Company and the Plymouth Company. To the former was granted the territory on the North American coast between 34 and 38 degrees north latitude, though these boundaries were somewhat extended in 1609. To the latter was assigned the region from 41 to 45 degrees. This left a section of unassigned territory between, extending from the Rappahannock to the Hudson rivers. This was open to settlement by either company, with the stipulation that neither was to plant a settlement within one hundred miles of a previous settlement of the other. Neither of these companies, however, ever made any very extensive achievements in colonization, and both gave up their charters in the course of a few years, the London Company in 1624 and the other in 1635.

Before the charters were surrendered, however, settlements had been started in both territories. In Virginia, the province of the London Company, the first shipload of adventurers from London arrived in the year 1607. But twelve years of hard and painful struggle were required to establish this settlement as a permanent and self-maintaining colony. It is interesting to note that at this time, and in this place, one of the greatest of our national racial problems had its commencement, through the introduction of a number of African slaves from a Dutch vessel in 1619. The settlers in this region were, in part, adventurers, younger sons of noble families, and other members of the aristocracy who found it advisable to leave England, and in part rather unworthy representatives of the lower classes. A combination of political, social, and economic causes was responsible for their coming.

The settlers of the northern colony, in the territory of the Plymouth Company, were of a different class of the population. Their motives for coming were also different, being primarily of a religious character. These colonists were separatists from the Church of England, who fled first to Holland, and from there came to America in 1620, landing in what is now Plymouth, Massachusetts. In this colony, also, the process of settlement was slow, and there were very few arrivals for ten years. In 1630, however, about one thousand colonists, Puritans but not separatists, came over, and settled in Massachusetts Bay. This was the real beginning of the history of the Massachusetts colony, which in time absorbed also the Plymouth colony. Once started, population in this colony advanced very rapidly, and overflowed into the neighboring regions, forming the colonies of Rhode Island, New Hampshire, and the river towns of Connecticut.

In the meantime the Dutch were taking possession of the unassigned central region. New Netherland was organized under the Dutch West India Company in 1621, and the city at the mouth of the Hudson was named New Amsterdam. Sweden, too, was trying to get a foothold in the new country and sent a party of colonists to Delaware Bay in 1638. This was not successful, however, and surrendered to the Dutch in 1655, so that Sweden never achieved prominence as a colonizing power in the New World. With the growth of the English colonies in the north and south, this central territory in the hands of a foreign power came to be recognized as a source of annoyance and danger, and on the occasion of a war with Holland, England sent over a fleet and took possession of the whole intervening region, forming the colonies of New York and New Jersey. In 1681 the territory of Pennsylvania was granted for settlement to William Penn, and thus the whole Atlantic coast from Canada to Florida became a field of colonization, subject to the English authority.

The study of the formation of the American people as a separate nation is of peculiar interest, because it has taken place within a recent historical period, and we can study the original elements from the time when they first settled in the country. This is not true of any of the nations of Europe.

The foundation of the new people consisted of colonists from England. They were the original settlers, and during the entire colonial period they continued to contribute to the growing population. In addition to these there was the Dutch element, which became well established when New York was a Dutch colony. Aside from the colonists, there was a large and important contribution from other European nations, people from practically every country on the continent. These were the true immigrants. The colonies which were most affected by arrivals of this sort were the central ones, particularly New York and Pennsylvania, and above all the latter. This was due to their location, the attitude of their proprietors, and the feeling and conduct of the original settlers. The attitude of William Penn was decidedly liberal, and Pennsylvania advanced in population accordingly. Penn advertised his colony widely, and when he came over in 1682 there were already six thousand Swedish, Dutch, and English settlers there. Other came rapidly, prominent among them English Quakers, Scottish and Irish Presbyterians, German Mennonites, and French Huguenots. These religious designations are significant of the preponderance of the religious element in the immigration of the day.

Throughout the colonial period this class of causes was an underlying factor in most of the important migrations to America, both colonization and immigration. The Protestant Reformation, and the intellectual and social movements which went with it, had a profound effect upon the contentment of large masses of the people of Europe, and made that continent a very undesirable place of residence for many of them. That political causes should have been closely combined with the religious ones was inevitable, on account of the intimate relation between religion and government, and the practice of using political power to secure religious ends, and *vice versa*. These two classes of causes were the prevailing and characteristic ones during this period.

The religious tolerance and freedom which characterized Pennsylvania was therefore one of the chief factors which drew immigrants of every nationality to it, and it quickly became the most cosmopolitan of all the colonies. Penn's agents were particularly active in Germany, with the result that in twenty years the Germans numbered nearly one half the population of the colony.

With the beginning of the eighteenth century two currents of immigration rapidly outdistanced all others in numbers, importance, and the amount of attention which they attracted. These were the Palatines and the Scotch-Irish. Throughout the rest of the colonial period they held the center of the stage in the immigration situation.

The Palatines were so called because their original home was in what was known as the Palatinate. This was a section of Germany lying on both sides of the Rhine from Cologne to Mannheim. It was divided into two parts, the upper and the lower, from the latter of which most of the immigration came. The position of this country brought it into close relations with the spirit of the Reformation, and large bodies of the population became Protestant, both Reformed and Lutheran. The rulers of the Palatinate, the Electors Palatine, swung back and forth between Lutheranism, Calvinism, and Roman Catholicism, and since each successive ruler wished his subjects to conform to his religious views, the miserable people suffered accordingly. Both of the two great wars between 1684 and 1713, the War of the Grand Alliance and the War of the Spanish Succession, had borne heavily on the Palatinate, which had long been the object of Louis XIV's most covetous desire. The second ruthless devastation which the country experienced during the latter of these wars reduced the people to the lowest pitch of misery and desperation. Meanwhile their ruler, John William, was trying to force the whole of the people back into Catholicism. "To the people already suffering from the intolerable hardships which the cruelest of wars had thrust upon them, this persecuting spirit of their prince came as the last impulse to break off their attachment to the fatherland and send them to make new homes in distant America." Thus began the great exodus, from a combination of political and religious causes, in entire harmony with the spirit of the age.

The Elector Palatine resisted the emigration, and adopted various measures to check it, among them an edict threatening death to all who should attempt to emigrate. As usual, such efforts were powerless to check a natural movement. The first detachment to leave was apparently a small band which, after many wanderings, settled in New Jersey in 1707. In 1708 a small company came to London and asked to be sent to America. They were sent to New York at public expense, and were furnished with farm implements; nevertheless, they fell into want and had to be aided by the colonial council. The next year about thirteen thousand Palatines arrived in London by way of Rotterdam. They were, for the most part, absolutely penniless, and in rags. England responded nobly to the burden thus cast upon her. Queen Anne allowed ninepence per day each for their subsistence, and they were housed in army tents set up in vacant lots, and in barns and warehouses. This piece of benevolence is said to have cost England, in public and private expenditures, the sum of £135,000. Some of these refugees were sent to Ireland, but large numbers of them eventually found their way to America. A large shipment arrived in the Carolinas in 1709.

The largest detachment, however, was a body of three thousand who arrived in New York, from England, in the early summer of 1710. This is said to have been the largest body of immigrants to have arrived in this country at one time during the colonial period. They have been characterized as perhaps the most miserable and most hopeful set of people ever set down on our shores. In spite of their poverty, they manifested a stern and determined spirit in their fight for their faith and home. To the shame of the New York colonists, it is recorded that they were welcomed with privation, distress, fraud, and cruel disappointment. They were cheated and oppressed by the heartless and rapacious settlers, to whom their helplessness made them easy victims. It was by such practices as these that New York diverted many streams of immigration from her territory to that of her neighbors, particularly Pennsylvania.[1]

The second great stream of immigration during the colonial period was composed of the Scotch-Irish, who were for a long time called merely "Irish." Neither name denominates them accurately, as, in the words of Professor Commons, they "are very little Scotch and much less Irish."[2] They are in fact the most composite of all the people of the British Isles, being a mixture of the primitive Scot and Pict, the primitive Briton and Irish, and a larger admixture of Norwegian, Dane, Saxon, and Angle. They were called Scots because they lived originally in Scotia, and Irish because they moved to Ireland.

James the First resolved to make Catholic Ireland a Protestant country, and with this in view dispossessed the native chiefs in Ulster, giving their lands to Scottish and English lords on condition that they settle the territory with tenants from Scotland and England. Thus about 1610 many people from Scotia moved to Ulster, and from that time on were called Irish, though there was only a slight trace of Irish blood in their veins. It was nearly a century later that conditions arose which began to predispose them to emigration in large numbers. In 1698, on the complaint, from English manufacturers, of Irish competition, the Irish Parliament, a tool of the

[1] Cobb, S. H., *The Story of the Palatines*. Cf., also, Faust, A. B., *The German Element in the United States*, Chs. II, III, IV; Bittinger, Lucy F., *The Germans in Colonial Times*, pp. 12–19; Proper, E. E., *Colonial Immigration Laws*, Columbia College Studies, Vol. 12, No. 2, pp. 40–42.

[2] Commons, J. R., *Races and Immigrants in America*, p. 32.

British crown, passed an act totally forbidding the exportation of Irish woolens, and another act forbidding the exportation of Irish wool to any country save England. The linen industry was also discriminated against. These acts nearly destroyed the industry of Ulster, and aroused great discontent. Next the people were compelled to take the communion of the established church in order to hold office, which practically deprived them of self-government, as they were unwilling to renounce their native Presbyterianism for political ends. Soon after, their hundred-year leases began to run out, and when the land was auctioned off the low-living Irish could offer higher rents than they, and consequently they lost much of their land. The ensuing large emigration was thus the result of dissatisfaction due to an interesting combination of economic, political, and religious causes.

It is said that in 1718 forty-two hundred of the Scotch-Irish left for America, and that after the famine of 1740 there were twelve thousand who departed annually. In the half century preceding the American Revolution, one hundred fifty thousand or more came to America. They were by far the largest contribution of any foreign race to the people of America during the eighteenth century, and constituted a strong element in the army at the time of the Revolution.

At the time of the arrival of the Scotch-Irish in America, the lands along the Atlantic coast were already well occupied, and they were compelled to move on into the interior. The traditional religious exclusiveness of Massachusetts and the well-settled character of the country prevented them from settling in the eastern portions of that colony. Consequently they chose as their destination New Hampshire, Vermont, western Massachusetts, and Maine, and most of all Pennsylvania and the foothill regions of Virginia and the Carolinas. They were by nature typical pioneers, and gradually pushed their way into western Pennsylvania, Ohio, Kentucky, and Tennessee. They were the one race sufficiently unified, endowed with the spirit of liberty, and scattered throughout the colonies, to serve as the amalgamating force binding all the other races into one — the American type.[1]

During the whole of the eighteenth century, up to the time of the Revolution, representatives of these two races continued to arrive in increasing numbers. The Palatines, though less numerous than the Scotch-Irish, seem to have attracted more attention. The general attitude of the colonists toward these immigrants was one of welcome, or at the least of toleration. This was natural under the conditions of the time. It must ever be borne in mind that the distinguishing feature of the situation in this country during the colonial period was a superabundance of fertile soil, rich in a variety of natural resources, and a scarcity of men. That is, the ratio between men and land was low. Hence there was a great demand for settlers, and newcomers were believed to be, and were, an asset to the community. A certain degree of rivalry and jealousy between the colonies, leading them to covet a rapid increase in population, contributed to this sentiment.

At the same time, there can be no doubt that there was a decided preference for colonists over immigrants.

[1] Cf., especially, Commons, *op. cit.*, pp. 31–38. Also Hanna, Charles A., *The Scotch-Irish*, esp. Vol. II, pp. 172–180; Green, S. S., *The Scotch-Irish in America;* MacLean, J. P., *Settlements of Scotch Highlanders in America*, pp. 40–61.

This was partly due to a natural race prejudice, but it was augmented by the character of the immigrants at that time. Considering the nature of the conditions which led to emigration from both Ireland and Germany, it is not surprising that a majority of the newcomers were characterized by extreme destitution. As might also be expected from the frightful shipping conditions which then existed, many of them arrived in wretched condition physically. The voyage was long, the ships were small, poorly ventilated, shockingly overcrowded, and totally unprovided with adequate provisions for sanitation, cleanliness, and culinary facilities. It seems to have been the expected thing that a large part of every shipload of immigrants, particularly of the Palatines, should arrive in a prostrated condition.

There is a record of one ship which made the voyage in 1731 on which there was such a scarcity of food provided for the passengers that they "had to live on rats and mice, which were considered dainties. The price on board for a rat was eighteen pence, and for a mouse an English sixpence. The captain was under the impression that the passengers had considerable money and valuables with them, and, believing that he might profit by it, he endeavored to reduce them to a state of starvation. He succeeded too well, for out of the 156 passengers only 48 reached America." [1]

These wretched victims were of course thrown upon the mercy of the citizens of the colony in which they landed; Pennsylvania, and particularly Philadelphia, were especially subject to visitations of this kind. The generosity with which these unfortunates were cared for

[1] Kapp, F., *Immigration and the Commissioners of Emigration of the State of New York*, p. 21.

in this colony is remarkable. Nevertheless, the burden was a heavy one, and the opposition which arose to the free admission of this class of persons is not to be wondered at. A new country, struggling to subdue the wilderness and to establish economic independence, welcomes hardy and industrious laborers, even though they bring little capital with them. If the poverty of the immigrant is due to no fault of his own, and is offset by a sound body and a determined spirit of industry, there is every hope that the influence of the new environment may set him permanently on his feet. But an influx of people so deficient in moral or physical stamina as to promise nothing, save an additional burden on the already strained resources of the community, is naturally and justly viewed with alarm. Very many of the immigrants of this period belonged to this type.

As suggested above, the low physical and economic state of many of the immigrants was due to the conditions and experiences attending the passage from the old country to the new. Many an immigrant who was hale and able-bodied when he started on the voyage was a physical wreck when he landed. Many others who were relatively well-off economically on leaving home arrived penniless. It was the practice of the "importers" to compel passengers who had means to settle the accounts of those who had not, and thus, it is stated, many who had been well-to-do were reduced to house-to-house beggary.[1] But many other of the immigrants were hopelessly destitute when they started. Still others were criminals. It was the practice of European nations at this time to empty not only their almshouses, but their jails, into their own colonies, or those of other nations.

[1] Pennsylvania Colonial Records, 6:385.

Thus many of the colonists, as well as of the immigrants, belonged to the pauper and criminal classes.[1]

This action of European states was naturally bitterly complained of by the colonies. But as long as they were colonies, and had no independent standing, it could be little more than a complaint.[2] After the War of the Revolution it became a matter of international relations, and, as will appear later, attracted no little attention.

Pennsylvania, being the destination of the largest number of immigrants, suffered most from troubles of this sort. Consequently, in this colony we find the most powerful body of opinion contrary to the free admission of aliens, and the most frequent and stringent measures to control it. Many of the stock arguments against immigration on the grounds of pauperism, criminality, and inability for self-support developed during this period.

One of the earliest Pennsylvania statutes covering this ground was an act passed in 1722, imposing a tax on every criminal landed, and making the shipowner responsible for the good conduct of his passengers.[3] This was followed by numerous other laws designed to help control the immigration situation. One of the most important of these was the act of September 21, 1727, which was passed at the suggestion of the colonial governor, who feared that the peace and security of the prov-

[1] Early examples of this practice are furnished by Holland, which in 1655 sent out large numbers of orphan boys and girls from its asylums. The action in this case was less grievous, however, as they were apparently bound out to service for a term of four years, so that they did not at once come on the community. Documents relating to the Colonial History of New York, 14: 166, 264, etc.

[2] Cf. Proper, E. E., *op. cit.*, pp. 19, 20.

[3] Diffenderffer, F. R., *German Immigration into Pennsylvania through Philadelphia*, p. 143.

ince was endangered by so many foreigners coming in, ignorant of the language, settling together and making, as it were, a separate people. This is one of the earliest instances of the use of the nonassimilation argument in connection with immigration legislation. The act in question provided that shipmasters bringing immigrants must declare whether they had permission from the court of Great Britain to do so, and must give lists of all passengers and their intentions in coming. The immigrants must take the oath of allegiance to the king, and of fidelity to the Proprietary of the Province. On the day the act was passed, an agreement was signed by 109 persons, representing about four hundred immigrants, who had arrived at the port and were waiting to be landed. A pathetic touch is given to the incident by the naïve statement, "Sundry of these forreigners lying sick on board, never came to be qualified."

This act remained in force for some time, but appears to have been more or less of a dead letter, for the shipmasters never seem to have had any license to bring immigrants, and yet the latter were always admitted.[1] This law was slightly modified in 1729, and a tax of forty shillings was laid on each immigrant. This is an early instance of the use of a head tax as a restrictive measure, for among the reasons assigned for its passage we find mention of the necessity "to discourage the great importation and coming in of foreigners and of lewd, idle, and ill-affected persons into this province, as well from parts beyond the seas as from the neighboring colonies," whereby the safety and quiet of the province are endangered, many of them becoming a great

[1] Pennsylvania Colonial Records, 2: 282 ff.

burden upon the community. It was asserted that shipmasters resorted to deceitful methods in the furtherance of the practice of bringing in convicts.[1] This accusation was substantiated by an event which occurred a short time previously, when "a vessel arrived at Annapolis with 66 indentures, signed by the Mayor of Dublin, and 22 wigs to disguise the convicts when they landed." [2] The provision imposing a head tax of forty shillings was repealed within a very few months.[3]

Through the discussions of this matter can be traced a frequent conflict of opinion between the colonial governor and the assembly. The former, representing the interests of the Proprietary, was inclined to welcome anything which tended to increase the population of the colony at whatever cost. The latter, representing the people, is concerned for the character of the settlers and the financial welfare of the colony.[4] This is well illustrated by the progress of the effort to secure an immigrant hospital in Philadelphia. The erection of such a building had been recommended to the assembly by Governor George Thomas as early as 1740, in the interests of humanity. But the house demurred on the ground of expense, and several years of haggling passed before a pest-house was finally erected. In the meantime much difficulty was experienced with "sickly vessels," and a law was passed requiring all ships to anchor a mile from the city, until inspected by the port physician. If sick passengers were found on board, the shipmaster was required to land them at a suitable distance

[1] Diffenderffer, *op. cit.*, pp. 51–53.

[2] *Ibid.*, p. 53, quoted from Watson's *Annals of Philadelphia*, 2 : 266–7.

[3] Proper, *op. cit.*, p. 50.

[4] The action of the governor in recommending the passage of the act of 1727 is exceptional.

from the city and convey them at his own expense to houses in the country prepared for them.[1]

The house, on its part, made vain attempts for a period of fifteen years or more to get a bill passed which should check the overcrowding of immigrants in ships. The ostensible reasons urged were mainly those of humanity, and they rested on an ample basis. The degree of overcrowding was frightful. It was stated that in many cases the chests of apparel belonging to immigrants were shipped in other vessels to make more room for passengers, so that the immigrants had no chance even to change their clothes during the long voyage of sometimes sixty days.[2] But underlying this there was undoubtedly the desire to reduce the number of immigrants. It was represented that whereas the German importations were at first of good class, people of substance, now they were the refuse of the country, and that "the very goals [*sic*] have contributed to the Supplies we are burdened with."

In the southern colonies we find much the same attitude of welcome to respectable settlers, and fear of criminals and paupers, with this difference, that as immigration was slower into these colonies, more active measures were occasionally taken by the colonies themselves to encourage it. Thus in 1669 North Carolina passed a law exempting new settlers from levies for one year, and from action for debt for five years. But they were debarred from holding office for three years.[3]

Maryland early experienced difficulties with imported

[1] Pennsylvania Colonial Records, 4: 516.

[2] William Penn in his day reckoned the average voyage at between six and nine weeks, though voyages sometimes took four months. Diffenderffer, *op. cit.*, pp. 29, 62.

[3] North Carolina Colonial Documents, 25: 120.

criminals. On account of the practice, which appears to have been common, of importing notorious criminals, the general assembly of this province in 1676 passed an act requiring all shipmasters to declare whether they had any convicts on board. If so, they were not to be allowed to land in the province. Any person presuming to import such convicts must pay a fine of 2000 pounds of tobacco, half to go to the Proprietary and half to the informer.[1] On December 9 of the same year the lieutenant governor issued a proclamation requiring all shipmasters who had landed convicts previous to this act going into effect to deposit a bond of £50 for their good behavior. Any landed without this bond were to be put in prison until the bond was paid.[2] This is one of the earliest instances of bonding shippers for the good conduct of their passengers.

On the other hand, settlers of good character were regarded as very valuable acquisitions, and measures were adopted from time to time to encourage their immigration.[3]

In New England the immigration question was less pressing than in either the central or southern colonies. There was less need of passing direct restrictive measures,[4] because the religious exclusiveness of this section kept away many who might otherwise have come. And there was little necessity of encouraging immigration,

[1] Archives of Maryland, 2 : 540. [2] *Ibid.*, 15 : 36.

[3] See, for instance, Archives of Maryland, 13 : 440 and 19 : 183.

[4] Yet in 1700 Massachusetts passed an elaborate immigration law, requiring shipmasters to furnish lists of their passengers, and prohibiting the introduction of lame, impotent, or infirm persons, or those incapable of maintaining themselves, except on security that the town should not become charged with them. In the absence of this security, shipmasters were compelled to take them back home. This statute was reënacted with amendments from time to time. Proper, *op. cit.*, pp. 29, 3.

as the natural increase of the population was sufficient to maintain an adequate number of inhabitants. In fact, the influx of population from Europe to New England was practically over by the middle of the seventeenth century. It is stated that from 1628 to 1641 about twenty thousand English came as permanent colonists to New England, and for the next century and a half more went from there to England than came from England there.[1] As a result of these conditions, the population of this region was much less mixed than in the other colonies. Nevertheless, it was a prolific and growing population, and "overflowed into the other colonies, without receiving corresponding additions from them."[2]

In spite of this fact, however, a certain jealousy was felt toward Pennsylvania, on account of the large number of foreigners who sought her shores. This feeling was expressed by Dr. Jonathan Mayhew in his election sermon before the governor and legislature of Massachusetts in 1754. While he surmised that Pennsylvania might in time experience some inconvenience from too large numbers of unassimilated Germans, yet he attributed much of her growth and prosperity to their presence. He was assured that the English element in Massachusetts was already too well established for there to be any fear of too great an admixture of alien elements, and expressed the opinion that all measures to encourage the immigration of foreign Protestants were to be favored.[3]

New York frankly shared this jealousy of Pennsylvania, and, when it was too late, made efforts to attract

[1] *Commercial Relations of the United States*, 1885–1886, Appendix III, p. 1967.

[2] Hall, Prescott F., *Immigration*, p. 4.

[3] *Mass. Election Sermons*, 1754, pp. 30, 48.

immigrants to her territory. Thus in 1736 Governor Clarke caused to be widely circulated in Germany an advertisement in which he proposed to give 500 acres of land to each of the first two hundred families who should come to New York from Europe. The measure met with no great success.[1] Possibly the treatment accorded to the would-be settlers of a generation earlier still lingered in the memory of their fellow-countrymen.

In addition to the legislation against paupers and criminals, most of the colonies had laws designed to prevent the entrance of religious sects who were not regarded with favor. The class most discriminated against was the Roman Catholics, and the eighteenth century found harsh statutes against them in the legislation of most of the colonies.[2] Virginia, and all the New England colonies except Rhode Island, had laws designed to prevent the coming in of Quakers.[3] Rhode Island resembled Pennsylvania in the religious tolerance which prevailed there.[4] Maryland started on the basis of religious toleration, but did not maintain this position.[5] A prejudice against Roman Catholics soon manifested itself, and occasionally found expression in legislation. Thus in the Maryland statutes for 1699 there is an act entitled, "An act for Raising a Supply towards the defraying of the Publick Charge of this Province and to prevent too great a number of Irish Papists being imported into this Province." The provisions of the act required shipmasters to pay twenty shillings per poll for all Irish servants imported, as well as for negroes.[6] None of these acts, of course, was absolutely prohibitive.

[1] Doc. Col. Hist. of N. Y., 6 : 60.

[2] Proper, E. E., *op. cit.*, p. 13.

[3] *Ibid.*, pp 25, 63.

[4] *Ibid.*, p. 36.

[5] *Ibid.*, pp. 13, 57, 62.

[6] Archives of Maryland, 22 : 497.

Among the settlers of this period there was one peculiar class which requires special mention. They were, for the most part, colonists rather than immigrants, though some of them came from foreign countries. These were the indented (or indentured) servants, or redemptioners.[1] There were two main classes of them — those who were brought under compulsion, and those who came voluntarily. Of the first class, many were convicted criminals, who were sent over in great numbers from the mother country, and on arrival were indented as servants for a term of years. Under the barbarous legal system of the day many persons were sentenced to death for insignificant crimes, such as stealing a joint of meat worth over a shilling, or counterfeiting a lottery ticket. Many humane judges welcomed exile as an alternative to the death penalty. It is estimated that possibly as many as fifty thousand criminals were sent to America from the British Isles, from the year 1717 until the practice was ended by the War of Independence. Besides the criminals, in this class of indented servants were many who were kidnaped and sent over to America. Press gangs were busy in London, Bristol, and other English seaports, seizing boys and girls, usually, but not always, from the lowest classes

[1] These terms are used somewhat loosely in the contemporary documents and in modern writings. "Indented servants" is the broader term, including all who signed indentures, or were sold under an indenture, whether they came willingly or under compulsion. "Redemptioners" is sometimes used to refer specifically to those who voluntarily sold themselves. But there is authority for the view that "redemptioner," strictly speaking, referred to one who came without an indenture, on the expectation of finding some one on this side who would pay for his passage. He was given a period of time after landing to accomplish this. Failing in this, he was to be sold by the captain to the highest bidder. See Geiser, K. F., *Redemptioners and Indentured Servants in the Colony and Commonwealth of Pennsylvania*, Ch. I. But the words are sometimes used interchangeably.

of society, and sending them over to labor as indented servants in the colonies.

Those who came voluntarily were respectable but destitute persons who, despairing of success or progress in the old country, sold themselves into temporary slavery to pay their passage over. Many of these came from very good classes of society. The southern colonies received a much larger number of indented servants of all classes than the northern colonies, as the semiplantation character of the former made a much larger demand for servile labor than in the farm colonies of the north.[1]

Shipmasters made an enormous profit from this traffic, adding as much as 100 per cent of the actual cost of transportation to cover risks. Adults were bound out for a term of three to six years, children from ten to fifteen years, and smaller children were, without charge, surrendered to masters who had to rear and board them.[2] As a rule the indented servants, on the arrival of a ship at an American port, were auctioned off to the highest bidder at a public auction very like a slave market. The last sales of this kind reported took place in Philadelphia in 1818 and 1819. These were mostly Germans. Many of the indented servants became eminent and respected citizens of the colonies, while others degenerated and became the progenitors of the "poor white trash" of the south.

As a result of this study of the colonial period the fact stands out prominently that during these years both colonization and immigration entered into the peopling of the Thirteen Colonies. The distinction between the two was clearly recognized by the colonists themselves,

[1] Fiske, J., *Old Virginia and her Neighbors*, Vol. II, pp. 177 ff.

[2] Evans-Gordon, W., *The Alien Immigrant*, pp. 192–193.

and immigrants were accorded different treatment from colonists. In the handling of the situation many of the stock arguments against unrestricted immigration were developed, and some of the important legislative expedients, such as the head tax, the bonding of shippers, the exclusion of paupers and criminals, etc., which have had a wide use in later years, were put into practice. It is very noteworthy, however, that in all the discussions of this question during this period one searches in vain for any trace of opposition to immigration on the grounds of the economic competition of the newcomer with the older residents. In the unsettled state of the country at this time, such a thing could hardly be thought of. The idea of any crowding of the industrial field, or any lack of economic opportunity for an unlimited number, was almost inconceivable. It is this, more than any other one thing, which differentiates the immigration situation during the colonial period from that at the present time.

Two other fundamental facts in reference to the formation of the new American people should also be noted in this connection. The first is that the actual transference of people from Europe to America during the entire colonial period was relatively slight. Benjamin Franklin stated that in 1741 a population of about one million had been produced from an immigration (used in the broad sense) of less than 80,000.[1] As an indication of how much less important this "immigration" was than the recent immigration into the United States has been, it may be noted that the ratio between immigrants and total population, at the period that Franklin mentioned, was one to twelve for a period of

[1] Hall, P. F., *Immigration*, p. 4.

120 years or more, while the ratio between immigrants since 1820 and population in 1900 — a period of only eighty years — was one to four. "After the first outflow from Old to New England, in 1630–31, emigration was checked, at first by the changing circumstances of the struggle between the people and the king, and, when the struggle was over, by the better-known difficulties of life in the colonies." [1]

The second of these facts is that such additions to population as there were, while containing a number of diverse elements, were predominantly English, and that those who were not English were almost wholly from races closely allied to the English. These were principally the Dutch, Swedes, Germans, and Scotch-Irish, which with the English, as Professor Commons has pointed out, were, less than two thousand years ago, all one Germanic race in the forests surrounding the North Sea. "It is the distinctive fact regarding colonial migration that it was Teutonic in blood and Protestant in religion." [2] This Protestantism was important, not so much because of the superiority of one form of religion over another, as because of the type of mind and character which Protestantism at that day represented. It stood for independence of thought, moral conviction, courage, and hardihood.

The English element, then, was sufficiently preëminent quickly to reduce all other elements to its type. As a result of the character of the migration assimilation was easy, quick, and complete. While it was said that every language of Europe could be found in Pennsylvania, this diversity was short-lived. "No matter how diverse the small immigration might have been on its arrival,

[1] *Encyc. Britannica*, article "United States." [2] Commons, *op. cit.*, p. 27.

there was a steady pressure on its descendants to turn them into Englishmen; and it was very successful. . . . The whole coast, from Nova Scotia to the Spanish possessions in Florida, was one in all essential circumstances."[1]

Such, then, was the American people at the time of the Revolution — a physically homogeneous race, composed almost wholly of native-born descendants of native-born ancestors, of a decidedly English type, but with a distinct character of its own. This was the great stock from which the people of the United States grew, and upon which all subsequent additions must be regarded as extraneous grafts.

[1] *Encyc. Britannica,* article "United States."

CHAPTER III

1783 TO 1820

WITH the beginning of the life of the United States as a separate nation, all strangers arriving at her shores, whencesoever they came, are to be classed as immigrants. From this time on colonization may be dropped out of the reckoning, and all increments of population from foreign sources be considered under the head of immigration.

The first forty-odd years of our national life are included in the second of the five periods which have been distinguished. During this period no accurate statistics were kept of the arrival of immigrants. The federal government took no control of the matter whatever, and the records of the states, taken mainly at the customhouses, were fragmentary and unreliable. Consequently there is no certainty as to the number or source of the arrivals during these years, and we are forced to rely on estimates. The best known are those of Seybert and Blodgett, which are generally taken as the basis of other estimates. The Bureau of Statistics in its pamphlet on "Immigration into the United States" (1903) says, "The best estimates of the total immigration into the United States prior to the official count puts [*sic*] the total number of arrivals at not to exceed 250,000 in the entire period between 1776 and 1820" (p. 4336). In an unpublished study of this question Mr. J. L. Leonard of Yale University finds this estimate probably too small, and thinks that the figure 345,000 would come nearer to representing the total number of immigrants from 1784 to 1810.

One thing is certain, however, that immigration during this period was far from being a burning issue, or from attracting any great amount of attention. An average of ten thousand arrivals a year was not a matter of great importance, and the young nation had enough more weighty matters to engage her attention to prevent her devoting much thought to immigration. It is true that the need of an increasing population was still felt, as it had been during colonial days, but the native population was multiplying at an extraordinary rate (doubling about every twenty-two years) and seemed thoroughly capable of supplying the entire need.

Yet we find occasional references to the matter in the contemporary literature, and the subject was evidently one which frequently came up for discussion. In general, foreigners were not regarded as such desirable citizens as natives, and it was considered unwise to give newcomers too much power or responsibility in the government.[1] Benjamin Franklin, writing in the *American Museum* for the year 1787, stated that the only encouragements which this government holds out to strangers are such as are derived from good laws and liberty. "Strangers are welcome, because there is room enough for them all, and therefore the old inhabitants are not jealous of them. . . . One or two years' residence give him [the immigrant] all the rights of a citizen; but the government does not at present, whatever it may have done in former times, hire people to become settlers, by paying their passage, giving land, negroes,

[1] *American Museum*, 1: 206.

utensils, stock, or any other kind of emolument whatsoever." [1]

A citizen of Pennsylvania, writing to a friend in Great Britain, enumerated the classes which could profitably come to America as follows: farmers, mechanics and manufacturers, laborers, indented servants, followers of the learned professions, and schoolmasters. "The encouragement held out to European immigrants is not the same in all the states. New England, New York, and New Jersey, being nearly filled with cultivators of the earth, afford encouragement chiefly to mechanics and laborers." Manufacture is said to be flourishing in these sections. "European artists, therefore, cannot fail of meeting with encouragement in each of the above states." Pennsylvania is said to welcome all people belonging to the classes mentioned above as needed, and the writer expresses his belief that the progress of art and science has been greatly favored by the extreme heterogeneity of population in that state, where, "we possess the virtues and weaknesses of most of the sects and nations of Europe." [2]

On April 20, 1787, a paper was read before the society for political inquiries at the house of Dr. Franklin. The subject was "An enquiry into the best means of encouraging emigration from abroad, consistently with the happiness and safety of the original citizens." The author admits at the outset that it is a question how much encouragement ought to be given to immigration. There seems to be a need for an increase of population. On the other hand, we have a right to restrict immigration whenever it appears likely to prove hurtful. Some prudent men have a well-grounded fear of the harm which may

[1] *Ibid.*, 7: 233. [2] *Ibid.*, 2: 213.

result from admitting foreigners too freely into participation in the rights of citizenship. Foreign powers might take advantage of such concessions to accomplish injury to the nation. The author doubts the validity of these fears, especially when it is considered that the usual motive for emigration is dissatisfaction with the old country.

The author reverts to the old question of imported criminals, remarking, "With a most preposterous policy, the former masters of this country were accustomed to discharge their jails of the violent part of their subjects, and to transmit shiploads of wretches, too worthless for the old world, to taint and corrupt the infancy of the new." With a somewhat unwarranted optimism he adds, "It is not now likely that these states will be insulted with transportations of this sort, directly ordered from any other sovereign power." Pennsylvania seems to be the only state which appears sensible of the danger from the poor quality of citizens. Referring to acts which have already been noted, the author says that Pennsylvania requires her naturalized citizens to be of good character, as far as this can be determined, and also remarks, "Pennsylvania, swelling hourly with arrivals of honest, industrious Germans and others, wisely discouraged by a duty, what she dared not openly prohibit."

The conclusion of the whole matter is that "the best means of encouraging emigration may therefore be truly said to be the cultivation of industry and virtue among ourselves, and the establishment of wholesome laws upon permanent foundations, which may render the comforts *we* enjoy objects of desire and pursuit to others." [1]

[1] *American Museum*, 10: 114.

The foregoing quotations may be taken as representative of the prevailing attitude toward immigration among the body of the American people. It is noteworthy that there is still no fear of the economic competition of the immigrants, though there is a faint foreshadowing of such a condition in the preference expressed for "artists" as against agriculturists, of which there already seemed to be enough in some states. On the whole, however, immigrants were regarded as assets, and there existed a vigorous sentiment in favor of encouraging them to come.

This sentiment occasionally found more active expression than that recommended in the passage quoted. North Carolina, for instance, by an act of the general assembly, passed in 1790, granted to Henry Emmanuel Lutterloh the right to raise $6000 per year for five years by lottery, for the purpose of introducing foreign artisans.[1] *Niles' Register* for November 9, 1816, states that "Col. Nicholas Gray, after having consulted with the governor of the Mississippi territory, is authorized to invite any number of industrious emigrants into that country, where they will be provided with lands, *rent free* for three years, and with cattle and corn at the usual rates."

The fear of foreign influence on our politics, to which reference has been made above, grew stronger during the next decade, and finally led to the passage of the Alien Bill in 1798, by which the president was empowered to deport all aliens whom he regarded as dangerous to the country. This act was a result of transitory unsettled conditions, particularly the expectation of a war with France, and contained a proviso that

[1] North Carolina Colonial Documents, 25: 120.

it should expire two years after passage. But it contains an important permanent principle — that of the right of deportation — which has been made much of in recent years.

The discussion of the question of naturalization brought out some decided opinions on both sides of the immigration problem.[1] The period of residence required for naturalization was set at two years by the act of 1790, but this was raised to five years in 1795. The war excitement which marked the closing years of the century led to the passage of an act in 1798 requiring a residence of fourteen years for naturalization. This was repealed after four years, and the provisions of the act of 1795 were again put in force. They have remained unchanged in their essentials ever since. In addition to the period of residence required, there was much discussion as to the charge to be made for naturalization. It was proposed by some to set this at $20, but this was regarded by others as too high, and the amount was finally fixed at $5.[2]

There was little change in the attitude toward immigration during the following years up to 1820. The number of arrivals remained relatively small. The immigrants, being mainly from Germany and the United Kingdom, were readily assimilated. In 1809 a French immigrant wrote a letter from Boston in which he said, "There is in general no enmity to strangers as such, but the most open, unguarded hospitality." [3]

[1] Jefferson is quoted as having expressed the wish that there were "an ocean of fire between this country and Europe, so that it might be impossible for any more immigrants to come hither." Hall, P. F., *op. cit.*, p. 206.

[2] McMaster, J. B., *History of the United States*, Vol. II, p. 332; "The Riotous Career of the Know Nothings," *Forum*, 17:524; Franklin, Frank G., *Legislative History of Naturalization*.

[3] *Monthly Anthology*, Boston, 6:383.

Shipping conditions were still very bad. We are told that in 1818 one ship from Amsterdam embarked about eleven hundred persons for America. Out of these, about five hundred died, some of them before leaving the shores of Europe.[1] Some ships seem to have followed the practice of sailing from Europe with a cargo of passengers, ostensibly for America, but instead of following this course, stopping at some near-by island, compelling their passengers to disembark, and then going back to the mainland for a fresh load. It follows, of course, that a large part of the immigrants who finally reached America arrived in a most deplorable condition.

During this period there occurred some important events which had the effect temporarily of interfering with the stream of immigration, but in their after results were largely responsible for conditions which gave to immigration an impetus such as it had never had before. Foremost among these were the Orders in Council, the Embargo, and the War of 1812. These great events resulted in powerfully stimulating the manufacturing industries of the United States. Up to this time, shipping and commerce had been among the most important, if not actually the leading, forms of enterprise for the citizens of the new nation, aside from agriculture. The Embargo, with the other restrictive conditions, struck a severe blow at this branch of industry, and forced great numbers of Americans to devote their energies to other forms of enterprise, notably manufacturing.

At the same time the need for such native manufactures was vastly augmented by the discontinuance of the supplies from England. This forced the youthful nation to be more self-sufficient and independent than

[1] *Niles' Register*, 15 . 378.

she had ever been before. At the close of the period of interrupted communication, England tried to dump the goods which had accumulated in her warehouses for a number of years upon the American market at cut prices. At this the Americans rebelled. They had had a taste of independence and liked it, and in the protection of their infant industries they inaugurated that long series of protective tariff measures which have continued to the present day. And whatever may be said of the utility of these measures at the present time, there can be no doubt that in the beginning they helped to establish the manufactures of this country upon a firm basis.

With the growth of manufactures, there arose a great demand for laborers, particularly skilled laborers, who knew the technique of industry. There was also a great need for common laborers who would be willing to go into factories and do the routine work. This supply was not forthcoming from the native population, who were, by instinct and training, independent workers, particularly agriculturists. It was extremely difficult to persuade any great number of them to forego the possibility of becoming independent landowners and cultivators, in order to become hired workers in somebody else's factory. The close of the second historical period, accordingly, is marked by a keen demand for foreign artisans, and the beginning of a general demand for immigrant labor, to which Europe was commencing to respond.

CHAPTER IV

1820 TO 1860

THE first act passed by the federal government of the United States which can in any way be called an immigration law was primarily designed, not to restrict or control the admission of immigrants into this country, but to make some provision for their comfort and safety while on the voyage — matters which had been shockingly neglected in the past, with the result of untold sufferings and horrors. These evils were largely due to the intolerable overcrowding on shipboard which was habitual. The act in question aimed to correct these evils by limiting the number of passengers which might be carried on any ship to two to every five tons of the ship's weight. It furthermore provided that each ship or vessel leaving an American port was to have on board for each passenger carried sixty gallons of water, one gallon of vinegar, one hundred pounds of salted provisions, and one hundred pounds of wholesome ship bread. It is very doubtful how much good either of these provisions ever did to the immigrants. The clause in regard to overcrowding, based as it was merely on the ship's total weight, was wholly inadequate to prevent extreme overcrowding in such parts of the vessel as might be assigned to passengers. And as far as the provision regarding supplies is concerned, it could have been of no help to the immigrants, as it applied only to ships leaving an American port. There was one provision of the law, however, which has been of permanent benefit. This was the stipulation that at the port of landing a full and complete report or manifest was to be made by the ship's officer to the customs authorities, which was to state the number of passengers carried, together with the name, sex, age, and occupation of each. This act was passed on March 2, 1819, and in the year ending September 30, 1820, the first official statistics of immigration were collected. From this time to the present we have a continuous record of arrivals, increasing in detail with subsequent legal requirements. Thus the year 1820 stands as a fitting beginning for our third period.

The decade of the twenties was one of great industrial activity on the part of the American people. Manufactures increased. The Erie Canal was completed, others were commenced, and there was a fever of excitement about them. The first railroads were projected, and vied with the canals in arousing public enthusiasm. There was a vast movement of population westward, and the Ohio River was a busy thoroughfare.

All of these enterprises aroused a demand for labor, which, as we have seen, the native population would not readily supply. By the middle of the decade the stream of immigration had begun to respond, so that in 1825 the number of arrivals for the year reached the ten thousand mark for the first time since statistics had been collected. By the end of the decade the number had more than doubled. In the fifteen months ending December 31, 1832, there were over sixty thousand arrivals, and in the year 1842, 104,565 — the first time the hundred thousand mark had been reached. Such an enormous increase in immigration as this could not fail to have its effect upon the social life of the nation, and to attract widespread attention. Coupled with the changing nature of industry, it brought many new problems before the American people — congestion, tenement house problems, unemployment, etc. Pauperism, intemperance, beggary, and prostitution increased.[1] For many of these evils it began to appear that the immigrants were partly responsible.

Yet during the twenties it seems that the immigrants were, on the whole, in good favor. The great economic need which they filled outweighed the social burden which they imposed, but which, as yet, was only vaguely felt. The hard manual labor on the construction enterprises of the period was mainly performed by Irish laborers, who flocked over in great numbers, constituting the largest single element in the immigration stream, amounting to probably nearly half of the entire number. It was believed by many Americans, as well as by foreign travelers and observers, that the canals and railroads could never have been built without these sturdy Irishmen. They were a turbulent and reckless lot, though perhaps not wholly through their own fault. Their miserable wages were supplemented by copious supplies of whisky, with the result that the labor camps were frequently the scenes of riotous demonstrations which shocked the sensibilities of the American community.

By the end of this decade, however, the evils attendant upon unregulated immigration were beginning to make themselves felt among the native population. Chief among these was the danger from an increase of pauperism. The frightful shipping conditions, which had marked previous periods, continued with practically no

[1] McMaster, J. B., *History of the United States*, Vol. V, pp. 121 ff.

amelioration. The records of the time are full of heart-rending tales of crowded, filthy, unventilated ships, and penniless, starved, diseased immigrants, often landed in a state of absolute destitution. The sickening details of these accounts make the most lurid description of present-day steerage conditions seem absolutely colorless. Under such circumstances it was inevitable that a very large number of these miserable victims should come immediately, or in a very short time, upon the public for support. The censuses of the poorhouses showed an altogether disproportionate number of foreign-born paupers among the inmates. In Philadelphia, for instance, it appears that at the beginning of the thirties the foreign-born paupers made up nearly one third of the total number, and by 1834 this proportion had increased to practically one half.[1] Such a state of affairs naturally aroused the consternation of the natives, and the feeling was made more intense by the belief that many of these paupers were taken directly from the almshouses of foreign countries, and shipped to this country at public expense. This matter has been the subject of so much debate that it will be worth while to examine the truth of these charges in this connection.

Mrs. Trollope, writing in 1832, said, "I frequently heard vehement complaints, and constantly met the same in the newspapers, of a practice stated to be very generally adopted in Britain of sending out cargoes of parish paupers to the United States. A Baltimore paper heads some such remarks with the words 'INFAMOUS CONDUCT' and then tells us of a cargo of aged paupers just arrived from England, adding 'John Bull has squeezed the orange and now insolently casts

[1] Hazard's *Register of Pennsylvania*, 6: 266; 11: 362, 416; 15: 157.

the skin in our faces.'" Mrs. Trollope states that careful investigation on her part failed to substantiate this charge.[1] The article referred to is one which appeared in *Niles' Register* for July 3, 1830. It gives an account of the ship *Anacreon* from Liverpool, which arrived at Norfolk with 168 passengers, three fourths of whom were transported English paupers, cast on our shores at about four pounds ten shillings per head. Many of them were very aged. The editor's vehement protest against such action contrasts sharply with the complacency with which the same journal had viewed the advent of a crowd of transported Irish paupers seven years earlier.[2]

An examination of the evidence on the question tends to support the statement of the Baltimore editor, rather than the denial of Mrs. Trollope. Other numbers of *Niles' Register* contain frequent accounts of such practices. A letter written from England, dated February 7, 1823, and published in this journal states, "I was down in the London docks and there were *twenty-six paupers* going out in the ship *Hudson*, to New York, sent by the parish of Eurbarst, in Sussex, in carriers' wagons, who paid their passage and gave them money to start with when they arrived in the U. States." The editor states that "this precious cargo has arrived safely." [3] Other numbers of the *Register* contain similar instances, some of them quoted from other papers.[4]

So far the evidence consists mostly of newspaper tales, and is perhaps open to reasonable doubt, though where there was so much smoke there must have been some fire. But more reliable testimony is available.

1 Trollope, Mrs. T. A., *Domestic Manners of the Americans*, p. 121.

2 *Niles' Register*, 24: 393.

3 *Ibid.*, April 26, 1823.

4 *Ibid.*, Aug. 23, 1823; July 21, 1827; Aug. 14, 1830.

Charges of the kind in question finally became so prevalent that the government ordered an investigation, and on May 15, 1838, Mr. John Forsyth, then Secretary of State, presented a report on the subject of pauperism and immigration. This contains a large amount of testimony, from which it will be sufficient to select a few typical cases.

On June 28, 1831, Mr. R. M. Harrison, United States consul at Kingston, Jamaica, reported that there was a local law compelling shipmasters who left that port to carry away paupers, for which they received $10 each as remuneration. If they refused to take them, they were fined $300. As various states had laws forbidding the landing of paupers, it was customary for shipmasters to sign the paupers as seamen. The pauper had the privilege of choosing his own vessel, and most of them went to the United States. Mr. Van Buren called the attention of Lord Palmerston, the British Foreign Secretary, to the affair, and requested a discontinuance of the practice. Lord Palmerston replied that the law was to expire December 31, and the governor of Jamaica had been instructed to withhold his assent to any similar law.[1]

Mr. Albert Davy, United States consul at Kingston-upon-Hull, Leeds, England, reported that while no reliable lists were kept at customhouses, distinguishing paupers from others, it was generally known that paupers emigrated, and several shipmasters admitted that passage was paid by parish overseers. If a pauper was an exceptionally hard case, he could demand considerable sums of money in addition to his passage, refusing to go unless they were paid.[2] Mr. F. List on March 8, 1837,

[1] Executive (House) Documents, 25th Cong., 2d Ses., 370. [2] *Ibid.*

reported from Leipsic that not only paupers, but criminals, were transported from the interior to seaports, to be embarked for the United States. A certain Mr. de Stein contracts with the governments to transport paupers for $75 per head, and several of the governments have accepted his proposition. There is a plan to empty the jails and workhouses in this way. It is a common practice in Germany to get rid of paupers and vicious characters by collecting money to send them to the United States.[1]

That it was customary to transport criminals as well as paupers is verified by the fact that during 1837 two lots of convicts arrived in Baltimore: one a party of fourteen convicts on a ship from Bremen, who had been embarked in irons, which had not been stricken off until near the fort; the other a shipload of 200 to 250 Hessian convicts, whose manacles and fetters remained upon their hands and feet until within the day of their arrival.[2]

A memorial of the corporation of the city of New York, January 25, 1847, states that within the last year the ships *Sardinia* and *Atlas* from Liverpool arrived in New York, one with 294 and the other with 314 steerage passengers, all paupers, sent by the parish of Grosszimmern, Hesse Darmstadt, to which they belonged and by which their expenses were paid. Two hundred and thirty-four of these immigrants, 117 from each ship, eventually found their way into the New York almshouse.[3]

On January 19, 1839, *Niles' Register* reported a crowd of paupers which had arrived in New York from England. Their passage had been paid by the overseers of the poor

[1] *Ibid.*

[2] Executive (House) Doc., 25th Cong., 2d Ses., 370, and House Reports of Committees, 34th Cong., 1st and 2d Ses., 359.

[3] Executive (House) Doc., 29th Cong., 2d Ses., 54.

at Edinburgh, and the majority of them were still wearing the uniform of the poorhouse. This naturally aroused objections, and the consignees of the vessel finally agreed to take them back to Europe, and to repay the city all expense that it had incurred on their account. The United States consul at Basle, Switzerland, reported in 1846 that it was the practice in that country for congregations or town authorities to send paupers to America.[1]

Instances of this sort might be multiplied, but these will suffice to prove that the practice of transporting paupers was a common one during the period we are considering. Just when it was finally stopped it is impossible to say.[2] It certainly played a large part in creating the feeling of hostility to immigrants which manifested itself strongly during the decade of the thirties.

That the situation was partially, at least, comprehended also in England is evidenced by a burlesque poem entitled "Immiscible Immigration," written in that country, which commences with the following words:

"The tide of emigration still flows fast;
Millions of souls remove their bodies corporate —
Columbia's shores will be o'erstocked at last,
And Yankees must support them by a pauper rate.
Others,
With their brothers,
Fathers and mothers,
Rush to Australia," etc.[3]

[1] Senate Doc., 29th Cong., 2d Ses., 161.

[2] As late as 1884–1885 thousands of immigrants were sent from Ireland to the United States and Canada, partly at state expense and partly at the expense of the "Tuke Fund." Some of these were admittedly paupers. Cf. Tuke, J. H., "State Aid to Emigrants," *Nineteenth Century*, 17 : 280.

[3] *Knickerbocker*, 7 : 78.

While the dangers from pauperism and criminality were probably the leading causes for opposition to immigration, at this time, other broader and deeper objections were beginning to be felt and to be expressed in current writings. In the *North American Review* for April, 1835 (p. 457), there is a very sane, calm and convincing article by Mr. A. H. Everett, in which the disadvantages of immigration are set forth. Many of the stock arguments of to-day are well set forth here, among them, of course, the dangers from pauperism and crime, but also the dangers of a heterogeneous population, of poor assimilation, congestion in cities, misuse of political power, and the growth of foreign colonies. The author questions whether the immigrants are really filling the demand for labor, and urges the necessity of furnishing the immigrants with information about different sections of the country, and advising them about their destination. He also feels the need of much greater discrimination in the admission of aliens.

In the same magazine, in the issue for January, 1841, there is an article entitled "The Irish in America," in which the author names as one of the great grievances against the immigrants that they do more work for less money than the native workingmen, and live on a lower standard, thereby decreasing wages. This is one of the earliest expressions which we find of this objection, and shows that by this time the country had passed beyond the primitive stage where there was room enough for everybody, and no fear of economic competition. It is the foreshadowing of modern conditions and modern thought.

There was still another ground for opposition to the immigrants which very possibly at the end of the thirties eclipsed all the others in positive influence.[1] This was the hatred and fear of the Roman Catholic religion, to which the great majority of the Irish adhered. The Protestant bias which had strongly characterized the early settlers still persisted among the great body of the American people. This motive was the leading one which led to the formation of the first political party which was openly based on opposition to immigration. This was the Native American party which came into prominence as a political movement about 1835, in which year there was a Nativist candidate for Congress in New York City. In the following year the party nominated a candidate for mayor of New York. Nativist societies were formed in Germantown, Pa., and in Washington, D.C., in 1837, and two years later the party was organized in Louisiana, where a state convention was held in 1841. The adherents of this movement did not confine themselves to peaceful and orderly methods, but resorted to anti-Catholic riots in 1844. Two Catholic churches were destroyed in Philadelphia, and a convent in Boston.[2]

In 1845 the Nativist movement claimed 48,000 members in New York, 42,000 in Pennsylvania, 14,000 in Massachusetts, and 6000 in other states. In Congress it had six representatives from New York and two from Pennsylvania. Its first national convention was held in Philadelphia in 1845.[3] A national platform was adopted, the chief demands being the repeal of the naturalization laws, and the appointment of native Americans only to office. They succeeded in securing

[1] It is said that the natives suspected a deliberate plan on the part of the Catholic powers to destroy the free institutions of America. McMaster, *Forum*, 17 : 524.

[2] Hall, P. F., *op. cit.*, p. 207.

[3] Franklin, F. G., *op. cit.*, p. 247.

a certain amount of congressional investigation in 1838, and a bill was presented by a committee appointed for the purpose, which proposed to fine shipmasters who tried to bring into the United States aliens who were idiots, lunatics, maniacs, or afflicted with any incurable disease, in the sum of $1000, and to require them to forfeit a like sum for every alien brought in who had not the ability to maintain himself. "Congress did not even consider this bill, and during the next ten years little attempt was made to secure legislation against the foreigner,"[1] though many petitions to extend the period of residence for naturalization were received. The ever increasing opposition to unregulated immigration had not yet become sufficiently widespread to accomplish any positive measures.

During this period the immigrants were almost wholly from the United Kingdom and Germany, with the Irish in the lead, as we have seen. There were also considerable numbers of French, who outnumbered the Germans in some years in the early part of the period, and small contingents from various other nations, particularly the Scandinavian countries. It was natural that the ties of relationship, language, etc., should put the United Kingdom at the head at this time, and conditions in Ireland were such as to make emigration a very welcome means of relief. The Irish tended to linger in the cities, where they went into domestic and personal service, or to go out into the construction camps. The Germans and Scandinavians, on the other hand, tended to move westward into the interior, and colonies of these races were becoming numerous in several of the middle western

[1] Report of the Immigration Commission, Federal Immigration Legislation, Abstract, pp. 7, 8.

states. The Germans of this period were mostly farmers from the thinly settled agricultural sections of the old country, and the great attraction which the United States had for them was the ease with which good farm lands might be secured in this country.[1]

Most of the agitation about immigration, as has been intimated, centered round the Irish, but there was also some feeling against the Germans. This was augmented by the decided clannishness of these people. There were many German societies and newspapers, and a strong and ill-disguised movement to form an independent German state in Texas, or elsewhere on the continent, which was not calculated to endear them to the native American.

Up to the year 1842 the total immigration did not reach one hundred thousand annually, and for the next three years it fell below that figure again.[2] During the last half of this decade, however, certain events occurred in Europe which vastly increased the immigration current, and brought the matter more forcibly to the notice of the American people than ever before. These were the potato famine in Ireland, and the political upheavals of 1848 in various nations of Europe, particularly in Germany. The result of the latter occurrences was to leave a large number of middle class liberalists in Germany in a very undesirable situation, in spite of the partial success of the revolution. The way out, for them, was emigration. This is one of the best examples in history of the political cause of emigration, though even here economic motives were also concerned. A

[1] Roscher-Jannasch, *Kolonien, Kolonialpolitik, und Auswanderung*, p. 380.

[2] The statistics at this period are confused by changes in the time of ending of the fiscal year, but the above statement corresponds with the figures of the Immigration Commission.

tremendous emigration followed, reaching its climax in 1854, when 215,009 immigrants from Germany reached this country. These were mainly persons of good character and independent spirit, as might be expected from the causes of their departure. Considerable numbers of Bohemians also emigrated at this period, similar in character to the Germans, and actuated by similar motives and conditions.

Conditions in Ireland at about the same time resulted in an emigration rivaling that from Germany in numbers, but by no means so desirable from the point of view of the United States. It was almost exclusively an economic movement. The introduction of the potato into Ireland by Raleigh in 1610 had seemed at first a blessing to the country. It furnished an easy and abundant food supply, and its cultivation spread rapidly. Population increased correspondingly, growing from 2,845,932 in 1785 to 5,356,594 in 1803 and 8,295,061 in 1845. By the latter year most of the population were dependent for their subsistence upon the potato. This was a precarious situation, for the potato furnishes the largest amount of food in proportion to the land used of almost any crop which is grown in temperate regions. In other words, the Irish were living on a very low standard as far as food was concerned, with no margin to fall back on in case of calamity. A people subsisting upon grains and meat may, in time of distress, resort to cheaper and more easily secured food materials temporarily. But a land which is densely populated by people living on the cheapest possible food has no resources when any misfortune attacks their staple supply. Ireland was in this situation in the middle forties, and the misfortune came in the shape of the potato murrain, which attacked the plants in 1845 and caused an almost complete failure of the crop for that year.

Extreme hardship, privation, and distress followed. From 200,000 to 300,000 died of starvation or of fever caused by insufficient food. All who could sought relief in flight. Benevolent agencies in England and Ireland came to their assistance, and enormous numbers of Irish, in one way or another, found the means for emigration, and embarked for Canada or the United States. Added to the great numbers of Germans who were coming at the same time, they caused the first great wave in the immigration current, reaching a maximum of 427,833 in the year 1854, a number which was not exceeded until 1873. After 1854 the immigration current dwindled rapidly, until in 1862 it amounted to only 72,183.

During this entire period, up to the time of the great influx from Germany and Ireland, immigration had been practically unregulated so far as the United States government was concerned, the only federal law bearing on the subject being the ineffective act of 1819. Many of the individual states, however, had attempted to cope with the evils of the situation by restrictive or protective measures. New York took the lead in this matter. In this state there were two sets of laws bearing on the question. The first of these had to do with the support of the marine hospital. As early as 1820 New York had passed a law (April 14, 1820, Chapter 229) levying a tax of $1.50 each for the captain and cabin passengers, and $1 each for steerage passengers, mates, sailors, and mariners, payable by the master of every vessel from a foreign port arriving at a New York port. The proceeds were to be used for the benefit of the marine hospital. This law was continued and reënacted, with slight changes in the amount of the tax, at frequent intervals during the next twenty-five years.[1] It was a real head tax, and may have had a slight restrictive influence upon immigration.

Much more important than this set of laws, however, was another group, specifically concerned with the immigration situation. The first [2] of these was the law of February 11, 1824, which required the master of every ship coming from any foreign country, or from any other state than New York, to report to the mayor in writing, within twenty-four hours after landing, the name, place of birth, last legal settlement, age, and occupation of all passengers, under a penalty of $75 for each person not reported, or reported falsely. The mayor might require a bond, not exceeding $300, for each passenger not a citizen of the United States, to indemnify the authorities of New York against any expense incurred in connection with such passengers, or their children born after landing, for the space of two years. Whenever any passenger, being a citizen of the United States, was deemed likely to become a public charge to the city, the master of the ship should at once remove him at his (the master's) expense to his place of last settlement, or else defray all expenses incurred by the city. Noncitizens entering the city with the intention of residing there must within twenty-four hours report themselves

[1] Mar. 21, 1823; Rev. Stat., 1827, Ch. XIV, Title IV, Sec. 7; Apr. 18, 1843; May 7, 1844.

[2] In 1818 a book was published under the title *Der Deutsche in Nord-Amerika*, by M. von Fürstenwärther. According to a review of this book which appeared in the *North American Review* for July, 1820, Mr. von Fürstenwärther mentions a New York State law requiring security from ship captains against their immigrant passengers becoming public burdens. This reference does, in fact, occur on page 38 of the book in question, but the present author, after a careful search, has not succeeded in finding any such law on the New York Statutes previous to 1824.

to the mayor, giving their name, birthplace, etc., the time and place of landing, the name of the ship and commander, under penalty of $300.

This law remained in force for twenty-three years. On May 5, 1847, a more inclusive immigration law was passed of which the most important provisions were as follows:

SECTION 1. The shipmaster shall report the name, place of birth, last legal residence, age, and occupation of every person or passenger arriving in the ship, not being a citizen of the United States. The report shall further specify whether any of the passengers reported are lunatic, idiot, deaf and dumb, blind or infirm, and if so, whether they are accompanied by relatives likely to be able to support them. A report is to be made of those who have died on the voyage. Penalty for violation, $75.

SECTION 2. For each person reported, the sum of one dollar is to be paid by the master within three days after arrival.

SECTION 3. The commissioners of emigration shall go on board of arriving vessels and examine their passengers. If any of the defective classes mentioned in Section 1 are found, not members of emigrating families, and likely to become a public charge, a bond of $300 for five years shall be required, in place of the commutation fee of one dollar.

SECTION 4. Commissioners of emigration are appointed, to have charge of the business of immigration.

SECTION 14. The commissioners of emigration are made recipients and custodians of the marine hospital funds.

SECTION 16. The commissioners are given power to

erect buildings for the handling of the immigration business.

SECTION 18. The act of February 11, 1824, is repealed.

Under this law a special body of officials took charge of the handling of immigrants for New York State, and a more systematic and effective method was introduced.

The foregoing law and the corresponding law of Massachusetts were both declared unconstitutional by the Supreme Court of the United States in January, 1849,[1] on the ground that the power to levy a head tax was conferred on Congress by Article 1, Section 8, of the Constitution, being included in the "power to regulate commerce with foreign nations." [2]

New York, however, at once (April 11, 1849) passed another law, even more stringent in its requirements than the foregoing one, but designed to avoid the constitutional difficulties. A bond of $300 was required for *all* alien passengers, which might be commuted for the sum of $1.50. If any alien passengers are "lunatic, idiot, deaf, dumb, blind, or infirm persons not members of emigrating families," or likely to become a public charge, or have been paupers in any other country, they are to be bonded in the sum of $500 for ten years, in addition to the commutation money. On such bonds the authorities were empowered to collect enough money to defray the expenses incurred in connection with the immigrants, not exceeding the amount of the bond.

By the act of July 11, 1851, the defective classes were added to by the inclusion of persons maimed, or above the age of sixty years, or under thirteen, widows having

[1] 7 Howard, 283. Passenger Cases, U. S. Supreme Court, Jan. Term, 1849.

[2] Endicott, William C., Jr., *Commercial Relations of the United States*, 1885–1886, pp. 1968 ff.

families, or women without husbands having families, or any person unable to take care of himself or herself without becoming a public charge. The bond of $500 for undesirables was retained, but the time limit was reduced to five years.

Practically all of the other states which received trans-Atlantic vessels had laws similar to the bonding law of New York, for their protection against pauper immigration. The Massachusetts law was much more severe than that of New York, and was believed to keep many immigrants away from that state. The Massachusetts law passed April 20, 1837, required shipmasters to deposit a bond of $1000 for ten years for each lunatic, idiot, maimed, aged, or infirm immigrant brought in, and for those incompetent to maintain themselves, or who have been paupers in any other country. For each other alien passenger the shipmaster was to pay the sum of $2.

In all of this legislation the states found themselves in the dilemma of wishing to frame laws which would keep out undesirable immigrants, and yet would not operate to discourage aliens of good quality. The desire for an increase of population by immigration, which was shared by practically all the states, and the fear of diverting the current from one state to another, led to a greater laxity in the attitude of each state than would probably have existed if each could have acted altogether independently. This made the state regulation of immigration most unsatisfactory.

It was inevitable, considering the immensity and suddenness of the immigration movement at this time, and the lack of experience in dealing with such a problem on the part of the American people, that grievous evils should arise. The immigrants, particularly the

Irish, were a destitute and helpless lot, and fell an easy prey to the machinations of the host of exploiters which at once sprang up to take advantage of the newly presented opportunities. Countless devices were put in practice for separating the immigrant from whatever valuable goods he brought with him. New York, in particular, as the center of the traffic, swarmed with a host of runners, agents, and solicitors of every kind, who fleeced the newcomers without remorse or pity. These runners were themselves mostly earlier immigrants, who could more readily gain the confidence of the aliens. The handling and inspection of these aliens by the officials was also a weighty problem. It was in the hope of checking the operations of the runners, as well as to provide suitable arrangements for the examination of arriving immigrants, that the Board of Commissioners of Emigration of New York State was created by the act of 1847. This timely action undoubtedly prevented the various evils connected with this immense movement from going to the extremes that they otherwise would have reached, and that they did reach in certain respects in Canada.[1]

[1] The following passage, quoted from J. T. Maguire's *The Irish in America*, gives a vivid picture of conditions on the voyage, and of the circumstances that attended landing in Canada. "But a crowded immigrant sailing ship of twenty years since [written in 1868], with fever on board! — the crew sullen or brutal from very desperation, or paralysed with terror of the plague — the miserable passengers unable to help themselves or afford the least relief to each other; one-fourth, or one-third, or one-half of the entire number in different stages of the disease; many dying, some dead; the fatal poison intensified by the indescribable foulness of the air breathed and rebreathed by the gasping sufferers — the wails of children, the raving of the delirious, the cries and groans of those in mortal agony!" The only provision for the reception of these sufferers at Grosse Isle, where many of them were landed, consisted of sheds which had stood there since 1832. "These sheds were rapidly filled with the miserable people, the sick and the dying, and round their walls lay groups of half-naked men, women and children, in the same condition — sick or dying. Hundreds were literally

In 1855 the commissioners leased an old fort at the foot of Manhattan Island, known as Castle Garden, to serve as an immigrant station. This did duty for many years and was considered one of the most interesting spots in the metropolis. It also proved of great service in restraining the operations of the immigrant runners.[1] It goes without saying that it was by no means successful in putting a permanent stop to them.

The bonding provision of the New York State law had one remarkable and unfortunate result. A class of brokers sprang up who took the responsibility of bonding the immigrants from the shipowners. It was obviously to their advantage to keep as many of the immigrants as possible from coming upon the public for support. To accomplish this, they established private hospitals and poorhouses on the outskirts of New York and Brooklyn, in which dependent aliens were placed. The effort to maintan them here at the least possible expense resulted in extreme neglect. A committee of the Board of Aldermen of New York City was appointed to look into this matter, in the year 1846. They found conditions which were almost unbelievable. In one apartment, fifty feet square, they discovered one hundred sick and dying immigrants lying on straw.

flung on the beach, left amid the mud and stones, to crawl on the dry land how they could. 'I have seen,' says the priest who was chaplain of the quarantine, . . . 'I have one day seen thirty-seven people lying on the beach, crawling on the mud, and dying like fish out of water.' Many of these, and many more besides, gasped out their last breath on that fatal shore, not able to drag themselves from the slime in which they lay." As many as 150 bodies, mostly half naked, were piled up in the dead-house at a time. (pp. 135,136.) The moral evils and dangers were said to be even worse than the physical.

[1] For accounts of the activities at Castle Garden, and of the operations of the runners, see Kapp, Friedrich, *Immigration and the Commissioners of Emigration of the State of New York; Chambers' Journal*, 23 : 141, "Emigrant Entrappers"; Bagger, L., "A Day in Castle Garden," *Harper's Monthly*, 42 : 547.

In their midst were the bodies of two others who had died four or five days earlier, and had been left there. The worst kind of food was specially purchased for the consumption of these victims. The conditions unearthed by this investigation contributed to the sentiment which brought about the passage of the law of 1847.[1]

The chaotic state of the immigration situation, the inadequacy of state control, and the increasing obviousness of the resulting evils led to a growing demand for federal action on the matter. This feeling found expression in numerous petitions and memorials presented to Congress by state legislatures, city councils, and private citizens. These began to appear about 1835, with the rise of the Native American party. With the increased immigration of the latter forties, the demand became more insistent. The immediate and crying evil, which attracted the greatest attention, lay in the unspeakable shipping conditions which still existed.[2] In 1847 Mr. Rathbun stated on the floor of Congress that emigrants from abroad were frequently landed in the port of New York in such a diseased condition, due to overcrowding on the ships which brought them, that they were unable to walk. They were carried in carts direct to the almshouse, and sometimes died on the way.[3] In the same year, out of ninety thousand immigrants who embarked for Canada in British vessels, fifteen thousand died on the way. This exceeded even the suffering in vessels bound for the United States.[4] On the whole, conditions seem to have been the best on the German and American vessels.

[1] Maguire, *op. cit.*, pp. 185–187.

[2] See Mr. Maguire's description, footnote, p. 79.

[3] *Congressional Globe*, Feb. 1, 1847, p. 304.

[4] Hale, E. E., *Letters on Irish Immigration.*

In response to these conditions, and to the growing demand for a remedy, Congress on February 22, 1847, passed a law, superseding that of 1819, and designed to remedy the evils of overcrowding. The provisions about victualing the ships remained the same as before, but the new law provided for a certain allotment of superficial, or square feet of, deck space per passenger, and also limited the number of passengers in proportion to the tonnage of the ship. This law was not satisfactory, however, and was very soon superseded by the act of May 17, 1848, which remained in force until 1855. In 1849 the British government passed a law, designed to secure the same ends as the American laws. It was under the operation of these three laws that the great flood of Irish immigration crossed the Atlantic.

The American statutes required that the deck space, unoccupied by stores or goods, except passengers' baggage, should average fourteen square feet for each passenger, man, woman, or child, excepting infants not one year old. If the space between decks was less than six feet, there must be sixteen square feet per passenger, and if less than five feet, twenty-two square feet (a significant commentary on the ship construction of the day). There were to be not more than two tiers of berths on any deck, and the berths were to be not less than six feet by one and one half feet in dimensions. The British statute set a limit of one passenger (exclusive of cabin) for every two tons registered tonnage, two children under fourteen years of age being counted as one, and children under one year not being counted.

Up to this time it had been customary on immigrant ships to require passengers to provide their own stores, but on account of the lack of intelligence and foresight on the part of the passengers, both the American and British statutes required ships to carry a certain amount and kind of provisions for each passenger, as follows:

	American Act	British Act
Water	60 gallons	$52\frac{1}{2}$ gallons
Ship bread	15 pounds	50 pounds
Wheat flour	10 pounds	20 pounds
Oatmeal	10 pounds	60 pounds
Rice	10 pounds	40 pounds
Salt pork	10 pounds	$22\frac{1}{2}$ pounds
Peas and beans	10 pounds	Potatoes may be substituted for meal or rice at the ratio of five pounds for one
Potatoes	35 pounds	

The passengers were still required to do their own cooking, and the American act provided for the building of cooking ranges for the use of steerage passengers, in proportion to the number carried.

Most of the Irish passengers were collected at Liverpool, though by 1847 there were also many direct sailings from Ireland. They were mainly booked through passenger brokers, who often imposed on them, but apparently not so much as might have been expected. There was a medical inspection at Liverpool, and emigrants were required to be certified against contagious diseases. The average length of the passage from Liverpool to New York in 1849 was about thirty-five days, and from London about forty-three and one half days. But voyages were often much prolonged. One ship, the *Speed* (!), in 1848 had a passage of twelve weeks, with great ensuing hardship. The British act provided that if ships had to turn back, the passengers must be transshipped to another vessel, and in the meantime maintained at the master's expense. This often resulted in hardship, instead of benefit, as ships sometimes kept on the voyage when they were not fitted to sail. In 1849 and 1850 some ships turned back after having been out seventy days. The British government tried to induce steamers to take steerage passengers by allowing them to provide provisions for only forty days, while sailing vessels had to provide for seventy. Very few immigrants, nevertheless, were carried on steam vessels during these years. The deaths on these voyages were mainly due to ship fever, a severe form of Irish typhus.[1]

Though the German immigrants at this time were at least as numerous as the Irish, they attracted much less attention. This was partly because they were less poverty-stricken, and partly because they mostly moved on to the west, and did not collect in the cities of the Atlantic seaboard. The Irish, in consequence of their native character, the circumstances which led to their coming, and the conditions of the voyage, were in a particularly helpless state when they arrived. They were the most prominent victims of the runners, and made the largest showing in the hospitals and almshouses. In spite of the good accomplished by the state and federal statutes, an extreme amount of destitution and suffering persisted. The burden of foreign pauperism, in particular, increased tremendously. In 1850 more than half the paupers wholly or partially supported in the United States were of foreign birth.

[1] Most of these details are taken from E. E. Hale's interesting *Letters on Irish Immigration*, written in 1851–1852.

In the North Atlantic coastal states the proportion was much larger.[1]

These considerations, added to the preponderance of Roman Catholics among the Irish immigrants, led to a renewal of the anti-immigration agitation, which had been so vigorous ten years earlier. This time the movement took the form of a secret organization, started probably in New York City in 1850. This society grew rapidly. Its meetings were held in secret, and the purpose and even the name of the organization were so much of a mystery at first that the rank and file of the members, either from necessity or from choice, were in the habit of answering all questions regarding it by saying, "I don't know." Hence it came to be known as the "Know Nothing" party, and as such has come down to history.[2]

The organization did not long maintain its ultra-secret character. This had mostly disappeared by 1854, and the society openly indorsed candidates, and put forward candidates of its own. It is recorded that in 1855 the governors and legislatures in New Hampshire, Massachusetts, Rhode Island, Connecticut, New York, California, and Kentucky were Know Nothings, and that they had secured many offices in other states. By 1855 they began to mature plans for the presidential election. They adopted a platform calling for a change in the existing naturalization laws, for the repeal of the state laws allowing unnaturalized foreigners to vote, and

[1] *Congressional Globe*, 33d Cong., 2d Ses., p. 391.

[2] Its real name was "The Supreme Order of the Star Spangled Banner." There appears to be some difference of opinion as to the exact date of organization. It began to attract public attention about 1852. See Hall, *op. cit.*, p. 207; Jenks and Lauck, *The Immigration Problem*, p. 297; Rept. Imm. Com., Federal Immigration Legislation, Abs., p. 8; McMaster, J. B., "The Riotous Career of the Know Nothings," *Forum*, 17:524.

the repeal by Congress of all acts making land grants to unnaturalized foreigners and allowing them to vote in the territories. In 1856 a national convention was held, and Millard Fillmore was nominated for president. The principles of the platform adopted were that Americans must rule America, that native-born citizens should be selected for all state, federal, and municipal government employment in preference to all others, that the naturalization law should be changed so as to require twenty-one years' residence, and that a law should be passed excluding from the United States all paupers or persons convicted of crime. This party had its greatest strength in the thirty-fourth Congress, 1854–1856, and in the discussions of the period many severe charges were made against the immigrants.

But the Know Nothings were in the minority and consequently had little real influence on legislation. The immigration laws proposed by them were, as a rule, confined to the exclusion of foreign paupers and criminals, and none of these was passed.[1] The diversion of public interest from immigration affairs to the great questions of slavery, and the events preliminary to the Civil War, coupled with the decline in the volume of immigration after 1854, led to the natural decline and final break-up of the Know Nothing party.

The agitation of the period, however, particularly in regard to steerage conditions, had its effect on Congress, and in 1853 a select committee of the Senate was appointed to investigate the conditions of steerage immigration and, in particular, "the causes and the extent of the sickness and mortality prevailing on board the emigrant ships on the voyage to this country," and to

[1] Rept. Imm. Com., Federal Immigration Legislation, Abs., pp. 8–10.

determine what legislation, if any, was necessary to secure better conditions. This committee reported on August 2, 1854, and on March 3, 1855, a bill was passed which, with slight modifications, governed the carriage of immigrants up to 1882. The design of this act was to improve steerage conditions, and "theoretically the law of 1855 provided for an increased air space, better ventilation, and improved accommodations in the way of berths, cooking facilities, the serving of food, free open deck space, and so forth. Although the evil of overcrowding, which had been attended with such disastrous results in former years, appears to have been especially aimed at by the makers of the law, the wording of the act was, unfortunately, such that the provisions relating to the number of passengers to be carried were inoperative, and there was practically no legal restraint in this regard, as far as the United States law was concerned, between 1855 and 1882." [1]

Practically the only amendment to the steerage law from 1855 to 1882 was an act of 1860, designed to secure much-needed protection for female passengers from immoral conduct on the part of members of the crew. A fine of $1000 was imposed on any person employed on any ship of the United States who was found guilty of such conduct, and members of the crew were forbidden to visit parts of the ship assigned to immigrants, except under the direction or with the permission of the commanding officer.

It will be observed that, while the various state laws had a slightly restrictive effect, all of the federal acts of this period, designed as they were to secure better accommodations on the voyage, served as an encourage-

[1] Rept. Imm. Com., Steerage Legislation, Abs., p. 11.

ment, rather than a deterrent, to immigration. And, on the whole, in spite of the violent anti-immigrant agitation of the nativistic and Know Nothing movements and the dread of foreign paupers and criminals, the preponderance of public opinion in the United States was probably favorable to the immigrant as such. It must be remembered that during this entire period the United States was still distinctly a new country. There was an abundance of unoccupied land which might be secured on easy terms. There was a large westward movement of population from the Atlantic seaboard, and the growing manufactures and internal improvements created a large demand for labor. It was, as a whole, a decidedly thinly settled country. All of these things combined to give the immigrant every advantage in the mind of the native citizen.

Reviewing the third period, we see that it was a period of rapidly increasing immigration, responding to the expanding industry and exceptionally favorable agricultural situation in this country. The movement culminated in the enormous immigration of the late forties and early fifties. These were mainly Germans, who left their home primarily for political reasons, and took up farm lands in the west, and Irish, who emigrated because of economic disaster, and tended to linger in the eastern cities, or to go out into the construction camps. Both of these races were closely allied to the American people, and easily assimilated. At the beginning of the period, the attitude of the American people was almost wholly one of welcome, but with the increase of the current, bringing as it did enormous numbers of destitute and helpless aliens, there arose a distinct feeling of opposition to unregulated immigration, based primarily upon the dislike of foreign paupers and criminals, and aided by the undeniable practice of foreign countries of emptying their poorhouses, and even their jails, upon our shores. This feeling later came to be intensified by a strong antipathy to Roman Catholics and the restriction of immigration was made a party policy. Nevertheless, the opposition to immigration did not, during this period, attain sufficient strength to secure any important legislation. Many of the states had laws designed to indemnify the communities against expense on account of foreign paupers, which may have had a slight restrictive effect. But such federal legislation as there was, was directed to the improvement of the conditions of the voyage, and hence had an encouraging rather than a restrictive tendency. With the approach of the Civil War immigration fell off, and public attention was diverted to other matters.

CHAPTER V

1860 TO 1882

THE disturbances connected with the Civil War, following the industrial depression of 1857, naturally produced a diminution in the immigration current, which in the year 1862 fell to 72,183, the lowest point it had reached for more than twenty years, and one which has never been reached since. This condition, which tended to allay the excessive fear of immigration which had marked the previous decade, was augmented by certain other factors. Foremost among these was the enormous internal migration of people from the east to the middle and farther west, encouraged by the liberal homestead act of 1862. This movement, in connection with the loss of life occasioned by the war, seemed to leave great gaps in the population of the eastern states, and put the foreigners who came to fill them in much better favor. Many of the immigrants themselves also moved on to the west and took up new land, where they crowded nobody and rendered a real service in the building up of the country.

These facts explain what would otherwise seem an extraordinary circumstance — namely, that the first federal law passed with the avowed intent of regulating the volume of immigration was an act to encourage immigration. This was the act of July 4, 1864, which provided for the appointment by the President of a Commissioner of Immigration, to be under the direction of the Department of State, and further provided that all contracts made in foreign countries by immigrants pledging the wages of their labor for a term not exceeding twelve months should be valid. An immigration office was to be established in New York City, in charge of a Superintendent of Immigration, to look after the transporting of immigrants to their final destination, and protecting them from imposition and fraud. Several companies, in pursuance of this act, were formed for the purpose of dealing in contract labor. But protests against the character of immigrants continued strong, and the law was repealed in 1868. The feeling of opposition to contract labor in general was also beginning to assert itself at this time, and continued to grow, so that the next federal legislation touching on contract labor was of a wholly different character.

This period witnessed another important change in the immigration situation — the transition from the sailing vessel to the steamship as the prevailing type of immigrant carrier. "Writers on the history of sail and steam navigation agree that steamships played no part prior to 1850 in the transportation of other than cabin passengers. In that year the Inman Line of steamships, then recently established, began to compete with sailing vessels by providing third-class, or steerage, accommodation. . . . . Once established in the emigrant carrying trade, steamships quickly monopolized the greater part of the business."[1] In 1856, of the passengers landed at Castle Garden, New York, 96.4 per cent were carried on sailing vessels, and 3.6 per cent on steamships. In 1873 the proportions were almost exactly reversed — 3.2 per cent on sailing vessels, and 96.8 per cent on

[1] Rept. Imm. Com., Steer. Legis., Abs., pp. 12, 13.

steamships. The turn of the balance came between the years 1864 and 1865; in the first of these years the sailing vessels carried 55.7 per cent of the passengers, and in the second, 41.7 per cent. "No consistent data are available to show the relative number of passengers carried on sailing vessels and steamships after 1873, but it was not long until steamships had practically a complete monopoly of the business."[1] This change did more to alleviate the conditions of the steerage than anything which had transpired previously.

The change from sail to steam was accompanied by the loss of the primary position in the immigrant carrying field by the United States. In the rivalry for the steamship business she was quickly outstripped by England. Chance played a part in this outcome through the loss of two of the largest ships of the Collins Line, but the conscious policy of the United States contributed to the result. The available capital of the country was diverted to manufactures and railroad building by the artificial stimulus given to these industries — by the tariff on the one hand, and the land grants on the other.

With the return of prosperity after the war, the volume of immigration began to increase again, and in 1873 culminated in the record figure of 459,803. The industrial depression of that year cut down the influx, and the next record was not reached until 1882, the year that inaugurates the modern period. During the entire period under discussion the two main elements in the immigration stream were the Irish and the Germans. The climax of the immigration from the United Kingdom (mostly Irish) had been reached in 1851, with a total of 272,240, a figure which has never been equaled since.

[1] Rept. Imm. Com., Steer. Legis., Abs., p. 13.

The immigration from Germany in the year 1854 had reached 215,009, a number which has been exceeded only once since then (in 1882). In 1854, 87.7 per cent of the entire immigration came from these two sources. In 1873, 68.8 per cent still showed the same origin.

During the closing years of this period people of Scandinavian origin occupied a noteworthy place in the immigration field. Small parties of Norwegians, Danes, and Swedes had appeared early in the nineteenth century, and had been followed by others from time to time. These early immigrants had formed settlements, for the most part agricultural, in various parts of the country, particularly in the middle west and northwest. But they were an inconsiderable part of the total immigration until after the Civil War. In 1873 they amounted to 7.7 per cent of the total immigration, and in 1882 to 13.4 per cent. The underlying causes which predisposed the natives of the Scandinavian countries to emigration were found in the rugged and inhospitable character of the soil, and the severe and uncertain climate. Only a small part of the total land area was available for cultivation, and there was little room for an expanding population. Thus the fundamental causes of emigration were economic. Religious differences and the demands of military service played minor parts. Political oppression entered in somewhat in the case of the Danes.

The more immediate causes are found in a period of financial depression between 1866 and 1870, the Dano-Prussian War of 1864, the activities of steamship agents, and more particularly the letters and visits from the earlier emigrants and adventurers, who told in person of the advantages and opportunities of life in America.

These, as always, had a profound effect in stirring up enthusiasm for emigration.

The Scandinavian emigrants came mainly from rural regions and rural occupations, and naturally tended to follow out the same bent in their new home, resembling in this respect their kinsmen, the Germans. Like them, too, they were easily assimilated, and aroused little opposition on the part of the Americans.[1]

It was in connection with one of these leading groups of immigrants — the Irish — that there developed one of the most unfortunate, and at the same time interesting, series of events that have occurred in connection with the immigrant situation during our entire history — one that had much to do with arousing antipathy toward foreigners, and was among the influences that led to the introduction of new races from southeastern Europe.[2] This was the Molly Maguire disturbance in the anthracite region of Pennsylvania.

When the anthracite coal districts of Pennsylvania were opened up, early in the second quarter of the nineteenth century, the social conditions in the new settlements resembled those of a gold mining region, in the prevalence of lawlessness, excitability, and turbulence. The country was still rough and thinly settled, and between the mining settlements were wide stretches of virgin wilds which furnished ideal hiding places for criminals and refugees. As the knowledge of mining was largely confined to foreigners, they came to occupy a large place in the colliery towns, and prominent among them were the Irish. As the numbers of Irish increased,

[1] See Flom, George T., *Norwegian Immigration into the United States*, and *Chapters on Scandinavian Immigration to Iowa;* also, Nelson, O. N., *History of the Scandinavians and Successful Scandinavians in the United States*.

[2] Commons, J. R., *op. cit.*, p. 129.

Irish customs and ideas came to practically dominate many places. Other foreign races represented were the Germans, English, Welsh, Scotch, and Poles. The immigrants from Ireland during the forties and fifties were not all worthy representatives of the race, as many of the more turbulent characters were practically compelled by the landlords to join the general exodus.

As early as 1854 there appeared among the Irish miners an organization known as the Molly Maguires — a name long known in Ireland, though there was no organic connection between the societies in the old and new world. Its members were all Irish and all professed adherents to the Roman Catholic Church, though both the church and the better elements of the race absolutely repudiated them and their acts. Also, practically all the Molly Maguires were members of the Ancient Order of Hibernians, and were able so to control this organization, legally chartered for beneficial purposes, as to use it as a cloak for their nefarious enterprises.

The power of the Molly Maguires was used primarily to further the ends of its members in their relations with the colliery owners and bosses; whenever a dispute arose between an employee and a boss, the latter would be served with a notice, frequently decorated with rude pictures of coffins, death's heads, and the like, warning him to desist in his course or to leave the region. If he failed to obey, he was almost sure soon after to be waylaid and cruelly beaten, as well as to suffer social ostracism. The perpetrators of the deed of violence always escaped, and thus confidence and a sense of power grew in the organization.

Soon after the breaking out of the Civil War, conditions in the anthracite region became such as to improve the situation of the miners and add to the power of the Molly Maguires. They became more and more insolent in their demands, and ambitious in their purposes. They tried to gain control of the Miners' Union, and also, with a measure of success, sought to dominate local politics, with their eye primarily upon the township funds. They succeeded in making the lives of the small mine owners such a burden that they were glad to sell out to the large combinations; thus the growth of large units and monopolies was fostered, as they alone could deal with the Molly Maguires on anything like terms of equality. In the meantime, the methods of the society increased in harshness and barbarity. Arson and murder took the place of beating. There arose a rivalry among the Mollies as to who should gain the greatest reputation for deeds of reckless savagery. Murder after murder was committed, without a conviction. The victims were often men of the highest repute and usefulness in their respective communities. The motives for the outrages increased in variety, including almost any injury, real or fancied, or any personal grudge on the part of a member of the society, though rarely were they committed for robbery. A general reign of terror settled down over the region, and vigilance committees were being formed for purposes of reprisal.

At this juncture, in 1873, Mr. Franklin B. Gowen, president of the Philadelphia and Reading Coal and Iron Company, and a man of remarkable character, enlisted the services of the Pinkerton Detective Agency in the effort to stamp out the organization. A young Irish detective, James McParlan, was chosen for the dangerous and difficult work. He was instructed to go to the anthracite region, join the Molly Maguires, and get as high in their counsels as possible, in order that he might reveal their secrets to the authorities, thereby preventing outrages when possible and securing convictions where he could not prevent. He was successful in both efforts. After many months of work and peril he finally succeeded in securing sufficient evidence to accomplish the conviction of a large number of the members of the society, breaking down completely their customary defense of an alibi. In all, nineteen Molly Maguires were hanged, and a larger number imprisoned, and the power of the organization was completely shattered.

This series of events is a remarkable illustration of the way in which customs, and habits of thought, and standards of conduct, which have grown up by a natural process, and are comprehensible if not excusable in one land, may develop most alarming and disgraceful features when transplanted to a new environment. The essential strength of the Molly Maguires lay in that deep-seated hatred of an informer which has become a pronounced feature of the Irish character, as a result of the conditions to which they have been subjected at home. Thus, while the great mass of the Irish settlers of the anthracite region abhorred the principles and deeds of the Molly Maguires, it was almost impossible to secure witnesses against criminals whose identity was a matter of general knowledge, because of the greater repugnance to the character of an informer. The traditional hatred of the Irish peasant towards the landlord was, in this country, diverted to the capitalist class in a wholly unreasonable but efficient manner.

There is here, also, a striking demonstration of the capacity of a relatively small group of turbulent and unassimilated foreigners so to conduct themselves as to bring an undeserved disrepute upon their whole group, and foster economic and social changes in society which will last on long after they are all dead.[1]

While the Irish and Germans were dominating the immigration situation on the Atlantic coast, the Chinese were occupying the center of the stage in the west. The stream of Chinese immigration became considerable at about the same time that the great increase in European immigration was taking place on the other side of the continent. As to its causes, Mrs. Mary Roberts Coolidge speaks as follows: "The first effective contact of China with Western nations was through the Opium War of 1840, which resulted in an increase of Chinese taxes, a general disturbance of the laboring classes, and the penetration of some slight knowledge of European ideas into the maritime provinces. Although this prepared the way for the emigration to the West, its precipitating cause lay in 'the Golden Romance' that had filled the world," — that is, the news of the discovery of gold in California. "Masters of foreign vessels afforded every facility to emigration, distributing placards, maps, and pamphlets with highly colored accounts of the Golden Hills. . . . But behind the opportunity afforded by foreign shipping and the enticement of the discovery of gold lay deeper causes for emigration — the poverty and ruin in which the inhabitants of Southeastern China were involved by the great Taiping rebellion which began in the summer of 1850. The terrors of war, famine, and plundering paralyzed all industry and trade, and the agricultural classes of the maritime dis-

[1] Dewees, F. P., *The Molly Maguires;* Rhodes, J. F., *The Molly Maguires in the Anthracite Region of Pennsylvania; Encyc. Britannica,* article "Molly Maguires."

tricts especially were driven to Hong Kong and Macao."[1] By the end of 1852 there were in the neighborhood of 25,000 Chinese on the Pacific coast, almost all of them in California.

During the first few years of their coming, the Chinese in California were welcomed, and were looked upon with favor. They were industrious, tractable, and inoffensive, and were willing to undertake the hard, menial, and disagreeable forms of labor — partly work generally done by women — for which native labor was not available under existing conditions. Their strange manners and customs aroused nothing more than feelings of curiosity. But gradually a feeling of opposition to them began to grow up, fomented by the jealousy and race prejudice of the miners. Their peculiar appearance and strange customs began to make them the objects of suspicion and hatred. This feeling was intensified by the presence of a large element of southerners in California, who classed all people of dark skin — "South Americans, South Europeans, Kanakas, Malays, or Chinese" — together as colored. Wild stories of their character and habits began to circulate, and with each repetition gained strength until they passed current as facts. Among these were the assertions that the Chinese were practically all coolies, or labor slaves, that they were highly immoral and vicious, that they had secret tribunals which inflicted the death penalty without due process of law, that they displaced native labor, that they could not be Christianized, that they had no intention of remaining as permanent residents of the country and would not assimilate with the natives, that they sent money out of the country, etc. Most of these

[1] Coolidge, Mary R., *Chinese Immigration*, pp. 16, 17.

charges have been proven to be either wholly false or highly exaggerated by recent investigations, and were so recognized by the more sober and fair minded students of the subject at the time. But for the mass of the people of the Pacific coast, and for many in other parts of the country, they acquired all the force of established dogma, and their reiteration passed for argument.

The Chinaman became the scapegoat for all the ills that afflicted the youthful community, from whatever cause they really arose, and in time an anti-Chinese declaration came to be essential for the success of any political party or candidate. In such a state of public opinion it was inevitable that their lot should be a hard one. They were robbed, beaten, murdered, and persecuted in a variety of ways. The foreign miners' license tax was used against them in a discriminating way which amounted to quasi legal plunder.

In 1876 the California State Legislature appointed a committee to look into the matter of Chinese immigration and to make a report. This was done in 1877, and although the resulting Address and Memorial to Congress have had a large influence in forming public opinion, and in shaping legislation, it appears that it was in fact a purely political document, and that everything was arranged in advance to secure a report which should accomplish a certain definite result — the satisfaction of the workingmen of the state, and the emphasizing of the necessity of federal legislation. The need of this was strongly felt, because nearly all the acts passed by the coast states against the Chinese had been declared either unconstitutional or a violation of treaty.

In response to the repeated demands of the coast states for some federal action, Congress in 1876 appointed a special committee on Chinese immigration, which made what purported to be a thorough investigation of the matter, and reported thereupon. The report was wholly anti-Chinese. But this was inevitable, as it is apparent from a careful study of the testimony, that the committee "came to its task committed to an anti-Chinese conclusion and that it had no judicial character whatever." [1] The evidence was willfully distorted to produce the desired result.

During all this time our relations with China had been nominally subject to a series of treaties, beginning with that of 1844, and including the famous Burlingame treaty of 1868. While the earlier agreements did not specifically mention the rights of Chinese to reside and trade in the United States, they were in fact allowed the same privileges in these respects as the citizens of other nations. By the treaty of 1868, however, the right of voluntary emigration was definitely recognized as between the two countries on the basis of the most favored nation; but the Chinese were not given the right of naturalization. From this privilege they were definitely excluded by the law of 1870.

It became evident in time that no federal legislation, satisfactory to the politicians of the western states, could be secured under the existing treaties. There arose accordingly a demand for a new treaty which would allow the passage of laws which would include the points desired by the western representatives, practically the exclusion of all Chinese not belonging to the merchant class. In response to this demand there was negotiated, after much conference between the representatives of the two nations, a new treaty in 1880. The most

[1] Coolidge, M. R., *op. cit.*, p. 107.

important feature of this new instrument was the right conferred upon the government of the United States reasonably to regulate, limit, or suspend, but not to prohibit, the coming or residence of Chinese laborers, whenever it deemed that the interests of the country demanded such action. It is under this treaty that the various Chinese exclusion acts have been passed.

The first of these acts was passed in 1882, and provided for the exclusion of Chinese laborers for a period of ten years. This was not to apply to Chinese who were already in the country, or who should enter within ninety days after the passage of the act. Such persons, who desired to leave the country and return, were required to secure a certificate, which by an amendatory act of 1884 was made the sole evidence of the right of a Chinaman to return. This act also required a certificate of the exempt classes, to be issued by the Chinese government or such other foreign governments as they might be subject to. The deportation of Chinese unlawfully in the country was also provided for by these acts.

These laws were in many respects carelessly drawn and extremely difficult of execution. In their application they entailed great expense upon the United States government, and worked extreme hardship and injustice to many Chinese. They were, nevertheless, effective as regards their main purpose, for the volume of Chinese immigration at once diminished exceedingly. The strictness of the exclusion was increased by the act of 1888, which refused return to any Chinese laborer unless he had a lawful wife, child, or parent in the United States, or owned property of the value of $1000 or had debts due him of like amount. The acts in force were extended for another ten years by the act of 1892, and again indefinitely in 1902, in each case with relatively unimportant modifications in detail.

This history of Chinese immigration is not a matter in which the citizen of the United States can take much pride. Race prejudice, bigotry, ignorance, and political ambition have played a prominent part in the agitation, and have been instrumental in securing much of the legislation. The attitude and conduct of the United States contrasts unfavorably with the position of China, which has been one of patient, courteous, dignified, but emphatic protest, and willingness to coöperate in securing reasonable and beneficial regulation. The boycott of 1905 has been her principal active reprisal. In spite of these facts, however, it would be rash to assert that the exclusion of Chinese laborers, by whatever unfortunate means accomplished, has not been of actual benefit to the United States. The assertion that the failure of the Chinese to assimilate has been due more to race prejudice and exclusiveness on the part of Americans than to unwillingness to be Americanized on the part of the Chinese, does not do away with the fact of nonassimilation. Until Americans are willing to fraternize on terms of social equality with members of any race, there is great danger to national institutions in the presence of large numbers of that race within the country.[1] And when we reflect how enormous Chinese immigration might easily have become in these recent years of quick and easy transportation, and excessive activity of steamship agents, contract labor agents, and others of their

[1] Professor Taussig justifies the exclusion of the Chinese on the ground that "a permanent group of helots is not a healthy constituent in a democratic society," *Principles of Economics*, Vol. II, p. 140.

kind, it is apparent that if free immigration had been allowed to these people of a widely diverse race, we might now be facing a Chinese problem in this country second in gravity only to the negro question.[1]

By the end of this period the conditions of life in America had so changed as to diminish the general feeling of complacency toward unlimited immigration. There was in particular a growing opposition to contract labor, and an increased demand for federal control of the immigration situation, especially as all state laws in regard to the regulation of foreign immigration had been declared unconstitutional in 1876. There was a conviction in the minds of some thinkers that the United States no longer stood in need of an increased labor force. These views were clearly expressed in an article by Mr. A. B. Mason, published in 1874. Some of his statements have a new ring. "The conditions that have hitherto greatly favored immigration no longer exist in their full force." "The labour market, *especially for agricultural labour*, is overstocked." "The especial disadvantages of American labour more than counterbalance its especial advantages." "English labour is in the main as well off as American labour."[2] It is

[1] The subject of Chinese immigration has been treated thus summarily because of the large amount of reliable material which is easily available on the question. It has been treated as a whole, rather than divided among the different periods, because in fact it has been a distinct phase of our immigration problem; only since 1900 has the administration of the Chinese exclusion law been a part of the duties of the Commissioner General of Immigration. Foremost among the books on the topic is Mrs. Coolidge's work, already quoted. A defense of the Chinese written in the heat of the controversy is George F. Seward's *Chinese Immigration*. Interesting chapters on the topic are to be found in Mayo-Smith, and Hall, and frequent references in Jenks and Lauck, and Commons. Cf. also Sparks, E. E., *National Development*, 1877–1885, pp. 229–250.

[2] Mason, A. B., "An American View of Emigration," *Fortnightly Review*, 22: 273.

evident that the time was at hand when the competition of the foreigner in the American labor market could no longer be regarded with equanimity.

This sentiment did not bear fruit, however, until the year 1882. The only federal legislation bearing on immigration after the repeal of the favorable contract labor law in 1868 up to this date, was the act of March 3, 1875, prohibiting the importation or immigration into the United States of women for the purpose of prostitution, and also prohibiting the immigration of criminals, convicted of other than political offenses. This law, while couched in general terms, was an outcome of the anti-Chinese agitation, and was passed with this race particularly in mind.

CHAPTER VI

MODERN PERIOD. FEDERAL LEGISLATION

THE year 1882 stands as a prominent landmark in the history of immigration into the United States. In that year the total immigration reached the figure of 788,992, a point which had never been reached before and was not reached again until 1903. It witnessed the climax of the movement from the Scandinavian countries, and from Germany; only once since then has the immigration from the United Kingdom reached the amount of that year. It coincides almost exactly with the appearance of the streams of immigration from Italy, Austria-Hungary, and Russia of sufficient volume to command attention. In that year the first Chinese exclusion act and the first inclusive federal immigration law were passed. Consequently the year 1882 stands as a natural and logical beginning of the modern period of immigration, a period during which the immigration movement has been marked by characteristics so peculiarly new and definite as to distinguish it sharply from anything which went before. The discussion of immigration during this period is in all its essentials the discussion of a present-day problem.

One of the most distinctive and obvious characteristics of this period has been the growth of a complicated body of federal immigration laws. These have put the whole immigration question on a new basis, an[illegible]erve to be considered in some detail. In the follov[illegible]w, only those sections of the successive laws which contain matter that is of general importance have been included. All merely technical details and many of the provisions regarding penalties and the practical administration of the laws have been omitted.

Act of August 3, 1882. SECTION 1. A duty (commonly known as a head tax) of fifty cents is to be levied for every passenger not a citizen of the United States, who comes from any foreign port to any port of the United States by steam or sail vessel. This duty is to be paid to the collector of customs of the port, by the master, owner, agent, or consignee of the vessel within twenty-four hours after entry. The money so collected is to constitute an Immigrant Fund, to be used to defray the expenses of regulating immigration, for the care of immigrants, and the relief of such as are in distress, and in general for carrying out the provisions of the act. This duty is to constitute a lien upon the vessel until paid.

SECTION 2. The Secretary of the Treasury is charged with the execution of this act, and with supervision over the business of immigration into the United States. He is authorized to make contracts with state boards and commissions, which are still charged with the duty of examining ships arriving at ports of the state. Any convict, lunatic, idiot, or any person unable to take care of himself or herself without becoming a public charge shall not be permitted to land.

SECTION 3. The Secretary of the Treasury is empowered to make provisions to protect immigrants from fraud and loss, and to carry out the law.

SECTION 4. All foreign convicts, except those convicted of political offenses, shall be returned to the nations to which they belong and from which they came. The expense of returning all persons not permitted to land is to be borne by the owners of the vessel in which they came.

SECTION 5. This act shall take effect immediately.

The salient points of this law are the imposition of a federal head tax, the beginning of a list of excluded classes, the return of excluded aliens, at the expense of the shipowners, and the assignment of the immigration business to the Secretary of the Treasury, the actual work of examination, however, still being done by the state boards.

The next act bearing on immigration was Section 22 of the act of June 26, 1884, and was designed to correct a discrimination in favor of land transportation contained in Section 1 of the act of 1882. It provided that until the provisions of this section should be made applicable to passengers coming into the United States by land carriage, they should not apply to passengers coming in vessels trading exclusively between ports of the United States and Canada and Mexico.

Act of February 26, 1885. SECTION 1. It shall be "unlawful for any person, company, partnership, or corporation, in any manner whatsoever, to prepay the transportation, or in any way to assist or encourage the importation or migration of any alien or aliens, any foreigner or foreigners, into the United States, its Territories, or the District of Columbia, under contract or agreement, parol or special, express or implied, made previously to the importation or migration of such alien or aliens, foreigner or foreigners, to perform labor or service of any kind in the United States, its Territories, or the District of Columbia."

SECTION 2. All contracts of the above nature shall be void.

SECTION 3. Provides for a fine of $1000 for every violation of the above provision, payable for each alien being party to such a contract.

SECTION 4. The master of any vessel who knowingly brings in contract laborers shall be fined not more than $500, and may also be imprisoned for not more than six months.

SECTION 5. The following classes shall be excepted from the provisions of the above sections: secretaries, servants, and domestics of foreigners temporarily residing in the United States; skilled workmen for any industry not now established in the United States, provided that such labor cannot be otherwise obtained; actors, artists, lecturers or singers, or persons employed strictly as personal or domestic servants. This act shall not prevent any individual from assisting any member of his family or any relative or personal friend to come in for the purpose of settlement.

On February 23, 1887, there was an amendatory act passed to the above act, specifically intrusting the Secretary of the Treasury with the carrying out of its provisions, and providing for the return of contract laborers in a manner similar to other excluded classes.

On October 19, 1888, the law of 1887 was amended, providing that a person who has entered the country contrary to the contract labor law, may be deported within one year at the expense of the owner of the importing vessel, or if he came by land, of the person contracting for his services.

The section containing the provision for excluding contract laborers has been quoted verbatim to emphasize its extremely strict and inclusive wording. It would be very difficult for any person who had the slightest idea of what he was going to do in this country to prove himself outside the letter of that law. The softening clauses of the law are put in the form of exceptions, thus throwing the burden of the proof upon the immigrant. The last amendment quoted is of especial interest as introducing the principle of deportation after landing.[1]

Act of March 3, 1891. SECTION 1. The following additions are made to the excluded classes: paupers or persons likely to become a public charge, persons suffering from a loathsome or a contagious disease, polygamists, and any person whose ticket or passage is paid for with the money of another, or who is assisted by others to come, unless it is specifically proved that he does not belong to one of the excluded classes, including contract laborers.

SECTION 3. Assisting or encouraging immigration by promise of employment through advertising in a foreign country is declared illegal, with the exception of the advertisements of state agencies.

[1] "Deportation" must be carefully distinguished from "exclusion," "debarment," or "returning." When either of the last three terms is used, it implies that the immigrant is never allowed to land in the country. The first term is applicable when the immigrant has landed in this country, and some time after, in accordance with some provision of the law, is sent back to the country from which he came.

This is the first provision for deportation in the federal laws, except the temporary provision of the Alien Bill. As early as 1837 the common council of New York City passed a resolution, authorizing the commissioners of the almshouse to send back to their native country such alien paupers as were, or were likely to become, paupers at the establishment at Bellevue or elsewhere, provided the pauper in question gave his consent. (Executive (House) Documents, 25th Cong., 2d Ses., 370, pp. 16–18.) It is amusing to note that at that period our right to send back alien paupers, — even though they had been officially transported to this country, — after they had once been admitted, was seriously questioned by foreign powers.

SECTION 4. Encouragement or solicitation of immigration by steamship or transportation companies, except by means of regular advertisements giving an account of sailings, facilities, and terms is declared illegal.

SECTION 5. The following are added to the excepted classes under the contract labor law: ministers of any religious denomination, persons belonging to any recognized profession, professors of colleges and seminaries. Relatives and friends of persons in this country are not hereafter to be excepted.

SECTION 6. Persons bringing in aliens not legally entitled to enter are made liable to a fine of not more than $1000, or imprisonment for not more than one year, or both.

SECTION 7. The office of Superintendent of Immigration is created, to be under the Secretary of the Treasury.

SECTION 8. Shipmasters shall file with the proper officers a manifest, giving the name, nationality, last residence, and destination of each alien passenger. Inspection is to be made by inspection officers before landing, or a temporary landing may be made at a specified place. The medical examination is to be made by surgeons of the Marine Hospital Service. During the temporary landing, aliens are to be properly fed and cared for. Right of appeal granted. Landing, or allowing to land, alien passengers at any other time or place than that specified by the inspectors is made an offense punishable by a (maximum) fine of $1000, or imprisonment for one year, or both. The Secretary of the Treasury is empowered to prescribe rules for the inspection of immigrants along the borders of Canada, British Columbia, and Mexico. The duties and powers previously vested in the state boards are now to go to the regular inspection officers of the United States.

SECTION 10. All aliens who unlawfully come to the United States are to be immediately sent back on the vessel in which they came, all expenses in the meantime to be borne by the shipowner.

SECTION 11. Any alien who comes into the United States in violation of law may be deported within one year, and any alien who becomes a public charge within one year after landing, from causes existing prior to this landing, may be deported. The expenses of all deportations are to be borne by the transportation agency responsible for bringing in the immigrant, if that is possible, and if not, by the United States.

The items in this act particularly worthy of notice are the following: extension of the excluded classes; prohibition of encouraging immigration by advertising or solicitation, an attempt to cure two serious evils, the success of which we shall have occasion to note later; relatives and personal friends in this country no longer excepted from the contract labor clause (this exception had almost vitiated the former law); requirement of manifests; the complete assumption of the work of inspection by the federal government; extension of the principle of deportation to public charges.

Act of March 3, 1893. SECTION 1. Manifests greatly enlarged in detail.

SECTION 2. Alien passengers are to be listed in convenient groups of not more than thirty each, and given tickets corresponding to their numbers on the manifests. The master of the vessel must certify that he and the ship's surgeon have made an examination of all the immigrants before sailing, and believe none of them to belong to the excluded classes.

SECTION 3. If the ship has no surgeon, examination must be made by a competent surgeon hired by the transportation company.

SECTION 5. Immigrants who are not beyond any doubt entitled to land are to be held for special inquiry by a board of not less than four inspectors.

The noteworthy features in this law are examination at the expense of the company at the port of embarkation, listing the immigrants in groups of thirty, the institution of the boards of special inquiry.

August 18, 1894. Head tax is raised to $1.

March 2, 1895. The Superintendent of Immigration is hereafter to be designated the Commissioner General of Immigration.

June 6, 1900. The Commissioner General of Immigration is made responsible for the administration of the Chinese Exclusion Acts.

March 3, 1903. SECTION 1. The head tax is raised to $2, and is not to apply to citizens of Canada, Cuba, or Mexico.

SECTION 2. The following are added to the debarred classes: epileptics, persons who have been insane within five years previous, persons who have had two or more attacks of insanity at any time previously; professional beggars, anarchists, or persons who believe in or advocate the overthrow by force or violence of the government of the United States, or of all government or of all forms of law, or the assassination of public officials; prostitutes, and persons who procure or attempt to bring in prostitutes or women for the purpose of prostitution; those who, within one year, have been deported under the contract labor clause.

SECTION 3. The importation of prostitutes is forbidden under a (maximum) penalty of five years' imprisonment and a fine of $5000.

SECTION 9. The bringing in of any person afflicted with a loathsome or a dangerous contagious disease by any person or company, except railway lines, is forbidden. A fine of $100 is attached if it appears that the disease might have been detected at the time of embarkation.

SECTION 11. If a rejected alien is helpless from sickness, physical disability, or infancy, and is accompanied by an alien whose protection is required, both shall be returned in the usual way.

SECTION 20. The period of deportation for aliens who have come into this country in violation of law, including those who have become public charges within two years after landing, is raised to two years.

SECTION 21. A similar provision for deportation within three years is made for the above classes of aliens, with the exception of public charges.

SECTION 24. The appointment of immigration inspectors and other employees is put under the Civil Service rules.

SECTION 25. The boards of special inquiry are to consist of three members. Either the alien or any dissenting member of the board may appeal.

SECTION 39. Anarchists, etc., are not to be naturalized.

The important features of this act are the further extension of the excluded classes; special attention and penalties with respect to prostitutes; the period of deportation raised to two and three years.

Act of February 14, 1903. The Department of Commerce and Labor is created, and the Commissioner General of Immigration is transferred to it from the Treasury Department.

March 22, 1904. Newfoundland is added to the countries exempt from the head tax.

June 29, 1906. The Bureau of Immigration is henceforth to be called the Bureau of Immigration and Naturalization, and is to have charge of the business of naturalization. A register is to be kept at immigration stations, giving full information in regard to all aliens arriving in the United States.

On February 20, 1907, there was passed an inclusive immigration law, designed to include all of the previous laws, and repealing such provisions of earlier laws as are not consistent with the present law. The principal changes introduced by the new law are as follows:

SECTION 1. The head tax is raised to $4. It is not to be levied on aliens who have resided for at least one year immediately preceding, in Canada, Newfoundland, Cuba, or Mexico, nor on aliens in transit through the United States.

SECTION 2. To the excluded classes are added imbeciles, feeble-minded persons, persons afflicted with tuberculosis, persons not included in any of the specifically excluded classes who have a mental or physical deficiency which may affect their ability to earn a living, persons who admit having committed a crime involving moral turpitude, persons who admit their belief in the practice of polygamy, women or girls coming into the United States for the purpose of prostitution, or for any other immoral purpose, or persons who attempt to bring in such women or girls, and all children under the age of sixteen unaccompanied by one or both of their parents, at the discretion of the Secretary of Commerce and Labor. Persons whose tickets are paid for with the money of another must show affirmatively that they were not paid for by any corporation, society, association, municipality, or foreign government, either directly or indirectly. This is not to apply to aliens in continuous transit through the United States to foreign contiguous territory.

SECTION 3. The harboring of immoral women and girls in houses of prostitution, or any other place for purposes of prostitution, within a period of three years after their arrival, is made an offense punishable in the same manner as importing them. Such women are liable to deportation within three years.

SECTION 9. A fine of $100 is imposed on any person bringing in aliens subject to any of the following disabilities: idiots, imbeciles, epileptics, or persons afflicted with tuberculosis (or with a loathsome or dangerous contagious disease), if these existed and might have been detected previous to embarkation.

SECTION 12. It is made the duty of shipmasters taking alien passengers out of the United States to furnish a report, before sailing, giving the name, age, sex, nationality, residence in the United States, occupation, and time of last arrival in the United States of each such alien passenger.

SECTION 20. All deportations may be within three years.[1]

SECTION 25. Appeal from a decision of a board of special inquiry may be made by the rejected alien or by any member of the board, through the commissioner of

[1] By an administrative rule of the department any alien, who is a lawful resident of the United States and becomes a public charge from physical disability arising subsequent to his landing, may, with his consent, and the approval of the bureau, be deported within one year at government expense.

the port and the Commissioner General of Immigration to the Secretary of Commerce and Labor, except in cases of tuberculosis, loathsome or dangerous contagious disease, or mental or physical disability, as previously provided for, in which case the decision of the board is final.

SECTION 26. Any alien who is not admissible because likely to become a public charge, or because of physical disability other than tuberculosis or loathsome or dangerous contagious disease, may be admitted on a suitable bond against becoming a public charge.

SECTION 39. An Immigration Commission is to be appointed.

SECTION 40. The establishment of a Divison of Information is authorized. Its duty is to promote a beneficial distribution of aliens admitted into the United States.

SECTION 42. Provisions regarding steerage accommodations.[1]

The especially noteworthy features of this act are the following: further extension of the excluded classes; more stringent provisions regarding immoral women, and their managers; the fine for bringing in inadmissible aliens extended to other classes; the beginning of statistics of departing aliens; appeal not allowed from the decision of a board of special inquiry in case of mental or physical disability; Immigration Commission authorized; Division of Information established.

The only important addition to immigration legislation since this act is the act of March 26, 1910, by which there were added to the excluded and deportable classes "persons who are supported by or receive in full or in part

[1] See page 118.

the proceeds of prostitution." The three-year limit for deportation was removed as regards sexually immoral aliens. Closely connected with this phase of the immigration statutes is a recent act prohibiting the importation from one state to another of persons for the purpose of prostitution. In accordance with an act just passed (1913) the business of immigration and naturalization passes over to the newly created Department of Labor.

We have seen that up to 1882 practically all the federal acts relating to immigration had to do with the regulation of steerage conditions. Until the year 1907 these acts, which were encouraging in tendency, were always considered as a separate body of legislation from the real immigration laws, which were primarily restrictive in character. In the act of that year, however, the control of the steerage was included in the immigration law, where it logically belonged. There had been one or two important pieces of steerage legislation passed previous to this time which we have not as yet noticed.

The last important steerage act which has been noted was the act of 1855. The principal law between that date and 1907 was the act of 1882. "Viewed from the standpoint of its predecessors the passenger act of 1882 was an excellent measure. Its framers had profited by observing the results of the legislative experiments of about sixty-two years. This advantage, together with the marvelous development and progress in the methods of passenger traffic, enabled the lawmakers to draft an intelligent and comprehensive bill. By its provisions the safety and comfort of emigrants were, theoretically at least, assured. No deck less than 6 feet in height on any vessel was allowed to be used for passengers. On the main deck and the deck next below 100 cubic feet of air space was allowed each passenger, and on the second deck below the main deck 120 cubic feet was allowed each person. Decks other than the three above mentioned were under no circumstances to be used for passengers. With the development of shipbuilding, however, other decks were added to ships, and this provision soon became obsolete. Sufficient berths for all passengers were to be provided, the dimensions of each berth to be not less than 2 feet in width and 6 feet in length, with suitable partitions dividing them. The sexes were to be properly separated. The steerage was to be amply supplied with fresh air by means of modern approved ventilators. Three cooked meals, consisting of wholesome food, were to be served regularly each day. Each ship was to have a fully equipped modern hospital for the use of sick passengers. A competent physician was to be in attendance and suitable medicines were to be carried. The ship's master was authorized to enforce such rules and regulations as would promote habits of cleanliness and good health. Dangerous articles, such as highly explosive substances and powerful acids, were forbidden on board."[1]

The above act remained in force until 1907, when it was superseded by Section 42 of the immigration act of that year. By this law the cubic air space system of the act of 1882 was abandoned in favor of the superficial area system of preventing overcrowding. Eighteen clear feet of deck space on the main deck or the deck next below were to be provided for each passenger, and 20 feet on the second deck below. If the height between the lower passenger deck and the one next above was less than 7 feet, there must be 30 clear feet

[1] Rept. Imm. Com., Steer. Legis., Abs., p. 14.

of deck space per passenger. There was also provision for light and ventilation. No passengers were to be carried on any other decks than those mentioned.

This act was unsatisfactory, as there was much uncertainty as to which was the main deck, inasmuch as ships with as many as eight decks were carrying immigrants. The British law was superior in this respect. It specified the lowest passenger deck as the one next below the water line. All above this were denominated passenger decks. This law required 18 clear superficial feet for each passenger carried on the lowest passenger deck, and 15 feet for each passenger on passenger decks. If the height of the lowest passenger deck was less than 7 feet, or if it was not properly lighted and ventilated, there must be 25 feet per passenger, and under similar conditions on passenger decks, 18 feet. There must be 5 feet of superficial open deck space for each passenger. In reckoning the space on the lowest passenger deck and passenger decks the space occupied by the baggage of passengers, public rooms, lavatories, and bathrooms used exclusively by steerage passengers might be counted, provided the actual sleeping space was not less than 15 feet on the lowest and 12 feet on the others. On December 19, 1908, the United States passed a law making our steerage provisions correspond with the British act, except that the last provisions are 18 feet and 15 feet respectively in the United States law.

In the practical application of such a complicated set of laws as these it is inevitable that many questions and uncertainties should arise. For the guidance of immigration officials in the performance of their duties, a long list of rules and regulations are prescribed by the Commissioner General. A few of these, which have an immediate bearing on the admission of aliens must be noted. Stowaways are considered *ipso facto* inadmissible, and as a rule are not even examined. Certain border ports are specified on the Canadian and Mexican borders, and any alien entering at any other port is assumed to have entered in violation of law. All aliens arriving in Canada, destined to the United States, are inspected at one of the following ports: Halifax, Nova Scotia; Quebec and Point Levi, Quebec; St. John, New Brunswick; Vancouver and Victoria, British Columbia. The United States maintains inspection stations at these points, and aliens examined there are given a certificate stating that the alien has been inspected and is admissible, accompanied by a personal description for purposes of identification. Special boards of inquiry are also established in other border cities for the examination of aliens, originally destined for Canada, but who later desire to be admitted to the United States within one year after their arrival in Canada. Aliens entering the United States by Mexican border ports are, in general, subject to the same inspection as if arriving by a seaport.

Aliens in transit are examined in the same manner as if desiring to remain in the United States, and if they are found to belong to the debarred classes they are refused permission to land. The head tax is charged on their account, as for other aliens, but it is refunded to the transportation company if the latter furnishes satisfactory proof that the alien has passed by a continuous journey through the territory of the United States, within thirty days, such proof to be furnished within sixty days after the arrival of the alien.

Throughout the development of this body of laws certain well-marked tendencies can be traced. In the first place, the criteria of admission have steadily increased in severity, until now the law provides for the exclusion of practically every class of applicants who might fairly be considered undesirable, with the exception, perhaps, of illiterates. Secondly, we may note a tendency to concentrate all business, connected with the admission of aliens into this country or into membership in the nation, in the hands of a single branch of the federal government, and the increasing power and importance of this branch. Thirdly, there is manifest an increasing recognition of the right of this country to protect itself against unwelcome additions to its population, not only by refusing them admission, but by expelling them from the country, if their subsequent conduct proves them unworthy of retention.

CHAPTER VII

VOLUME AND RACIAL COMPOSITION OF THE IMMIGRATION STREAM

As regards the volume of the immigration current the modern period has witnessed a continuation of the same general process which has been going on since 1820. The same succession of crests and depressions in the great wave has continued, the only difference being that the apex reached a much higher point than ever before. And, as in other periods, the great determining factor in the volume of immigration has been the economic situation in this country. Prosperity has always been attended by large immigration, hard times by the reverse. As already remarked, the year 1882 was marked by the largest annual immigration which had hitherto been recorded. The next low-water mark was reached in the middle nineties, following the depression of 1893. As the country recovered from this, immigration began to increase again, and rose almost steadily until in 1907 it reached the highest record which it has ever attained, a grand total of 1,285,349 immigrants in one year.[1] The crisis of that year interrupted the course of affairs, and immigration fell off sharply, and has not since completely recovered.

There is one matter connected with the volume of immigration which marks the last few years of the modern period and is of the greatest importance. This

[1] The figures since 1858 have [illegible] r the fiscal year ending June 30.

is the provision for estimating the exact net gain or loss in population each year through immigration movements. Until very recently the only immigration figures which were considered worth while were those of arriving aliens. It was tacitly assumed that our immigrant traffic was a wholly one-sided one. But gradually people began to realize that there was a large counter-current of departing aliens. In the Report of the Commissioner General of Immigration for 1906 (p. 56) an effort is made to supply as far as possible these data for the years 1890 to 1906. But in the absence of any legislation requiring shipmasters to furnish lists of departing passengers, these figures are admittedly incomplete, and no attempt is made to distinguish aliens from citizens of the United States. The nearest approach that can be made to ascertaining the number of departing aliens is to assume that all the passengers other than cabin belonged to this class. This is probably not very far from the truth, and taking these figures as a guide, we can get some idea of how large the outward movement has been at certain times, particularly during the period of commercial depression which marked the middle nineties. Thus in 1895 while there were 258,536 arrivals of immigrant aliens, there were 216,665 departures of the class mentioned, making a total gain of only 41,871; in 1898 the net gain was only 98,442 against a total immigration of 229,299. Unfortunately, figures are not available for 1896–1897. The importance of this phase of the subject eventually became so evident that in the immigration law of 1907 a provision was included requiring masters of departing vessels to file accurate and detailed lists of their alien passengers, giving certain important facts concerning them. Accordingly, in the fiscal year 1908 we have for the first time complete and accurate data regarding departing aliens.

In that year another important distinction is made, that between immigrant and nonimmigrant aliens on the inward passage, and emigrant and nonemigrant aliens on the outward passage. Immigrant aliens are those whose place of last permanent residence was in some foreign country, and who are coming here with the intention of residing permanently. Nonimmigrant aliens are of two classes: those whose place of last permanent residence was the United States, but who have been abroad for a short period of time, and those whose place of last permanent residence was in a foreign country, and who are coming to the United States without the intention of residing permanently, including aliens in transit. Departing aliens are classified in a corresponding way. Emigrant aliens are those whose place of last permanent residence was the United States, and who are going abroad with the intention of residing there permanently. Nonemigrant aliens are of two classes: those whose place of last permanent residence was the United States, and who are going abroad for a short visit only, and those whose place of last permanent residence was abroad, but who have been in the United States for a short time, including aliens in transit. In all cases the expressed intention of the alien is regarded as final concerning residence, and an intended future residence of twelve months is considered a permanent residence. The recent reports of the Commissioner General contain tables almost as detailed for departing as for arriving aliens.

Thus it is now possible to make an exact reckoning of the net gain or loss in population each year through immigration movements. The classes in which we are particularly interested are naturally the immigrant and emigrant aliens, for they are the only participants in true immigration movements, according to our definition. The others are merely travelers. Yet they are important and interesting travelers, and the modern problems of immigration cannot be thoroughly understood without taking some consideration of them. As for the aliens in transit, they can be quickly disposed of. They are counted as nonimmigrant aliens on their arrival, and nonemigrant aliens at their departure, which is supposed to occur within a period of thirty days. Thus they cancel, and do not in any important way affect the life of the United States. The other class of nonimmigrants and nonemigrants is much more important, for they include a group of aliens who have attracted considerable attention of late — the so-called "birds of passage." These are, in the strictest sense, aliens who have chosen the United States as their place of permanent residence, but who go back to the old country for brief sojourns on certain occasions. In a broader sense, the birds of passage may also be taken to include aliens whose permanent residence is abroad, but who come to this country for a brief stay.[1]

As an illustration of the method of reckoning the gain or loss in population, let us take the year 1910. In that year there were 1,041,570 immigrant aliens, and 156,467 nonimmigrant aliens admitted, making a total of 1,198,037. There were 202,436 departures of emigrant aliens and 177,982 of nonemigrant aliens, making a total of 380,418. Thus there was a net gain in the year of 817,619 aliens all together. But not all of these were

[1] For a fuller discussion of this class see the discussion of crises, p. 359.

permanent residents. To get an idea of the actual increase of permanent residents we need to add together two classes, — the immigrant aliens, who come here for the first time with the intention of residing permanently, and those nonimmigrant aliens who are such, not because they do not expect to reside here permanently, but because their permanent residence has already been established here and who have been abroad for a brief period. Of the former class, the immigrant aliens, there were 1,041,570; of the second class, nonimmigrants whose places of last permanent residence and of intended future residence were both the United States, there were 94,075. This makes a total of 1,135,645 permanent alien residents who came into the United States in the year in question. The actual decrease in permanent residents may be computed in a similar way. In the year in question there were 202,436 emigrant aliens who departed, and 89,754 nonemigrant aliens whose places of last permanent residence and intended future residence were both the United States, — that is, permanent residents of this country who left for a brief period only. This makes a total of 292,190 permanent residents of this country who left it in the year in question. Subtracting this number from the total of permanent residents who arrived, we have a remainder of 843,455. This represents the actual gain in permanent alien residents during the year in question. This figure, in the year in question, happens to come very near to the gross gain estimated in the simplest way. But it is not necessarily so, and in the year 1908 there was considerable difference between the two figures. It is not always necessary to make this somewhat involved calculation. In many cases, the mere comparison of the figures for immigrant and emigrant aliens is sufficient for the purpose. But there are many other instances in which accuracy and consistency require this exact calculation to be made, and it is a decided acquisition to the study of immigration to have these data available.[1] Thus in the year 1909 the net gain in permanent alien residents was 584,513, while in 1908 it was only 341,075; yet there were more immigrant aliens admitted in 1908 than in 1909.

In respect to the composition of this great current, the period in question has witnessed a profound and most significant change. We have seen that prior to 1882 practically the entire body of immigrants was made up of individuals from Germany, the United Kingdom, and the Scandinavian countries. From that year on, these have steadily decreased in importance, and their places have been taken by contingents from Italy, Austria-Hungary, Russia, and other south European countries. This change has been so pronounced as to lead to a separation of immigrants into the "old immigration" and the "new immigration," a distinction which has become familiar to every casual student of the subject. The Immigration Commission has recently given its official sanction to this classification, and in its reports follows this scheme: the old immigration includes those from England, Ireland, Scotland, Wales, Belgium, Denmark, France, Germany, the Netherlands, Norway, Sweden, and Switzerland; the new immigration, those from Austria-Hungary, Bulgaria, Greece, Italy, Montenegro, Poland, Portugal, Roumania, Russia, Servia, Spain, Syria, and Turkey. This schedule refers only to European countries (with the exception of Syria and

[1] As, for instance, in the study of the effects of crises (see pp. 347–361.

Turkey, which ethnically belong to Europe), without reference to non-European sources. But immigration to the United States is as yet almost wholly a European movement, so that other countries may be neglected in any general consideration. In so far as there are any immigrants from non-European sources they would naturally be classed with the new immigration. Roughly speaking, the old immigration came from the north and west of Europe, the new immigration comes from the south and east of that continent.

The sweeping nature of this change can be comprehended only through the comparison of figures. The immigration from the United Kingdom and Germany, which up to 1882 had made up so nearly all of the total, never again reached the same figure, and gradually dwindled, both relatively and positively, until in 1907 it amounted to only 11.8 per cent of the total immigration for the year. On the other hand the currents from Austria-Hungary, Italy, and Russia, all of which, as we have seen, began to attain prominence approximately in 1882, grew steadily until in the year 1907 they amounted respectively to 26.3 per cent, 22.2 per cent, and 20.1 per cent of the total. Putting them together, we have a total for these three countries of 68.6 per cent of the total immigration, and adding to them the immigration from the other countries belonging to the new movement, we have a total of 81 per cent of the European immigrants admitted to the United States in 1907. In the years from 1819 to 1883 the old immigration had furnished about 95 per cent of the total movement from Europe to the United States. Comparing the two years 1882 and 1907, it appears that the old immigration made up 87.1 per cent of the total immigration in the first year, and 19 per cent in the latter, and the new immigration 12.9 per cent in the former and 81 per cent in the latter.[1]

This is a most radical change, the importance of which can hardly be overestimated. The old immigrants, as we have before observed, were of a racial stock very closely related to the early settlers of the country, and to the original type of the American people. Their language was the same or similar, and their national traditions wholly harmonious. Consequently assimilation was a comparatively simple matter. It was practically a reforming, on American soil, of the English race, from the same component elements which had gone into it from the beginning in England. The new immigration is made up from people of a very different racial stock, representing the Slavic and Mediterranean branches of the Caucasian race rather than the Teutonic. With the difference in race go differences in mental characteristics, traditions, and habits of life. As a result, the problem of assimilation in this country has taken on a completely different aspect. Moreover, this change is a very recent one. It was not until the year 1896 that the three currents from Austria-Hungary, Italy, and Russia exceeded in volume the contributions of the United Kingdom, Germany, and Scandinavia. The real dilution of the original American stock is a matter of scarcely half a generation. These facts will become clearer by glancing at the following table:

[1] Rept. Imm. Com., Emigration Conditions in Europe, Abs., p. 9.

PER CENT OF TOTAL IMMIGRATION COMING FROM SPECIFIED COUNTRIES BY DECADES, FROM 1861 TO 1910.

Country	Years				
	1861-70	1871-80	1881-90	1891-00	1901-10
Austria-Hungary	0.33	2.6	6.7	16	24.4
German Empire	35	25.5	28	14	3.9
Italy, Sicily, and Sardinia	0.51	2	5.9	18	23.3
Russian Empire and Finland	0.2	1.9	4.4	14	18.2
United Kingdom:	38				
England		15.6	12	6	4.4
Ireland		15.5	12	10	3.9

In seeking to determine the causes of this change it will be well to note first certain general causes which have underlain the whole movement, and then to consider the specific causes which have operated to stimulate immigration in certain of the more important countries.

Among the general causes may be mentioned first of all the great development of transportation during the last thirty years. As has been previously observed, emigration movements are very dependent upon easy and cheap transportation facilities. One great reason why there were so many more immigrants from the United Kingdom, France, Germany, and the Scandinavian countries, during the first three quarters of the nineteenth century, was that communication between those countries and the United States was so much easier than with southeastern Europe. The latter part of this century saw the establishment of many direct steamship lines from Mediterranean ports to the United States, which served to open up this new territory.

There was also a great improvement in internal transportation in the more backward countries of Europe, which completed the line of access from the United States to the more remote interior districts of Europe.

With the establishment of these new lines of communication, it followed inevitably that the transportation companies should put forth every effort to attract as much business as possible to them. So we find the activities of transportation and emigration agents extending farther and farther into Europe, with the growth of lines that demanded their services. The importance of these agents in stimulating emigration will be discussed in another connection. Along with these changes, and incident to the beginnings of emigration from some of these new sources, there grew up in these countries a better knowledge of the United States, its attractions, and the means of getting there. This knowledge was very meager and faulty at first, and willfully distorted by the agents, but it served to awaken the people to the possibilities of emigration, and to stimulate them to take the step. This influence was abetted by a growing sense of independence and ambition on the part of the people of these regions, which made it more possible for them to act on their own initiative. They could never have emigrated under the conditions of difficulty, uncertainty, and hardship which marked the earlier movement, and which the more hardy, adventurous, and daring northern races faced without hesitation.

There are two further causes of this shifting of the sources of immigration from northern to southern Europe, which are even more significant than the foregoing. The first of these is that, with the filling up of the United States, and the industrial improvements of northern Europe, the economic situation in this country no longer presents the same marked advantages over the older nations that it did during most of the nineteenth century. The immigrant from England, Ireland, Germany, or Sweden no longer finds his lot so much easier here than at home. The United States has now its own problems of congestion, pauperism, and competition of labor. Consequently it is much less worth while for the northern immigrant to come. But as compared with the more backward countries of Europe, there is still a sufficient margin of advantage in the United States to make it well worth while for the peasant to make the change. The comparison of the conditions which exist, or which he believes to exist, in the United States, with those in his own land has still sufficient power to arouse those feelings of discontent which are necessary to migration.

The second of these causes is that when the representatives of more backward countries, representing a lower standard of living and of industrial demands, have once begun to come, the members of more advanced races cease coming. They are unwilling to take up residence in a country where they must enter into competition with their inferiors, and where all will be classed together by the natives. Our immigration started from the most advanced nations of Europe. Each inferior reservoir which we have successively tapped, and allowed to drain freely into our nation, has tended to check the flow from the earlier sources. This will continue to be true to the end. Canada recognizes this fact frankly, and while making every effort to attract immigrants from the United Kingdom and northwestern Europe places serious obstacles in the way of immigrants from the other half of the continent.[1]

In considering the specific causes of the rise of the new immigration we will confine our attention primarily to the countries of Austria-Hungary, Italy, and Russia, which send us the great bulk of the immigrants, and in which conditions are sufficiently representative to give a satisfactory idea of the nature of the new movement in general. Let us first consider Austria-Hungary.

The early immigration from Bohemia in the middle of the nineteenth century belongs in every way rather to the old than to the new immigration, and need not be considered here. As for the recent immigration from Austria-Hungary, it may be said that the underlying, fundamental factor is the racial diversity which characterizes that country. Austria-Hungary is not in any sense a nation, but a mixture of diverse and hostile races, held together primarily by the outside pressure of Russia, Germany, Italy, and Turkey. The attempt to get a clear and definite understanding of the racial composition of the empire is baffling to one who has not had the opportunity to make an exhaustive study of the situation at first hand, and even the authorities do not wholly agree as to the racial classification. The following sketch, taken from Professor Commons,[2] will give a sufficient idea of the complicated conditions which exist. In the territory of Austria-Hungary may be found considerable numbers of five important sections of the human family, as follows:

German.

Slav: Czechs or Bohemians, Moravians, Slovaks,

[1] Rept. Imm. Com., The Immigration Situation in Canada, p. 15.

[2] Commons, J. R., *op. cit.*, pp. 79 ff.

Poles, and Ruthenians in the northern part; Croatians, Servians, Dalmatians, and Slovenians in the southern part.

Magyar.

Latin: Italians and Roumanians (Latinized Slavs).

Jewish.

From such a conglomeration of races it is impossible that political and social entanglements and difficulties should not arise. In the words of Miss Balch, "Politically, the dual monarchy is nothing short of a monstrosity." [1]

In general, the Germans and Magyars are the ruling element, and the Slavs are held in subjection. The former races constitute the nobility, and own the land; the latter are the peasants and laborers. The management of public and private financial affairs has largely been monopolized by the Jews, who have been more liberally treated here than in any other country of modern Europe. Along with this political inequality there has gone a pronounced economic inequality, and while universal manhood suffrage has recently been granted by the emperor, it yet remains to be seen whether it will bring about an improvement of the economic conditions, which are the great immediate stimulus to emigration.

One of the greatest blights of Austria-Hungary is the system of landlordism, and the antiquated system of landholding and agriculture, which still persists, and seriously handicaps the country in competition with more advanced nations. These economic disabilities are accompanied by various social and political disturbances. Taxes are high and fall unequally upon different classes of the population, exempting the great landowners from their fair share of the burden. The

[1] Balch, Emily G., *Our Slavic Fellow-Citizens*, p. 29.

terms of military service are severe. The birth rate and death rate are both high, and the poverty, ignorance, inequality, and helplessness of the people make the over-population seem greater than it is. The emigration is almost wholly from the peasant class, which does not, however, represent the lowest section of the population. Below the peasant in the social scale are the cottager, the laborer, and the farm servant.

We thus have, in the case of Austria-Hungary, an interesting combination of economic, political, and social causes, all resting upon racial heterogeneity.[1]

Turning to Italy, we find somewhat the same combination of economic and political causes, without, however, a corresponding basis of racial diversity. It is true that the population of Italy is divided into two distinct groups, but these are also geographically separated, and the result is a dual stream of immigration, rather than a single outflow due to racial antagonism. The inhabitants of northern Italy, the "north Italians" as they are called, are Teutonic in blood and in appearance. Their home is in a relatively well-developed manufacturing section, and a large proportion of the emigrants are skilled artisans, and come from the cities. The southern Italians belong to the Mediterranean branch of the Caucasian race, are shorter in stature and more swarthy, and on the whole much inferior in intelligence to their northern compatriots. The majority of the emigrants are peasants from the great landed estates, accustomed to wages about one third of those in the north. Naturally the conditions which lead to emigration are somewhat different in the north and the south, and it is in the latter

[1] For a detailed account of Slavic immigration, the reader is referred to Miss Emily G. Balch's monumental work, *Our Slavic Fellow-Citizens*.

region that we are particularly interested, for, unfortunately from our point of view, the great majority of our Italian immigrants belong to the southern branch. The distinction between these two groups is so marked that for years the immigration authorities of the United States have recognized it, and have listed them separately in the statistics. In 1910 there were 192,673 south Italian immigrants to this country, and only 30,780 north Italians. The north Italians go to Argentina, Uruguay, and Brazil in about the same numbers that the south Italians come to us.

In southern Italy and Sicily the power of the landlord, which as in Austria-Hungary is one of the great curses of Italy, is greatest. The land is divided up into large estates held by the nobility, and let out to tenant farmers at enormously high rents. As much as $160 per year per acre is paid for an orange garden. The leases are short. The wages of all classes are very low. An agricultural laborer earns from 8 cents to 38 cents per day, an unskilled laborer from 25 cents to 50 cents, and a skilled laborer, such as a mason or carpenter, from 27 cents to $1.40.[1]

It is true that prices are lower than in the United States, so that these wages are not so extremely inadequate as might at first appear. Nevertheless, the difference between prices in this country and in Italy is not nearly so great as the difference in wages, so that the wage scale is in fact much lower there. Living expenses are seriously increased by an exaggerated system of indirect taxes, which are so severe in the case of food as to make food alone cost the peasants about 85 per

[1] Commons, J. R., *op. cit.*, p. 73. For fuller figures see King, B., and Okey, T., *Italy To-day*, p. 126.

cent of their wages. These taxes are so arranged as to fall with undue weight upon the poor and working classes, forcing them to pay over one half of the entire amount of taxes. The amount thus paid, exclusive of the tax on wine, amounts to from 10 to 20 per cent of their wages. Moreover, this is an increasing burden. Since 1870 the wealth of the country has increased 17 per cent and taxes 30 per cent.

The army and navy are a tremendous drain upon the people, in two ways. First, they vastly increase the national expenditures. The money spent for this purpose amounts to one fourth more of the national income than is spent by France or Germany, and nearly three times as much as by the United States. Secondly, they interfere with production, as every able-bodied peasant is required to serve in the army for a term of two years.

Another, and more profound, cause of economic distress is found in the rapid increase of population. This is both a cause and a result of poverty, and the birth rate is highest in the poorest districts. While this high birth rate is accompanied by a high death rate, there is still difference enough between the two to bring about an extreme density of population, exceeded only by the islands of Great Britain and Japan, and the states of Rhode Island and Massachusetts, and the little country of Belgium. In such a densely populated country, where both the birth rate and death rate are high, we are almost always sure to find economic pressure and distress.[1]

As a result of the foregoing conditions, the annual emigration from Italy is very heavy. In addition to the true emigration, where there is a permanent change of residence, there is a large amount of temporary or periodic

[1] Cf. *Americans in Process*, p. 46.

migration, in which case the individual leaves his home only for a short space of time, with the fixed intention of returning. Much of this temporary emigration is directed to France and Germany, where work is obtainable during the summer season. Some of it turns toward North America, and a large amount to South America. Many Italians take advantage of the difference in seasons, and put in two seasons of summer work in each year, one on each side of the equator. It is estimated that about one third of the total migration from Italy is of this temporary or periodic character.[1]

Of the total number of immigrants to the United States from Russia, somewhat less than one tenth are Russians. The balance are Poles, Lithuanians, Finns, Germans, and Jews. Agricultural, social, and political conditions in Russia are sufficiently well understood to make it no cause for wonder that almost any of its common citizens should be glad to leave. The Russian peasant is said to be the most oppressed in Europe, but he is also probably the most ignorant and degraded, and as yet is only beginning to learn to emigrate. There is a great reservoir there which will be ready to furnish us untold millions when the current gets well started. But so far the great stream from Russia is made up principally of other races. Of these, we are particularly interested in the Jews, partly because they are the most numerous, partly because they are a unique and striking people, partly because the reasons for their coming are more definite and easily comprehended.

We have seen that during the Middle Ages the Jews were expelled from almost every country of Europe. Almost the only region where they were allowed a settle-

[1] Bodio, Luigi, "Dell' Emigrazione Italiana," *Nuova Antologia*, 183 : 529.

ment was in Poland, and hence they gathered there in large numbers. Under Russian domination this has been made the "Pale of Settlement" for the Jews, and now contains about one third of the 11,000,000 people of that race in the world. Life in any other part of the Empire is made practically impossible for them, and it is far from easy there. Among the other restrictions put upon the Jews during the Middle Ages was a prohibition of engaging in agriculture. But they were allowed to take usury, which was forbidden to Christians. The natural result was that they were driven almost entirely into trade, and particularly into money lending, so that those pursuits which seem to be so well adapted to the natural proclivities of the Jews were in a sense thrust upon them. As a result the Jews in Russia are engaged primarily in the two businesses of lending money and selling liquor. When the Russian serfs were liberated in 1861, and left in a most helpless state without either capital or land, the Jews became their merchants, middlemen, and usurers. It was perfectly natural that the ignorant peasant should come to blame the money lender and the saloon keeper for evils which were really due to the wretched political, social, and economic organization, but of which they seemed to be the immediate agents. There is reason to believe that the government encouraged this popular antipathy toward an unpopular race for the sake of diverting the indignation of the masses from itself. Certain it is that the attitude of the government has been most hostile to the Jews. In 1881 this antagonism culminated in a series of terrible anti-Semitic riots, and then began the exodus to America.

In the next year, 1882, were passed a set of laws, known

as the May Laws, which, with other subsequent ones of a similar nature, have made existence for the Jews almost intolerable in the Russian Empire. These laws, inspired largely by the Greek Orthodox Church, have made it impossible for the Jew " to foreclose a mortgage or to lease or purchase land; he cannot do business on Sundays or Christian holidays; he cannot hold office; he cannot worship or assemble without police permit; he must serve in the army, but cannot become an officer; he is excluded from schools and universities; he is fined for conducting manufactures and commerce; he is almost prohibited from the learned professions."[1] The press is against them. Here in America we hear of only the climaxes of this persecution, but the oppression is constant and untiring. Is it any wonder that the Jews seek relief in flight?

It will become evident from time to time that our Jewish immigration is in many respects unique, and stands as an exception to many of the general principles which one might lay down concerning immigration. So in respect to the causes of their emigration it is not surprising to find a situation somewhat different from other branches of the new immigration, or from any other immigration, in fact. The Jews have always been a "peculiar people," and religion has played a larger part in their history than in the case of probably any other modern people. The persecutions to which they have been subjected from age to age have had religious diversity as their ostensible and obvious, if not always their only, motive. And in the modern emigration from

[1] Commons, J. R., *op. cit.*, p. 92. Cf. *Americans in Process*, p. 48; Rubinow, I. M., "The Jews in Russia," *Yale Review*, August, 1906, p. 147; Antin, Mary, *The Promised Land;* Evans-Gordon, *The Alien Immigrant*, Chs. IV, V.

Russia, while the oppression under which they suffer touches almost every phase of their life, and imposes numberless economic handicaps, it rests ultimately upon religious grounds. Russia is the only modern country from which numerous emigrants are driven by actual persecution, though it is said that Roumania has within the last ten years passed anti-Jewish laws more stringent than those of Russia.

Conditions in Austria-Hungary and Italy, and to a less extent in Russia, may be taken as typical of the circumstances which prevail in other countries of southern and eastern Europe, and Asia Minor, from which our new immigrants come. In Bulgaria the following four particular reasons have been assigned for emigration:

(1) Bulgaria is distinctively an agricultural country, and while a large per cent of the people own their farms, the holdings are too small to enable them to make a sufficient living, and the methods of cultivation are poor.

(2) There is a great dearth of manufacturing industry. In 1907 there were only 166 factories of any size, with 6149 workers.

(3) Taxes are very heavy, amounting to one fifth, one fourth, or even one third of the earnings of families.

(4) There is much dissatisfaction with the government among the peasants on the grounds of expense, and of the very oppressive terms of military service.[1]

Summing up the facts regarding the volume and racial character of immigration during this period, it appears that, as regards the former, the series of waves has been continued, responding to the economic conditions, but reaching a much higher culmination than ever before. As regards the latter, there has been a most distinct and

[1] Marsh, Benjamin C., *Charities*, XXI: 15, p. 649.

profound change. The main source of the immigrant current has shifted away from northern and western Europe, to the southern and eastern portions of the continent, whose people are by no means so closely related in physique or so similar in mental characteristics to the people of the United States as the immigrants of earlier periods. The causes of this change lie primarily in altered conditions in the United States which make it less attractive to the residents of the more advanced nations of Europe than formerly. In the more backward countries the political and economic situation is still so inferior to the United States that an ample motive for emigration exists. All that was needed to start a large movement was a knowledge of the possibilities across the Atlantic, and the means of getting there. Both of these have been provided within the period in question.

CHAPTER VIII

THE CAUSES OF IMMIGRATION

THERE are two things which the student of sociological problems — like every other scientist — wishes to know about the phenomena which fall within his field. These are the causes and the effects. Hitherto we have said a good deal about the causes of immigration and very little about the effects. In truth, it is much simpler to predicate causes of such a movement than effects. The causes lie in the past; the effects are largely a matter of the future. It is possible to state with a fair degree of certainty what are the causes of the modern immigration to the United States. The reader will have already formed a general idea from the examples of the new immigration which we have given.

In general the causes of our recent and present immigration may be divided into two classes, the natural and the artificial. Most of what has been said thus far refers to the former; the latter has been merely hinted at. Another distinction which is often helpful is that between the permanent or predisposing causes, and the temporary or immediate causes. It frequently happens that in a given country there are conditions of long standing — perhaps inherent in the character of the country itself — which make life hard and disagreeable for the resident. Yet no immigration takes place until some relatively trivial event, of a temporary nature, occurs, which serves as the final impulse to emigration. To the superficial view this temporary event appears as the cause of emigration, when in point of fact its weight in the total amount of dissatisfactions is insignificant.[1] The natural causes of immigration at the present time lie primarily in the superiority of the economic conditions in the United States over those in the countries from which the immigrants come. Modern immigration is essentially an economic phenomenon. Religious and political causes have played the leading part in the past, and still enter in as contributory factors in many cases. But the one prevailing reason why the immigrant of to-day leaves his native village is that he is dissatisfied with his economic lot, as compared with what it might be in the new world. The European peasant comes to America because he can — or believes he can — secure a greater return in material welfare for the amount of labor expended in this country than in his home land. This fact is recognized by practically all careful students of the subject, and is frequently emphasized in the recent report of the Immigration Commission. It is worthy of notice, also, that the changes which affect the volume of the immigration current, and cause those repeated fluctuations which we have observed, are changes in the economic situation in this country, rather than in the countries of source. A period of good times in this country attracts large numbers of immigrants by promising large rewards for labor; an industrial depression checks the incoming current, and sends away many of those who are here. This is probably accounted for by the fact that economic conditions in this country are subject to greater oscillations than in European

[1] The instances given by Mrs. Houghton of economic causes of immigration are mainly of this temporary nature, though not all trifling. See Houghton, Louise S., "Syrians in the United States," *Survey*, July 1, 1911, p. 482.

countries which are relatively static, rather than dynamic. An example of the opposite condition is furnished by the Irish emigration of the middle of the nineteenth century, when a great economic disaster in the country of source occasioned a large increase in emigration. This relation between the economic situation in this country and the volume of immigration has been worked out statistically by Professor Commons, and is presented in graphic form in a table in his book, *Races and Immigrants in America* (opposite page 64). In this table he takes imports as an index of the prosperity of the United States and shows how closely the curve representing immigration follows the curve of imports per capita. If he could have taken account of the departing aliens as well, the showing would probably have been still more striking.

The search for the reasons for this economic superiority of the United States involves an investigation too complicated and extensive to be undertaken in the present connection. There are two factors, however, which may be pointed out, which, at the beginning of our national life, gave us an advantage possessed by no other modern nation. The first of these was the small ratio between men and land, which we have commented on before. The territory of the United States was a vast, newly discovered region, with untold natural resources and every advantage of climate and configuration, inhabited by a mere handful of settlers, at a time when the nations of Europe had long since struck a balance between population and land, on the customary standard of living. The countries of Europe have also profited, it is true, by the opening up of this great new world. But their benefit has been transmitted and indirect, while the American people have been the direct and immediate recipients of this great advantage. The importance of this factor can hardly be overestimated.

The second of these great factors is the character of the American people themselves. We have seen that this was well formed and distinctive at the time of the Revolution. The early settlers of the North American continent were in many respects a picked body, taken from the best of the populations of Europe. Their descendants were also subjected to the stern selective processes of the struggle with, and conquest of, the wilderness, and the establishment of their own economic and political independence. As a result, the American people at the beginning of our national life had certain qualities both of physical and intellectual character, — hardihood, enterprise, daring, independence, love of freedom, perseverance, etc., — which set them apart from any of their contemporaries.

It has been the combination of these two factors — a unique people in a rich virgin land — which, more than anything else, has accounted for the eminent position attained by the American nation in the economic life of the world. Many other circumstances have doubtless contributed to the result, but they would have been powerless to accomplish the end, without these two essential prerequisites. With the disappearance of these two distinguishing features the United States will begin to lose her position of economic superiority.

The statement made in a previous paragraph, that the immigrant comes to America because he can — or believes he can — better his economic lot by so doing, suggested that great class of causes which we have called the artificial. The advantages of the economic life in the

United States all too frequently exist, not in fact, but in the mind of the prospective emigrant. And this belief is equally potent in stirring up emigration, whether it is grounded on fact or not. There are hosts of immigrants passing through the portals of Ellis Island every year whose venture is based on a sad misconception. There are also countless numbers who would never have engaged in the undertaking had not the idea of doing so been forcibly and persistently instilled into their minds by some outside agency. In other words, a very large part of our present immigration is not spontaneous and due to natural causes, but is artificial and stimulated. This stimulation consists in creating the desire and determination to migrate, by inducing dissatisfaction with existing conditions as compared with what the new world has to offer. Its source is in some interested person or agency whose motive may, or may not, be selfish.

There are three principal sources from which this stimulation or encouragement to immigration emanates — the transportation companies, the labor agents, and the previous immigrants. The motive of the first two is an economic and wholly selfish one; that of the latter may or may not be selfish.

The carrying of immigrants from Europe to America is a very vast and lucrative business. The customary charge for steerage passage averages at least $30, and as the large immigrant ships carry 2000 or more steerage passengers there is a possibility of receiving as much as $60,000 from steerage passengers on a single voyage. It is, furthermore, a business which can be almost indefinitely expanded by vigorous pushing. A skillful agent can induce almost any number of the simple and credulous peasants of a backward European country to emigrate, who had scarcely had such an idea in their heads before. Consequently it pays the transportation companies to have an immense army of such agents, continually working over the field, and opening up new territory. The motive is not so much rivalry for a given amount of business between the different companies; a mutual agreement between different lines or groups of lines, dividing up the territory from which they shall draw their steerage passengers, practically precludes this.[1] It is rather the possibility of actually creating new business by energetic canvassing.

It is obvious that the activity of these agents may be of the most pernicious nature. The welfare of the immigrant, or the benefit of either country concerned, are of no concern to them. Their sole aim is to get business. So long as the immigrant has the wherewithal to pay his passage, it matters not to them where he got it, nor are they deterred by any doubts as to the fitness of the immigrant for American life, or of the probability of his success there. In fact, it is claimed that the steamship companies prefer a class of immigrants which is likely, eventually, to return to the old country, as this creates a traffic going the other way. The only checks to their operations are such as are imposed by their own scruples, and the possession of too many of these does not help a man to qualify for the position of agent.

The methods used by these agents to encourage emigration are most ingenious and insidious. Every possible means is used to make the peasant dissatisfied with his present lot, and to impress him with the glories and joys of life in America. Many, perhaps the majority,

[1] Rept. Imm. Com., Steer. Cond., p. 8.

of the agents are themselves returned immigrants, who give glittering accounts of their experiences in America, and display gold watches, diamond pins, and various other proofs of their prosperity. The methods of to-day are not quite so crude and bizarre as they used to be. The stories of the richness of America and the ease of life there which used to be current were so overdrawn as to undeceive any but the most ignorant and gullible. Immigrants have left for America expecting to be able to pick up unlimited dollars lying loose in the streets, and stories are told of steerage passengers who threw away the cooking utensils they had brought with them, as the vessel neared New York, supposing that they could get a new lot for nothing as soon as they landed. A better knowledge of actual conditions in America, which now prevails in most European countries, has precluded the continued circulation of such fictions as these. In fact, if there were not real advantages in the United States, and many cases of successful emigrants, the agents would not be able to operate successfully for an indefinite time. But as yet there does exist a sufficient difference between conditions in the new world and in the old to give them a basis of truth, which they may embellish as occasion demands. Many of these agents make a practice of advancing money to the emigrants to pay for their passage, taking a mortgage on their property for an amount far in advance of that actually furnished. These debts are met with a strange faithfulness by the immigrants, even when they have been woefully deceived and cheated. In Greece it is asserted that the agents work through the priests, and thus largely increase their influence.[1]

Immigration which is inspired by such stimulation as

[1] Caro, L., *Auswanderung und Auswanderungspolitik in Österreich*, pp. 59–71.

this is far from being so desirable as that which is natural and spontaneous. It follows no natural laws, and responds to no economic demand in this country. It is likely to be of injury rather than of benefit to the United States, and works untold injustice to the immigrants. It is regarded as pernicious by all fair-minded observers, and the United States government has made serious efforts to check it. This is the purpose of the clause in the immigration law limiting the nature of solicitation that may be done by transportation lines. The solicitation of immigration is no new thing. Hale, in his *Letters on Irish Immigration*, written in 1851–1852, said that competition between the different lines of packets and different shipping houses had made the means of emigration familiar in the remotest corners of Ireland, and that advertising was fully utilized. Professor Mayo-Smith in 1892 wrote that the Inman Steamship Company had 3500 agents in Europe and an equal number in the United States selling prepaid tickets. In Switzerland in 1885 there were 400 licensed emigration agents.[1] The laws passed since then have forced the agents to proceed more cautiously, and conceal their activities. They have not put a stop to their operations.

These emigration agents are by no means all accredited representatives of the steamship lines over which they send their recruits. There are, to be sure, plenty of official agents of the various transportation companies, who are openly acknowledged as such. The region around the harbor, in many of the Mediterranean seaports, is thronged with steamship ticket offices, often flying the American flag, and with emigration agencies, and the line between the two is frequently very difficult

[1] Mayo-Smith, R., *Emigration and Immigration*, p. 46.

to draw. But the traveling agents, or "runners," are often free lances as far as appearances go. It is very hard to establish any connection between them and any transportation company. Yet all who have investigated the subject are convinced that there is a close understanding and coöperation between the two, even if there is no official relation. It is contrary to human nature, when so much money is to be made by such canvassing, and there are plenty of people ready to do it, that the transportation companies should neglect the opportunity. On this subject the Immigration Commission says, "It does not appear that the steamship lines as a rule openly direct the operations of these agents, but the existence of the propaganda is a matter of common knowledge in the emigrant-furnishing countries, and, it is fair to assume, is acquiesced in, if not stimulated, by the steamship lines as well."[1]

The Commissioner General of Immigration is much more emphatic in his statements. The report for 1909 contains the following passages (p. 112): "The promoter is usually a steamship ticket agent, employed on a commission basis, or a professional money lender, or a combination of the two. . . . He is employed by the steamship lines, large and small, without scruple, and to the enormous profit of such lines. . . . To say that the steamship lines are responsible, directly or indirectly, for this unnatural immigration is not the statement of a theory, but of a fact, and of a fact that sometimes becomes, indeed, if it is not always, a crying shame. . . . [Referring to Contract Labor Inspector John Gruenberg] He shows quite clearly that all of the steamship lines

[1] Rept. Imm. Com., Brief Statement of Conclusions and Recommendations, p. 17.

engaged in bringing aliens from Europe to this country have persistently and systematically violated the law, both in its letter and spirit, by making use of every possible means to encourage the peasants of Europe to purchase tickets over their lines to this country. They have issued circulars and advertisements, and made use of extensive correspondence, through their own agents in this country and in Europe."

The law referred to is Section 7 of the Act of 1907, repeating in substance Section 4, Act of 1891 (p. 111). The ease and persistency with which this provision, carefully worded as it is, is violated, furnishes a striking example of the difficulty of passing statutes which shall be capable of enforcement, especially in foreign countries, to put a stop to practices which are universally conceded to be undesirable.

The second great source of stimulation to emigration is the labor agent. His operations are extensive and diversified, and always in direct violation of the contract labor law. That section of the immigration statutes, as previously pointed out, is so sweepingly drawn as to make any immigrant, not in the excepted classes, who has received the slightest intimation that there is work awaiting him in this country, a violator of the law. But the economic advantage to employers in this country of importing European labor under contract to perform services in the United States at much less than the market rate of wages, is so great, that, as in the previous case, human nature cannot resist the temptation, provided the chances of escaping detection are sufficiently good. And this part of the law, like that relating to advertising, is of such a nature as to make it susceptible of continued and extensive evasion by unscrupulous persons, possessed of such skill and craftiness as characterize the typical contract labor agent. While there is no way of estimating the extent of this practice, there is no doubt that only a very small proportion of the present immigration, from the Mediterranean countries at least, is innocent of the letter of the law, strictly interpreted. This is not to say that they are under actual contract to labor, but that their coming has been encouraged by some sort of intimation that there would be work awaiting them.

By a recent opinion of the Attorney-General, two essential points have been laid down in the construction of the contract labor laws, as follows:

"(1) That they 'prohibit any offer or promise of employment which is of such a definite character that an acceptance thereof would constitute a contract.'

"(2) That the prohibition to encourage the immigration of an alien by a promise of employment is 'directed against a promise which specially designates the particular job or work or employment for which the alien's labor is desired.'"[1]

Even under this somewhat liberal interpretation of the laws, wholesale violations undoubtedly go on. In the words of the Immigration Commission, "In this way hundreds of immigrants are annually debarred at United States ports as contract laborers, while doubtless hundreds of thousands more are admitted who have practically definite assurances as to the place and nature of their employment in this country."

A fuller description of contract labor in general, and of that particular form of it which is known as the padrone system, will be given in another connection. The point to be emphasized here is that it operates as one of

[1] Rept. Imm. Com., Contract Labor, etc., Abs., p. 12.

the great causes of our present immigration, and that it continues to exert a powerful, and probably increasing, influence, in spite of all the efforts of the legislators and officials of the United States to check it.

The third source of stimulation to emigration is the earlier immigrant himself. He is probably the greatest factor of all in induced immigration, and his influence is utilized in various ways by both emigration agents and labor agents, and made to contribute to the success of their efforts.

Every stream of immigration must have its origin in some few individuals, who, the first of their region, break the ties of home and fatherland, and go to seek their fortune in a new and far-away land. Upon their success depends the question whether others from the same district shall follow in their footsteps. If they fail in their venture, it serves as a discouraging factor as respects further emigration from that region. But if they succeed, and win a position which makes them envied in the eyes of their fellow-countrymen, it furnishes a powerful stimulus to further emigration. Sooner or later, there will be some who succeed from every region, and the example of a few successful ones is likely to far outweigh numerous failures. Something like this is going on in countless remote districts of the south European countries, and has gone on for decades in every country which has sent us numbers of immigrants.

Take a typical example. Some Slav peasant, in a little village of Austria-Hungary, of a more ambitious and adventurous disposition than most of his fellows, hears of the opportunities in America, and being dissatisfied with his present lot, decides to try his fortune in the new world. His first "job" is in a mine in some small town of Pennsylvania. Accustomed as he is to a low standard of living, he is able to save a considerable part of the wages which seem munificent to him. From time to time he writes letters home, telling of his prosperity. Eventually he saves up enough to purchase a little store or saloon. Of course there will be a letter telling about that. These letters are wonderful documents in the eyes of his friends and relatives at home. Correspondence does not flourish in these regions, and the receipt of any letter is a matter of great importance. The arrival of a message from across the sea creates an impression which it is almost impossible for an American to comprehend. The precious missive is read aloud in the coffee-houses, and passed from hand to hand throughout the village. It may even travel to neighboring hamlets, and make its impression there. The neighbor in America, and his career, become the foremost topic of conversation for miles around.

In time all this has its effect. A small group of the original emigrant's former neighbors resolve to try their luck too. The most natural thing, of course, is for them to go to the place where their friend is. He helps them to find work, tides them over difficulties, and in various ways makes their life easier and simpler than his had been. Each of these newcomers also writes letters home, which go through the same round, and add to the growing knowledge of America, and the discontent with European life in comparison. Once started, the movement grows with great rapidity, and the letters from America increase in geometrical proportion. Other nuclei start up in other places, recruits are drawn from more distant villages, and the first little trickling stream becomes a swelling tide.

This is what has come to be known as the chain-letter system. Multiplied by hundreds of thousands, the foregoing example serves to illustrate the irresistible network of communications which is drawing the peasants of Europe to every part of the United States. This is recognized by all authorities as probably the most powerful single factor in stirring up emigration from such countries as Italy, Austria-Hungary, Greece, Bulgaria, etc. Its effect has been graphically described by a Greek writer in the following words:

"'Such a one, from such a village, sent home so many dollars within a year,' is heard in some village or city, and this news, passed like lightning from village to village and from city to city, and magnified from mouth to mouth, causes the farmer to forsake his plow, the shepherd to sell his sheep, the mechanic to throw away his tools, the small-grocer to break up his store, the teacher to forsake his rostrum, and all to hasten to provide passage money, so that they may embark, if possible, on the first ship for America, and gather up the dollars in the streets before they are all gone."[1]

This is a perfectly natural influence, and obviously beyond the power of any legislation to check, even if that were desirable. When inspired merely by a friendly interest in the home neighbors, a desire to keep in touch with them, and a little personal vanity, it is probably the most harmless of any of the forms of stimulation. When, as all too frequently happens, the underlying motive is sinister and selfish, it becomes a source of the greatest deceit and injustice.

When the pioneer emigrant returns to his native village, after some years of prosperous life in America,

[1] Canoutas, S. G., *Greek-American Guide*, 1909, p. 39.

his influence and importance are unbounded. He becomes in truth the "observed of all observers." Groups of interested listeners and questioners gather round him wherever he goes, and hang on his words in breathless awe. His fine, strange clothes, his sparkling jewelry and gold watch, his easy, worldly manners, all arouse the greatest admiration. He has to tell over and over again the story of his career, and describe the wonders of that far-away land. If such a one is returning to the United States, it takes no urging on his part to induce a number of his countrymen to accompany him; they are fairly clinging to the skirts of his garments, to be taken back. Even if he has come home to remain, his constant example is there to inspire the youth of the village to follow in his path. So the "visit home" and the "returned immigrant" add their weight to the influence of the stream of letters. How universal this condition has become is evidenced by the fact that in 1909 only 6.3 per cent of all the immigrants admitted to the United States were not going to join either relatives or friends, according to their statement; in 1910 the percentage was only 4.9. In 1912 it rose to 7.5. About six times as many go to join relatives as friends.

Many of the letters from America contain remittances from the immigrants to their friends and relatives at home. Often these remittances take the form of prepaid tickets,[1] complete from some European center or port to the city in America, where the sender is waiting. Then their influence is absolutely irresistible. The transportation companies make every effort to make the passage as simple as possible, and railroad companies in this country

[1] These prepaid tickets are commonly orders, to be exchanged by the traveler, in Europe, for the actual certificate of transportation. Cf. Rept. N. Y. Com. of Imm., pp. 38 ff.

make special immigrant rates, to be used in connection with such tickets. A large part of the induced immigration of the present day is also assisted immigration. It is a perfectly natural thing that an immigrant in this country should wish to be joined by certain of his relatives on the other side, and, if he is able, should send them the means to come. This has always been done. In the middle of the nineteenth century E. E. Hale wrote that a large part of the letters from Irish to their friends in this country consisted in acknowledgments of remittances, and requests for more. The remittances in 1850 are said to have amounted to about four and one half million dollars. Prepaid tickets were also in use at that date. It is manifestly impossible to estimate correctly the extent of this business at the present time. According to the official reports, in 1910, 72.5 per cent of the immigrants had paid for their own tickets, 26.5 per cent had their tickets paid for by a relative, and 1 per cent by some one other than self or relative. But this showing rests solely upon the immigrant's own statement, and is undoubtedly an underestimate. The suspicion of immigrants whose passage is paid for them, which characterizes our law, leads many to practice deceit in this matter. For instance, it is almost impossible to believe that all but 5.4 per cent of the Greeks had paid their own passage. An examination of the figures shows that there is a larger proportion of passages paid by some one besides the immigrant among the old immigration than among the new. This is explained by the fact that the old immigration has more of a family character, and that immigrants are sending for wives and children. This can be understood only by comparison with the sex and age tables.[1]

[1] See pp. 192, 194.

Even when these remittances are not in the form of prepaid tickets, nor are even intended to pay passage in any way, they exert a powerful influence in stirring up immigration, through the tangible evidence which they furnish of American possibilities. There could be no stronger proof of the success of immigrants in the United States than the constant stream of gold which is flowing from this country to Europe.

For the sake of clearness, these different forms of stimulation have been discussed separately. In practice, they overlap and combine in a variety of complicated relations. The emigration agent is often himself a returned immigrant; if not, he utilizes all the influences which arise from the letters, visits, and remittances of actual immigrants to further his ends. The letters from America are often misleading or spurious, used by labor agents in this country to entice others to come. The prepaid ticket is susceptible of a wide variety of uses. Assistance to emigrants is often furnished, not by well-disposed friends and relatives, but by loan-sharks, whose motives are wholly selfish, and whose sole aim is to secure usurious rates of interest for sums advanced, which are amply protected by mortgages.

As a result of this complex of motives and forces, America has become a household word even to the remote corners of Europe, and he who wishes, for any reason, to stir up emigration from any region finds a fertile field already prepared for him. It is amazing to find how much an ignorant Greek peasant knows about conditions in America. The economic situation is, of course, the prime interest. But there is also a good fund of information about social and political subjects. There are of course many misconceptions and errors, but it is evident that the lines of communication between the European village and the American city are very well established. Similar conditions prevail in all the immigrant-furnishing countries.

It is impossible to say to just what extent our present immigration ought to be classified as induced. It is probable that only a very small part of the total immigration is wholly free from stimulation to some degree. Certain it is that a very large proportion of it is thoroughly artificial and induced. The getting of immigrants is now a thoroughly developed system, planned to serve the needs of every form of interest which might profit thereby.[1] As to the quality of such immigration, something has already been said. There is evidently nothing about the immigrants themselves, or the way in which they are secured, that serves as a guarantee of their serviceability or value to this country; as to their own prospects, we can do no better in closing this chapter than to quote the words of the Commissioner General; these various operations "often result in placing upon our shores large numbers of aliens who, if the facts were only known at the time, are worse than destitute, are burdened with obligations to which they and all their relatives are parties, — debts secured with mortgages on such small holdings as they and their relatives possess, and on which usurious interest must be paid. Pitiable indeed is their condition, and pitiable it must remain unless good fortune accompanies the alien while he is struggling to exist and is denying himself the necessaries of decent living in order to clear himself of the incubus of accumulated debt. If he secures and retains employment at fair wages, escapes the wiles of that large class

[1] See Whelpley, Jas. D., *The Problem of the Immigrant*, p. 3.

of aliens living here who prey upon their ignorant compatriots, and retains his health under often adverse circumstances, all may terminate well for him and his; if he does not, disaster is the result to him and them."[1]

[1] Report, 1910, p. 116.

CHAPTER IX

THE EFFECTS OF IMMIGRATION. CONDITIONS OF EMBARKATION AND TRANSPORTATION

IT was remarked in an earlier paragraph that the effects of immigration were largely a matter of the future. This may have seemed like too sweeping a statement. Yet it will prove true upon consideration. In the case of the old immigration there are, to be sure, certain immediate and superficial effects which may be postulated with a fair degree of certainty. As an example, we may be reasonably sure that the old immigration has increased the proportion of Irish, German, and Scandinavian blood in the composite American people. But as to the ultimate effects of this movement upon the social, religious, moral, and economic aspects of our national life, we can, at best, hazard only a forecast. The reason is that the effects have not transpired as yet.

"One of the commonest errors of writers on sociological topics is to allow too little time for the action of social forces. We are inclined to think that the effects of a certain social phenomenon, which we are able to detect in our lifetime, are the permanent and final effects. We forget that these matters may require many generations to work themselves out. No better illustration of this could be asked for than that furnished by the case of the negroes in the United States. The importation of these people began many generations ago. To our ancestors it undoubtedly seemed a perfectly natural thing to do, and for centuries it did not occur to anybody to even question its rightfulness or its expediency. When objections began to be raised, they were feeble and easily put aside. But at last the presence of this peculiar class of people in the country involved the nation in a terrible and bloody conflict, which worked irreparable injury to the American stock by the annihilation of the flower of southern manhood, and left us a problem which is probably the greatest one before the American people to-day — one which we have hardly begun to solve. There is much of similarity between the case of the negroes and that of the modern immigrants. To be sure, the newcomers of to-day are for the most part white-skinned, instead of colored, which gives a different aspect to the matter. Yet in the mind of the average American, the modern immigrants are generally regarded as inferior peoples — races which he looks down on, and with which he does not wish to associate on terms of social equality. Like the negroes, they are brought in for economic reasons, to do the hard and menial work to which an American does not wish to stoop."[1]

Even in the case of the old immigration, then, the effects are largely in the future; in the case of the new immigration they are almost wholly so. We have seen that in regard to racial stock the new immigration has been predominant for scarcely half a generation. There are a number of circumstances besides this which make the immigration problem practically a new one. Certain of the most important factors which condition it, and many of the aspects which it presents to the

[1] Quoted from the author's book, *Greek Immigration*, pp. 236–237. Cf. Cooke-Taylor, W., *The Modern Factory System*, p. 419.

public mind, are new to the men of this generation. The verification of this statement is to be found in the following pages; in the present connection it must suffice merely to suggest the circumstances in which these differences may be looked for. These may be grouped under six main heads, as follows: (1) the racial stock of the immigrants; (2) the volume of the immigration current; (3) the distribution of immigrants in the United States; (4) the economic conditions of this country; (5) the native birth rate; (6) the quality of the immigrants.

If the effects of immigration are mainly in the future, the discussion of them must be, for the most part, theoretical. It is a discussion of something which is going to happen, or which is likely to happen, not of something that has happened. This gives it an element of uncertainty and speculation which is not wholly desirable in a scientific study. Yet this is the phase of the subject which is by far the most interesting and important to the average American citizen who wants to know how this great sociological phenomenon is going to affect him, and his country, and his relatives and friends. His attitude toward the question will depend upon what he believes these effects will be. If it appears to him that immigration will benefit himself, his country, the immigrants, or humanity in general, he will favor it; if his belief is to the contrary, his attitude will be one of opposition. Since there is no certainty as to what the effects will be, the arguments about immigration are largely composed of attempts to prove that certain effects have transpired, or to demonstrate that they will transpire. As a consequence, it comes about that the discussion of the effects of immigration practically resolves itself into a consideration of the arguments for and against immigration, and it will be so treated, for the most part, in the following chapters.

There are three classes of effects of immigration which may be clearly distinguished, and which will interest different persons in different degrees. These are the effects upon the United States, the effects upon the countries of source, and the effects upon the immigrants themselves. The second and third of these interest the American citizen only as he is open to broad humanitarian considerations; the first touches him directly, and may have an intimate bearing on his personal and selfish interests and pursuits. If a seemingly disproportionate space is given in this volume to effects in general, and effects upon the United States in particular, it is because this is the vital and imperative part of the whole subject to the people of this nation.

Although the effects of immigration are largely a matter of speculation and debate, one step may be taken which will help to make the deductions arrived at as reliable as is possible under the circumstances. This is a careful investigation of the actual conditions which surround immigration at the present time, and a comparison of them with those of the past. Only upon a solid basis of such facts can any trustworthy predictions be made as to what may be expected to come about in the future. Accordingly, in preparation for the discussion of effects, we will attempt to get a clear picture of the circumstances which surround the immigrant on his journey from the old world to the new; of his condition when he arrives; of the character of his life and labor in his new home. In general, the plan followed will be to take up each set of conditions in turn, and having ascertained the facts, to try to determine what bearing these seem likely to have upon the final effects of immigration. This will at times involve a departure from the strictly logical method of treatment, but this is unavoidable in such a complicated discussion.

With the sources of our present immigration we are already familiar. We have seen how they have shifted from the north and west of Europe to the south and east. It has been stated that the movement is essentially a European one. This is still emphatically true. In 1912, 85.8 per cent of all our immigrants came from Europe, and if we exclude Turkey in Asia (which really is a part of Europe in the ethnical sense), British North America, Mexico, and the West Indies, there is very little left of the non-European portion. So it is still correct, for all important purposes, to regard immigration to the United States as having its origin in Europe. How long this will continue, it is of course impossible to say. There are vast reservoirs of population in Asia, to say nothing of the other continents, which we have scarcely as yet tapped, and which may reach the point of emigration with advancing civilization. Whether or not we are to receive large contingents from these countries in the future will depend largely upon the attitude of our government. So far, we have put up the bars before the Chinese, and unless they are lowered, which hardly seems likely, we need not anticipate any considerable number of arrivals of this race. Up to 1900 there were only a comparatively few Japanese in this country. Since then, the rising tide of immigration from Japan, which threatened to reach large proportions, has been checked, partly by "a series of measures which permits the greater part of the administrative problem to rest with the Japanese government,"[1] which is avowedly opposed to the emigration of its laboring population, and partly by a presidential order from the White House on March 14, 1907,[2] denying admission to Japanese and Korean laborers, who had received passports to go to Canada, Mexico, or Hawaii, and were using them to secure admittance to continental United States. While the new treaty between this country and Japan contains no specific prohibition of immigration, it is understood that the Japanese government agrees to prevent the emigration of laborers from that country to this. A new problem has recently appeared in the Pacific coast states in the form of an East Indian immigration. The manifestly undesirable character of this immigration, however, has led the immigration officials in the Pacific seaports to apply the law to members of this race with the greatest strictness, so that most, if not all, of the Hindu laborers applying for admission have been debarred on the grounds of belief in polygamy, liability to become a public charge, or some other provision of the statutes. A similar attitude on the part of the Canadian immigration officials has been of assistance in stopping at the outset what might have grown into a very important current of immigration.[3]

Whatever the future may bring forth, then, our immigration at present springs from European sources.[4] Every country on the continent furnishes its contingent,

[1] Rept. Imm. Com., Japanese and Other Immigrant Races, etc., Abs., p. 46.

[2] Under authority conferred by Section 1 of the Immigration Law of 1907.

[3] Millis, H. A., "East Indian Immigration to British Columbia and the Pacific Coast States," *Am. Econ. Rev.*, Vol. I, No. 1, p. 72. Rept. Comm. Gen. of Imm., 1910, p. 148.

[4] For a picturesque description of "The Beginning of the Trail" the reader is referred to the first chapter of Professor Steiner's fascinating book, *On the Trail of the Immigrant*.

large or small. From the cities, towns, and villages, most of all from the rural sections, even to the most remote corners of the back districts, they come, inspired with great hopes by the emigration agents and the labor contractors, aided by friends or relatives or future employers on the other side. Homes and property are mortgaged, the labor of their bodies — even their very souls — are pledged, to pay their passage. Wives, children, and sweethearts are left behind. On foot, on donkey back, in rude carriages and wagons, they travel till the nearest railroad station is reached. The way is made as easy as possible for them, through the agency of interested parties, who profit by their coming. The prepaid ticket avoids much confusion and perplexity. Friends are awaiting them on the other side. In every large group there are almost certain to be some who have been over the road before. All the emigrant needs to do is to allow himself to be passed along submissively from one stage to another — provided he has the money to pay. For those who make the way easy must have an ample recompense.

As the seacoast and the port of embarkation draw near, the groups of emigrants increase in size by constant additions. In the important emigration ports they arrive by thousands during the busy season. The provisions for their entertainment, while awaiting the sailing of the vessel upon which they are to embark, differ in different ports. In many ports they are required to put up in the cheap hotels and lodging houses, which, in such cases, abound in the neighborhood of the harbor. In other ports, the steamship companies maintain extensive emigrant stations, where emigrants are lodged and cared for while awaiting transportation. Probably the most elaborate of these is the emigrant village of the Hamburg-American Line, at Hamburg. This is located on the left bank of the Elbe, completely segregated from the city, and is designed to receive only immigrants from countries where the standard of health is low. It consists of about twenty-five buildings, and accommodates 5000 persons. Among the buildings are a large inspection building, a simple hotel, and a number of living pavilions, each consisting of a dormitory, living room, baths, etc. There is one large dining hall, with a special section for Jews, for whom also a separate kitchen is provided. The religious needs of the emigrants are provided for by a synagogue, a Catholic church, and a Protestant church.[1]

The provision of the United States law, which requires an examination and medical inspection at the port of embarkation, is observed with different degrees of care in different countries and by different lines. It is to the advantage of the steamship company to refuse transportation to any individuals who are manifestly inadmissible to the United States, as their refusal involves their return at the expense of the company, and in many instances an additional fine of $100. On the other hand, if there is a fair chance that the immigrant may succeed in passing the examination, there is a strong temptation for the steamship company to take him, for the sake of his passage money. There is a practice, believed to be quite extensive, among the transportation companies, of compelling an alien who seems in danger of being debarred, to deposit with the foreign agent from whom he purchases his ticket a sum sufficient to cover the cost of

[1] Clapp, Edwin J., *The Port of Hamburg*, pp. 667–688; Evans-Gordon, *op. cit.*, Ch. XIII.

his return in case he is refused admission. This is in direct violation of the United States law, but the difficulty of securing evidence has prevented the authorities from putting an effective stop to the practice.[1] Large numbers of would-be emigrants are nevertheless turned back before embarkation, as a result of the examination by the steamship company. The proportion of those detained in this manner to those debarred at the ports of arrival in the United States is at least four to one.[2] Some companies have had such a bitter experience in the matter of having their passengers refused as to lead them to exercise great caution. The Austro-American Company, which carries a large share of the Greek traffic, had over 300 emigrants refused at the United States port on one of their early voyages, and returned to Europe. Since then, they have adopted the system of having physicians provided for their forty subagencies in various parts of Greece, who inspect applicants for tickets, and pass upon them before any document is issued to them by the agent. If this physician accepts an emigrant, he is given a medical certificate, makes a deposit toward his ticket, and has space reserved for him on the steamer. He is then sent on to the port of embarkation, where the final examination takes place.[3] In this way large numbers of inadmissible immigrants are kept from leaving their native village, and are spared the expense and disappointment of the trip to the port of embarkation.

The examination at the port of embarkation is differently conducted at different seaports. As a rule the medical examination is made by a physician employed

[1] Rept. Com. Gen. of Imm., 1910, p. 118.

[2] Rept. Imm. Com., Emig. Cond. in Eur., Abs., p. 37. [3] *Ibid.*, p. 38.

by the steamship company, either the ship's doctor, or a specially engaged physician. But at some ports the American consul chooses the physician, though the steamship company pays him. At Naples, Palermo, and Messina, by a special arrangement between the two governments, the examination is made by officers of the United States Public Health and Marine Hospital Service, who examine steerage passengers and recommend the rejection of those who are likely to be refused admission to the United States. Their action is unofficial, but their suggestions are always complied with. Under the quarantine law of the United States the American consular officers are also required to satisfy themselves of the sanitary condition of passengers and ships sailing for United States ports. In addition to the medical examination, a long list of questions is put to the immigrant, in accordance with the requirements of the United States law. His answers are recorded on the manifest, which is later put into the hands of the inspecting officer at the port of arrival, who repeats the same questions and notes whether the answers tally. Vaccination and the disinfection of the passenger's baggage are important parts of the preparation of emigrants for the journey to America. The differing degree of care exercised in this examination at the different ports is indicated by the fact that the proportion of immigrants refused at the port of arrival for medical causes, to the total number embarked from the different ports, varies from 1 to 163 at the Piræus and 1 to 165 at Bremen, to 1 to 565 at Antwerp and 1 to 597 at Fiume.

A large amount of transatlantic traffic passes through Germany from neighboring states, and to protect herself against having large numbers of foreign emigrants refused at her ports, and left in a destitute and helpless condition in her territory, Germany has compelled the steamship companies to establish control-stations on the German-Russian and German-Austrian borders. There are fourteen of these stations, thirteen on the frontier, and one near Berlin. All emigrants from eastern Europe who are intending to pass through German territory to ports of embarkation are examined at these stations, and those who do not comply with the German law, or who are evidently inadmissible to the United States, are turned back. This is a wise and humane provision, for the condition of the emigrant, who, having spent his all to pay his passage to America, and traveled a long distance to the seaboard, finds himself refused at the port of embarkation, is often pitiable in the extreme.[1]

The governments of most European countries do not regard a large emigration with favor, partly because of the withdrawal of men from military service, partly because of the economic loss resulting from the departure of so large a part of the laboring class. Most of them exercise some control over emigration, and, in particular, endeavor to combat the activities of the emigration agents, which, however, they are as powerless to check as is the United States. Nevertheless, there is practically no effort to prohibit emigration altogether, as it is recognized as a natural and irresistible movement. Italy exercises the greatest care for the welfare of her immigrants of any European nation.

Practically all of the immigrants who are crossing for

[1] For a fuller description of the system of medical examination, see the Report of the Immigration Commission, Emig. Cond. in Eur., Abs., pp. 35 ff., from which many of the above facts are taken.

the first time, and probably a majority of those who have made the trip before, travel in the steerage. The second cabin is patronized by the more prosperous of the immigrants who have been in the United States previously, and by others who know themselves to be inadmissible, and hope in this way to avoid a searching inspection. The great bulk of the emigrants, however, having passed their preliminary examination, flock up the steerage gangway into the ship which is to convey them to America. At the top of the ladder stands a ship's officer who examines their tickets and their certificates of vaccination (sometimes a little purple mark stamped on the wrist), and in certain cases searches them for concealed weapons. They are then allowed to proceed to the interior of the ship, and find their way to such berths as suit their fancy, and are not already occupied, within the limits of the section of the ship assigned to them. Steerages are usually divided into three compartments, more or less completely separated from each other; one is for men without wives, another for women traveling alone, and the third for families.

Steerages on the transatlantic vessels are divided into two main classes, designated by the Immigration Commission as the old-type or old steerage, and the new-type or new steerage. The former class predominates on the Mediterranean lines; the latter is found on some of the better ships of the north Atlantic service. Some ships are equipped with both kinds. The old-type steerage is still the typical one, and is found on the majority of vessels bringing immigrants to the United States. It is in such a steerage that the average immigrant gets his first introduction to America — for everything after he leaves the port of embarkation is closely identified with America in his mind. It is in this type of steerage that the student of immigration is primarily interested.

Steerages of this type all bear a general resemblance to each other, and once seen can never be forgotten. Imagine a large room, perhaps seven feet in height, extending the entire breadth of the ship, and about one third of its length. The floor and ceiling are sometimes of iron, but more often of wood. Through the center of the room, very probably, descends the shaft to the hold. This room is filled with a framework of iron pipes, with only sufficient space left to serve as aisles or passageways. This framework is so constructed as to form a series of berths or bunks, adjoining each other laterally, and in two tiers vertically. The dimensions of these berths are usually about six feet by two, with approximately two and one half feet between berths, and about the same space between the lower berth and the deck below, and the upper berth and the deck above. In each berth a network of strap iron serves for the support of a coarse mattress, upon which a pillow and a cheap blanket are the only bedding. Often a life-preserver takes the place of the pillow. Thus the room is filled with a double layer of beds, with only space enough between for the passengers to reach them. On some of the older ships wooden bunks may still be found. Such a room will sometimes accommodate as many as three hundred passengers, and is duplicated in other parts of the ship, and on the successive decks upon which immigrants are carried.

In their provisions for steerage passengers most transportation lines aim to trim as close to the minimum requirements of the law as possible. The immigrant-carrying business is a purely money-making enterprise, and humanitarian considerations have no place in it. The good effects which might result from free competition are practically eliminated by the recent agreement dividing territory, which has been mentioned above.[1] There is no other force to compel transportation companies to go one whit beyond the legal requirements in an effort to make their steerage passengers comfortable.

The open deck space reserved for steerage passengers is usually very limited, and situated in the worst part of the ship, subject to the most violent motion, to the dirt from the stacks and the odors from the hold and galleys. The only provisions for eating are frequently shelves or benches along the sides or in the passageways of sleeping compartments. Some ships have separate rooms, used for dining and recreation purposes, but these are usually wholly inadequate to accommodate all the steerage passengers. Frequently, too, they are planned without the least regard to cleanliness, as when the dining table, upon which the dishes remain set, is placed directly below an open grating, through which the filth and dirt may fall from the shoes of passers-by. Toilet rooms are wholly inadequate in number, are poorly designed, and often wholly uncared for during most of the voyage. The resulting conditions are almost unbelievable. Toilets are sometimes placed directly alongside the only passages leading to the steerage quarters, so that one must pass them, and breathe their horrible stench, every time he passes in or out. The law requires separate wash rooms for men and women, but this is a distinction which is frequently ignored, men and women using the same rooms promiscuously. The provisions for washing are wholly inadequate. There

[1] See p. 149.

are only a few taps, and usually the only water provided is cold salt water, which must be used for all purposes, including the washing of dishes. The law requires that hospitals for steerage passengers be provided, but as they are not open to seasick passengers, they fail of their greatest usefulness.

The arrangements for feeding steerage passengers differ on different vessels, but there are two main systems. In the first, each passenger is furnished a cheap set of eating utensils at the beginning of the voyage, which remain in his possession till the close, and sometimes permanently. At meal time the passengers form in line, and pass before stewards who have large kettles of food, and serve out the rations to each. Passengers may eat at tables if there are any and they can find places; otherwise, wherever they can. After the meal, they must wash their own dishes, and stow them away for future use. Under the second system, the women and children receive slightly better attention, being given first place at such tables as there are. The most essential utensils are placed by stewards, and washed by them afterwards. The food is served in large pans, one for each table, which are passed along a line of stewards from the galley, in the manner of a bucket brigade. This is all the table service there is. The men receive even less attention. They are divided into groups of six, and each group is given two large tin pans, and tin plates, tin cups, and cutlery enough for all. Each man takes his turn at going after the food, and in caring for the dishes. The men eat wherever they can find a place.

Life under such circumstances must of necessity be disgusting and degrading, whatever the character or desires of the individual. The only part of the whole ship which the steerage passenger has a right to call in any sense his own is the few square feet contained in his berth. Here he must keep all of his personal belongings. His hand baggage must be stored in it, or hung from the pipes above his head. If there are eating utensils committed to his keeping, they must be concealed in some corner of the bunk when not in use. This is the only place to which he may retire in the search of even the semblance of privacy. It is the only place where he can recline during the daytime, except upon the open deck. The berths receive absolutely no attention from the stewards from the beginning of the voyage to the end. Is it any wonder that they become untidy, mussed, and ill smelling? The blankets provided are usually wholly inadequate for cold weather, so that passengers are absolutely compelled to sleep in their day clothing for warmth.

The ventilation of the steerage is almost always inadequate, growing worse the farther down one goes. The congestion is intense, and even if every provision were made for cleanliness, the air would inevitably become foul. Unfortunately such provision is not made. There are no sick-cans provided for the use of steerage passengers, and the vomitings of the seasick are allowed to lie unattended to for hours. Sometimes a steward comes around with a can of sawdust or sand, but that is of little avail. Add to this the odors of bodies not too clean, the reek of food, and the awful stench of the toilet rooms, and the atmosphere of the steerage becomes such that it is a marvel that human flesh can endure it. It is a fact that many of the passengers lie in their berths for the greater part of the voyage, in a stupor caused by breathing the vitiated air, indifferent to everything around them, unless it be to their meals. If one attempts to better things by going on deck, and remains above for any length of time, he finds it almost impossible to go below again. There are practically only two alternatives; either to go below for only a few hours of sleep, and spend practically all the time on deck, or to spend all the time below.

Even if the immigrants desired to keep personally clean, there is practically no opportunity, owing to the inadequacy of the wash rooms, the absence of towels, soap, etc., and the absolute lack of privacy. Only one who was trained to make the very most of such facilities could maintain his decency under such conditions; the bulk of the immigrants lack even the elements of such training.

The food served to steerage passengers is, according to almost all investigators, usually sufficient in quantity, and originally of good quality. But in the majority of cases it is so poorly cooked and served in such an unappetizing way as to render it most unsatisfactory. An average menu reads very well; it is only when one actually undertakes to eat the food, as served to the immigrants, that the real quality appears. There is usually a canteen, or bar, where drinks, candy, fruit, etc., may be secured by those who can pay for them, and stewards sometimes turn an extra penny by securing food from the second cabin for steerage passengers who make the arrangement with them.

One of the worst conditions prevailing in the steerage, upon which the investigators of the Immigration Commission lay great stress, is the indecent and immoral attitude and conduct of the men, including the crew as well as the passengers, toward the women. The stories which are told of the constant persecution of immigrant women, — unprovided as they are with any means of privacy, — even by those whose duty it is to protect them, are almost unbelievable, but are well substantiated. As one investigator wrote, only a set of instantaneous photographs could give an adequate idea of the demoralizing attentions to which women and girls are subjected, until even the most self-respecting of them sometimes weaken under the strain. The United States law, of course, aims to prevent these abuses, but it is powerless, without better machinery for enforcement than is provided.

All of these conditions are naturally aggravated by crowding, and are usually more pronounced on the westward than on the eastward trip, since the steerage is ordinarily more congested coming to the United States. It is a marvel that even the ignorant, uncultured, stolid peasants of Europe can find life tolerable under such conditions. Yet they do, and manage to get some enjoyment out of it besides. There are songs and games and dances to while away the time. Especially when the ship stops at any intermediate port the deck throngs with immigrants, men, women, and children, seeking recreation in their own way.

On the whole, the old-type steerage is the poorest possible introduction to, and preparation for, American life. It inevitably lowers the standards of decency, even of the immigrants, and often breaks down their moral and physical stamina. It shatters their bright visions of American life, and lands them cynical and embittered. One of the first steps in the improvement of the immigration situation should be the abolition of the old-type steerage.

The new-type steerage, which is found on some lines carrying immigrants from north Europe, was the result of competition for the traffic, which led certain companies to improve their facilities. The traffic agreement above referred to, by eliminating this competition, has prevented the extension of this type of steerage to other lines, and other ships. In general, the new-type steerage is a modified second cabin, with simpler and plainer accommodations, and less attendance. Separate staterooms are provided, having from two to eight berths in each; in some cases the berths are of the old steerage type. The blankets are adequate, and towels, mirrors, etc., are provided. On some lines the stewards are responsible for the care of the berths and staterooms. There are regular dining rooms, properly cared for; the food is abundant, and when carefully prepared, of good quality. Facilities for washing and toilet are superior to the old steerage, and greater segregation of the sexes is secured. The air is still bad, but not so absolutely intolerable, and most of the flagrant abuses of the old-type steerage are avoided. Old and new steerages are sometimes found on the same vessel, in which case the latter is known as third class. The difference in price between the two does not at all correspond to the wide difference in accommodations; in general, the price of steerage passage is much nearer to that of second cabin than the relative service would seem to warrant. This tends to disprove the claim sometimes made that the steamship companies cannot afford to furnish better accommodations to steerage passengers without materially raising the price, as does the fact that passengers are actually being carried in the new-type steerage, with a profit, at a moderate charge.

Throughout their long journey from their native villages to the portals of America, the immigrants are very much at the mercy of those into whose hands they have committed themselves for transportation. Their treatment differs with different companies, but all too often they are handled like so many cattle, or even worse, like so many articles of inanimate freight.[1]

The Immigration Commission recommends that a law be passed requiring United States government officials, both men and women, to be placed on all ships carrying third class or steerage passengers, at the expense of the companies, and that inspectors in the guise of immigrants should occasionally be sent across in the steerage. This ought certainly to bring about a decided improvement in conditions, for at present there is no provision, on the part of this government, for enforcing the steerage laws, or looking after the welfare of passengers on the voyage. Ships are subject to inspection after they arrive in port, but conditions are very different then from what they are in mid-ocean. As the ship approaches shore, toilet rooms and wash rooms are cleaned up, disinfectants are used, and everything is made to appear more proper and orderly. That such supervision and inspection is capable of producing beneficial results is proved by the fact that on ships carrying an Italian royal commissioner, conditions are very much superior to those on others.

[1] For fuller accounts of the steerage and life therein, see Rept. Imm. Com., Steerage Conditions; Steiner, E. A., *On the Trail of the Immigrant;* Brandenburg, B., *Imported Americans,* Chs. III, XIV, XV.

CHAPTER X

INSPECTION. SOCIAL AND ECONOMIC CONDITIONS OF ARRIVING IMMIGRANTS

The immigrant first comes under the official control of the United States government when he arrives at the port of destination. There are a number of seaports on the Atlantic and Pacific coasts designated by the Bureau as ports of entry for immigrants. Entry at any other ports is illegal. The facilities for the inspection and care of immigrants differ in extent in the different ports with the demands placed upon them, but the general line of procedure is the same in all. As New York has the most elaborate and complete immigrant station in the country and receives three quarters or more of all the immigrants, it may be taken as typical of the fullest development of our inspection system.

A ship arriving in New York is first subject to examination by the quarantine officials. Then the immigrants are turned over to the officers of the Immigration Bureau. All aliens entering a port of the United States are subject to the immigration law, and have to submit to inspection. First or second class passage does not, contrary to a common impression, secure immunity. Cabin passengers are given a preliminary inspection by the officials on board the vessel, and if they are plainly admissible, they are allowed to land without further formality. If there is any question as to their eligibility, they are taken to Ellis Island, and subjected to a closer examination. While there, they have to put up with the same accommodations as are accorded to steerage passengers. During three months of the spring of 1910 twenty-five hundred cabin passengers were thus taken over to Ellis Island, and the commissioner in charge at that port was led to recommend that better facilities be provided for this class of immigrants.[1] This recommendation was repeated in 1912.

The steerage passengers are loaded on to barges, rented by the steamship companies, and transferred to the immigrant station. This is located on Ellis Island, a group of small islands in the harbor, not far from the Statue of Liberty. It consists of two main parts, on one of which is located the main building, containing offices, sleeping rooms, restaurant, inspection rooms, ticket offices, etc.; on the other are the hospitals, etc. This temporary disembarkment does not constitute a legal landing; the immigrants are still nominally on shipboard, and the transportation companies are responsible for their support until they are legally landed.

After landing on the Island, the immigrants pass through a detailed process of examination, during which all the facts required by the statutes are ascertained and recorded, as far as possible. This examination consists of three main parts. The first is the medical examination made by officers of the United States Public Health and Marine Hospital Service. These inspect the immigrants for all physical weaknesses or diseases which make them liable to exclusion. The next stage is the examination by an inspector who asks the long list of questions required by the law, in order to determine whether the alien is, for any nonphysical reason,

[1] Rept. Com. Gen. of Imm., 1910, p. 135.

inadmissible. If the immigrant appears to be "clearly and beyond a doubt" entitled to admission, he passes on to the discharging quarters, where is he turned over to the agents of the appropriate transportation company, or to a "missionary," or is set free to take his way to the city by the ferry.

If any alien is not clearly entitled to admission, he must appear before a board of special inquiry, which goes into his case more deliberately and thoroughly, in order to determine whether he is legally admissible. Appeal from the decision of these boards, in cases provided for by the statutes, may be made either by the alien or by a dissenting member of the board. Such appeal goes through the Commissioner and the Commissioner General of Immigration to the Secretary of Commerce and Labor, whose decision is final.

Many aliens must of necessity be detained on the Island, either during investigation, or, in case they are excluded, while awaiting their return to the country from which they came. The feeding of these aliens, along with certain other services, is intrusted to "privilege holders," selected carefully by government authority.

The volume of business transacted on Ellis Island each year is immense. There are in all about six hundred and ten officials, including ninety-five medical officers and hospital attendants, engaged in administering the law at this station. The force of interpreters is probably the largest in the world, gathered under a single roof. At other immigrant stations the course of procedure follows the same general lines, though the amount of business is very much less.[1]

[1] Cf. Brandenburg, B., *Imported Americans*, Chs. XVII and XVIII.

This is obviously one of the most difficult and delicate of all the branches of government service. Questions involving the breaking up of families, the annihilation of long-cherished plans, and a host of other intimate human relations, even of life and death itself, present themselves in a steady stream before the inspectors. Every instinct of humanity argues on the side of leniency to the ignorant, stolid, abused, and deceived immigrant. On the other hand, the inspector knows that he is placed as a guardian of the safety and welfare of his country. He is charged with the execution of an intricate and iron-bound set of laws and regulations, into which his personal feelings and inclinations must not be allowed to enter. Any lapse into too great leniency is a betrayal of his trust. One who has not actually reviewed the cases can have no conception of the intricacy of the problems which are constantly brought up for decision.

Is it surprising that the casual and tender-hearted visitor who leans over the balcony railing or strolls through the passages, blissfully ignorant of the laws and of the meaning of the whole procedure, should think that he detects instances of brutality and hard-heartedness? To him, the immigrants are a crowd of poor but ambitious foreigners, who have left all for the sake of sharing in the glories of American life, and are now being ruthlessly and inconsiderately turned back at the very door by a lot of cruel and indifferent officials. He writes a letter to his home paper, telling of the "Brutality at Ellis Island." Even worse than these ignorant and sentimental critics are those clever and malicious writers who, inspired by the transportation companies or other selfish interests, paint distorted, misleading, and exaggerated pictures of affairs on Ellis

Island, and to serve their own ends strive to bring into disrepute government officials who are conscientiously doing their best to perform a most difficult public duty.[1]

It would not be safe to say that there never has been any brutality on Ellis Island, or that there is none now. Investigators of some reputation have given specific instances.[2] It would be almost beyond the realm of possibility that in so large a number of officials, coming in daily contact with thousands of immigrants, there should be none who were careless, irritable, impatient, or vicious. How much of maltreatment there may be depends very largely upon the character and competency of the commissioner in charge. The point is, that no one is qualified to pass an opinion upon the treatment of immigrants, except a thoroughly trained investigator, equipped with a full knowledge of the laws and regulations, and an unbiased mind.

One thing in particular which impresses the dilettante observer is the haste with which proceedings are conducted, and the physical force which is frequently employed to push an immigrant in one direction, or hold him back from another. It must be admitted that both of these exist — and they are necessary. During the year 1907 five thousand was fixed as the maximum number of immigrants who could be examined at Ellis Island in one day;[3] yet during the spring of that year more than fifteen thousand immigrants arrived at the port of New York in a single day. It is evident that under such conditions haste becomes a necessity.

The work has to be done with the equipment provided, and greater hardship may sometimes be caused by delay

[1] See an editorial in the *New York Evening Journal*, May 24, 1911.

[2] Brandenburg, *op. cit.*, p. 214. [3] Rept. Com. Gen. of Imm., 1907, p. 77.

than by haste. As to the physical handling of immigrants, this is necessitated by the need for haste, combined with the condition of the immigrants. We have seen that the conditions of the voyage are not calculated to land the immigrant in an alert and clear-headed state. The bustle, confusion, rush, and size of Ellis Island complete the work, and leave the average alien in a state of stupor and bewilderment. He is in no condition to understand or appreciate a carefully worded explanation of what he must do, or why he must do it, even if the inspector had time to give it. The one suggestion which is immediately comprehensible to him is a pull or a push; if this is not administered with actual violence, there is no unkindness in it. An amusing illustration of the dazed state in which the average immigrant goes through the inspection is furnished by a story told by one of the officials on the Island. It is related that President Roosevelt once visited the Island, in company with other distinguished citizens. He wished to observe the effect of a gift of money on an immigrant woman, and fearing to be recognized, handed a five-dollar gold piece to another member of the party, requesting him to hand it to the first woman with a child in her arms who passed along the line. It was done. The woman took the coin, slipped it into her dress, and passed on, without even raising her eyes or giving the slightest indication that the incident had made any different impression on her than any of the regular steps in the inspection. It would be a remarkable man, indeed, who could deal with a steady stream of foreigners, stolid and unresponsive to begin with and reduced to such a pitch of stupor, day after day, without occasionally losing his patience.

The information collected at the port of entry is

sufficient, when compiled and tabulated, to give a very complete and detailed picture of the character of the arriving immigrants, in so far as that can be statistically portrayed. The reports of the Commissioner General contain an elaborate set of tables, which are the principal source of accurate information on the subject. In the following pages these tables will be summarized, with the intent of bringing out the most important facts which condition the immigration problem in this country. Data from other reliable sources will be added as occasion requires.

During the period 1820 to 1912 a total of 29,611,052 immigrants have entered the United States. Of these, the Germans have made up a larger proportion than any other single race, amounting in all to 5,400,899 persons from the German Empire. Until very recently the Irish have stood second; but as far as can be determined from the figures the Italians and natives of Austria-Hungary have now passed them. There have been, in the period mentioned, 3,511,730 immigrants from Austria-Hungary, 3,426,070 immigrants from Italy, including Sicily and Sardinia, and 3,069,625 from Ireland. But if the 1,945,812 immigrants from the United Kingdom not specified could be properly assigned, it would probably appear that Ireland could still lay claim to second place. The other most important sources, with their respective contributions, are as follows: Russian Empire, 2,680,525; England, 2,264,284; British North American possessions, 1,322,085; Sweden, 1,095,940.[1] When it is considered how recent is the origin of the im-

[1] Rept. Imm. Com., Statistical Review, Abs., p. 17, and Rept. Comr. Gen. of Imm., 1912, pp. 68, 129. The figures of the Commission do not tally in all respects with those given in the annual Reports.

migration from Italy, Russia, and Austria-Hungary, the significance of these figures becomes apparent. The figures for a single recent year show very different proportions. Thus in the year 1907, 28.2 per cent of the total European immigration came from Austria-Hungary, 23.8 per cent from Italy,[1] and 21.6 per cent from the Russian Empire, while only 3.2 per cent came from the German Empire, 1.7 per cent from Sweden, 2.9 per cent from Ireland, and 4.7 per cent from England.[2] What the ultimate effect of this sweeping change in nationality will be it is impossible to predict with any certainty; it is one of the greatest of all the problems connected with immigration, and can better be discussed in another connection. Suffice it to say for the present, that it has put an entirely new face on the question of the assimilation of the immigrant in this country.

In regard to the sex of the immigrants, the males have always had the predominance. During the period from 1820 to 1910, 63.8 per cent of the immigrants were males, and 36.2 per cent females.[3] This is what might naturally be expected. The first emigration from a region is almost always an emigration of men. They have the necessary hardihood and daring to a greater extent than women, and are better fitted by nature for the work of pioneering. After the current of emigration becomes well established, women are found joining in. Early emigrants send for their families, young men send for their sweethearts, and even some single women venture to go to a country where there are friends and relatives.

[1] Figures for Italy, unless otherwise specified, include Sicily and Sardinia.

[2] Rept. Imm. Com., Emig. Cond. in Eur., Abs., p. 9.

[3] *Ibid.*, Stat. Rev., Abs., p. 11.

But in the majority of cases the number of males continues to exceed that of females. In the long run, there will be a greater proportion of men than of women, because of the natural differences of the sexes. In this respect, however, there has also been a change in recent years. The proportion of males is considerably larger among the new immigrants than among the old. In the decade 1820–1830, when immigration was still in its beginning, there was a large proportion of males, amounting to 70 per cent of the total. In the decades of the forties and fifties, however, the proportion of males fell to 59.5 per cent and 58 per cent, respectively. But in the decade ending 1910, 69.8 per cent of all the immigrants were males. There is a general tendency for the proportion of males to rise in a year of large immigration, and fall as immigration diminishes. This can be traced with a remarkable degree of regularity throughout the modern period. It is well exemplified in the last six years. In the year 1907, when the total immigration reached its highest record, the proportion of males also reached the highest point since 1830, 72.4 per cent. After the crisis of that year the total immigration fell off decidedly, and in 1908 the proportion of males was only 64.8 per cent. In the next year the percentage of males rose to 69.2, while the total immigration decreased slightly; but since the net gain by immigration increased in that year,[1] this is not a serious exception to the rule. In 1910 the total immigration again showed a marked increase, and the percentage of males rose to 70.7.[2] In 1911 there was another marked decline in immigration and the percentage of males fell to 64.9, while a further slight decline in 1912 was accompanied by a

[1] See page 128. [2] Rept. Imm. Com., Stat. Rev., Abs., pp. 9, 10, 11.

fall in the percentage of males to 63.2.[1] This phenomenon is undoubtedly accounted for by the fact that the men come in more direct response to the economic demands of this country than the women, and hence respond to economic fluctuations more readily. Many of the female immigrants come to join men who have established themselves on a footing of fair prosperity in this country, and are able to have them come even in a year of hard times.

An examination of the sex distribution of some of the leading races shows how thoroughly characteristic of the new immigration this excess of males is. The following table shows the percentages of the two sexes of certain chosen races for the eleven-year period 1899 to 1909:

SEX DISTRIBUTION OF IMMIGRANTS OF SPECIFIED RACES, BY PER CENTS, 1899 TO 1909

Race or People	Per Cent	
	Male	Female
Bulgarian, Servian, Montenegrin	96.0	4.0
Croatian and Slovenian	85.1	14.9
English	61.7	38.3
German	59.4	40.6
Greek	95.4	4.6
Hebrew	56.7	43.3
Irish	47.2	52.8
Italian, north	78.4	21.6
Italian, south	78.6	21.4
Lithuanian	71.1	28.9
Magyar	72.7	27.3
Polish	69.2	30.8
Ruthenian	74.0	26.0
Scandinavian	61.3	38.7
Slovak	70.3	29.7

[1] Repts. Comr. Gen. of Imm., 1911, 1912.

Comparing the entire old immigration for the period specified with the entire new immigration (European only), we find that of the former 58.5 per cent were male and 41.5 per cent female; of the latter 73 per cent were male, and 27 per cent female.[1] It is evident that the new immigration is in no sense an immigration of families, but of men, either single men, or married men who have left their wives on the other side. This is due in part to the very fact that it is a new immigration, partly to the fact that it is, to such a large degree, temporary or provisional. An immigrant who expects to return to his native land after a few years in America is more likely to leave his wife behind him than one who bids farewell to his old home forever. The typical old immigrant, when he has secured his competency, sends for his wife to come and join him; the typical new immigrant, under the same circumstances, in many cases returns to his native land to spend the remainder of his days in the enjoyment of his accumulated wealth. The only exception to this rule is that furnished by the Hebrews, among whom the sexes are nearly equally distributed. This is one of the many respects in which they stand apart from the rest of the new immigration. The only race in which the female immigrants exceed the males is the Irish, and this has been the case only within recent years. During the years of the great Irish immigration the males predominated.

The matter of sex is one of the greatest importance to the United States. It is one thing to have foreign families coming here to cast in their lots with this nation permanently; it is quite another to have large groups of males coming over, either with the expectation of re-

[1] Rept. Imm. Com., Emig. Cond. in Eur., Abs., p. 13.

turning ultimately to their native land, or of living in this country without family connections, for an indefinite number of years. Such groups form an unnatural element in our population, and alter the problem of assimilation very considerably. They are willing to work for a lower wage than if they were trying to support families in this country, and are not nearly so likely to be brought into touch with the molding forces of American life as are foreign family groups. Their habits of life, as will appear later,[1] are abnormal, and tend to result in depreciated morals and physique. Many of the most unfortunate conditions surrounding the present immigration situation may be traced to this great preponderance of males.

The one thing that can be said in favor of this state of affairs is that such a group of immigrants furnishes a larger number of workers than one more evenly distributed between the sexes. This is an argument which will appeal to many; but to many others, who have the best welfare of the country at heart, it will appear wholly inadequate to offset the serious disadvantages which result from the situation. The Immigration Commission expresses its opinion that, in the effort to reduce the oversupply of unskilled labor in this country by restricting immigration, special discrimination should be made against men unaccompanied by wives or children.[2]

In regard to the age of immigrants the most striking fact is that the great bulk of them are in the middle age groups. In the year 1912 the distribution of the total immigration among the different age groups was as follows: under fourteen years, 13.6 per cent; fourteen to forty-four years, 80.9 per cent; forty-five years and

[1] See page 247. [2] Rept. Imm. Com., Brief Statement, p. 39.

over, 5.5 per cent. In the total population of the United States the respective percentages in these groups are about 30, 51, and 19. There is only a slight difference in this respect between the new and the old immigration. Of the total European immigration for the years 1899 to 1909, the old immigration had 12.8 per cent in the first age group, 80.4 per cent in the second, and 6.8 per cent in the third; the new immigration had 12.2 per cent in the first, 83.5 per cent in the second, and 4.3 per cent in the third.[1] There is, however, a very marked difference between the races. This will be brought out by the following table, which shows the age distribution of certain selected races, for the year 1910:

DISTRIBUTION OF IMMIGRANTS OF SPECIFIED RACES AMONG THE AGE GROUPS, BY PER CENTS, 1910

Race or People	Age, Per Cent		
	Under 14 Years	14 to 44 Years	45 Years and Over
Croatian and Slovenian	4.7	91.0	3.3
German	17.0	75.9	7.1
Greek	2.6	96.0	1.4
Hebrew	25.9	67.9	6.2
Irish	7.4	88.3	4.3
Italian, south	10.4	83.5	6.1
Polish	7.6	89.7	2.7

Here, again, the Hebrews appear as an exception to the general rule as regards the new immigration and, in this case, as regards the total immigration.

The showing in regard to age substantiates the ob-

[1] *Ibid.*, Emig. Cond. in Eur., Abs., p. 14.

servation already made that our modern immigration is in no sense an immigration of families. This, too, affects the chances for assimilation very considerably. As regards the economic efficiency of the immigrants, the age distribution, added to the sex distribution, marks them as a selected group. When it is further considered that the physically and mentally feeble, and those who are unlikely to be able to earn their own living are weeded out in the process of inspection, it appears that those who look upon the immigrant as nothing more than a source of cheap labor have much reason to be pleased with the quality of our immigration. The productive power of a group of immigrants averages very much higher than a corresponding number of persons taken from the general population of the race from which they come.

Herein lies perhaps the greatest and most popular argument for immigration. It is claimed that without our foreign laboring force it would have been impossible to develop the resources of the country so rapidly and completely as they have been developed, and that if the supply were cut off now, it would seriously cripple the entire industry of the country. It is certainly true that under the present organization of industry in this country, production in many lines depends to a very important degree upon foreign labor. How much of truth there is in the deduction that without the immigrants this country would be much farther back in the industrial race than it is to-day, will be considered in another connection.[1]

There are many citizens of the United States, however, who look upon the immigrant as something more than a mere productive machine. To them the proof of

[1] See page 341.

his economic efficiency is not sufficient. They wish to know something of his adaptability to assimilation into the American life, and of his probable contribution to the ethnic type of the United States. To such as these, there are a number of further conditions which must be considered, and which are of at least equal significance in determining the final effects of immigration upon this country.

Prominent among these is the intellectual quality of the immigrant. This is naturally a very difficult thing to measure. Beyond actual feeble-mindedness, the only test of intellectual capacity which has received wide application is the literacy — or, as it is more frequently expressed, the illiteracy — test. This concerns the ability to read and write, and is given a great deal of weight by many students of the subject. It is not, however, necessarily an indication of intellectual capacity, but rather of education. The inability to read or write may be due to lack of early opportunity, rather than to inferior mental caliber. Nevertheless, the matter of literacy has received sufficient attention, and is in fact of sufficient importance, so that it is desirable to have the facts in this respect before us.

Two forms of illiteracy are recognized by the immigration authorities, inability to either read or write, and inability to write coupled with ability to read. The latter class is a very small one, and for all practical purposes those who are spoken of as illiterates are those who can neither read nor write. For the period of 1899–1909 the average illiteracy of all European immigrants fourteen years of age or over was 26.6 per cent. There is a marked difference between the old and new immigrants in this respect. Of the former class, during the period mentioned, only 2.7 per cent of the immigrants fourteen years of age or over was illiterate; of the latter class, 35.6 per cent. The same difference is brought out by the following table, showing the illiteracy of certain specified races:

PERCENTAGE OF ILLITERACY[1] OF IMMIGRANTS OF THE SPECIFIED RACES, 14 YEARS OF AGE OR OVER, FOR THE YEARS 1899 TO 1909[2]

Race or People	Per Cent	Race or People	Per Cent
Scandinavian	0.4	Greek	27.0
English	1.1	Roumanian	34.7
Irish	2.7	Polish	35.4
German	5.1	Croatian and Slovenian	36.4
Italian, north	11.8	Italian, south	54.2
Magyar	11.4	Portuguese	68.2
Hebrew	25.7		

Where there is such a marked difference between races as is exhibited in the foregoing table, it seems fair to assume that there is a corresponding difference in the intellectual condition of the respective peoples — if not in their potential capacity, at least in the actual mental equipment of the immigrants themselves.[3] In fact, it is quite customary to take the degree of illiteracy as a reasonable index of the desirability of a given stream of immigration. There seems to be considerable basis for this idea, for it appears probable that an immigrant who has had the ability and the opportunity to secure, in his home land, such a degree of education as is indicated by the ability to read and write, is better equipped for adapting himself to life in a new country than one who has not. On the other hand, there is considerable testimony to the effect that the immigrants

[1] Those who can neither read nor write.

[2] Rept. Imm. Com., Emig. Cond. in Eur., Abs., p. 17.

[3] The per cent of illiteracy in the general population of the United States, ten years of age or over, is 10.7.

who have the hardest time to get along in this country are those who have a moderate degree of education, bookkeepers, mediocre musicians, clerks, etc. They are either unable or unwilling to do the menial work which their less educated countrymen perform, and are not able to compete with persons trained in this country in the occupations which they followed at home. There are relatively few of the occupations into which the typical immigrant of to-day goes, and for which he is encouraged to come to this country, in which the ability to read and write adds to the efficiency of the worker to any considerable degree. It is possible that the ability to read and write may hasten the process of assimilation somewhat; it is questionable whether it adds appreciably to the economic fitness of the immigrant for life in this country.

The question of literacy as a test of immigrants has received a large amount of attention recently through its inclusion in the proposed immigration bill which barely failed of becoming a law early in the year 1913. This bill was the result of the investigations of the Immigration Commission, and embodied several of the recommendations of that body. The one upon which most of the opposition was centered was a clause providing a reading test for adult aliens. There were certain exceptions to the rule, however, so that in its actual application the exclusion would have been limited almost wholly to adult males. The bill passed both houses of Congress, but was vetoed by the President, after a careful and judicial consideration. The Senate promptly passed the bill over the veto, but a similar action in the House failed by the narrow margin of half a dozen votes.

The agitation for a literacy test rests upon two main groups of arguments. The first class includes the efforts to show that literacy, in itself, is a desirable qualification for citizenship, economically, socially, and politically. The second group rests on the belief that the total number of immigrants ought to be cut down, and that a literacy test is a good way to accomplish the result. It is not unlikely that this latter set of opinions predominated over the former in the minds of the adherents of the proposed measure, though it was not necessarily expressed openly. And there is much to be said in favor of the literacy test from this point of view. In the first place, it is a perfectly definite and comprehensible test, which could be applied by the immigrant to himself before he left his native village. In the second place, it is a test which any normal alien could prepare himself to meet if he were willing to make the effort. It does not seem too much to require of one who wishes to become a member of the American body politic, that he take the pains to equip himself with the rudiments of an education before presenting himself. Finally, as Miss Claghorn has pointed out,[1] it is a test which would react favorably upon the immigrant himself. It is impossible to tell, as noted above, just how much value attaches to literacy in the effort of the alien to maintain himself in this country. Yet without doubt there is some advantage. And perhaps there would be even more in the strengthening of character and purpose which would result from the effort to attain it. A glance at the preceding table will show which of the immigrant races, as the immigration stream is now constituted, would be most affected by such a test. But it is not at all impossible that the

[1] Claghorn, Kate H., "The Immigration Bill," *The Survey*, Feb. 8, 1913.

passage of a literacy test by this government would have the effect of materially stimulating the progress of education in some of the more backward countries of Europe.

This tendency to illiteracy on the part of immigrants is apparently well overcome in the second generation, for among the employees in manufacturing studied by the Immigration Commission the percentage of illiteracy was lower among the native-born descendants of foreign fathers than among the native-born of native fathers.[1]

In the year 1910 information was collected for the first time in regard to the conjugal condition of immigrants. The figures on this point are summarized in the following table, which gives the percentages of each sex, in the different age groups, who are in the different classifications as to conjugal condition.

CONJUGAL CONDITION OF IMMIGRANTS, 1910

Sex	Percentages							
	14 to 44 Years[1]				45 Years and Over			
	Single	Married	Widowed	Divorced	Single	Married	Widowed	Divorced
Male .	55.3	44.2	0.5	*a*	5.2	86.8	7.9	*a*
Female .	57.7	39.9	2.3	*a*	6.6	52.8	40.5	0.1

[1] All the immigrants under 14 were single, with the exception of one female.
[a] Less than one tenth of 1 per cent.

This table furnishes further verification of the fact that our present immigration is in no sense an immigration of families. More than half of all the immigrants fourteen years of age or over, of both sexes, are single.

[1] Rept. Imm. Com., Immigrants in Manufacturing and Mining, Abs., p. 165.

This affects the problem of assimilation very deeply. One of the greatest forces for Americanization in immigrant families is the growing children. Where these are absent, the adults have much less contact with assimilating influences. If there was a large degree of intermarriage between these single immigrants and native Americans, the aspect of the case would be very different; but thus far, this is not the case.

Much has been said and written about the absolute economic gain to this country through immigration. It is pointed out that each year an army of able-bodied laborers, in the prime of life, is added to our working force. To the expense of their rearing we have contributed nothing; they come to us as a free gift from the nations of Europe. Various efforts have been made to estimate the actual cash value of these alien laborers. Professor Mayo-Smith enumerates three different ways of attacking the problem. The first is by estimating the cost of bringing up the immigrant, up to the time of his arrival in the United States. The second is by estimating his value as if he were a slave. The third is by estimating the amount of wealth he will contribute to the community before he dies, minus the cost of his maintenance — in other words, his net earnings.[1]

The lack of uniformity in the results obtained by different methods and by different investigators gives weight to the opinion that it is, after all, a rather fruitless undertaking. To estimate the monetary value of a man seems to be, as yet, too much for economic science.

There is one economic contribution, however, which the immigrants make to this country which is capable of fairly accurate measurement. This is the amount of

[1] Mayo-Smith, R., *Emigration and Immigration*, pp. 104 ff.

money which they bring with them when they come. For many years immigrants have been compelled to show the amount of money in their possession, and this information has been recorded, and incorporated in the annual reports. Up to 1904, immigrants were divided into those showing less than $30 and those showing that amount or more. In that year this dividing line was raised to $50. The total amount of money shown is also given. Thus it is possible to estimate the average amount of money shown by the immigrants of different races, and also to ascertain what proportion of them showed above or below the specified amount. Unfortunately for the conclusiveness of the statistics, immigrants very commonly do not show all the money in their possession, but only so much as they think is necessary to secure their admission. So the total amount of money shown does not represent the total amount brought in; all that can be positively stated is that at least so much was brought in.

In 1909 the total amount of money shown was $17,331,828; in 1910, $28,197,745; in 1911, $29,411,488; and in 1912, $30,353,721. The average per capita showings of the European immigrants for the period 1905 to 1909 was as follows:[1]

Class	Average per Capita	
	Based on Total Coming	Based on Total Showing
Old immigration	$39.90	$55.20
New immigration	15.83	20.99
Total	$22.47	$30.14

[1] Rept. Imm. Com., Emig. Cond. in Eur., Abs., p. 20.

Those not showing money were for the most part children and other dependents. This shows how baseless is the impression, quite prevalent among Americans and aliens alike, that a certain specified amount of money is necessary to secure admission to this country. Thirty dollars or fifty dollars are the amounts commonly mentioned. But since the average based on the total number showing money is barely over thirty dollars, it is plain that there must be a large number showing less than thirty dollars. In fact, some races, as, for instance, the Polish, Lithuanians, and south Italians, have an average of from twenty to twenty-five dollars for all showing money. There is no monetary requirement for admission to the United States. While the possession of a certain amount of money is considered to add to the probability of an immigrant being able to support himself without becoming a public charge, a sturdy laborer with ten dollars in his pocket is more likely to secure admission than a decrepit old man with a good-sized bank account.

Against these large amounts of money brought in by immigrants, which represent a net gain to the total wealth of the country, must be set off the enormous amounts of money annually sent abroad by alien residents of the United States. Various efforts have been made to estimate these sums. The best is probably that of the Immigration Commission which sets the figure at a total of $275,000,000 for the year 1907, which was a prosperous year.[1]

The following table gives the distribution of immigrants among the different classes of occupations.

[1] Rept. Imm. Com., Immigrant Banks, p. 69.

OCCUPATION OF EUROPEAN IMMIGRANTS FOR THE YEARS 1898 TO 1909, PERCENTAGES[1]

Occupation	Per Cent	Occupation	Per Cent
Professional	1.0	Common laborers	27.8
Skilled laborers	15.2	Servants	10.8
Farm laborers	15.7	Miscellaneous	2.1
Farmers	1.0	No occupation[2]	26.4

These figures are taken from the statements of the immigrants themselves, and represent, in so far as they are correct, the economic position of the immigrant in the country from which he came. They are not a reliable indication of the occupation into which he goes in this country.

It is evident that the great majority of the immigrants belong in general to the unskilled labor class. This is the class of labor for which there is a special demand in this country, and for which the immigrants are desired. At the same time, as Professor Commons has pointed out,[3] there is also a considerable demand for skilled artisans in this country, as the peculiar conditions of American industry prevent the training of a sufficient number of all-round mechanics at home. This demand is also met from European sources. There is a great difference in this respect between the different races.[4] For instance, 29.8 per cent of the English immigrants were skilled laborers, 37.9 per cent of the Scotch, and 35.2 per cent of the Welsh, while only 4.7 per cent of the Croatians and Slovenians, 2.7 per cent of the Roumanians, 1.8 per cent of the Ruthenians, and 3.5 per cent of

[1] *Ibid.*, Emig. Cond. in Eur., Abs., p. 15. [2] Including women and children.
[3] *Races and Immigrants in America*, pp. 124–125.
[4] For detailed figures of occupation by races see Rept. Imm. Com., Stat. Rev., Abs., pp. 52, 53.

the Slovaks belonged to that class, during the period mentioned. The highest proportion of professional is shown by the French, with 6.2 per cent. In general, the old immigration has a larger proportion in the professional and skilled groups than the new, and this difference would be much more marked if the Hebrews were excepted, as they again furnish a marked exception to the general rule of the new immigration, with 36.7 per cent in the skilled labor group.

Thus far, the facts which have been brought out all have to do with the condition of the immigrants upon their arrival. They furnish a sort of a composite picture of the raw material. This is about as far as the regular statistics go. After the immigrants have left the port of arrival, the Bureau furnishes practically no information about them until they leave the country again, except an occasional special report, and, in recent years, figures concerning naturalization. This is typical of the general attitude which characterizes the entire immigration system and legislation, and rests on the assumption that if sufficient care is exercised in the selection of immigrants, all will thenceforth be well, and no attention need be paid to them after they are in the country. The final piece of information furnished in the reports is the alleged destination of the immigrants. This is of course somewhat uncertain, but in so far as it is conclusive it furnishes a preliminary clew to the distribution of our alien residents throughout the country.

The significance of the figures regarding destination, or intended future residence, may best be brought out by showing the percentages destined to the different territorial divisions of the United States. In 1910 these were as follows:

PER CENT OF TOTAL IMMIGRATION DESTINED TO EACH OF THE SPECIFIED DIVISIONS, 1910

Division	Per Cent
North Atlantic	62.3
South Atlantic	2.5
North Central	26.1
South Central	2.3
Western	6.1
Total	99.3 [1]

The fact that in a typical year 88.4 per cent of the total immigration gave their intended future residence as the North Atlantic or North Central divisions, introduces us to some of the peculiarities of the distribution of immigrants in the United States, which will be further considered later.

Before closing our consideration of arriving immigrants it will be well to glance briefly at those who arrive, but are not admitted — in other words, the debarred. We have seen that the law has grown more and more stringent in its conditions for admission, and each new statute has tended to raise the standard. These laws have had a powerful influence in improving the character of the applicants for admission, and with the coöperation of the transportation companies have operated to check the emigration of the manifestly undesirable to an ever greater extent. Yet there are every year considerable numbers of would-be immigrants who have to be turned back at the portals of the United States. The lot of these unfortunates is undeniably a hard one, and they are the objects of much well-deserved sympathy. Everything possible ought to be done to limit the number of inadmissible aliens who are allowed to present themselves at the immigrant stations of this country. The farther

[1] Balance to Alaska, Hawaii, Philippine Islands, and Porto Rico.

back on the road they can be stopped, the better will the interests of humanity be served. At the same time, pity for the rejected alien ought not to be allowed to express itself in unreasonable and unwarranted attacks upon our system of admission, and the officials who administer it, as is sometimes done.[1]

The statistics of debarments may be indicative of the character of the applicants, of the stringency of the laws and the faithfulness of their enforcement, or of the care of the transportation companies in prosecuting their examination on the other side. It is impossible to tell from the figures themselves which of these factors account for the different fluctuations. It is undoubtedly true that there has been, in general, a steady improvement in the care with which immigrants are selected. If, next year, a million immigrants of the same general character as prevailed sixty years ago should present themselves at our gates, the proportion of refusals would soar tremendously. The following table gives the proportion of debarments to admissions since 1892.

PROPORTION OF ALIENS DEBARRED, EXPRESSED IN PERCENTAGES OF IMMIGRANTS ADMITTED, 1892–1912

Year	1892	1893	1894	1895	1896	1897	1898
Per cent	.37	.24	.49	.94	.62	.70	1.32
Year	**1899**	**1900**	**1901**	**1902**	**1903**	**1904**	**1905**
Per cent	1.22	.95	.72	.76	1.02	.98	1.15
Year	**1906**	**1907**	**1908**	**1909**	**1910**	**1911**	**1912**
Per cent	1.12	1.02	1.18	1.09	2.33	2.54	1.92

[1] See Brandenburg, B., "The Tragedy of the Rejected Immigrant," *Outlook*, Oct. 13, 1906.

In the years 1892 to 1912, 169,132 aliens were refused admission to the United States. Of these, 58.2 per cent were debarred on the grounds of pauperism or likelihood of becoming a public charge, 15.8 per cent were afflicted with loathsome or dangerous contagious diseases, and 12.7 per cent were contract laborers. These three leading causes account for 86.7 per cent of all the debarments. The other classes of debarred aliens specified in the reports are as follows: idiots, imbeciles, feeble-minded, epileptics, insane, tuberculosis (non-contagious), professional beggars, mental or physical defects likely to affect ability to earn a living, accompanying aliens, under sixteen years of age unaccompanied by parent, assisted aliens, criminals, polygamists, anarchists, prostitutes, etc., aliens who procure prostitutes, etc., under passport provision, Section 1, under provisions Chinese exclusion act, supported by proceeds of prostitution.

There has been a change in the relative importance of the three leading causes of debarment since 1892. In that year almost all the debarred aliens were paupers or likely to become a public charge or contract laborers. The first of these classes has held its own down to the present, and still stands far in advance of any other cause as regards the number refused. The contract labor class has declined in relative importance. Loathsome and dangerous contagious diseases were comparatively unimportant until 1898, when they sprang into prominence, and have since outstripped contract laborers. This was due to the classification, in 1897, of trachoma as a dangerous contagious disease. It has since led the list of diseases by a large margin. In 1910 there were 2618 cases of trachoma out of a total of 3123 loathsome or dangerous contagious diseases. Favus comes next with 111 cases, tuberculosis next with 90, and others 304. The proportions were about the same in 1908 and 1909. In 1912 the proportion of trachoma was even greater.

Trachoma is the disease popularly known as granular lids. It attacks the conjunctiva, or mucous lining of the lids, setting up inflammation. It affects the cornea, forming ulcers, and may result in partial or total opacity, which may be permanent or temporary. The determination of cases of true trachoma appears to be a matter of some difficulty; the examiners on Ellis Island are "instructed to regard as trachoma any case wherein the conjunctiva presents firm, well-marked granulations which do not have a tendency to disappear when the case is placed in hygienic surroundings a few days, or does not yield rapidly to ordinary treatment, even though there be no evidence of active inflammation at the time of the examination, nor appreciable discharge, nor as yet any signs of degenerative or destructive processes." [1] The necessity for great caution in this matter is increased by the fact that it is possible by medical treatment to remove the outward symptoms of trachoma so as to make it very difficult of detection, though there is no real cure, and the disease will return later. Many immigrants who are suffering from this malady take treatment of this sort before emigrating. It is stated that in London there are institutions which make a business of preparing immigrants for admission.[2] Statements emanating from medical sources have recently appeared in the newspapers to the effect that trachoma is not so

[1] Stoner, Dr. George W., *Immigration — The Medical Treatment of Immigrants*, etc., p. 10.

[2] There is also a flourishing business of this sort in Liverpool, Marseilles, etc. Rept. Commissioner General of Immigration, 1905, pp. 50 ff.

contagious or dangerous as has been supposed, but they appear to lack substantiation.

Favus is another name for the disease known as ring worm. It is a vegetable parasite which attacks the hair, causing it to become dry, brittle, dull, and easily pulled out. Favus is also susceptible to temporary "cures."

On the whole, the new immigration is more subject to debarment than the old, particularly for the cause of trachoma. This is a disease to which the races of south-eastern Europe and Asia Minor are especially liable. A large part of the Syrians have it. In 1910 more than 3 per cent of all the Syrians who presented themselves for admission were refused for this cause alone. Inability for self-support is also much more common among the new than the old.

Reviewing this survey of the arriving immigrants, we find that as respects age and sex they are a body of persons remarkably well qualified for productive labor. The predominating races are now those of southern and eastern Europe, which are of a decidedly different stock from the original settlers of this country. There is a large percentage of illiteracy. The statistics of conjugal condition, combined with those of sex and age, show that our present immigration is in no sense an immigration of families. The great majority of the immigrants belong to the unskilled or common labor class, or else have no occupation. The bulk of the immigrants are destined to the North Atlantic and North Central divisions of the United States. The immigrants are a selected body, as far as this can be accomplished by a strict examination under the law. In spite of the care exercised by transportation companies on the other side, a considerable number of aliens are debarred each year, mainly for the causes of disease, inability for self-support, or labor contracts. In almost all of these respects the old immigration differs to a greater or less extent from the new, with the exception of the Hebrews, who stand apart from the rest of the new immigration in a number of important particulars.

CHAPTER XI

CONDITIONS OF IMMIGRANTS IN THE UNITED STATES. EFFECTS ON POPULATION. DISTRIBUTION

THE student who turns to the investigation of immigration conditions within the United States at once finds himself hindered by a serious lack of material. As has been stated above, the Immigration Bureau furnishes practically no data concerning our alien residents after it bids them farewell at the immigration station. The Census Bureau furnishes certain valuable data, and the Immigration Commission has recently collected a vast amount of useful information. Occasional articles appear in the periodicals, and there are a few books touching on the subject. But there is a great need for more concrete, exhaustive, and sympathetic studies of single racial groups of immigrants, such as has been made by Miss Emily G. Balch in regard to the Slavs. There ought also to be a number of conscientious studies of different phases of immigrant life in this country — what might be called transverse sections of the problem, as the other studies are longitudinal sections. A number of valuable studies of the latter sort have been made by the Immigration Commission in its reports upon immigrants in industries, immigrants in cities, immigrants as charity seekers, etc. Other topics which might well be considered in a similar manner will be suggested by the following subjects: housing conditions among immigrants, the food of immigrants, the problem of assimilation, family life of the immigrants, religious life of the immigrants, etc. Until more work of this sort has been done most general conclusions must be admittedly tentative and subject to revision. Nevertheless, knowledge grows from the general to the particular, as well as in the reverse order, and it will not be without profit to review the data which are already at hand, and establish as many conclusions with a fair degree of certainty as may be possible.

At the time of the census of 1900 the population of the United States numbered 76,303,387. Of these 10,460,085 were foreign-born. In 1910 out of a total population of 91,972,266 there were 13,515,886 foreign-born. Out of about forty-five different groups, designated by the country of origin, the following are the most important:

FOREIGN-BORN POPULATION OF THE UNITED STATES WHOSE BIRTHPLACE WAS IN THE COUNTRY SPECIFIED

Birthplace	1900 Number	1910 Number
Austria	276,702	1,174,973
Canada (English or other)	787,798	819,554
Canada (French)	395,427	385,083
England	843,491	877,719
Germany	2,669,164	2,501,333
Ireland	1,619,469	1,352,251
Italy	484,703	1,343,125
Norway	338,426	403,877
Poland (all)	383,595	[1]
Russia	424,372	1,602,782
Sweden	574,625	665,207

When we remember the remarkable homogeneity of the inhabitants of the United States at the time of the Revolution, we seem justified in saying that one conclusion, at least, is established beyond any doubt, viz. that immigration to the United States since 1820 has

[1] Distributed under Austria, Germany, and Russia.

resulted in a decided mixture of racial stock. For good or ill, the racial unity of the American people is a thing of the past.

There is another conclusion which might be drawn from the above figures, and which is in fact assumed by many writers, and in most popular discussions of the subject, which is not so well supported by facts. This is, that these foreign-born residents of the country, amounting to one seventh of the total, constitute a net addition to the population; in other words, that immigration has increased the total population of the country by an amount approximately equal to the number of immigrants, allowing, of course, for removals and deaths.

At first glance this may seem almost a self-evident proposition. That it is not, however, is evidenced by the strikingly large number of the deeper thinkers on the subject who hold the opposite view. Of these, the best known in this connection is General Francis A. Walker. In his discussion of this problem he says: "Space would not serve for a full statistical demonstration of the proposition that immigration, during the period from 1830 to 1860 instead of constituting a net reënforcement to the population, simply resulted in a replacement of native by foreign elements; but I believe it would be practicable to prove this to the satisfaction of every fair-minded man." [1] Mr. Prescott F. Hall, who quotes this passage, holds firmly to the same opinion himself, and cites a number of other writers who are more or less positive in their statements of the causal relation between immigration and the diminishing native birth rate.

Mr. F. A. Bushee, whose authority on matters of

[1] Quoted by Prescott F. Hall, *Immigration*, p. 107. See also Walker, F. A., "The Restriction of Immigration," *Atlantic Monthly*, 77:822.

population is well recognized, says, "The multiplication of foreign peoples has seriously checked the growth of the old American stock."[1] Mr. Robert Hunter is a pronounced advocate of this view, and says, "The immigrants are not additional inhabitants. Their coming displaces the native stock."[2] Professor John R. Commons supports this position throughout his discussions of the subject. An extreme but convincing opinion is that expressed by Mr. S. G. Fisher in the *Popular Science Monthly* for December, 1895. After a careful statistical survey of the growth of population in the United States he states his conviction that "immigration has not materially increased, but, on the contrary, has somewhat decreased the American population. . . . All the immigrants and all their increase cannot make up for the loss of the old rate of increase of the natives."

In view of this imposing weight of authoritative opinion, it is perhaps surprising that the popular mind still holds so tenaciously and universally to the belief that immigration directly increases population. The explanation probably lies in ignorance of the facts of the case and of the fundamental laws of population and in the somewhat abstruse nature of the reasoning by which the expert conclusions are reached. For it must be admitted frankly that this is not a proposition which can be demonstrated in an absolutely conclusive mathematical way, which will leave no further ground for argument. The factors affecting population are many and complicated, including not only immigration, but war,

[1] Bushee, F. A., "The Declining Birth Rate and Its Cause," *Pop. Sci. Month.*, 63: 355.

[2] Hunter, Robert, "Immigration the Annihilator of our Native Stock," *The Commons*, April, 1904.

vice, hard times, marriage customs, the growth of cities, and a host of other things. It is far beyond the present power of social science to define positively the relative importance of each of the forces involved in producing a certain phenomenon.

The line of argument by which, in general, all writers such as those to whom reference was made above have reached their conclusions is as follows. The population of the United States at the time it became a nation was almost wholly of native origin. It was a homogeneous people, of one stock, one language, and one set of traditions, customs, and beliefs. For the first forty years of our national life the increase of population was phenomenal, doubling every twenty-two or twenty-three years. Malthus chose the North American colonies as an example of the extreme possibilities of increase under favorable conditions, and the rate continued for many years after they ceased to be colonies. Between 1790 and 1830 the population increased from less than 4,000,000 to nearly 13,000,000, or 227 per cent in forty years. An estimate made in 1815, based on the first three censuses, reckoned the probable population of the United States in 1900 at 100,235,985. The fact that it was, instead, only 76,303,387, in spite of the incoming of 19,115,221 aliens since 1820, shows that there must have been a tremendous falling-off in the native birth rate. Careful study reveals the fact that the birth rate first began to decline appreciably about 1830, just the period when the effects of immigration first began to be strongly felt in this country, and that it diminished progressively with the swelling volume of the immigration current. Moreover, it was in just those sections where the immigrants congregated most thickly that the fall in the native birth rate was most pronounced, even down to such minor divisions as counties. New England, which, at the time of the Revolution, held the most homogeneous population in the country, and had the highest birth rate, has now the greatest proportion of foreigners and, as far as the natives at least are concerned, the lowest birth rate. To such an extent has this decline gone, that at the present time the native stock in large sections of New England is not even maintaining itself. Coincidences of time and place between the phenomena of immigration and those of the declining birth rate are so numerous and so striking that, in the words of General Walker, they "constitute a statistical demonstration such as is rarely attained in regard to the operation of any social or economic force."

This line of argument has been so thoroughly and convincingly expounded by a number of writers that it need not be dwelt upon further here. Its great weakness is that which has been anticipated — it lacks mathematical positiveness. An opponent might readily claim that the appalling decline in the native birth rate (the existence of which no one would care to deny) was due to some one or other of a variety of different causes, or to several operating together. The sections where the birth rate is the lowest are not only those where immigration has been the heaviest. They are also to a large extent those which are characterized most distinctively by manufacturing industry, or where the population is the densest. Why not assign the falling birth rate to one of these causes? [1]

[1] For a statement of the importance of the growth of cities, as opposed to immigration, in affecting the birth rate, see Goldenweiser, E. A., "Walker's Theory of Immigration," *Am. Jour. of Soc.*, 18: 342.

The best answer to this counterargument is to strengthen the original position by another and wholly different course of reasoning. This may be done very effectively by applying the fundamental and accepted laws of population to the question in hand, and seeing how they would work out in such a case. If the conclusion thus reached coincides with that resulting from the other method of proof, it will furnish a demonstration amounting almost to a certainty.

For this purpose we must go back to the set of doctrines first consistently expounded by Malthus, and known by his name. Though they are now more than a century old, they still stand as one of the profoundest contributions to human knowledge. These doctrines are so familiar to all students of social subjects that the merest summary will serve the present purpose. This may be given in the following words.

Under favorable circumstances, the reproductive power of the human species is very great.[1] Actual cases of doubling of population in from twenty to twenty-five years have been known, and this may be taken as a maximum standard. But man is dependent for his existence on the food supply, and, owing to the actual conditions of production, there is no ground for the hope that the amount of subsistence of the world or of any nation can ever be increased at a rate corresponding to the possible increase of mankind. Consequently, the growth of the species is always limited by the possibilities of the increase of the food supply, and as the strength of the reproductive instinct is very great, population will always be pressing hard on the limits of subsistence. The only means of providing for a greater population is

[1] See page 217.

by increasing the amount of productive land, or, by improvements in the arts, by making the land already under cultivation produce more food. Briefly stated, in any society, population tends to increase up to the supporting power of the soil. The forces which retard the growth of population, however, are something more than starvation in the strictest sense of the word. They are enumerated by Malthus in a list of what he calls checks. These naturally fall under two heads: First, the positive checks, which increase the death rate, viz. war, famine, pestilence, vice, etc.; these all produce misery and arise whenever population becomes too dense. Second, the preventive checks, which limit the birth rate, such as deferred marriage, celibacy, and voluntary restriction of births, vicious or otherwise; these are under the control of the human reason and will, and while they too entail a degree of suffering, it is not comparable to that caused by the other class of checks. All civilized societies have come more and more to employ the preventive checks, particularly that which is known as moral restraint.

The basic principles of Malthusianism remain as unassailable as when they were first propounded. But there have been certain modifications made necessary by the changing conditions of human society. As already suggested the preventive checks hold a much larger place than formerly, and great weight is now attached to what are known as the institutional checks, such as the demands of education, late marriages, social obligations, the "emancipation" of women, and a host of other customs and conventions which tend more or less imperceptibly to limit the number of births. Still more important, in the place of a bare subsistence as the limit upon which population is always pressing, has been substituted the standard of living. This includes all those necessaries, comforts, and even luxuries which are customary in the social group in which the individual or family finds itself placed. The limits of the family group are not now determined by the amount of bare necessaries which are essential for the preservation of life — probably they never were absolutely — but rather by the amount of advantages which are required to keep the family in the social stratum to which it belongs or to which the parents aspire, either for themselves or for their children. Particularly is this true in a democratic country like the United States, where social position depends not so much on rank or birth, as on wealth and education, both of which are attainable by effort and sacrifice. It is the desire for the "concentration of advantages" of this sort which leads to the restriction of the size of families.

With this set of laws in mind, let us seek to determine the effect which might reasonably be expected to follow the introduction of a large number of immigrants from European countries into the American body politic. In the first place, it will be conceded that the great bulk of our immigrants represent a much lower standard of living than is customary among native American workmen in the occupations into which they go.[1] Observation of conditions in the countries from which the immigrants come, and in the communities in which they settle after they arrive, establishes this fact beyond the necessity of proof. In fact, this difference, as has been shown, is the underlying reason for their coming.[2] Undoubtedly

[1] See review of Levasseur's "American Workman," *Pol. Sci. Quart.*, 13:321.
[2] See page 145.

many of the immigrants raise their standard of living somewhat after their arrival in this country, but not nearly up to the American level.

Since the immigrant has a lower standard than the native, he can afford to work for lower wages, and since the amount of alien labor is so abundant and so easily available, the standard of wages in the occupations into which the immigrants go is set by the amount for which they are willing to work. This amount is lowered still further by the fact that the immigrant is generally quite willing to add to the income of his family by putting his children to work as soon as the law allows — or earlier if possible — whereas the native ordinarily prefers to keep his children at home and in school as long as possible.[1] Thus large families become a source of revenue for one, and an item of expense for the other. It is obviously impossible for the native to support the same-sized family in the same degree of comfort on the new scale of wages as on the old. He is compelled to choose between two alternatives. Either he may lower his standard of living and keep the same-sized family, or limit the size of his family for the sake of the standard of living. But the lowering of the standard of living is something which every people — particularly the Americans — resist strenuously. If it is a question of the possibility of raising the standard, people often prefer larger families. This is instanced by the very significant fact that immigrants to this country do, as a rule, raise their birth rate very considerably. The foreign-born birth rate in Massachusetts in 1895 was 50.40, which

[1] See Report of Committee on Standard of Living, 8th N. Y. State Conference of Charities and Corrections, Albany, 1907, p. 20. Also Van Vorst, Mrs. John, *The Cry of the Children*, p. 213.

is from 12 to 20 higher than in most European countries.[1] But if it is a question of lowering the standard of living, the opposite course is taken. The standard of living is a matter of custom, and, when once established, has a tremendous tenacity. The American laborer chooses the other alternative. *He limits the size of his family.*

Multiplied by tens of thousands, this expedient results in seriously checking the growth of population. This decrease in the number of native children destined to enter certain occupations makes a greater demand for alien labor, which is promptly supplied. Thus the invasion of the American standard goes on progressively, and gradually these occupations come to be resigned more and more to foreign labor. Already certain classes of work are commonly known as "Dago labor," others as "Hunkie labor," etc., and a self-respecting American parent shudders at the thought of having his child enter them.

This very fact is sometimes used as an excuse for the whole procedure. It is claimed that the natives are not displaced, but are simply forced into higher occupations. Those who were formerly common laborers are now in positions of authority. While this argument holds true of individuals, its fallacy when applied to groups is obvious. There are not nearly enough places of authority to receive those who are forced out from below. The introduction of five hundred Slav laborers into a community may make a demand for a dozen or a score of Americans in higher positions, but hardly for five hundred. Furthermore, in so far as this process does actually take place,

[1] Bailey, W. B., *Modern Social Conditions*, p. 104, and Gonnard, René, *L'Émigration européenne au XIXe siècle*, p. 120.

it must result in a lowering of the native birth rate, for it is a well-known fact that in all modern societies the higher the social class, the smaller is the average family.

What has been said thus far refers to the limitation of families after marriage. The same influences work to produce the same result in another way. The increased difficulty in earning enough to support a family, due to immigration, leads countless American young men to postpone marriage for many years, and perhaps an equal number to give up marrying altogether. Both result in a great decrease in the birth rate for society as a whole.[1]

The processes sketched above are mainly volitional. There is a variety of other influences, which work unconsciously, but perhaps none the less powerfully, to accomplish the same result. General Walker asserted that the shock produced on the American mind by the miserable class of immigrants in the thirties and forties, in itself, had a profoundly detrimental effect on the natural rate of reproduction. Immigration has the effect of vastly increasing congestion of population, and congestion limits its growth. Furthermore, in an average group of immigrants, the males exceed the females by more than two to one.[2] The introduction of such an unnatural element into the population must limit its reproductive power.

It is thus apparent that the laws of population would

[1] For discussions of the sensitiveness of the marriage rate to economic conditions, see Schooling, J. Holt, "The English Marriage Rate," *Fortnightly Review*, 75:959; Willcox, W. F., "Marriage Rate in Michigan, 1870–1890," *Quart. Publ. Amer. Stat. Assn.*, 4:1; and Crum, F. S., "The Marriage Rate in Massachusetts," *Quart. Publ. Amer. Stat. Assn.*, 4:322.

[2] See page 191.

lead us to expect exactly the result which the statistical data indicate — a decided fall in the native birth rate, due to the enormous and ever increasing immigration into this country. The conclusion thus reached is corroborated and verified by a host of social workers, who testify from their own experience and observation. As an example, note the words of Rev. Walter A. Rauschenbusch, whose keen insight into social questions has placed him in the front rank of American thinkers: "The natives, who suffer by the competition of the immigrants and who feel the tightening grip of our industrial development, refuse to bring children into a world which threatens them with poverty."[1] Whether this decline in the native birth rate has been sufficient to offset the high birth rate of the foreign-born, and produce an actually smaller population than we would have had without any immigrants since 1820, is impossible of proof. It seems wholly probable that it has. The second generation of immigrants themselves feel the effect of the newcomers, and our foreign population shows a sharp decline in its birth rate after a generation of American life.[2] At least, if immigration has not positively lessened our population, we may be certain that it has failed to increase it to any considerable extent. Its net result, as far as size of population is concerned, has been to substitute a very large foreign element, from various sources, for a native element which would otherwise have come into being.

The size and diversity of this foreign element in the United States is constantly increasing. The representatives of different foreign nationalities are becoming ever

[1] *Christianity and the Social Crisis*, p. 273.

[2] Cf. Commons, J. R., *op. cit.*, pp. 203–204.

more numerous and more important in the life of the country. In them is embodied the "problem of the immigrant."

One of the most essential factors conditioning this problem is the distribution of these foreign residents. The importance of this aspect of the situation is becoming more and more felt, and will manifest itself in the succeeding pages. There are two main sources of official information on this point. The first of these, the immigration reports, has already been considered, and its data taken for what they are worth.[1] The other is the reports of the Bureau of the Census, which give the actual distribution of the foreign-born, at ten-year intervals. According to this authority, the per cent distribution of the foreign-born among the various territorial divisions in 1900 was as follows:

PER CENT DISTRIBUTION OF FOREIGN-BORN POPULATION IN THE UNITED STATES (EXCLUSIVE OF ALASKA AND HAWAII) AMONG THE DIVISIONS, 1900[2]

Total foreign-born, exclusive of Alaska and Hawaii, 10,356,644

Division	Per Cent
North Atlantic	46.0
South Atlantic	2.1
North Central	40.2
South Central	3.5
Western	8.2
Total	100.0

According to the division adopted in the census of 1910, 84.8 per cent of the foreign-born were in the North, 5.4 per cent in the South, and 9.7 per cent in the West.

[1] See page 207.

[2] Twelfth Census, Vol. I, p. civ.

The distribution shown by these figures accords closely with the statement of destinations made by the immigrants at the time of their arrival.[1] Whereas 88.4 per cent of the immigrants in 1910 gave their destination as either the North Atlantic or North Central divisions, in 1900 the census enumerators found 86.2 per cent of the foreign-born residents actually residing in those divisions, and in 1910, 84.8 per cent in the North.

There is a marked difference, however, in the distribution of the various races. This is shown by the following table, which gives the proportional distribution of some of the leading races of the foreign-born among the divisions:

PER 10,000 DISTRIBUTION OF FOREIGN-BORN POPULATION OF THE UNITED STATES, ACCORDING TO DIVISIONS AND COUNTRY OF BIRTH, 1900[2]

Birthplace	North Atlantic	South Atlantic	North Central	South Central	West
United Kingdom	6152	234	2558	220	806
Scandinavia	1653	37	7066	105	1087
Germany	3312	274	5475	410	508
Poland (Russian)	7070	261	2389	145	132
Hungary	7297	144	2260	126	167
Italy	7264	216	1136	540	830
Roumania	8491	144	1142	92	124
Austria	6187	134	2543	365	743
Russia	6580	387	2535	211	272

The most striking fact exhibited by this table is the exceptionally large proportion of the Germans and Scandinavians who have settled in the North Central division. It also illustrates further the minor part that

[1] See page 207. [2] Twelfth Census, Supp. Anal. and Deriv. Tables, Table 67.

the Southern and Western divisions have played in the immigration of all races. The same general showing is made by the figures for 1910. Thus 74.1 per cent of the foreign-born from Austria, 86.8 per cent of those from Hungary, 69.3 per cent of those from Italy, and 72.9 per cent of those from Russia were in the Middle Atlantic and East North Central divisions. But 35.2 per cent of the foreign-born from Denmark, 17.1 per cent of those from Germany, 49.2 per cent of those from Norway, and 32.1 per cent of those from Sweden were in the West North Central division alone.[1]

The significance of these figures can be fully comprehended only by taking into consideration the questions of area and density. The statement is often made that the density of population in the United States is so small that we still have ample room for an indefinite number of immigrants. It is pointed out that the average density of population in the United States is only 25.6 per square mile (1900), as against 400, 500, or even more in European countries. If the immigrants were evenly distributed over the entire territory of the United States, this argument would have some weight. But we see that they are not. This is one of the cases where an average is misleading. The immigrants are really being concentrated in the most thickly populated portions of the country. This becomes more evident if we examine the conditions in certain states. Thus in 1907, according to the Immigration Report, 6.5 per cent of the immigrants were destined to Massachusetts, which in 1900 had a density of 348.9; 30 per cent of the immigrants were destined to New York, with a density of 152.6; 17.9 per cent to Pennsylvania, with a

[1] Abstract, Thirteenth Census, p. 197.

density of 140.1; 8.1 per cent to Illinois, with a density of 86.1; 5.5 per cent to New Jersey, with a density of 250.3; while little Rhode Island, with a density of 407, was credited with .9 per cent. It thus appears that these six states, containing only 5.6 per cent of the total area of the United States, and with a density in each case far above the average, received 68.9 per cent of the total immigration for the year.

It is thus apparent that our foreign-born residents tend irresistibly to congregate in the most densely settled portions of the country, and in the most densely populated states. But this is not all. They also tend to congregate in the largest cities, and in the most congested sections of those cities. In 1890, 61.4 per cent of the foreign-born population of the United States were living in cities of at least 2500 population. In 1900 the percentage had increased to 66.3, while 38.8 per cent of the entire foreign-born population were huddled into the few great cities having a population of over 100,000. In the same year only 36.1 per cent of the native-born population were living in cities of over 2500. This tendency appears to be increasing in strength, and is more marked among the members of the new immigration than among the older immigrants.[1] Thus in 1910 the percentage of foreign-born living in cities of the specified size had risen to 72.2.

The reasons for this tendency of the foreign-born to congregate in the most densely settled districts may be briefly summarized as follows. (1) They land, almost

[1] For a full statement of opposite opinions on this subject, see Willcox, W. F., "The Distribution of Immigrants in the United States," *Quart. Jour. of Econ.*, August, 1906; and Fairchild, H. P., "Distribution of Immigrants," *Yale Review*, November, 1907.

without exception, in cities, and it is often the easiest thing for them to stay there. It takes some capital, knowledge, and enterprise to carry the immigrant any distance from the port of arrival, unless he has a definite connection in some other place. Yet it is claimed that, land them where you would, about the same number of immigrants would find their way to New York within a few weeks. (2) Economic opportunities are much more abundant and varied in the cities than in the country. (3) Such occupations as are obtainable in the city require much less capital than the characteristic country occupations. With a few dollars, an immigrant in the city can set himself up in some independent business, depending on turning over his capital rapidly to make a living. There are so many people in the city, that if one can manage to serve the most trivial want satisfactorily, he can get along. But any independent business in the country requires a larger outlay of capital than the average immigrant can hope for. The only country occupation open to him is common farm labor, and there are other reasons which make him ill adapted for this. (4) In the cities, the newly arrived immigrant can keep in close touch with others of his own race and tongue. In the compact colony of his fellow-countrymen, he may be sure of companionship, encouragement, and assistance when needed. It is the most natural thing in the world for an immigrant to want to settle where there are numbers of others of his immediate kind. (5) Knowledge of the English language is much less essential in the city than in the country. The presence of others who can speak the same tongue makes it possible for an immigrant to make a living without knowing a word of the language of his adopted country, as many of them do for year after year. In the rural districts, however, it is almost impossible for a newly arrived immigrant to get along at all without a knowledge of the English language, either in independent business, or as an employee, unless he settles in a farm colony of people of his own race, of which there are, of course, many to be found. (6) Not only is there more chance of friendly relief from fellow-countrymen, in case of necessity, in the cities, but public relief agencies and private benevolences are much more available there than in the country. (7) The excitement and novelty of American city life is very attractive to many immigrants — just as it is to the natives. Trolley cars, skyscrapers, and moving picture shows are wonderfully alluring features. In fact, in addition to the considerations which are peculiar to himself, the immigrant has all the general incentives to seek the city, which operate upon the general population, and which have produced so decided a change in the distribution of population within the last few decades.[1]

The matter of distribution has been treated thus at length because it is one of the most important aspects of the entire situation. Many, if not most, of the practical problems of immigration hinge directly upon the matter of distribution. Upon it depends the question whether the immigrant and the economic opportunity, which is his justification for being in the country, shall come together. The question of assimilation, which is largely a question of contact between the newcomer and the native-born population, is primarily a matter of distribution. Crime, pauperism, disease, the standard

[1] Cf. Balch, Emily G., *Our Slavic Fellow Citizens*, pp. 317–319; and Addams, Jane, *Newer Ideals of Peace*, pp. 65–68.

of living, morality, education — all, to a greater or less extent, are dependent upon distribution. No practical program for the treatment of immigrants, which is not calculated directly to improve distribution, can hope for any considerable measure of success.

CHAPTER XII

CONDITIONS (*continued*). THE STANDARD OF LIVING

WE turn now to a closer study of the life conditions of the immigrants after they have been admitted to this country, and have become a part of our body politic. These conditions affect all the life interests of the alien, and must, in the end, have a determining influence upon the desirability of immigration, both from the point of view of the immigrant and of the United States. They are manifestly so diverse and complicated as to make it difficult to frame any classification which will not overlap, and confuse rather than clarify. In general, however, we may divide these conditions into two categories, which are not absolutely exclusive and definite, but will serve the purposes of arrangement. These are as follows: (1) Those conditions which are primarily individual to the immigrant himself, and affect the general life of the nation only indirectly, because the immigrant is a resident of that nation. (2) Those conditions which have to do directly with the life of the immigrant as a member of society, and immediately affect the interests and welfare of others besides himself. To the first category belong such matters as housing conditions, food, and standard of living in general, wages, recreations, religious life, certain forms of vice, education, etc. To the second, pauperism, crime, sex vice, insanity, contagious diseases, industrial efficiency, trade-union affiliations, political activities and affiliations, money brought into and sent out of the country, and anything which increases or lightens the burdens of the average citizen of the country. In each of these two classes, there are conditions which may be considered as political, religious, economic, and social. Many life interests belong partly in one category, and partly in the other. This is especially true of that great class of facts having to do with marriages, births, and deaths, which affect first of all the immigrant, but through him the general population of the country.

Among those conditions which are primarily individual, many of the most important come under the head of the economic. And many of the most significant economic conditions may be considered under the head of the standard of living. It has been said, with a great deal of truth, that the immigration problem in this country is largely a matter of a competitive struggle between different standards of living.

Probably no other department of the standard of living of the immigrants has received such careful study in recent years as the matter of housing. As a result, we are now able to draw more accurate general conclusions in regard to this matter than is possible in respect to almost any other phase of the standard. Particularly is this true in regard to conditions in the compact colonies of our large cities, which, as we have seen, constitute the characteristic home of the new immigrant, and where the problem is the greatest. There is also a mass of reliable information in respect to another characteristic home of the immigrant, the residence portions of mining camps, and the smaller manufacturing cities.

Up to the present the slum, in spite of all the attacks upon it, has maintained itself as a permanent feature of most of our large cities. But the population of the slum is not a permanent but an ever changing one. The unsuccessful, unfortunate, and incapable individuals remain, but the more ambitious, progressive, and successful move on to other and better sections. Nevertheless, the slums are always full; and grow rather than diminish. There is a never failing supply of new recruits, in the body of recent immigrants, to take the places of those who move up. Thus the slum becomes the great sifting ground of the foreign-born, and tends to become more and more the abode of the poorest classes of our population. Not only is there a progression of individuals through the slum, but some of our cities have witnessed a most interesting and significant succession of races along the same course. The natives were displaced by the Irish; they in turn were crowded out by the Italians and Jews, and now the Greeks, Syrians, and allied races are driving out the Italians. Races may come and races may go, but the slum goes on — forever?

The character of the modern tenement has been sufficiently described by many writers to obviate the necessity of going into any detailed account of it in the present connection. Our main concern is the life of the immigrant within this tenement. The most recent and reliable information upon this point is that furnished by the Immigration Commission in their report on Immigrants in Cities.[1] The agents of the Commission made a detailed study of the most densely congested districts of New York, Chicago, Philadelphia, Boston, Cleveland, Buffalo, and Milwaukee. They found the population of these districts to consist mainly of members of the recently

[1] Quotations are from the abstract of that report.

immigrating races. In all seven of these cities Russian Hebrews and south Italians are among the principal races represented in the congested districts, while in the cities on the Great Lakes Poles, Bohemians, and other Slavic races are relatively more numerous than in the Atlantic coast cities. Very few families whose heads were native-born of native fathers were found in these districts. Nearly one half of the foreign-born heads of households had come within the last ten years, and over one fifth within five years. Not only were there very few native families, but only the remnants of colonies of Germans, Irish, and Swedes were found.

The first point to demand our attention in regard to the life of the foreign-born within the tenements is the amount of congestion. Among the households studied by the Immigration Commission, the average numbers of rooms per apartment was 3.72. The average number of rooms per apartment for the households whose head was native-born white of native father was 4.47, of the native-born of foreign father 4.34, of the foreign-born 3.64. The average number of persons per household for the native-born white of native father was 4.14, for the native-born of foreign father 4.39, for the foreign-born 5.16. An interesting indication of the habits of life of some of the newer immigrating races is given by the fact that while, among the Greeks, 32.7 per cent of the households consisted of two persons, and 18.4 per cent of three persons, 8.2 per cent consisted of ten or more persons. Among the Servians 18.2 per cent of the households consisted of ten or more persons, and among the Slovenians 11.2 per cent. This is the result, as will appear later, not of large families, but of the tendency on the part of the male representatives of these races to group themselves together into large coöperative "households" (pp. 21, 22, 23).

The average number of persons per room in the households studied was as follows: native-born white of native father, .93; native-born of foreign father, 1.01; foreign-born, 1.42 (p. 24). Only 51.9 per cent of the native-born white of native father had one or more persons per room, 54.7 per cent of the German households, 68.5 per cent of the Irish, south Italians 91.9 per cent, and Greeks 98 per cent. Of the Slovaks, Slovenians, and Syrians, 90 per cent or more of the households had one or more persons per room. Two per cent of the Greeks, 2.6 per cent of the south Italians, and 3 per cent of the Syrians had four or more persons per room. The number of occupants, per *sleeping* room, is of course somewhat higher. The total average number of persons per sleeping room in the households whose heads were native-born white of native father was 1.93; of the foreign-born, 2.39. Two per cent of the Greek households studied had six or more persons per sleeping room, as did 2 per cent of the south Italians and 5.2 per cent of the Slovenians. Fourteen per cent of all the foreign-born households slept in all the rooms in their apartments, and 41.1 per cent in all the rooms except one, while among the native-born whites of native fathers 2.3 per cent slept in all the rooms, and 20.2 per cent in all the rooms but one.

The foregoing figures may be taken as giving a reliable summary of the amount of congestion in the crowded districts of the seven great cities mentioned. It is painfully evident that conditions exist on a wide scale in these centers, which are a disgrace to any civilized country. A large proportion of the lower classes of our cities are living under conditions which render self-respect, cleanliness, and even decency almost impossible. Moreover, it is apparent that the native-born whites of native fathers, studied in this investigation, although representing the lowest portions of that class, rank decidedly above the foreign-born as far as can be judged by the degree of congestion. The native-born of foreign fathers stand between the other two classes. A more vivid and vital aspect may be given to the picture by taking some specific instances of life conditions among various groups of the foreign-born.

Among the Italians extreme congestion had manifested itself as long ago as the decade of the nineties. The average density of population in the Italian quarter of the North End of Boston was said to be nearly 1.40 persons per room.[1] In the Italian quarter of Philadelphia investigators found 30 Italian families, numbering 123 persons, living in 34 rooms. In some of the Italian tenements in this city, lamps were kept burning all day in some of the rooms, where day could scarcely be distinguished from night.[2] The Jews at this time were only a little less densely crowded than the Italians. In 1891 nearly one fourth of the whole number of Jews living in two of the precincts of the North End of Boston were living with an average of more than two persons to a room and were found to be very uncleanly in the care of their homes. Among the Irish an average of 1.24 persons per room was found in Boston in 1891. On the whole they kept their tenements cleaner than did the Jews or Italians.[3]

Since the beginning of the twentieth century, interest in the slum population of our cities has centered itself

[1] Lord, Trenor, and Barrows, *Italians in America*, p. 70; Bushee, F. A., *Ethnic Factors in the Population of Boston*, p. 29.

[2] Lord, Trenor, and Barrows, *op. cit.*, p. 72. [3] Bushee, *op. cit.*, p. 30.

about the Slavic and other races of southeastern Europe, even more than about the Italians and Jews. About one sixth of the entire population of Buffalo, or 80,000 individuals, is Polish. Of these, about 4000 families, representing 20,000 persons, own their homes. They are said to be thrifty, clean, willing, and neglected. Nearly all the Poles live in small one and two story wooden cottages. Good tenement work thirty years ago avoided the serious structural conditions which prevail in most cities. The principal evil now in the Polish section is room-overcrowding. The two-story cottages hold six or more families, while the older one-story cottage was built for four families, though the owner is likely to occupy two of the rear apartments. There are 15,000 of these cottages, all subject to the tenement law. A Pole was recently made health commissioner, and gave promise of being the best incumbent of that office that Buffalo has ever had. That there is plenty of work for him to do may be judged from the description of some of the conditions which prevail.

"Counting little bedrooms, living rooms, and kitchens (and they are pretty nearly indistinguishable), Mr. Daniels tells us that half the Polish families in Buffalo, or 40,000 people, average two occupants to a room. There are beds under beds (trundle beds, by the way, were once quite respectable), and mattresses piled high on one bed during the day will cover all the floors at night. Lodgers in addition to the family are in some sections almost the rule rather than the exception. Under such conditions privacy of living, privacy of sleeping, privacy of dressing, privacy of toilet, privacy for study, are all impossible, especially in the winter season; and those who have nerves, which are not confined to the rich in spite of an impression to the contrary, are led near to insanity. Brothers and sisters sleep together far beyond the age of safety. It begins so, and parents do not realize how fast children grow, or how dangerous it all is."[1]

Even in Buffalo, the congestion problem is not limited to the Poles. The author just quoted describes the Italians as tending to establish residences in old hotels, warehouses, and abandoned homesteads, and says, "As late as 1906 we found Italians living in large rooms, subdivided by head-high partitions of rope and calico, with a separate family in each division."

In Milwaukee there are three foci of the tenement evil, the Italian quarter, the Polish quarter, and the Jewish quarter. While there are not the large tenement houses that prevail in larger cities, there are the same evil conditions in the small cottages of the laboring class. The following paragraphs give a vivid picture of some of the conditions in each of these three sections.

In the Italian district, "Entering one of these dwellings we had to duck our heads to escape a shower bath from leaking pipes above the door. Incidentally, we had to dodge a crowd of the canine family which did not seem to be particularly pleased with our visit. The rooms were dark. Something, which I supposed was food or intended for food, was bubbling on a little stove. A friendly goat was playing with the baby on the floor, and the pigeons cooed cheerily near by. Through the door of the kitchen we got the odor of the stable. The horses had the best room. In the middle room, which was absolutely dark, on a bed of indescribable filth, lay

[1] Almy, Frederic, "The Huddled Poles of Buffalo," *The Survey*, Feb. 4, 1911.

an aged woman, groaning with pain from what I judged to be ulcerated teeth, but which for aught she knew might have been a more malignant disease. In this single dwelling, which is not unlike many we saw, there lived together in ignorant misery one man, two women, ten children, six dogs, two goats, five pigeons, two horses, and other animal life which escaped our hurried observation."

"In the Ghetto, in one building, live seventy-one people, representing seventeen families. The toilets in the yard freeze in winter and are clogged in summer. The overcrowding here is fearful and the filth defies description. Within the same block are crowded a number of tenements three and four stories high with basement dwellings. One of these is used as a Jewish synagogue. Above and beneath and to the rear this building is crowded with tenement dwellers. The stairways are rickety, the rooms filthy, and all are overcrowded. The toilets for the whole population are in the cellar adjoining some of the dwelling rooms, reached by a short stairway. At the time of our visit the floors of this toilet, both inside and outside, were covered with human excrement and refuse to a depth of eight to twelve inches. Into this den of horrors all the population, male and female, had to go."

A typical dwelling of the Polish working people is thus described. "There is an entrance, perhaps under the steps, which leads to the apartments below. In this semibasement in the front lives a family. There are perhaps two rooms, sometimes only one. In the rear of this same basement lives another family. Above, on the first floor, lives another family, likewise in two or three small rooms; and in the rear is another. Thus four or more families live in one small cottage — and, often, in true tenement style, they 'take in' boarders. . . . Here, together, live men, women, children, dogs, pigeons, and goats in regular tenement and slum conditions."[1]

Such instances as these, which might be multiplied almost indefinitely, are individual manifestations of conditions which are represented *en masse* by the figures of the Immigration Commission. It is apparent that slum conditions exist, fully developed, in other places than the great cities, and in other types of building than the regulation tenement. As will be seen later, they may be found in communities which do not come under the head of cities at all. The slum is a condition, not a place, and will crop up in the most unexpected places, whenever vigilance is relaxed. The slum can never be eradicated by erecting model dwellings, however well planned, nor by any other superficial method alone. The foundation of the slum rests in the social and economic relations of society, and can be effectually attacked only through them.

In the foregoing quotations, frequent reference is made to the filthy condition in which the dwellings of the foreign-born are kept. It is the current idea among a large class of people that extreme uncleanliness characterizes the great majority of immigrant homes. Unfortunately there is all too large a basis of truth for this impression. Yet there is undoubtedly much exaggeration on this point in the popular mind. The Immigration Commission found that out of every 100 homes investigated in its study of city conditions, 45 were

[1] Thompson, Carl D., "Socialists and Slums," Milwaukee, *The Survey*, Dec. 3, 1910. Cf. Byington, Margaret F., *Homestead*, pp. 131–136.

kept in good condition, and 84 in either good or fair condition, though the foreign-born were inferior in this respect to the native-born. In many cases the filthy appearance of the streets in the tenement districts is due to negligence on the part of city authorities, rather than to indifference on the part of the householders. "In frequent cases the streets are dirty, while the homes are clean." [1] Not only is it an error to suppose that all immigrants are filthy, but it is also untrue that all immigrants who are filthy are so from choice. While the standards of decency and cleanliness of many of our immigrant races are undoubtedly much below those of the natives, there are many alien families who would gladly live in a different manner, did not the very conditions of their existence seem to thrust this one upon them, or the hardship and sordidness of their daily life quench whatever native ambition for better things they might originally have had.

In the foregoing paragraphs mention has been made of the boarder as a characteristic feature of life in the tenements. He is, in fact, a characteristic feature of the family life of the newer immigrant wherever found. Since so large a proportion of the modern immigrants are single men, or men unaccompanied by their wives (see p. 191), there is an enormous demand for accommodations for male immigrants who have no homes of their own. This demand is met in two main ways. The most natural, and perhaps the least objectionable, of the two, where there are a certain number of immigrant families of the specified race already in this country, is for a family which has a small apartment to take in one or more

[1] Cf. description of conditions in a manufacturing town, Fitch, John A., Lackawanna, *The Survey*, Oct. 7, 1911, p. 936.

boarders or lodgers of their own nationality. In this way they are able to add to their meager income, and thereby to increase the amount of their monthly savings, or perhaps to help pay off the mortgage on the house if they happen to be the owners. The motive is not always a financial one, however, but occasionally the desire to furnish a home for some newcomer from the native land, with whom they are acquainted, or in whom they are interested for some other reason.[1] The second way of solving the problem is for a number of men to band themselves together, hire an apartment of some sort, and carry on coöperative housekeeping in one way or another. A description of these households will be given later (p. 247).

The keeping of boarders or lodgers[2] is a very widespread practice among our recently immigrating families.

Among the households studied by the Immigration Commission in its investigation of cities, 13 per cent of the native-born white households kept boarders, and 27.2 per cent of the foreign-born. The following foreign-born nationalities had high percentages, as shown by the figures: Russian Hebrews, 32.1 per cent; north Italians, 42.9 per cent; Slovaks, 41 per cent; Magyars, 47.3 per cent; Lithuanians, 70.3 per cent. A similar showing is made by the figures given in the report of the Immigration Commission on Immigrants in Manufacturing and Mining (abstract quoted). The percentage of households keeping boarders, as shown in that report, is as follows:

[1] Balch, Emily G., *Our Slavic Fellow Citizens*, p. 349.

[2] For convenience' sake, the term "boarder" will hereafter be used in the place of the clumsy phrase "boarders and lodgers."

PERCENTAGE OF HOUSEHOLDS KEEPING BOARDERS[1]

Nativity	Per Cent
Native-born white of native father	10.0
Native-born of foreign father	10.9
Foreign-born	32.9
Race (foreign-born) —	
Norwegian	3.8
Bohemian and Moravian	8.8
Croatian	59.5
South Italian	33.5
Magyar	53.6
Polish	48.4
Roumanian	77.9
Servian	92.8

The average number of boarders per household, based on the number of households keeping boarders, was as follows:

AVERAGE NUMBER OF BOARDERS PER HOUSEHOLD BASED ON THE NUMBER OF HOUSEHOLDS KEEPING BOARDERS[2]

Nativity	Number
Native-born white of native father	1.68
Native-born of foreign father	1.52
Foreign-born	3.53
Race (foreign-born) —	
Bulgarian	8.29
Croatian	6.39
Roumanian	12.23
Servian	7.25

This prevalent custom of taking boarders brings numerous evils in its train. Foremost among these is the absolute sacrifice of family life in the households. It is

[1] Rept. Imm. Com., Imms. in Mfg. and Min., Abs., p. 147. [2] *Ibid.*, p. 149.

difficult at best to maintain a decent degree of privacy when the family is left to itself; the intrusion of outsiders makes it wholly impossible. Secondly, the taking of boarders tends to increase a congestion which is likely already to be extreme. Thirdly, it lays additional burdens upon the already overworked housewife. Its great advantage is, of course, the increase of the family income, sometimes to an amount almost double that which could be obtained without the boarders. Among the Slavs, for example, women are rare, and are regarded as very valuable, first as wives, and second as a means whereby a man may take boarders.[1] The arrangements between the boarders and the housewife differ in different localities, and under different conditions. In a Colorado mining camp $10 a month is the customary price for a regular boarder. A very common arrangement is for the men to buy each his own food, and pay the woman to cook it. The sums paid range from $2 to $4 a month for lodging, washing, and cooking.

The life of such a housewife in a coal mining community has been described in the following words: "The status of the immigrant housewife from the south and east of Europe is deplorable. The boarding system followed is one whereby a fixed sum is paid for lodging, cooking, washing, and mending; an individual food account being kept with each lodger. The housewife has the beds to make each day for a dozen men, their clothing to wash and mend, their meals to prepare. In many cases she has also to buy the food, which necessitates many visits to the store and separate purchases for each boarder. She has also to carry all the water used from the hydrant or well, which may be ten or one hundred yards distant.

[1] Balch, *op. cit.*, p. 349.

When the men return from work it is a part of her duties to help them in their ablutions by scrubbing their backs. There are also numerous children to care for and scores of other tasks demanding her attention. Under these conditions the marked untidiness of the immigrant households is not to be wondered at."[1]

The second typical method of providing for the single male immigrant, mentioned above, is coöperative housekeeping on the part of a group of men, either with or without a female housekeeper. This practice is very common among many of the newer races of immigrants, as has been suggested. It is a makeshift to which the foreigner is driven by the absence of a normal number of women of his own race. In households of this sort are developed some of the very worst conditions to be found among our foreign residents.

Under this system, a number of men of a certain foreign race club together and hire an apartment, consisting of a few rooms in a regular tenement house, or, very frequently, a large storeroom or warehouse, which thereupon becomes their home. In order to minimize expense, the greatest possible number of beds are provided in each room. If the apartment consists of a storeroom, it is often fitted up with tiers of bunks along the sides. Such a room may be used by two sets of men, one during the day and one during the night. If some of the men are peddlers, the peanut stands or barrows will be kept at night in the unoccupied spaces in the room. The lack of woman's care in the upkeep of such apartments is very manifest.

[1] Lauck, W. Jett, "The Bituminous Coal Miner and Coke Worker of Western Pennsylvania," *The Survey*, April 1, 1911. Cf. also Roberts, Peter, *Anthracite Coal Communities*, p. 137.

The meals are either prepared in the apartment or secured at some near-by restaurant, or the two methods are combined. In the absence of all semblance of family life, every possible expedient to reduce expense is adopted, with the unfortunate results that might be expected. The following description of such a household will give a concrete idea of the type:

"To-day, in a certain mining town, there are fourteen Slavs, all unmarried, and with only themselves to support, who rent one large, formerly abandoned, storeroom. This is taken care of by a housekeeper, who also prepares the meals for the men. Each man has his own tin plate, tin knife, fork, and cup; he has his own ham and bread, and a place in which to keep them. Some things they buy in common, the distribution being made by the housekeeper. For beds the men sleep on bunks arranged along the walls and resembling shelves in a grocery store. Each has his own blanket; each carries it out-of-doors to air when he gets up in the morning, and back again when he returns from his work at night. The monthly cost of living to each of these men is not over four dollars. They spend but little on clothes the year round, contenting themselves with the cheapest kind of material, and not infrequently wearing cast-off garments purchased of some second-hand dealer. For fuel they burn coal from the culm-banks or wood from along the highway, which costs them nothing but their labor in gathering it."[1]

That housing conditions such as have been portrayed above should prevail so generally all over the country is a serious indictment against the social and industrial organization of the United States. It has been intimated

[1] Warne, F. J., *The Slav Invasion*, p. 68. Cf. Hunt, Milton B., "The Housing of Non-Family Groups of Men in Chicago," *Am. Jour. of Soc.*, 16: 145.

that these conditions are not in all cases due to the choice of the immigrant, or to the lack of desire for better things on his part. Whether they are not, to a large degree, actually due to the presence of the immigrant in this country is quite another matter, upon the decision of which must rest much of the final judgment as to the desirability of immigration under the present system.

Throughout the study of housing conditions among the foreign-born, it becomes more and more evident that there is a marked distinction not only between the homes of the native-born and the foreign-born, but between those of the older and newer immigrants. By whatever test the standards of each class are measured, there is almost invariably a decided discrepancy in favor of the older races. As regards the number of rooms per apartment, the size of households, the number of persons per room, the number of boarders, the care and upkeep of the apartment, the English, Scandinavians, Germans, and Irish come much nearer to what might be considered a reasonable American standard than do the Italians, either north or south, the Slavs (except perhaps the Bohemians and Moravians), the Greeks, Syrians, Bulgarians, etc. This distinction is well brought out in mining localities, where the newer races have displaced the older within recent years. A graphic comparison is given by Mr. F. J. Warne in his book, *The Slav Invasion and the Mine Workers.*[1] He says that, by the time of the coming of the Slavs, the Irish, English, Welsh, Scotch, and German mine workers had grown accustomed to a "social life of some dignity and comfort." The English-speaking mine worker wanted a home and family. That home was usually a neat, two-story frame house, with porch and yard. Within were pictures on the walls, and carpets on the floors of the best rooms. He wished to have no one as a permanent resident of the house save his own family, or very near relatives. He desired his wife to be well dressed and comfortable, and his children to have the benefits of school. His wants were always just beyond his wages, and always increasing.

The Slav had no wife and children, and wished none. "He was satisfied to live in almost any kind of a place, to wear almost anything that would clothe his nakedness, and to eat any kind of food that would keep body and soul together." He was content to live in a one-room hut, built of driftwood and roofed with tin from old powder cans. In the mining towns he drifted to the poorer and cheaper sections to live. He did not care with whom or with how many he lived, provided they were of his own nationality. When two such standards are brought into competition, it is inevitable that the higher should yield in some way or other.

This difference in standards is undoubtedly due in part to a difference in natural instincts and aptitudes for decency and cleanliness between the common classes of northern and southern Europe, but probably more to the customary standards to which they have become habituated in their native land. The effect is the same, whatever the cause. The new immigrant desires a certain improvement in his standard as a reward for emigration, but the new standard need not be by any means the equivalent of that of the immigrant races which have preceded him. As long as we continue to draw our immigrants from more and more backward and undeveloped nations and races we may expect to see a progressive degradation in the customary standard of the working people.

There are many other considerations besides congestion which determine the character of life in the slums. Many of these have already been suggested in preceding paragraphs. Prominent among them are ventilation, sanitary and cooking facilities, light, water supply, healthfulness of surroundings, and play room for children. The degree in which evils exist in these particulars, in any locality, depends primarily upon the stringency of the local tenement and public health laws, and the energy and faithfulness of their enforcement. Much is being accomplished and has been accomplished in recent years in the direction of securing better conditions. Yet there is almost infinite room for improvement. The futility of relying upon the individual benevolence and humanity of builders, owners, and agents was demonstrated long ago. Here, of all places, eternal vigilance on the part of the better classes of society is the price of safety. Descriptions of the homes of the foreign-born are full of accounts of dark and absolutely unventilated bedrooms, houses unprovided with any water supply, filthy outdoor closets and privy vaults, toilets used by ten or twelve families conjointly, buildings covering the entire lot, dooryards flooded with stagnant water and refuse, basements half filled with water, domestic animals sharing the limited accommodations with the family, and a host of other horrors. Detailed descriptions of these dwellings are unnecessary. Any one interested may find them in abundance in the accounts of housing conditions in the poorer sections of our cities and towns, for, as the Immigration Commission has amply demonstrated, the slum, wherever found, is distinctively the home of the foreign-born.[1]

[1] See, for instance, Riis, Jacob, *How the Other Half Lives*; Breckenridge, Sophonisba, and Abbott, Edith, "Housing Conditions in Chicago," *Am. Jour. of Soc.*, 16: 4 and 17: 1, 2; "The Housing Awakening," series in *The Survey*, beginning Nov. 19, 1910.

It is almost superfluous to add that there are thousands of immigrants, even of the newer races, who live in conditions wholly different from those we have been discussing. Individuals of every race, in large numbers, have succeeded in raising themselves from the lowly estate of their compatriots, and establishing homes of culture and refinement, even of luxury. Examples of this class are prominent, and are frequently referred to. Yet in spite of this, the slum remains the characteristic home of the average immigrant to this country, and as such it must be reckoned with.

The influence of the slum must of necessity be hampering and degrading to its denizens. No poorer training school for American citizens could be devised. Not only is the life prejudicial to health and morals, and destructive of ambition, but it precludes practically all incidental or unconscious contact with the uplifting influences of American life. Almost the only actively assimilating agency with which the slum dweller comes into immediate relationship is the public school, and this lacks much of its value as an assimilating force in districts which are so largely foreign that the pupils meet few, if any, children of native-born parents. Any practical program for solving the immigration problem must attack the slum boldly. In the words of Mr. Frederic Almy, "You cannot make a silk purse out of a sow's ear, and you cannot make an American citizen out of a tenement slum. The slum must go. If you spare the slum, you will spoil the child." [1]

In regard to the housing conditions of the foreign-born outside of the larger centers of population it is more difficult to make generalizations. Fortunately, it is

[1] *The Survey*, Feb. 4, 1911, p. 771.

also less necessary. Some of the foremost housing evils are essentially city matters. Particularly is it true of immigrants who have established themselves in independent agriculture, that they have made a long step toward Americanization. While every grade of dwelling may be found among foreign-born agriculturists, from the wretched hovel of the Italian market gardener to the home of the Swedish farmer of the Northwest which ranks with the finest in the land, yet the alien who takes up his abode in the country has, in many respects, removed himself from the general problem of the immigrant, and his living conditions can, with a reasonable degree of safety, be left to look after themselves. Yet it has been abundantly proved that slum conditions can exist even in the country, and in small towns. This is especially true in mining camps, and in the smaller manufacturing communities. Some of the worst conditions of the most crowded sections of the cities are reproduced in the shacks of the miners or the dwellings of the factory hands. Overcrowding, bad ventilation, unsanitary toilet facilities, inadequate heating, and filth are not city monopolies. The taking of boarders is especially common in these communities, and, in the mining towns, brings a peculiar evil with it, in addition to all the regular disadvantages. This lies in the necessity which every mine worker is under of bathing every day after work. In the absence of bathrooms, ablutions are customarily performed in a tub set in the kitchen, and in the crowded quarters of the miner's cabin, the children of the household are accustomed to the sight of nudity from their infancy up, to the serious injury of their moral sense.[1]

[1] Roberts, *op. cit.*, p. 143.

It is too often true that the worst conditions prevail in the company houses. The extreme monotony of these identical rows of ugly dwellings is in itself sufficiently depressing. But in addition, it appears that many employers are wholly oblivious to the higher needs of their employees, and provide the most meager shelter which will suffice to keep body and soul together, charging therefor exorbitant rates. To say that these men and women are treated like beasts, is putting the case too mildly, for no well-to-do person would house a valuable animal as some of these human workers are housed. The shifting character of the population and the uncertain duration of a mining camp offer a quasi justification for some of these evils. Yet a self-respecting nation should not permit any type of industry to persist which requires its army of workers to live as do hundreds of thousands of these faithful toilers.[1]

In regard to the food of our immigrant population, such studies of individual races as have been made seem to indicate that, while the dietary of the average foreign family falls far short of what a native American would consider a satisfactory standard and is very deficient in variety, yet it is ordinarily sufficient in quantity and in amount of nourishment. Of course there are countless immigrant families of the poorer sort, just as there are of natives, who are habitually undernourished; yet the ordinary immigrant working family or individual appears not to suffer for lack of sustaining food. This con-

[1] For full descriptions of life in mining and manufacturing villages, see Roberts, *op. cit.*, Chs. IV and V; Lauck, W. Jett, *The Survey*, Apr. 1, 1911; Fitch, John A., *The Survey*, Oct. 7, 1911; Balch, *op. cit.*, pp. 372–375; Warne, *op. cit.*, Ch. VI. For an account of the life of some of our foreign agriculturists, see Cance, Alexander E., "Piedmontese on the Mississippi," *The Survey*, Sept. 2, 1911; Lord, Trenor, and Barrows, *op. cit.*, Ch. VI; Balch, *op. cit.*, Ch. XV.

dition is made possible by a long habitude in European countries to an exceedingly simple diet, and by a resulting knowledge of cheap and nourishing foods. The food item in the budget of an immigrant family from southern or eastern Europe is almost incredible to an American. The average cost of food for an individual immigrant mine worker in Pennsylvania runs from about $4 to $10 per month. Among the Italians in Boston, during the winter months, about a dollar a week will suffice for the food of a man. The south Italian berry pickers in New Jersey are said to be able to get along on as little as 25 cents per week, and other races live almost as cheaply.[1]

There appears to be a considerable difference in this respect between the different races, even among the newer immigrants. The lowest standard prevails among the south Italians, Greeks, Syrians, Bravas, etc. The Slavs are inclined to spend more of their increasing income on food; particularly is meat a more important part of their diet. The Jews are said to rank well above the Italians in this regard.

The quality and preparation of food leaves much to be desired. Italian children are sent to the markets of Boston to gather vegetables which have been thrown away as unfit for use. A brief walk through the East Side of New York, with an eye on the push carts, will convince one of the undesirable quality of some, at least, of the food eaten by the residents of that section. On the other hand, the Greek laborers on the railroads of the West are said to live remarkably well, and themselves

[1] Cf. Balch, *op. cit.*, pp. 363–364; Lauck, *The Survey*, Apr. 1, 1911, p. 48; Roberts, *op. cit.*, pp. 103 ff.; Bushee, *op. cit.*, p. 29; Rept. Imm. Com., Recent Imms. in Agr., Abs., p. 59; *Americans in Process*, p. 141.

complain of the staleness of American food, and object to our practice of putting everything up in "boxes."[1] In general, the conclusion of investigators in regard to the food of our working classes seems to be that the faults of their dietary lie, not so much in the failure to spend an adequate amount of money for food, as in wasteful and ill-judged purchases, unsatisfactory preparation, and improper balance between the essential food elements (especially lack of sufficient proteids) and too much fat. It is not unlikely that in this particular the immigrants fare better than the natives in the same class. It is certainly probable that, taken on the whole, the standard of food of the immigrant families in this country is superior to that to which they were accustomed in their native land.

There is probably no other aspect of life in which the immigrant shows at least a superficial Americanization more quickly than in the matter of clothing. It is a matter where imitation is easy, and in fact almost inevitable. Any purchases of clothing made after the immigrant's arrival in this country must, almost of necessity, be American in type. And the younger generation, at least, are eager to have their exterior appearance correspond to that of the older residents of their adopted country,— so eager, often, as to lead them to adopt the most extreme of the new fashions in cut and fitting, however cheap and flimsy the materials may be. In fact, this Americanization affects the immigrants even before they leave their native home. Officials on Ellis Island say that it is rare nowadays to see groups of immigrants arriving clad in their picturesque European costumes; the prevailing garb now is of the American

[1] Cf. Streightoff, F. H., *Standard of Living*, Ch. VI.

type. It is a strange fact that some writers, apparently oblivious of the ease of this transition, seem to regard American clothes as an evidence of real assimilation.

As regards physical adequacy of clothing, the immigrant is probably as well off on the average as his native fellow-worker. It is not likely that any large proportion of our working classes actually suffer physical harm from insufficient clothing, unless it be through lack of proper protection against dampness, particularly in the matter of shoes.[1] In respect to cleanliness, and even decency, there is frequently room for improvement among the immigrants, just as there is among the native-born. There is, on the other hand, a recognized danger that the desire for a fashionable appearance, particularly on the part of the women, may lead to an extreme expenditure for dress, unwarranted by the family income.[2]

[1] *Ibid.*, p. 106. [2] *Americans in Process*, pp. 142–143.

CHAPTER XIII

THE STANDARD OF LIVING (*continued*)

THE standard of living of any family or individual[1] is the resultant of two principal factors. These are the desires and appetites of the individual or family and the amount of income available for the gratification of those desires and appetites. The casual observer, in forming his estimate of the immigrant, is in danger of forgetting the second of these factors, and of assuming that because the immigrant is found living in a certain status, he is therefore satisfied with that status and has no ambition to change it. It has already been hinted, in the foregoing paragraphs, that this is not the case. A full understanding of the limitations under which the immigrant is placed can come only with a study of the customary wages or income of the class to which he belongs.

The matter of wages is one of the easiest aspects of the life of the immigrant about which to secure reliable data. It lends itself readily to exact measurement, averaging, and tabulation. It is a subject upon which the immigrant himself can give accurate information if he is so inclined. As a result, there is a considerable mass of data in regard to the earnings of the foreign-born, and it is possible to make trustworthy generalizations thereupon. The latest and most inclusive figures on this point are those furnished by the Immigration Commis-

[1] Conditioned, of course, by the general standard of the society.

AVERAGE ANNUAL EARNINGS OF EMPLOYEES IN THE INDUSTRIES SPECIFIED[1]

Industry	Per Cent of Employees Foreign-born	Average Annual Earnings		
		Males, 18 or Over	Male Heads of Families	Average Family Income
Iron and steel manufacturing	57.7	$346	$409	$568
Slaughtering and meat packing	60.7	557	578	781
Bituminous coal mining	61.9	443	451	577
Glass manufacturing	39.3	574	596	755
Woolen and worsted manufacturing	61.9	346	400	661
Silk goods manufacturing and dyeing	34.3	431	448	635
Cotton goods manufacturing	68.7	[2]	470	491
Clothing manufacturing	72.2	513	530	713
Boot and shoe manufacturing	27.3	502	573	765
Furniture manufacturing	59.1	575	598	769
Collar, cuff, and shirt manufacturing	13.4	637	662	861
Leather tanning, currying, and finishing	67.0	431	511	671
Glove manufacturing	33.5	625	650	904
Oil refining	66.7	591	662	828
Sugar refining	85.3	522	549	661
Cigars and tobacco manufacturing	32.6	1.92[3]		

[1] Compiled from Rept. Imm. Com., Imms. in Mfg. and Min., Abs.
[2] Not given.
[3] Daily wage only given.

sion in its various reports. Foremost among these stands the report of Immigrants in Manufacturing and Mining, which presents the results of a thoroughgoing investigation of twenty of the leading industries of the country, and a less detailed study of sixteen others, covering in all 17,141 households and 503,732 individuals. The great majority of these are foreign-born, but there is a sufficient number of native-born, both of native and foreign parentage, to serve the purposes of comparison. The table on the previous page gives the average annual earnings of employees and the average family income in the different industries.

A noteworthy feature of the above table is the general excess of average family earnings over the average earnings of heads of families, showing the extent to which other members of the family besides the head contribute to the family support.

The average weekly earnings of male employees, 18 years of age or over, distributed according to nativity, are as follows. (The table includes over 200,000 individuals.)

AVERAGE WEEKLY EARNINGS OF MALE EMPLOYEES, 18 YEARS OF AGE OR OVER, BY NATIVITY[1]

Nativity	Average Weekly Earnings
Native-born white of native father	$14.37
Native-born of foreign father	13.89
Foreign-born	11.92

There is a marked difference between races in this respect. The lowest figures among the foreign-born were: Albanian, $8.07; Greek, $8.41; Portuguese, $8.10; Syrian, $8.12; Turkish, $7.65. Some of the foreign-born rank well above the natives, as, for instance: Norwegian, $15.28; Scotch, $15.24; Scotch-Irish, $15.13; Swedish, $15.36; Welsh, $22.02.

[1] Rept. Imm. Com., Imms. in Mfg. and Min., Abs., p. 91.

The average yearly earnings (approximate) of male employees 18 years of age or over were as follows:

AVERAGE YEARLY EARNINGS (APPROXIMATE) OF MALE EMPLOYEES, 18 YEARS OF AGE OR OVER, BY NATIVITY[1]

Nativity	Average Yearly Earnings
Native-born white of native father	$666
Native-born of foreign father	566
Foreign-born	455

In this table, the decrease of earnings of approximately $100 from class to class is striking.

The average family income was as follows:

AVERAGE ANNUAL FAMILY INCOME, BY NATIVITY OF HEAD OF FAMILY[2]

Nativity	Average Family Income
Native-born white of native father	$865
Native-born of foreign father	866
Foreign-born	704

Comparing the last two tables, and noting that while the average yearly earnings of native-born male employees of foreign parentage are $100 less than those of the native-born of native parentage, yet the family income of the native-born of foreign parentage is $1 more than that of the native-born of native parentage, the obvious conclusion might be that the native-born of foreign parentage are more inclined to rely upon some one besides the head of the family for part of the income than are the native-born of native parentage. Closer examination, however, proves that this is not the case. The following table gives the percentages of families of different nativities which receive the entire income from the husband.

[1] *Ibid.*, p. 131.

[2] *Ibid.*, p. 136.

PER CENT OF FAMILIES HAVING ENTIRE INCOME FROM THE HUSBAND, BY NATIVITY[1]

Nativity	Per Cent
Native-born white of native father	58.4
Native-born of foreign father	61.3
Foreign-born	38.0

Thus there is a smaller proportion of families among the native-born of foreign fathers who rely upon other members of the family than the husband for part of the family income than of the native-born of native father. It appears that the explanation of the peculiarity which has been noticed must be either that only the more prosperous of the native-born of foreign parentage are heads of families, or that those families of this class which do receive income from other sources than the husband receive a much greater total amount than among the native-born of native father, so as to raise the average. The former explanation seems the more probable, for while 67.3 per cent of the male native-born white employees of native fathers, 20 years of age or over, were married, only 56.5 per cent of the native-born of foreign fathers of the same age were married. Native-born employees of foreign parentage who are old enough to be the heads of families are predominantly representatives of the old immigration, and hence stand high on the wage scale. The very small percentage of families among the foreign-born which derive their entire income from the husband indicates the extent to which the children of this class contribute to the family support, and also the extent to which boarders are taken.

Figures from other sources corroborate, in general, the showing made in the foregoing tables, with some

[1] Rept. Imm. Com., Imms. in Mfg. and Min., Abs., p. 139.

differences in detail. The Immigration Commission in one of its other reports, namely that on Immigrants in Cities, gives the average approximate yearly earnings of over 10,000 male wage workers 18 years of age or over as follows: native-born white of native father, $595; native-born of foreign father, $526; foreign-born, $385.[1] These figures are less, throughout, than those presented in the foregoing tables, and seem to indicate that the average of wages in cities is less than in the general run of organized industries throughout the country. It is probable that a census of city workers would include many in insignificant industries, and in occupations which could hardly be classed as industries, where the wage scale is low.

The earnings of agricultural laborers on the farms of western New York range from $1.25 to $1.75 per day of ten hours. South Italian families of four or five members, engaged in this kind of work, average from $350 to $450 for the season, extending from April to November. Poles, working as general farm laborers the year round, earn from $18 to $20 per month.[2] Among the anthracite coal miners of Pennsylvania, the average yearly wage of the contract miners, who make up about twenty-five per cent of persons employed about the mines, is estimated at about $600 per year, while "adults in other classes of mine workers, who form over sixty per cent of the labor force, do not receive an annual average wage of $450."[3] In the extensive array of wage figures given by Mr. Streightoff, distinction is not made between natives and immigrants, but the general showing harmonizes so well with what has already been given as to obviate the necessity of going into this question in further detail.[4]

[1] *Ibid.*, Imms. in Cities, Abs., p. 44.

[2] *Ibid.*, Recent Imms. in Agr., Abs., p. 57.

[3] Roberts, *op. cit.*, p. 346.

[4] *Standard of Living*, Ch. IV.

We are justified in setting down the average earnings of wage-working adult male immigrants as from $350 to $650 per year, and the average annual income of immigrant families at from $500 to $900.

The figures given for individual immigrant incomes have been confined to male workers, for the reasons that they are representative, and are of primary importance in determining the status of the immigrant family in this country. The wages of female workers range on the average from 30 to 40 per cent below those of males. Full comparisons are given in the volume of the Immigration Commission Report on Immigrants in Manufacturing and Mining.

The next question which arises is, to what degree are these incomes, of individuals and families, adequate to furnish proper support to an average family of five persons? This problem involves the determination of the minimum amount on which a family can live in decency under existing conditions in America. Numerous efforts have been made to solve this question. The estimate of the Bureau of Statistics of Massachusetts is $754.[1] The Charity Organization Society of Buffalo regards $634 a year as the "lowest tolerable budget which will allow the bare decencies of life for a family of five."[2] A special committee of the New York State Conference of Charities and Corrections in 1907 made the following estimates as to the income necessary for a family of five persons in New York City.

"$600–$700 is wholly inadequate to maintain a proper standard of living, and no self-respecting family should be asked or expected to live on such an income."

"With an income of between $700–$800 a family can

[1] Roberts, *op. cit.*, p. 346. [2] *The Survey*, Feb. 4, 1911, p. 767.

barely support itself, provided it is subject to no extraordinary expenditures by reason of sickness, death, or other untoward circumstances. Such a family can live without charitable assistance through exceptional management and in the absence of emergencies."

"$825 is sufficient for the average family of five individuals, comprising the father, mother, and three children under 14 years of age to maintain a fairly proper standard of living in the Borough of Manhattan."

Mr. Streightoff summarizes the evidence in the following words: "It is, then, conservative to set $650 as the extreme low limit of the Living Wage in cities of the North, East, and West. Probably $600 is high enough for the cities of the South. At this wage there can be no saving, and a minimum of pleasure." [1]

The close correspondence of these various estimates gives them a high degree of credibility. If we fix these standards in mind, and then look back over the wage scales given on the foregoing pages, we are struck with the utter inadequacy of the annual incomes of the foreign-born to meet even these minimum requirements of decency. It is obvious that an enormous number of immigrant families, if dependent solely on the earnings of the head of the family, would fall far below any of these standards, and that many of them, even when adding to their resources by the labors of wife and children, and the contributions of boarders, cannot possibly bring the total income up to the minimum limit. Even the average income in many occupations is far below this minimum, and it must be considered that while an average indicates that there are some above, there must also be many below, the line. What must be the condition

[1] Streightoff, *op. cit.*, p. 162.

of those below! The average family income of the foreign-born studied in the Immigration Commission's investigation of the manufacturing and mining industries was $704. Mr. Frederic Almy states that 96 per cent of the Poles under investigation in Buffalo earn less by $110 than the $634 per year which was set as the "lowest tolerable budget."[1]

A vast amount of information covering a number of miscellaneous aspects of human life, which fall under the general head of the standard of living, is furnished by the Immigration Commission, in its report on the manufacturing and mining industries. Some of the most important of these facts are summarized in the following tables.

First, as to the situation of young children in the homes of immigrants.

PER CENT OF CHILDREN 6 AND UNDER 16 YEARS OF AGE[2]

	Male			Female		
	At Home	At School	At Work	At Home	At School	At Work
Native-born white of native father	5.4	90.9	3.6	6.9	90.5	2.6
Native-born of foreign father	10.2	83.9	5.9	12.6	83.5	3.9
Foreign-born	13.2	77.0	9.9	19.1	73.6	7.3

Among the following races the following per cent of foreign-born male children of the specified age were at work: German, 13.9; south Italian, 13.3; Lithuanian,

[1] *The Survey*, Feb. 4, 1911, p. 767.

[2] Rept. Imm. Com., Imms. in Mfg. and Min., Abs., pp. 194–195.

14.3; Portuguese, 15.7; Ruthenian, 14.6; Scotch, 19.0; Syrian, 22.6.

The following table, showing the per cent of literacy of the employees studied in these industries, is based on information for 500,329 employees, and hence has a remarkable trustworthiness:

LITERACY OF EMPLOYEES IN MINING AND MANUFACTURING[1]

NATIVITY	MALES		FEMALES	
	PER CENT WHO		PER CENT WHO	
	Read	Read and Write	Read	Read and Write
Native-born white of native father	98.2	97.9	98.8	98.4
Native-born of foreign father	99.0	98.7	99.0	98.8
Foreign-born	85.6	83.6	90.8	89.2

Foreign-born male employees of the following races have the following literacy, as shown by the per cent who can read and write: south Italian, 67.6; Macedonian, 67.1; Portuguese, 46.1; Ruthenian, 63.6; Servian, 69.5; Turkish, 54.1.

From the foregoing table it appears that in respect to literacy the native-born employees of foreign fathers are superior to the native-born whites of native fathers, and that the foreign-born females are superior to the foreign-born males.

The important matter of ability to speak English is forcibly portrayed in the following table:

[1] *Ibid.*, pp. 162–165.

PER CENT OF FOREIGN-BORN EMPLOYEES (EXCLUSIVE OF THE ENGLISH-SPEAKING RACES) WHO SPEAK ENGLISH[1]

Nativity	Male	Female	Total
Total	55.6	38.6	53.2
Bulgarian	20.3	80.0 (only 5)	20.6
Danish	96.5	98.3	96.6
German	87.5	80.2	86.8
Greek	33.5	12.3	31.5
Hebrew, Russian	74.7	75.7	75.0
Herzegovinian	14.6		14.6
Italian, south	48.7	25.8	44.4
Magyar	46.4	24.0	45.2
Norwegian	96.9	91.8	96.5
Polish	43.5	15.5	39.1
Portuguese	45.2	27.0	37.8
Slovak	55.6	26.6	55.1
Slovenian	51.7	30.3	50.9
Swedish	94.7	94.2	94.7

It is thus apparent how large a proportion of our foreign-born laborers have not even taken the first essential step toward assimilation. This evil is, of course, practically overcome in the second generation. Almost all of the native-born persons of foreign fathers, six years of age or over, speak English, though some races show from 6 to 8 per cent who do not.

The percentage who can speak English naturally increases with the length of residence in the United States, until a percentage of 83.1 is reached for all foreign-born employees who have been in the United States ten years or more. But even in this group a very low percentage is found among the Cuban and Spanish cigar makers, of

[1] Rept. Imm. Com., Imms. in Mfg. and Min., Abs., p. 198.

whom almost three fifths are unable to speak the English language.

The age of the immigrant at the time of arriving in the United States has a great deal to do with the ability to speak English. The percentage of those who were under fourteen when they arrived who can speak English is nearly twice as large as that of those who were fourteen or over. The reasons for this are the greater adaptability of the younger immigrants, and their greater opportunities of going to school. The relatively poor showing of the females is probably due to their greater segregation, which prevents them from coming in touch with Americans or older immigrants of other races.

One of the special reports of the Immigration Commission deals with the children of immigrants in schools and brings out some very significant facts. Practically all of the information was secured in December, 1908. Naturally this investigation involved a study of the children of native-born fathers also. A general investigation was made in the public schools of thirty cities, including the first twenty cities in point of population, as shown by the census of 1900, with the exception of Washington, D.C., Louisville, Ky., and Jersey City, N.J. An investigation was also carried on in regard to parochial schools in twenty-four cities, and an investigation of the students in seventy-seven institutions of higher learning. In addition to this general investigation, an intensive investigation was made in twelve cities, including seven cities not in the previous list, making a total of thirty-seven cities in which public schools were studied. The total number of public school pupils for whom information was secured was 1,815,217. Thus the investigation was a very inclusive one, and the results may be taken as representative of educational conditions in the cities of the entire country.

Of the total number of public school children studied in the thirty-seven cities, 766,727 were of native-born fathers, and 1,048,490 of foreign-born fathers. The children of native-born white fathers constituted 39.5 per cent of the total, while among the children of foreign-born fathers there were the following percentages of the total number: Hebrews, 17.6; Germans, 11.6; Italians (north and south), 6.4; total, native-born father, 42.2 per cent; total, foreign-born father, 57.8 per cent.

The different cities show a marked difference in the proportion of children who come from foreign-born fathers, as the following table will show:

PER CENT OF PUPILS IN PUBLIC SCHOOLS OF FOREIGN-BORN FATHERS IN SPECIFIED CITIES

City	Per Cent	City	Per Cent
Chelsea	74.1	Fall River	67.2
Duluth	74.1	Shenandoah	67.1
New York	71.5	New Britain	65.3
New Bedford	68.8	Boston	63.5
Chicago	67.3		
New Orleans	18.1	St. Louis	31.9
Kansas City	21.3	Los Angeles	32.0
Johnstown	24.8	Cedar Rapids	34.2
Cincinnati	27.1	Haverhill	39.1
Baltimore	28.5		

"In only 7 of the 37 cities is the proportion of pupils who are children of native-born white fathers as high as 60 per cent." Four cities have less than 30 per cent. The children of German foreign-born fathers are most numerous in Milwaukee, Detroit, Buffalo, Cleveland, Meriden, Chicago, Cincinnati, and St. Louis; those of foreign-born Russian Hebrew fathers in Chelsea, New York, Boston, Philadelphia, Newark, and Baltimore, those of foreign-born south Italian fathers in Providence, Newark, New York, Yonkers, Buffalo, and Boston.

A smaller proportion of the total number of children of foreign-born fathers are in the higher grades of the public schools than of the children of native-born white fathers, as the following table shows:

PER CENT OF PUPILS OF SPECIFIED NATIVITY IN THE SPECIFIED GRADES

Grade	Native-born White Father	Foreign-born Father
Kindergarten	4.3	4.4
Primary grades	52.1	57.6
Grammar grades	34.5	33.3
High school	9.1	4.7
Total	100.0	100.0

The Slovaks, south Italians, and Magyars have the largest percentages in the kindergartens, and the Portuguese, Lithuanians, Slovaks, south Italians, and Polish the largest percentages in the primary grades. In the high schools, the Canadians, other than French, the Scotch, the native-born white, the Welsh, Germans, Hebrews, and English stand highest. This is due to two main facts, — the longer residence of these latter races in the United States, and their greater desire for a high education for their children, coupled with a greater ability to give it to them. Especially in the case of the kindergartens are the newer immigrating races very eager to have their young children looked after so that the mother can be free to work, or otherwise occupy herself.

Another interesting set of figures is that referring to the amount of retardation among the pupils of different nativities. By "retardation" is meant that a pupil is above the "normal" age for the grade in which he is. In this respect the children of foreign-born fathers of the newer immigration are decidedly inferior to those of the older immigration. The latter, in fact, are on the whole superior to the children of native-born white fathers. Of the total number of children of foreign-born fathers for whom this information was secured, 77.2 per cent were born in the United States, and 28.8 per cent were born abroad. There is a considerably larger proportion of retardation for those children eight years of age or over who were born abroad than among those born in the United States. The proportion retarded increases as the age at the time of arrival in the United States advances. The proportion of retardation is greater among those children whose fathers cannot speak English than among those who can, and greater among those whose fathers have not taken out naturalization papers than among those who have.

When we turn to the institutions of higher learning, we find a comparatively small number of foreign-born students, as might be expected.[1] The percentages for a total of 32,887 students are as follows:

Nativity of Student	Per Cent of Total
Native-born white of native father	64.0
Native-born of foreign father	25.3
Foreign-born	10.2

The Hebrews stand foremost among the foreign-born.

[1] In this investigation pupils are listed by their own nativity, rather than by that of the father.

Of the 221,159 pupils included in the parochial school investigation, 36.5 per cent are children of native-born fathers (36.3 per cent of native-born white fathers), and 63.5 per cent of foreign-born fathers. Children of foreign-born Irish fathers number 26.9 per cent of the total number of pupils, foreign-born German fathers, 9.7 per cent, Polish, 7.1 per cent, and Italian, 7 per cent. In the twenty-four cities in which information was secured for both public and parochial schools, there were 1,322,053 pupils in the public schools, and 221,159 pupils in the parochial schools. In Philadelphia nearly one fourth of the pupils were in parochial schools.

Information was also secured for teachers in the kindergartens and elementary grades of the public schools in thirty cities, including 49,067 individuals. Of these, 49.8 per cent were native-born of native white fathers, and 42.8 per cent native-born of foreign fathers, and 5.8 per cent foreign-born. Of the foreign-born, only six races were represented by as many as one hundred teachers each, viz. Hebrew, English, Irish, German, Canadian (other than French), and Scotch.

CHAPTER XIV

THE EXPLOITATION OF IMMIGRANTS. RELIGION. BIRTHS, MARRIAGES, AND DEATHS. RECREATION

There is a group of peculiar economic institutions which have been developed by the immigrants in this country, and which are especially characteristic of the new immigration. This group includes the padrone system, the contract labor system, the immigrant bank, and two or three similar institutions, particularly the sweating system, which is now practically dependent on immigrants.

The word "padrone" is adopted from the Italian, and signifies master or "boss." In its application to American conditions, it refers to a system of practical slavery, introduced into this country by the Italians, and subsequently utilized by a number of other southeastern European races. When immigration from Italy began to assume considerable proportions, there were already in the United States a few Italians who had been here some time, and had acquired a certain familiarity with the language and customs of the land. They were thereby especially fitted to be of assistance to their newly arrived fellow-countrymen, and also, unfortunately, to exploit them. In fact, they did both of these things. By way of assistance, they put the green immigrants in touch with employers of labor, helped them to find lodgings, and, in brief, acted as the go-between in every case of contact between the immigrant and the life of the people around him. On the other hand, the padrone charged the newcomer well for every service rendered, and in too many cases subjected him to various forms of extortion, which his ignorance kept him from either recognizing or preventing. As certain of the newer immigrants became familiar with the speech and customs of their new home, they in turn became padrones, and extended their operations over the ever-increasing numbers of new arrivals. Thus the system spread.

There are certain businesses or occupations which are particularly adapted to the application of this system, such as railroad labor, peddling, boot-blacking, etc. The Italians developed it primarily in respect to the first of these. This race has now practically abandoned this system in this country, but it has been taken up by others, and is at present practiced by the Bulgarians, Turks, Macedonians, Greeks, and Mexicans, and in some cases among Austrians and Italians.[1]

A more concrete idea of the workings of this system may be gained by an examination of its operation in a single industry, as, for instance, the shoe-shining industry among the Greeks. This business, in a marked degree, combines the necessary elements for the successful application of the system, — small capital, cheap unskilled labor, close supervision, etc., — and this race is well adapted to apply it to its extreme extent, partly from natural aptitude, and partly from custom and training. For the system, in its main outlines, has long been familiar in Greece, though some of the most unfortunate aspects do not develop there.

The padrone is a Greek who has been in this country

[1] Rept. Imm. Com., Greek Padrone System, pp. 7, 8. For an account of the operation of the system in England, see Wilkins, W. H., *The Alien Invasion*.

for some time, and knows the ways of the land. He decides to engage in the boot-blacking trade, and to secure his necessary helpers contracts for a number of boys from his native land to come over and work for him for a certain length of time, for a specified sum. The arrangement is sometimes made with the boys, sometimes with the parents, but almost always with the parents' consent. When these boys arrive, they are taken to a room or set of rooms, which the padrone has engaged and which thenceforth are their "home." They are at once put to work in the shop of the boss, and kept at work continuously thereafter, with practically no time off which they can call their own, except the meager allowance made for sleep. The hours are long — twelve, fourteen, or even more hours per day. The boss furnishes board and lodging, and pays a small sum in cash, perhaps $200 per year. The rooms are frightfully overcrowded, miserably ventilated, and wholly unhygienic. The boys do their own cooking, usually in relays of two, and the noon meal is eaten hurriedly in a room in the rear of the shop. The boys are prevented from attending night school, and are forbidden to talk to patrons. In every way the padrone tries to discourage their acquiring knowledge of American ways, for the system rests on ignorance. In a majority of cases the padrone takes all the tips given to the boys, and the boys excuse him on the grounds that wages are high and expenses great.

It is obvious that the boys are wholly at the mercy of their boss, a mercy the quality of which is sadly strained. And when a boy does manage to get a grasp of the English language, and acquire a little independence, instead of turning traitor to the system, he sets up as a padrone himself. All investigators, and a number of the better class of Greeks in this country, agree that this system is a disgrace to the Greek race, or to any other race that practices it.[1]

The contract labor system is next of kin to the padrone system. The main differences are that the control of the boss, outside of working hours, is not so complete, and the relationship is likely to be of shorter duration. This system arises from the necessity of the capitalistic employer of labor getting in touch with the alien workman. Differences of language, ignorance of the sources and the means of communication, and a variety of other perfectly comprehensible reasons, prevent the employer from enlisting his workers directly, and the laborer from applying for work in his own person. The natural and inevitable intermediary is the immigrant who has been in this country long enough to know the language and have some influence and acquaintance among employers. Given this starting point, the process of bringing the immigrants and the employer together goes along wholly natural channels, with only minor modifications in the details. In some cases the employer pays the agent certain specified wages for each laborer furnished, and the agent pays whatever is necessary — below that figure — to secure the workers; sometimes the employer pays fixed wages to the laborers, and allows the agent a stated commission for each worker secured. This is much the more desirable system of the two. In many cases the agent is retained as overseer in charge of the men he has secured. The degree of definiteness in these

[1] For a fuller description of the system, and a more detailed account of its crying evils, see Fairchild, H. P., *Greek Immigration*, and Rept. Imm. Com., The Greek Padrone System in the United States.

arrangements varies all the way from cases where agents go over to foreign countries, definitely charged with securing laborers for some employer, to those where the employer simply lets it be known among his employees that there will be work for all their friends or relatives who wish to come, and leaves the leaven to work. It is becoming more rare for agents in this country to go abroad in person; the tendency is for them to work in connection with agents established on the other side.

The possibilities of abuse in this system are manifestly great. The agent customarily advances the passage money of those brought from abroad, taking a mortgage far in excess of his actual expense on whatever property the immigrant has to offer. Rates of interest are exorbitant, and the terms of the contract all in favor of the importer.[1] Sometimes the immigrant agrees to work for him seven or eight months, in return for an initial outlay of not over $100 or $125. In extreme cases, when an importer has taken mortgages far in excess of his actual expenditure, he will discharge an entire set of men, in order to make room for a new lot brought over on similar terms. The debts of the original group are still binding, and it is astonishing to note the faithfulness with which these poor unfortunates, thus thrown on their own resources, will labor on to pay off these obligations.

Not all of the laborers employed under this system are secured directly from abroad. Many of the more recent immigrants, who have been in this country for some time, are almost equally dependent on the contractor with the absolute "greeners." Chicago is a great clearing house for the labor market of the western

[1] For an illustration of such a contract, see Rept. Imm. Com., Greek Padrone System, Abs., pp. 23–24.

railroads, and labor agencies, often connected with a restaurant, or some similar place of business, abound in the foreign sections.[1]

A great deal of business of this general nature is carried on by aliens who are not real agents. It is very frequent for an immigrant to tell a newcomer that if he will pay him a certain sum of money he will secure him a position in the establishment where he is himself employed. All that he really does is to take the newcomer around and introduce him to the foreman, who gives him work, if there is any. But the new arrival considers himself much in the debt of his "friend," and more than that, thereafter regards the job as his own because he has paid for it, and resents discharge for any reason as an injustice. Conscientious employers naturally do all they can to discourage such practices, but are powerless to prevent them. In fact, the eagerness of earlier immigrants to exploit their newly arrived fellow-countrymen, not only in this way, but in any other that promises a profit, is one of the most disheartening features of the whole immigration situation.

It goes without saying that all of these operations, which involve bringing immigrants into the country under agreement to labor, are in direct violation of law. The contract labor clause of the immigration law, if strictly interpreted and enforced, would exclude practically every immigrant who had the slightest assurance of employment awaiting him. In fact, however, as has been shown above (page 154), the courts have so interpreted the act as to include under contract laborers only those who have a definite contract, or those who come in response to a specific offer or promise of employ-

[1] Cf. Addams, Jane, *Twenty Years at Hull-House*, p. 221.

ment.[1] This kind of a promise or offer is relatively rare. Nothing so definite is required to induce unskilled laborers to emigrate. Broad and general assurances of employment awaiting them are sufficient. The wide discrepancy between the letter and the interpretation of the law is unfortunate. This section of the law is the one upon which immigrants are coached more thoroughly than on any other, and in addition to the large number of immigrants who violate the most lenient interpretation, there must be many others whom the courts would not hold guilty, who nevertheless believe themselves so and suffer a corresponding degradation of character. A third element in the situation, which complicates it still further, is the interpretation practically placed on the law by the immigration authorities, which is apparently more strict than that of the courts. The whole matter of contract labor needs to be thoroughly reconsidered.

In addition to the activities of labor agents and employers, state boards do a good deal to encourage immigration, sometimes keeping within the spirit of the law, and sometimes exceeding it.

Another member of this same nefarious family is the peonage system. For a general description of the system the reader is referred to Professor Commons, *Races and Immigrants in America*, chapter on Labor. It has been judicially defined in the following words: "Peonage is a status or condition of compulsory service based upon the indebtedness of the peon to the master. The basic fact is indebtedness."[2] The customary or typical case is where a laborer receives advances of some sort from his employer, and then leaves his service

[1] Rept. Imm. Com., Contract Labor, Abs., p. 12, which compare throughout.
[2] Clyatt case, 197 U. S. 207.

before the terms of his engagement have been fulfilled, certainly before he has repaid his employer for the advances. His employer then procures his arrest, either under a charge of obtaining money under false pretenses, or under the labor statutes of the various states. The employer makes a new agreement with the laborer, that if he will return to his employment, and work out the balance of his indebtedness, the criminal procedure will be dropped.

This might seem, on the face of it, a thoroughly just proceeding. The trouble is that the employer has every advantage. The laborer is ignorant, and very often the conditions under which he is to work are grossly misrepresented to him. Lack of forethought, moreover, is one of the chief characteristics of ignorant and unintelligent men. The money or goods advanced to them occupy a very disproportionate place in their minds, compared to the work which they agree to perform in the future. The employer, on the other hand, knows all about the conditions, and just how much he can afford to pay, and is able to give himself the best of the bargain by a broad margin.

The Immigration Commission made a thorough investigation of this subject, and found evidences of peonage in every state in the Union, except Oklahoma and Connecticut. In the south, where peonage is supposed to be most rampant, it was discovered that most of the peons were supplied by labor agents in New York City, who seriously misrepresented the conditions under which they were to work, and in many cases sent out men wholly unfitted for the work which they were to do. In the south, however, in spite of the existence of many cases, it appears that the vigorous prosecutions, and the willingness of juries to convict, have pretty well broken up the tendency toward peonage in connection with aliens.

In the west and northwest, cases of technical peonage were found in the shoe-shining industry, and in some lumber and railroad camps. But there have been practically no attempts at prosecution for peonage in these states.

The most surprising fact established by the Commission in this respect is that probably the most complete system of peonage in the whole country has existed, not in the south, but in Maine. Here the employers of labor in the lumber camps have been obliged to secure their labor mostly from other states and in the main from immigrants. Boston is the great labor market for this industry. The immigrants are given very misleading accounts of the conditions of their labor, and are engaged to work for their employers for a specified time. They are then taken into the forests, sometimes having to walk sixty or seventy miles to their place of labor, and kept in the forest all winter.

When they learn the extent to which they have been deceived, many of them are inclined to run away. However, in February, 1907, a law was passed making it a criminal offense for a person to "enter into an agreement to labor for any lumbering operation or in driving logs and in consideration thereof receive any advances of goods, money, or transportation, and unreasonably and with intent to defraud, fail to enter into said employment as agreed and labor a sufficient length of time to reimburse his employer for said advances and expenses." The general interpretation of the courts has been to ignore the provision about intent to defraud, or at least to put the burden of proof on the defendant, though it is not specifically provided in the law that failure or refusal to fulfill the terms of the contract shall be *prima facie* evidence of an intent to defraud, as is the case in the contract labor law of Minnesota and other states. Employers in other branches of industry have sought to secure the same protection, but in vain, so that this law is iniquitous, not only from the point of view of peonage, but also because it is class legislation. A considerable amount of peonage has resulted from this law in Maine.[1]

The basis of all the evils which have just been discussed has been seen to lie in the ignorance and helplessness of the newly arrived immigrant. Knowing nothing of the language of the country, or of its methods of doing business, and having no connections with the industrial system of the country, he is forced to rely on some one who can supply these factors. Most naturally he turns to some one of his fellow-countrymen who has been in this country longer. From that time on, sometimes for many years, his career is dominated by the older immigrant to a remarkable degree. Out of this connection has grown up a peculiar set of institutions, commonly known as immigrant banks, which have the power for great good or evil to the immigrant, according to the character of the men who have them in charge. The origin and nature of these banks is as follows:

The foremost ambition of the average immigrant is the saving of money. The purposes of this saving are many — to guarantee his own future prosperity, to ease the lot of friends and relatives at home, to pay off mortgages and other debts, and, perhaps the most important of all, to provide the means whereby friends and relatives

[1] Cf. Rept. Imm. Com., Peonage, etc.

on the other side may join him in the new world. The prepaid ticket is the final end of much of the saving of aliens. These accumulations naturally come in small amounts. Out of a month's earnings, the immigrant may save $10 or $15 or even as high as $30. The living conditions of many of the immigrants make it unsafe for them to try to keep this money in their lodgings; they are unfamiliar with, and distrustful of, American banks. The disposition of their savings which seems to them the wisest and safest is to intrust them to a fellow-countryman who is familiar with the ways of the country and has some means of keeping them safe. This individual may be the padrone or boss, the lodging-house keeper, a saloon keeper or grocer, or the steamship agent from whom the immigrant expects eventually to purchase the prepaid ticket. In time, immigrants in these positions get into the habit of receiving small sums from their fellow-countrymen for safe keeping or on deposit against some future purchase. As these amounts accumulate, they become of considerable value to the holder, who may deposit them in a regular savings bank at interest, to his own profit, or may invest them in his business, or may make other speculative investments with them. To attract such deposits, and increase their amount, he adds the term "bank" to the name of his business, so that he now becomes a "Grocer and Banker," a "Ticket Agent and Banker," etc. This adds a dignity to his position and increases the confidence of the people in his integrity.

It has been intimated in the preceding paragraph that the immigrant "banker" makes no distinction between the funds deposited with him and his own property. This is generally the case. Occasionally the banker will keep the deposits in his safe, in the original wallets in which they were delivered to him,[1] or deposit them in a bank in his wife's name,[2] but these are exceptional instances. Ordinarily all the money in the banker's possession is lumped together, so that the assets of the "bank" are identical with the general resources of the proprietor. Furthermore, there is a great amount of laxity in the giving of receipts to depositors. Sometimes no written acknowledgment whatever is given; from this point the character of the receipt varies all the way up to a regular pass book, and a thorough system of bookkeeping.

From such a beginning as this, these banks have developed a variety of forms, varying in functions and in stability. They have been classified by the Immigration Commission into three main groups, as follows:

"I. State and incorporated banks or highly organized private institutions thoroughly responsible and operated in a regular manner almost exclusively as a bank. There are comparatively few of these institutions.

"II. Privately owned steamship agencies, and real-estate offices which masquerade under the name of a bank, but which are not legally authorized as such. To this class should be added groceries and saloons in which the banking functions are clearly defined as apart from other business. The majority of the banks investigated are of this class.

"III. Banks which may or may not be known as such, but in which the functions of caring for deposits and receiving money for transmission abroad are extended more as an accommodation or as incidental to the main business of the concern. Saloon keepers, grocers,

[1] Rept. Imm. Com., Immigrant Banks, p. 35. [2] *Ibid.*, p. 35.

boarding houses, barbers, and men engaged in similar occupations usually conduct this class of banks. It has been claimed by some that every immigrant saloon keeper will be found doing a banking business of this character. This is the largest, as it also is the most irresponsible, class. It is undoubtedly the hardest class to regulate, as it is the one about which it is the most difficult to obtain accurate information."[1]

The hold which these bankers have over their patrons is due in the first instance to the ignorance of the latter, and the feeling of security which they have in dealing with people of their own race. It is increased by the familiarity which the banker has with business methods in this country, and names, places, and methods in the old country. The immigrant banker assumes a decidedly paternalistic attitude toward his patrons, and renders them many services not ordinarily associated with a banking business, such as writing and translating letters, securing employment, giving legal advice, etc. The greater the hold thus secured, the wider are the opportunities for exploitation. In the absence of proper control, and of the ordinary safeguards of such businesses, the immigrant depositor is made to suffer extortion and loss in countless cases. In many cases this is due to the ignorance of the banker, and his total unfitness for the assumption of such responsibilities; in many others, it is due to dishonesty, greed, and willful intent to defraud. In the panic year of 1907 large numbers of these banks failed, and sums of money were lost to immigrants, the importance of which is to be judged, not so much by the total amounts, as by the fact that they represented the savings of a large number

[1] Rept. Imm. Com., Immigrant Banks, p. 27.

of individuals in meager circumstances. In normal years, there is a steady loss, due to failures, defalcations, and abscondings on the part of bankers, and also to the continual petty frauds, habitually practiced by many of these men. The trustfulness of the immigrants towards men of this character is surprising. Instances are known where men have come into a community, advertised a bank, and in a few weeks accumulated large sums of money from the foreigners, with which they promptly decamped, leaving absolutely no means of redress to their creditors.

The primary functions of these banks are the safe keeping of money and the transmission of remittances abroad. Only in exceptional cases do the other banking functions play an important part. It is estimated that in 1907 approximately $137,500,000 in foreign remittances passed through the hands of immigrant bankers, in sums averaging about $35.[1]

These banks are mostly in the hands of the recently immigrating races. The reasons for their existence — ignorance of language and customs, illiteracy, inconvenient hours kept by American banks, and their luxurious appearance and requirements of cleanliness — appeal much less strongly to the immigrants from northwestern Europe.

Another functionary who exercises an extensive, and often baleful, influence over the immigant is the notary public. The position of dignity and influence held by corresponding officials in foreign countries leads the immigrant to accord too much confidence and trust to such persons in the United States, who are often ignorant and in many cases dishonest men. The nature of the cases

[1] *Ibid.*, pp. 69, 85, 86.

in which the immigrant has recourse to them gives them a large amount of power over the foreigner, and opens the way to many petty extortions.

All of these exploiting agencies become inextricably mingled in actual life. The functions of the padrone, the labor contractor, the employment agent, the steamship agent, the boarding boss, the saloon keeper, the grocer, the banker, the notary public — any two or more of these may be combined in the person of a given individual, who exercises a corresponding control over the destiny of those who are dependent on him. His hold over them rests upon the fact that they are not Americanized, and it is wholly to his interest to keep them so.[1]

The sweat shop is manifestly an institution of the same general character as those which have just been discussed, and while it may not owe its origin to the immigrants, it is now practically dependent on them for its existence. The main features of this system are familiar. Its distinctive characteristic is the giving out of work by manufacturers to contractors, in order that certain processes may be carried on in the homes of the workers. It finds its fullest development in the clothing trade, which at the present time is almost wholly in the hands of the Jews.

The chief evils of the system are the unsanitary conditions of labor, the long hours, the extensive employment of women and children, the difficulty of proper supervision, the low wages, and the complete subjection

[1] For a full description of the nature, organization, and functions of the immigrant bank, and of efforts which have been made to correct its evils, the reader is referred to the Report of the Immigration Commission on Immigrant Banks, to which reference has been made, and also to the Report of the New York Commission of Immigration. This latter volume also contains an extended discussion of the position of the notary public. Cf. also Roberts, Peter, *The New Immigration*, Ch. XV.

of the workers to the control of the boss. The contractor himself is often in a precarious financial situation, being himself a victim of the system. Like the foregoing institutions, it results from the ignorance and lack of connection of the workers. Its persistence and wide spread in this country are due to the constant accessions of low-grade workers, unassimilated to the conditions of the country, which immigration furnishes. These supply the raw material upon which the system feeds. By so doing they have blocked the efforts of the cities of the United States to control or abolish this evil.[1]

There is another class of institutions which rests upon the helplessness of the newly arrived immigrant, which is, however, an alleviating, rather than an exploiting agency, and which belongs to the social rather than to the economic life. This is the immigrant home or aid society. These institutions are numerous in the seaport cities where immigrants arrive; there are said to be not less than sixteen in operation in New York City.[2] They are for the most part benevolent or philanthropic organizations (at least nominally), and many of them are under the control of some religious organization. Many of them work primarily with a single race or people. Their functions are looking after newly arrived immigrants who are not met by friends, and forwarding them to their destinations, furnishing them board and lodging while in the port of arrival, helping them to find work or to locate missing acquaintances, and in general safeguarding them while they are establishing a connection with some responsible party in this country.

[1] Addams, Jane, *Twenty Years at Hull-House*, p. 99; Adams, T. S., and Sumner, Helen L., *Labor Problems*, Ch. IV.

[2] Rept. New York Com. of Imm., p. 88.

Most of the immigrants who come to this country come to join relatives or friends, who generally meet them at the port of arrival, or send money or transportation to take them to their destination. But it frequently happens that the friends or relatives fail to put in an appearance. In that case the immigration authorities are unwilling to turn the immigrant adrift unprotected, especially in the case of unaccompanied women or girls. Consequently the government has allowed representatives of homes and aid societies to visit the immigrant stations, and offer their aid to the immigrants. At Ellis Island, immigrants whose relatives or friends fail to call for them are detained five days, and then given the choice of being sent back to Europe or of leaving the station in company with some representative of a home or aid society, often called a "missionary." If the latter alternative is chosen, the immigrant is said to be "discharged" to the given person, who is thereupon held theoretically responsible that the immigrant shall not become a public charge. There are three general classes of immigrants who are thus discharged: (1) Immigrants whose friends or relatives fail to meet them, and whom the authorities do not deem it wise to land unless some one becomes responsible for them. (2) Immigrants who are without sufficient money to take them to their destination, and who must be cared for until the necessary funds are forthcoming. (3) Immigrants, particularly girls and women, who have no friends or relatives in this country, and need a home until they can secure employment. These homes and aid societies necessarily have something of the nature of employment agencies, and do a good deal of work of that kind.

The amount of work done by these organizations is

very great. In the calendar year 1907, over 14,800 immigrants were discharged to such representatives at Ellis Island by the New York discharging division. This does not include the total number discharged, as the boards of special inquiry and the commissioners of immigration also discharge immigrants.[1] Six homes in New York City cared for a total of 48,275 immigrants in 1908.[2]

It will be seen at once that these homes and societies have great power over the immigrants, and are in positions of immense advantage and responsibility, inasmuch as the authorities give their representatives a semiofficial standing, and intrust immigrants to them without reserve. Unscrupulous and grasping persons, once admitted to the stations as missionaries, have large opportunities and every advantage to exploit the immigrants at will. This is especially true of the homes, where the immigrants can be charged — and overcharged — for every possible kind of service.

It might appear at first sight that the authorities would exercise every caution, not only in regard to the character of the representatives, but as to the character and conduct of the homes. The investigations of the Immigration Commission, however, revealed that this has not always been the case. Not only have many of the authorities used very little care or discretion in granting privileges to representatives in their stations, but they exercised practically no supervision over the homes themselves, and when the immigrant had once been discharged to the representative, they paid no more attention to him or his welfare. The Commission in-

[1] Rept. Imm. Com., Imm. Homes and Aid Socs., Abs., p. 8.
[2] Rept. New York Com. of Imm., p. 90.

vestigated carefully 102 immigrant homes and aid societies, in addition to twenty-five employment agencies, most of which had some connection with an immigrant home or aid society. A large amount of misconduct on the part of representatives was discovered, as well as undesirable conditions in the homes themselves. Many of the homes were found to be purely money-making institutions, where the immigrant was fleeced to the limit of his resources. The sanitary conditions in some of them were terrible. Some of the representatives seemed to care for nothing but to have as many immigrants as possible discharged to them, and were little more than runners for their respective homes. "It was the testimony of some of the leading officials at Ellis Island that the majority of missionaries and representatives there care only to secure the discharge of immigrants who have money and can pay for food and lodging." [1] Some of the representatives were instrumental in securing the admission of contract laborers. "About two-thirds of the homes investigated were clean, comfortable, and sanitary, and about one-third were overcrowded, badly ventilated, filthy and insanitary." [2] Many of the homes where bad conditions were found were supported by honest conscientious people, who had been duped and betrayed by their representatives and managers; others were intentionally nothing but money-making schemes.

These conditions are bad enough in themselves, but the most serious feature of the situation is the lack of responsibility and care in placing women and girls out in employment. The majority of the homes investigated showed absolutely no sense of their duty and responsibility in this matter. Only one sixth of them refused

[1] Rept. Imm. Com., Imm. Homes and Aid Socs., Abs., p. 14. [2] *Ibid.*, p. 16.

to place girls in situations where their morals would be seriously endangered. Many of them were perfectly willing to supply girls to work in houses of immoral character.[1] There was also a great deal of carelessness in the investigation of addresses to which girls were sent. Many of the addresses reported by the societies were found to be fictitious, many were false, that is, the girls had never been there, and some of them were admittedly immoral resorts. It is encouraging to note that since the investigation of the Commission vigorous measures have been employed in correcting these evils, and conditions have greatly improved.

The case of the immigrant homes and aid societies is a remarkable illustration of the eternal vigilance which is necessary to prevent exploitation and corruption from flourishing, even in connection with professedly benevolent agencies, when plastic material is furnished in such abundance as exists in the immigrant body.[2]

The effects of immigration upon the religious life of the immigrants and of the United States constitute a great field of research which has been surprisingly neglected, perhaps because of the difficulty of securing reliable data and establishing definite conclusions, perhaps because it has not seemed of sufficient importance to warrant exhaustive study.

One result which has certainly followed the immigration of the nineteenth century and the beginning of the twentieth is a vast increase in the number of denominations and sects organized in this country. The position of the Roman Catholic Church as a product of immigration is too obvious to be dwelt upon. The predomi-

[1] Cf. Rept. N. Y. Com. of Imm., p. 92.

[2] New York now has a state law, which went into effect Sept. 1, 1911, for the regulation of these lodging houses. *The Survey*, Sept. 30, 1911.

nance of this form of belief among the Irish of the first half of the nineteenth century, which more than anything else motived the Native American and Know Nothing movements, has been maintained to a certain extent among the Germans, and in later days among the Italians and Slavs.[1]

The census reports on religious bodies unfortunately give no information as to the nationality of members and communicants, so that it is impossible to distribute the adherents of the various sects among the constituent races. However, out of the list of denominations given we can pick a number of manifestly foreign origin which indicate the tremendous diversity of religious forms which are represented in this country. Among them are the following: Armenian Church; Buddhists, Chinese and Japanese; Dunkers; Eastern Orthodox churches, Russian, Servian, Syrian, and Greek; various German Evangelical bodies; various Scandinavian Lutheran bodies; Slovak Evangelical Lutheran Synod; Moravian bodies; Jewish congregations; Polish national church; Swedish Evangelical bodies; Hungarian Reformed Church; Bahais, etc.

The total number of organizations covered by the report of the census for 1906 is 212,230 as reported by

[1] That the spirit of Know Nothingism dies hard, and is likely to crop out even in modern times, is evidenced by the so-called A. P. A. agitation of the early nineties. The A. P. A., or American Protective Association, was the most prominent of several secret organizations, formed about this time, the purposes and methods of which were strikingly similar to those of the Native American and Know Nothing parties. The object of their antagonism was the Roman Catholic Church, and particularly the body of Irish Catholics. This agitation was carried to such an extent that many people, even of the intelligent and thoughtful, feared that a religious war was impending. For details see Winston, E. M., "The Threatening Conflict with Romanism," *Forum*, 17:425 (June, 1894); Coudert, Frederic R., "The American Protective Association," *Forum*, 17:513 (July, 1894); Gladden, W., "The Anti-Catholic Crusade," *Century*, 25:789 (March, 1894).

186 denominations. One hundred and fourteen of these denominations reported the use of some foreign language in some of their organizations. Of the denominations so reporting 12.5 per cent of their organizations, with 26.3 per cent of their membership, report the use of foreign languages, either alone or with English. There are forty-one individual languages included in the report.

These facts indicate that, whatever changes the removal to a new environment involves, and however much of American life the immigrants adopt, a large percentage of our foreign population brings its religion with it, and keeps it. This is not to be wondered at, as we know that men hold on to their traditional religion more tenaciously than to almost any other of their mores and resent interference here most of all. More than this, it is probably well that it is so. For religion is the great conserving force of morality, the principal bulwark of traditional conduct. The perils of the moral nature of the immigrant in his new home are many. Trained to repression, restriction, and control, he finds himself suddenly endowed with liberty and opportunity. This liberty he is all too likely to interpret as license. Finding people all around him doing things which have hitherto seemed to him sinful or immoral, he adopts the practices, without having acquired the principles and restraints which safeguard them, and make them innocuous for Americans. If, along with this shifting of ethical standards, he loses also his religious sanctions, his moral danger is great indeed.[1] This process has been

[1] Professor Mayo-Smith says on this point, "The commands of morality are absolute and must have the sanction of perfect faith in order to be effective. To destroy the credibility of the sanction, without putting anything in its place, must for the time being be destructive of ethical action." *Emigration and Immigration*, p. 7.

particularly observed among the second generation of Hebrews. In the light of American civilization and public thought, they find the religion of their fathers discredited. It appears to them antiquated and unworthy. They throw it over unreservedly, and with it goes the whole body of admirable moral precepts and guides, and the remarkable ethical standards, which have been indissolubly associated with religious belief in their minds. The unfortunate part of the process is that nothing takes the place, either of the religious faith, or of the moral code. The old, which was good, is forsaken without adopting the new, which is perhaps better. As a result, juvenile crime is very prevalent among the Jews, and a large proportion of those concerned in the white slave traffic, both men and women, are Hebrews.[1] It would be difficult to say to what extent the bad record of the second generation of immigrants in regard to criminality and general lawlessness may be due to similar causes.

While the majority of our immigrants are nominally Christians, there is nevertheless a sufficient demand for religious guidance to constitute a tremendous foreign missionary problem within the borders of our own land — the more so when it is remembered that a large part of the efforts of some of our foreign missionary boards is directed toward people who are already nominally Christians, in their home lands. Many of the religious denominations are beginning to feel this call, and are responding to it by special services or organizations, planned to meet the needs of foreign residents. As stated above, many religious bodies support missionaries

[1] Cf. Bingham, T. A., "Foreign Criminals in New York," *North American Review*, September, 1908, p. 381. Also, Rept. Imm. Com., Importing Women for Immoral Purposes, pp. 12, 14.

on Ellis Island. The Young Men's Christian Association devotes especial attention to the foreign-born. Many foreign groups have societies of a religious character, aside from their regular church organizations.

Yet in spite of all that can be said on this side of the question, there remains an astonishing apathy on the part of the body of American Protestant churches toward the religious and moral needs and dangers of the foreign population, and of the opportunities for service which it offers. This service might be made of incalculable benefit not only to the immigrants themselves, but to their adopted country, whose destiny hangs in the same balance as theirs. It is true that a group of ignorant, stolid, perhaps dirty, European peasants on the streets of one's own city does not make the same appeal to his emotions and sympathies as the half-clad savages which he reads of in the missionary journals. Yet the spiritual needs of the immigrant group are probably the greater of the two — at least they are more immediate — and the receptive attitude of the newly arrived immigrant toward all elevating influences makes him a uniquely promising subject for missionary work.

The unwillingness on the part of many wealthy and fashionable churches to accept this responsibility in the spirit of the founder of the Christian religion may be attributed to ignorance of actual conditions, to fastidiousness, or to race prejudice, if not to actual indifference. But if the church is to fulfill its mission in twentieth century America, the efforts toward serving the spiritual needs of the alien must be immensely widened and strengthened. Reverend Charles Stelzle gives an ironical epitome of the situation in the story of the church in New York City which sold its fine building because there were too many foreigners in the neighborhood, and sent the proceeds to the Board of Foreign Missions.[1]

In regard to that set of social conditions which are represented by statistics of births, marriages, and deaths, no definite statistical data for the country at large are available. The census reports do not make the necessary distinctions between native and foreign born to serve as a basis of comparison. Such a comparison is, in fact, practically impossible, for the composition of the foreign-born element of the population in respect to sex, age, and conjugal condition differs so widely from that of a normal population that any comparative rates, based on general statistics, would be meaningless. Thus a foreign-born death rate, based simply on total deaths and total population, would probably be remarkably low. For, as has been shown, the foreign-born population is largely in the middle age groups. They have passed the dangerous period of childhood, and many of them, with advancing age, go home to die. But if compared with a selected group of native-born, of the same sex and age, the foreign-born would probably show a high death rate, on account of the prevalence of industrial accidents and diseases, and unhygienic living conditions.

Similar considerations hold true as regards the birth rate and marriage rate. In respect to the former, it has been observed in another connection that the birth rate of the foreign-born is extraordinarily high for the first generation. As the length of residence of any foreign group in this country increases, its birth rate tends to approach that of the native-born until, as has been said,

[1] *The Workingman and Social Problems*, p. 32. Cf. White, Gaylord S., "The Protestant Church and the Immigrant," *The Survey*, Sept. 25, 1909.

"the probability is that when immigrants have lived with us so long that their grandparents were born in the land, there is little more difference between the two stocks in reproductivity than between any other equally extensive groups taken at random."[1] The study made by the Immigration Commission of the fecundity of immigrant women shows that women born of foreign parents have a much greater fecundity than those born of native parents.

In respect to marriages, comparative rates would have little meaning unless they could be very carefully refined. The relative number of foreign-born women is so small, and the number of men who have left wives on the other side so large, and the temporary character of the residence of many aliens so marked, as to put the entire question of marriage among the foreign-born into an abnormal status. Many obstacles prevent the free intermarriage of foreigners with natives. Marriages between the foreign-born in this country are probably much more infrequent than would be the case in a normal population of the same size. Even in the case of the second generation of immigrants Professor Commons finds that the proportion of marriages is smaller than among the native-born.[2] The effect of this is to increase the tendency, already noticed, to augment the population of this country by new immigration, rather than by the reproduction of elements already here.

For recreation the foreign-born are limited to virtually the same resources as the natives of the working class. The dance hall, the moving picture show, the cheap theater, and the recreation park hold the prom-

[1] Anderson, W. L., *The Country Town*, p. 164.

[2] Commons, J. R., *op. cit.*, p. 203.

inent places. For the men of some races the saloon, and for others the imported coffeehouse, furnish a place for meeting and social relaxation. The need of recreational facilities for the working classes, so long neglected in this country, is beginning to be recognized and met in every up-to-date American city. In all such advantages the foreign-born will have their share. There are also other efforts, such as the revival of folk dancing among foreign groups, and the giving of dramas which appeal to the immigrants, which have the foreigner directly in view. These merit hearty commendation. Yet much remains to be done. The problem of recreation can be solved only in connection with the problem of general industrial conditions. The average adult worker in many of our industries is too much exhausted at the close of his day's work to take much interest in recreation of any kind. All too often, also, the time and the pecuniary means are alike lacking for forms of recreation which would be of great value. There needs to be more recognition of the fact that the workman, though a foreigner, must have relaxation and diversion to promote his highest welfare, just as truly as those in higher stations.[1]

[1] It is a suggestive fact that the word "recreation" does not occur in the indexes of Hall's *Immigration*, Jenks and Lauck's *The Immigration Problem*, Commons' *Races and Immigrants in America*, Coolidge's *Chinese Immigration*, or Balch's *Our Slavic Fellow Citizens*. For descriptions of the recreations of the foreign-born see Kenngott, George F., *The Record of a City*, Ch. VIII; *City Wilderness*, Ch. VIII; *Americans in Process*, Ch. VIII; Roberts, Peter, *The New Immigration*, Ch. XVIII.

CHAPTER XV

CONDITIONS AFFECTING THE COUNTRY. WAGES. PAUPERISM. CRIME. INSANITY

TURNING to those aspects of the immigration situation in this country which more immediately affect the life of the American people as a whole, we find that they group themselves under nine main heads, as follows: wages and standard of living, pauperism, crime, insanity, industrial efficiency and progress, amount and distribution of wealth, crises, social stratification, and politics. In each of these categories certain preliminary effects are already observable, and other much more extensive ones may be predicted on a theoretic and hypothetical basis.

As regards wages, we have already made a careful study of what may be taken as typical immigrant wages. The question now is, how have these wages affected the earnings of the great body of American workmen? Has this admittedly low wage scale of the foreign labor body exercised a depressing effect upon the remuneration of the native American, or has the latter been enabled, by relinquishing the lower grades of labor to the foreigner, to avail himself of higher and better paid positions?

This question, like many others of its class, involves the problem of determining what would have happened if history had been different in some single particular. It is a most perilous, and often profitless, field to enter. It is apparently impossible for statisticians to determine with certainty what has been the course of real wages within the past half century or so. There is no doubt that money wages have gone up. There is also no doubt that the average price of commodities has gone up. The question is whether average prices or average wages have gone up the faster. The most reliable tables covering this subject are probably those of the Bureau of Labor, and these have been discontinued since 1907. As far as the showing which they make can be depended upon, it seems to indicate that there has been a very slight rise in the purchasing power of full-time weekly wages since 1890.[1] Granting this, the question still remains, would not the American workman have enjoyed a much greater increase in real wages during this period, if he had been allowed to reap the full advantage of his economic position in the country, without having to meet the competition of vast numbers of foreign laborers? The answer to this question must rest on pure theory, as its statistical proof would involve a reënactment of past history, which is a manifest impossibility.

According to the established laws of economics there are two ways in which immigration may operate to lower wages. First, by increasing the supply of labor in the country, and thereby diminishing the amount of remuneration which the individual laborer can command. Second, by introducing a body of laborers whose customary wage in the countries they come from, and whose corresponding standard of living, is much lower than the prevailing standard in the new country. This factor operates, not by increasing the number of laborers bidding for employment, but by lowering the amount of the

[1] Statistical Abstract of the U. S., 1910, p. 251. Cf. also Ely, R. T., *Outlines of Economics*, p. 340, and Streightoff, F. H., *Standard of Living*, p. 55.

initial bid on the part of a sufficient number of laborers to fix the remuneration for the whole lot. As to the first of these ways, if the argument contained in Chapter XI is valid, it is not probable that in the long run immigration has materially increased the total population of the United States. But it has, from time to time, caused a marked temporary increase in the body of unskilled labor, and this, as will be shown later, is an important matter. However this may be, the second of these two ways has undoubtedly been by far the more instrumental in reducing the average wage of the American workman. It is not because he has had to compete with more laborers, so much as with cheaper laborers, that the American workman has failed to secure a higher remuneration for his services. It is what Professor Commons has called the "competitive struggle for standards of living"[1] which has been the determining factor, and the whole matter can be best understood by taking it up in the light of the general standard of living, rather than of mere wages.

The standard of living is the index of the comfort and true prosperity of a nation. A high standard is a priceless heritage, which ought to be guarded at all cost. The United States has always prided itself on the high standard of living of its common people, but has not always understood on what that standard rests. The standard of living is the resultant of two great factors, the stage of the arts, and the ratio of men to land. It may be improved by bettering the methods of production and utilization of natural resources, or by reducing the ratio between men and land, *i.e.* by limiting the increase of population. It may be lowered either by a

[1] *Races and Immigrants in America*, p. 115.

retrogression in the stage of the arts — something which can hardly be conceived of under our present civilization — or by an increase in the ratio between men and land. Both of these suppositions assume that the amount of land remains stationary. If large tracts of good land are made available by any means, it gives opportunity for a decided improvement in the standard of living, and if we can conceive of large areas of good land being actually lost, there would be an inevitable lowering in the standard. In point of fact, standards of living are much more likely to go up than down. The history of civilization has been that of increasing standards. A retrogression in the stage of the arts is not likely to take place on a large scale; neither is it probable that, other things being equal, men will increase their rate of reproduction, for the very reason that such an increase would involve a lowering in the standard of living.

A standard of living, once established, has great tenacity, and people will suffer almost anything in the way of hardship before they will reduce it. If, for any reason, the dilemma is presented to a people of lowering their standard or of limiting their rate of increase, they will in general adopt the latter alternative. This will come about, not so much as the result of a conscious choice, as by the unconscious adaptation to surrounding conditions.[1] On the other hand, if natural conditions are gradually and steadily improving, it may frequently

[1] Professor Taussig says that there is evidence that "a standard of living so tenaciously held as to affect natural increase" is a force which acts on the numbers of the well-to-do in modern countries and is coming into operation in the upper tier of manual workmen. *Prin. of Econ.*, Vol. II, p. 152. In these upper groups it operates mainly upon the birth rate. In the lower groups, where there is less conscious control of the rate of reproduction, a decrease in the means of subsistence must almost inevitably result in an increase of the death rate, particularly of infants.

happen that the rate of reproduction will keep pace therewith, so that the standard of living will remain essentially the same. But if some sudden improvement in conditions appears — like the opening up of great stretches of new land, or some far-reaching improvement in the arts — the standard of living may rise appreciably before the forces of reproduction have had time to offset the new advantage. In other words, the rise of standards of living does not take place ordinarily by a steady and unvarying progress, so much as by successive steps or waves. The regular, continuous improvements in conditions account for lifted standards less than the exceptional, epochal occurrences. Such occurrences, being inherent in the cosmic laws and in the constitution of human nature, transpire with sufficient frequency to make possible great advances in standards of living over long periods of time.

Let us apply these principles to the case of the United States, and seek to determine what part immigration has played in their operation.[1] At the beginning of its career the United States was most favorably circumstanced as regards its standard of living. A people whose knowledge of the arts represented the highest product of the civilization of the day was set down in a practically uninhabited country, apparently unlimited in extent, and of marvelous fertility and abundance of natural resources. All of the old checks to population were removed, and there resulted a natural increase of numbers unprecedented for a corresponding area and extent of time in the annals of the race. But even this

[1] A certain amount of repetition of matter already given — particularly in the discussion of the effects of immigration on population — has seemed unavoidable in the following paragraphs. The matters of population, wages, and standards of living are obviously closely associated.

could not keep up with the development of natural resources, and a general standard of living was established far ahead of any other nation of the period.

Into this favored section of the earth's surface have been introduced ever increasing numbers of the lower classes of foreign nations. What has been their effect upon the prevailing standard of living? As a major premise, it will be granted that the standard of living of the working classes of the United States has been and still is superior to that of the nations which have furnished the bulk of the immigrants. Common observation and general testimony establish this beyond the need of proof. Particularly at the present time, if this were not so, very few of our immigrants would come, for, as we have seen, this is the great incentive which draws them.[1] It is significant, however, that the bulk of immigration has been recruited from more and more backward races of Europe as the decades have succeeded each other. There is not now the relative advantage for the peasant of England, Germany, or Scandinavia that there was during the first two thirds of the nineteenth century.[2] As regards the new immigrants — those who have come during the last thirty years — the one great reason for their coming is that they believe that on the wage which they can receive in America they can establish a higher standard than the one to which they have been accustomed. And this wage for which they are willing to sell their labor is in general appreciably below that which the native American workman

[1] See page 145.

[2] Mr. Earle Clark has shown by a comparison of recent figures that "the wages paid in the Massachusetts cotton mills do not enable the men employed to maintain a standard of living higher than that which the men employed in English mills can maintain upon English wages." *The Survey*, March 23, 1912.

requires to support his standard.[1] What does this mean? It means in the first place that the American workman is continually underbid in the labor market by vast numbers of alien laborers who can do his work approximately as well as he. But it means more than this. It means that he is denied the opportunity of profiting by those exceptionally advantageous periods which as we have seen recur from time to time, and provide the possibility of an improved standard. From his point of view these periods include any circumstances which occasion a sudden increase in the demand for labor — such as the establishment of a great new industry or the opening up of new territory by the completion of a railroad or recurring "good times" after a period of depression. If this new demand must perforce be met by the labor already in the country, there would be an opportunity for an increase in wages to the working man. But the condition which actually confronts the American workman at such a time is this — not only is the amount of wages which can be successfully demanded by labor profoundly influenced by the number and grade of foreign workers already in the country, but there comes at once, in response to improved conditions, a sudden and enormous increase in the volume of immigration. Thus the potential advantage which might accrue to the laborers already in the country is wholly neutralized. The fluctuating nature of the im-

[1] A further consideration, in addition to the difference in standards, which gives the foreigner an advantage over the native, is found in the different price levels here and abroad. In general the price levels in the countries from which the new immigration comes are lower than in the United States. This means that the immigrant, who saves part of his earnings for the support of a family in Europe, finds it possible to accept a lower wage than the native, who supports his family in this country, and yet keep his family on a standard equivalent to that of the American workman.

migration current is of vital importance to the American workman. It means that for him the problem is not that of taking the fullest advantage of a possibility of an improved standard, but of maintaining intact the standard which he has. We have seen that, in the long run, the only way in which he can do this is by limiting the size of his family.

The familiar argument that the immigrants simply force the native laborers up into higher positions is often urged in this connection. It is hard to see how any one can seriously hold this opinion. The fallacy of it has already been shown. It is, of course, perfectly obvious that at the present time most of the native workmen in industry are in the better paid positions, and that the lower grades are occupied by foreigners. But the question is, are there as many native workmen in high positions as there would have been in all positions if there had been no immigration? This is what the "forcing up" argument assumes, and the falsity of the position seems self-evident. It appears much more reasonable to believe that while a few native workers have been forced up, a vastly larger number are working side by side with the immigrants and earning approximately the same wages — to say nothing of that other body of native labor which the immigrants have prevented from ever being brought into existence.

Even if it were true that the native American himself is as well off as he would have been without immigration, that would not settle the matter. The question is that of the standard of living of the American workman. If the American workman happens to be a foreigner, it is just as important for the welfare of the nation, and of humanity, that he be properly housed, fed, clothed, educated, and amused as if he were a native. We would still have to face the fact of a standard continually retarded by accessions of newcomers, representing ever lower economic strata. Can we afford, as a nation, to allow the standard of living of the workman, whoever he is, to suffer in this way?

It appears that the forces whose working has been outlined in the preceding paragraphs can have only one logical outcome — namely, the depression of the wage scale of the American workman. If immigration has not absolutely lowered the wages and the standard of living of the American workman, it certainly has kept them from rising to the level that they otherwise would have reached. This is the opinion reached by many of the most careful students of immigration in the country, and it seems the only tenable one.[1] And after all, this is the really important thing. For it must not be forgotten that poverty, and riches, and standards of living are all purely relative terms. It is not a question of how much a man has, absolutely, as of how much he has in comparison with thosc around him, or how much he might have had. So that the common statement that the American workman of to-day has more of the comforts and luxuries of life than one in the same class fifty or one hundred years ago, by no means meets the case.

[1] Professor Taussig says, "The position of common laborers in the United States (that is, in the Northern and Western States) has been kept at its low level only by the continued inflow of immigrants. . . . These constant new arrivals have kept down the wages of the lowest group, and have accentuated also the lines of social demarcation between this group and others." *Principles of Economics*, Vol. II, p. 139. See also p. 234.

The same general opinion is expressed by Jenks and Lauck, *The Immigration Problem*, p. 195; by Hall, *Immigration*, pp. 123–131; by Commons, *Races and Immigrants in America*, pp. 151, 152, 159; by Miss Balch, *Our Slavic Fellow Citizens*, pp. 288–289; and by Wilkins (with reference to England), *The Alien Invasion*, p. 68.

If his share in the wonderful prosperity of the nation has not increased at least in the same proportion as that of the capitalist, or the professional man, or other members of society, then he has really suffered loss.

Immigration has seriously complicated the problems of the trade-unions in this country. Both the need and the difficulty of organization have been greatly increased. The traditional attitude of the unions toward immigration has been one of opposition. Restrictive measures, in particular the contract labor law, have met with their approval and support. But when the immigrants are once admitted to the country, the unions are under the necessity of either receiving them or suffering from their competition. A large body of unskilled laborers, with low standards, unaffiliated with the unions, is most prejudicial to the success of unionism. Alien races differ as to their adaptability to union control. Some of the races of southeastern Europe are looked upon as natural strike-breakers. The Irish, on the othe hand, are natural organizers, and at the present time tend to monopolize the direction of the unions. In some cases a large influx of foreigners has practically put the unions out of the running.[1] In others, the unions come to be made up largely of foreigners. At times it is necessary to organize the different racial elements into separate subgroups.[2]

On the other hand, the unions exercise a great educative influence on the immigrants — often practically the only one with which the adult foreigner comes in contact. They encourage him to learn English, imbue him with higher standards of living, and teach him the

[1] Cf. Byington, M., *Homestead*, pp. 6–11.

[2] Cf. Ripley, William Z., "Race Factors in Labor Unions," *Atlantic Monthly*, 93 : 299.

principles of independent thought and self-government.[1]

One of the chief objections to unrestricted immigration has always been the belief that it seriously increased the amount of pauperism and crime in the country, and added to the burden of relief and correction. We have seen how large a part this objection played in the early opposition to immigration, not only in colonial days, but during the first half of the nineteenth century. Even in our day, in spite of the laws prohibiting the entrance of criminals, paupers, and persons likely to become a public charge, there is a widespread impression that these two evils are increased through immigration.

The prominence of pauperism as an item in the immigration agitation has led to the production of a large amount of material on the subject. Nevertheless, most of it has been fragmentary and untrustworthy. This has been largely due to the incompleteness and lack of uniformity of the records of various eleemosynary institutions, and the difficulty of securing returns from all the manifold agencies of relief. At the present time, however, as a result of careful studies by the Immigration Commission, this is one of the very few effects of immigration about which we may feel justified in setting down definite conclusions.

According to statistics for the year 1850 a native-born population of 21,947,274 contributed 66,434 of the paupers who were wholly or partially supported in the country, while a foreign-born population of 2,244,602 contributed 68,538.[2] This was manifestly enough to arouse deep

[1] Cf. Stewart, Ethelbert, "Influence of Trade-Unions on Immigrants," in LaFollette, R. M., *The Making of America*, Vol. VIII, pp. 226 ff.

[2] Congressional Globe, 33d Cong., 2d Ses., 391.

consternation, and had not the current of immigration fallen off in the latter fifties we should probably have had a pauper restriction clause in the federal statutes long before we did. The enactment and enforcement of such a statute has prevented the recurrence of any such state of affairs in recent years. Nevertheless, as one glances at random over the reports of various charitable organizations he is impressed with the fact that the number of foreign-born paupers is out of all proportion to the total number of foreign-born inhabitants. Thus in Massachusetts in 1895 a foreign-born population of 30.6 per cent furnished 47.1 per cent of the paupers.[1] The report of the Associated Charities of Boston for 1894 stated that nearly all of their applicants were of foreign birth or parentage,[2] while in the same city, three years later, the Industrial Aid Society reported that 56 per cent of the men given work in the men's department were foreign-born, while 66 per cent of those aided by the Provident Aid Society were of this class.[3] The reports of the Wisconsin State Board of Charities for the years 1871 to 1898 show that, on the average, the foreign-born paupers considerably outnumber the native-born. Similar figures may be obtained from many sources.[4]

But the question can be settled only by taking the whole country into account. The Special Report of the Census Bureau on Paupers in Almshouses, 1904, gives the following figures as to the proportions of foreign and native paupers in the almshouses of the country (p. 6):

[1] Hall, P. F., *Immigration*, p. 161. [2] *Ibid.*, p. 165. [3] *Ibid.*, p. 161.

[4] See, for example, Mass. Report on the Unemployed, 1895, pp. 18, 116. Report Ohio State Board of Charities, 1902, pp. 178 ff.

Nativity	Per Cent Distribution of Paupers			Per Cent Distribution of General Population		
	1903	1890	1880	1903	1890	1880
Native white .	51.6	50.2	56.8	74.5	73.2	73.4
Foreign white .	39.3	37.8	34.6	13.4	14.6	13.1

These figures are the most authoritative and inclusive which there are, covering the almshouses of the country, and show a ratio of paupers among the foreign-born vastly in excess of the ratio of total population.

The paupers in almshouses, however, do not by any means include the total number of persons who belong in that category. There are large numbers of persons receiving relief, who never get inside the almshouses. To cover this class, the Immigration Commission made a special study of immigrants as charity seekers, which included the work done by the charity organization societies in forty-three cities, during the six months from December 1, 1908, to May 31, 1909. The cities were distributed as follows: North Atlantic states, 17; North Central states, 18; Southern states, 4; Western states, 4.

In the terminology of this report, a "case" means an individual or family assisted. The head of the case is the husband, if he is living at home, or the wife if widowed or deserted. If there are no parents or real family, the one upon whom the responsibility falls is the head of the case, or otherwise, the one asking assistance. The total number of cases for which information was secured is 31,685. Of these, the head of the case was foreign-born in 38.3 per cent of the cases, native-born of foreign father in 10.7 per cent, native-born white of native father, 39.9 per cent, and native-born of native negro father, 11 per cent. Of the persons represented, 37.5 per cent were native white of native father, and 42.3 per cent foreign-born. For exact conclusions, comparison should be made of the relation of the percentage of foreign-born paupers to the percentage of foreign-born in the total population in each separate city. For general purposes it is sufficient to note that in the cities of 25,000 or over in 1910 — which include all of the forty-three cities studied — the percentages of foreign-born were 20.2 for cities of 25,000 to 100,000, 22.1 for cities of 100,000 to 500,000, and 33.6 for cities of 500,000 and over.[1]

In fifteen out of the forty-three cities one half or more of the cases, classed by the head of the case, were foreign-born, Milwaukee standing at the head of the list with 67 per cent. In twelve out of the forty-three cities, more than 15 per cent of the cases were immigrants of the second generation, Milwaukee again standing at the head with 25.5 per cent. These two classes make up 92.5 per cent of all the cases for this city. There is evidently more than one thing that makes Milwaukee famous, with a possible connection between them.

In regard to the relative importance of the various foreign races in this respect, we find that the Germans show the largest proportion, amounting to 6.8 per cent of the total number of cases and 7.1 per cent of the total number of persons. The next in order are the Polish, with 6.5 per cent of the cases and 8.6 per cent of the persons, and the Irish, with 6.2 per cent of the cases, and 6.3 per cent of the persons.

As might be expected, the proportion of foreign-born is much larger (more than half) in the cities of the North Atlantic states than in the rest of the country, and very

[1] Abstract of Thirteenth Census, pp. 92, 95, 96.

small (10 per cent) in the southern cities. It is interesting to see how each city has its special problem. For instance, in Buffalo 32 per cent of all the cases were foreign-born Poles, and in Chicago 20 per cent were of the same class. In Hartford 15.1 per cent of the cases were foreign-born Irish, in Lynn 10.7 per cent were foreign-born Canadians (other than French), and 19.3 per cent foreign-born Irish. In Milwaukee 33.3 per cent were German, in Newport 22.2 per cent were Irish, in Orange 26.4 per cent Irish, in Rochester 14.6 per cent south Italian, in San Francisco 23.7 per cent were "other races." By way of comparison, it is interesting to note that in Washington 56.9 per cent of the cases were native-born negroes of native father. In ten of the cities, the native-born whites of native father were less than one fourth of the cases.

The Hebrews are noted for looking after their own poor, yet in six cities more than 5 per cent of all the cases were foreign-born Hebrews. In Brooklyn they made up 18.1 per cent, and in Malden 15.7 per cent. The Germans rank first among the foreign races in 18 cities, and tie with other races in three more. The Irish rank first in nine cities and tie with the Germans in one more. The Polish rank first in four cities and tie in one more.

One more piece of evidence may be taken from the Report of the Commissioner General of Immigration for 1908 (p. 98). It is there shown that in the charitable institutions (other than for the insane) in the United States, including Alaska, Hawaii, and Porto Rico, both public and private, there were, at the time this investigation was made, 288,395 inmates, of whom 19,572 were aliens, 40,453 naturalized citizens, and 228,370 native-born. The percentages are native-born 79.2 per cent and foreign-born 20.8 per cent. It appears that the proportion of foreign-born in institutions is not so extremely excessive as among those seeking a more temporary relief. This is what might be expected in the light of certain considerations respecting the make-up of the foreign-born group which are now to be considered.

It thus becomes evident that from whatever source the figures are taken, the percentage of foreign-born dependents is sadly out of proportion to their relative number in the general population. The absolute figures themselves are bad enough. But a further consideration of the composition of the foreign-born element will demonstrate that the actual showing is much worse than the figures would indicate on their face.

We have seen that as respects their economic efficiency the immigrants are a picked group. The same is true of the foreign-born in the country. This is especially evident as regards the age distribution. The following table, taken from the census of 1910, illustrates this point:

PER CENT OF NATIVE-BORN AND FOREIGN-BORN OF THE GENERAL POPULATION IN THE DIFFERENT AGE GROUPS[1]

Age Period	Native White				Foreign-born White	
	Native Parentage		Foreign or Mixed Parentage			
Under 5 years	13.2		14.2		0.8	
5 to 14 years	22.6		24.1		4.9	
15 to 24 years	19.7		21.6		15.8	
25 to 44 years	26.2	59.5	27.6	60.4	44.1	85.3
45 to 64 years	13.6		11.2		25.4	
65 years and over	4.4		1.4		8.9	

[1] Abstract of Thirteenth Census, p. 126.

It will be seen that there is a much larger proportion of the foreign-born in the middle-age groups, that is, in the period of greatest productivity, than of the native-born. There ought accordingly to be a smaller percentage of pauperism, rather than a larger one.

The sex distribution contributes a further element to this disparity. In 1910, in the native-born white population there were 102.7 males to 100 females. In the foreign-born white population there were 129.2 males to 100 females. This should lessen the liability of the foreign-born to pauperism.

Another factor which enters in to complicate statistical comparisons of pauperism among immigrants and native-born is the matter of the age at which persons become dependent, or, in the case of the immigrants, the number of years they have resided in the United States before they become dependent. There are two periods at which the immigrant is most likely to need relief. The first is immediately after landing, when he has exhausted his slender store of money, and has not yet found means of self-support. Seven per cent of the entire Jewish immigration to the United States, in one year, found it necessary to apply at the office of the United Hebrew Charities in New York, within a short time after their arrival. Relief granted at this time is liable to be temporary, and the immigrant cannot justly be considered a pauper. If he actually becomes dependent, he is of course liable to deportation.

The second, and vastly more important, period is several years after arrival, when the immigrant has exhausted the prime of his strength, and becomes one of the unfit in the keen struggle for economic existence. Those who become dependent at this time are likely to remain so for life. They are those who have been unable or unwilling to make provision for old age, perhaps being so dazzled by the apparent richness of America that they gave no thought to a possible future dearth, perhaps having sent all their meager savings year by year back to friends or relatives in the old country, possibly never having been able to earn more than a bare living wage. Individuals of this class make up the vast majority of the foreign-born paupers in our almshouses. The census of 1890 showed that 92 per cent of the foreign-born male paupers in the almshouses of the United States had been in this country ten years or more. The corresponding figures for the twelfth census show that out of 27,230 foreign-born paupers whose length of residence in this country is known, 26,171, or 96 per cent, had been here ten years or more.[1] The facts furnished by the investigation of the Immigration Commission in respect to persons aided by the Charity Organization societies are similar; it must be borne in mind, also, in respect to these cases, that they largely represent instances of temporary distress, rather than settled dependence. Of all the foreign-born heads of cases aided by these societies, 44 per cent had been in the United States twenty years or more, and 70.7 per cent ten years or more. When it is recollected how small a proportion of our foreign-born population have been in this country twenty years or over, or even ten years or over, it is manifest how misleading are comparisons in respect to pauperism between native-born and foreign-born, based on the total population of the two classes. Thus, according to the census of 1910, only 62.2 per cent of the total foreign-born population, and 60.2 per cent of the foreign-born population in the urban communities, had immigrated in

[1] *Paupers in Almshouses*, p. 101.

the year 1900 or earlier.[1] These facts also point to a possible great increase of pauperism among the foreign-born, as the average length of residence of this class increases.

The age of admission to the almshouse of the different population groups gives corroborative evidence along the same line. The following figures, taken from the census report on Paupers in Almshouses (p. 129), give the average age at admission of the different groups in 1904: native white of native parentage, 45.6 years; native white of foreign parentage, 41.7 years; native white of mixed parentage, 38.3 years; foreign-born white, 56.9 years. The high average age of the foreign-born is due in part to the relatively small number of foreign-born children in the country. But it is undoubtedly also an indication of the effectiveness of the system of examination in weeding out those whose liability to dependence in the near future can be detected. It furthermore adds to the apprehension with which we must look forward to the time when a greater proportion of our foreign-born residents will be above the specified age.

These considerations have an especial bearing on the effort to establish the relative tendency toward dependence of the different immigrating races. As one runs over tables of dependence or pauperism, arranged by nationality, he is impressed by the immense preponderance of the Germans and Irish among those listed. His first conclusion is likely to be that the popular idea of the greater desirability of these races over the newer immigrants is an error; but as soon as he recalls how much longer these races have been in this country, on the average, than the southeastern Europeans, he realizes that these tables, taken by themselves, are wholly unreliable

[1] Abstract of Thirteenth Census, pp. 215, 218.

as indicating relative tendencies among races. The following table will serve as an illustration:

PER CENT OF FOREIGN-BORN PAUPERS IN ALMS-HOUSES BY COUNTRY OF BIRTH[1]

Country of Birth	Enumerated, 1903	Admitted, 1904	Per Cent of Total Foreign-born Pop.
Ireland	46.4	41.2	15.6
Germany	23.3	18.4	25.8
England and Wales	8.7	8.8	9.0
Canada	4.8	6.5	11.4
Scandinavia	4.9	4.9	10.3
Scotland	2.5	2.6	2.3
Italy	1.0	3.1	4.7
France	1.4	1.3	1.0
Hungary and Bohemia	1.0	1.5	2.9
Russia and Poland	1.5	3.4	7.8
Other countries	4.5	8.3	9.2
	100.0	100.0	100.0

Taking these figures as they stand, we may say roughly that the Irish have thirty times as many paupers as those born in Russia and Poland, and forty-six times as many as the natives of Italy or Hungary and Bohemia, and twice as many as the Germans. But this evidently does not represent the relative tendencies to pauperism of these races. The first correction to be made is in regard to the relative numbers of each group in the total population. The Irish have 3.3 times as large a total population as the Italians, which reduces the ratio of relative tendency to pauperism down to about fourteen to one. By a similar reckoning we find that the Germans manifest only about one third the tendency to pauperism

[1] *Paupers in Almshouses*, pp. 19, 20.

that the Irish do, but 4.2 times as great as the Italians. But before even approximately accurate figures for the relative tendencies of these races can be secured, a further correction must be made for the relative average length of residence of the different groups. This unfortunately cannot be done in the present state of our information.

The figures in the preceding paragraph are of course merely the rudest approximations, but they serve to convey an idea of the extreme complexity of the problem of determining relative tendencies toward pauperism, and illustrate the utter worthlessness of the ordinary hit-and-miss comparisons which are made.

The Immigration Commission also made a study of the patients admitted to Bellevue and Allied Hospitals for the seven months period August 1, 1908, to February 28, 1909. The total number of charity patients or cases was 23,758. Of these 18.5 per cent were native-born of native father (2.5 per cent negro), 28.5 per cent native-born of foreign father, and 52.3 per cent foreign-born. The Irish foreign-born are far in the lead, having approximately one fifth of all the cases treated. If we add the Irish native-born of foreign father, we have over one third of the total.

In regard to the length of residence in the United States, the two danger periods noted above are well marked, as the following figures show:

PER CENT OF FOREIGN-BORN PATIENTS ACCORDING TO LENGTH OF RESIDENCE IN THE UNITED STATES

	Under 5 Years	5 to 9	10 to 14	15 to 19	20 or Over
Per cent . . .	28.0	14.2	8.9	10.8	38.1

The same distinction appears here between the old and new immigrants that we should expect — a high percentage for the old immigrants in the group over twenty, and a high percentage for the new immigrants in the group under five.

Whether the newer races, as their average length of residence in this country increases, will approach the degree of pauperism of the Irish and Germans, time alone can tell. The strictness of the tests of admission to the United States has steadily increased, and this has had the effect of giving the later immigrants a better showing, as a body, than the earlier ones. It is not impossible that time will prove that thrift and foresight are more distinguishing features of the southern races than of the northern, purchased though they are at the cost of a very low standard of living. A large amount of relief is undoubtedly sought by members of the newer races of immigrants. Among the Charity Organization cases studied by the Immigration Commission, 14.2 per cent of the Russian foreign-born heads of cases had been in the United States less than one year, and the following percentages of foreign-born heads of cases had been in the United States less than five years: Magyar, 44.1 per cent; Russian, 38.7 per cent; Italian, south, 26.6 per cent; Syrian, 25.8 per cent; Italian, north, 25.6 per cent. The races having the largest percentages of foreign-born heads of cases residing in the United States twenty years or over were: Irish, 71.3 per cent; Welsh, 70.4 per cent; French, 62.9 per cent; German, 62.8 per cent; Canadian, French, 58.5 per cent.

The Hebrews exhibit a large amount of dependence, but as they are almost wholly looked after by their own race they seldom appear in large numbers in the public reports. The United Hebrew Charities of New York, in the year 1904, received 10,334 applications at their relief bureau, representing 43,938 individuals, and expended for relief alone $124,694.45. In 1912 the number of applications had fallen to 7140, representing 31,835 individuals, but the expenditure for relief had risen to $254,188.71. This indicates, as the report points out, that the present applicants are in need of permanent relief to a much greater extent than those of a decade ago. The report of the same organization for October 1, 1901, gives the estimate that from 75,000 to 100,000 Jews in New York alone are not self-supporting.

There can be but one conclusion from the foregoing discussion, namely, that our foreign-born residents add to the burden of public and private relief an amount largely out of proportion to their relative numbers in the general population, and that this burden is likely to be an increasing one. Mr. Prescott F. Hall publishes an estimate that the total annual cost of caring for the foreign-born poor of New York State alone equals $12,000,000.[1] It is worth noting that while the expense of this burden of relief is borne by the public and by benevolent individuals, the real benefit goes to the employer of cheap labor. He secures his labor at a wage which will barely maintain its efficiency for a period of years, without any provision for the future, and when that period is over, and the laborer is no longer an efficient producer, he is cast aside with absolutely no responsibility resting on the employer for his future support or care.[2] At the

[1] *Immigration*, p. 168.

[2] Mr. Streightoff points out that even in a year of prosperity about half of the laboring families are not able to save anything, even on the close margin of living which they maintain. *Standard of Living*, pp. 24, 25.

customary rate of wages there seem to be but two alternatives open to the workingman's family — either to live on a frightfully low standard, and make some slight provision for the future, or to live on a somewhat higher standard and run the risk of dependence in old age or misfortune.[1] It is obvious that both of these are unqualifiedly bad.

As to the causes of this abnormal amount of pauperism Miss K. H. Claghorn makes the following statement: "While it is plain enough that foreign immigration has some connection with the problem of pauperism since common observation and all the statistics available unite in showing that the majority of the recipients of our charity, public and private, are of foreign birth, it is equally certain on the other hand that pauperism is not something that the immigrant brings with him, but is the result of a considerable period of life and experiences here."[2] This opinion, coming from so high a source, emphasizes two facts — first, that it is not altogether, if at all, the immigrant's "fault" that there is so much pauperism among this class. Those who have been paupers before, or seem likely to become so, are refused admission. Second, that there is something radically wrong in the industrial adjustment of the United States when so large a number of foreigners, who come here primarily for motives of financial betterment, and who are not by nature thriftless, are unable during a long period of faithful labor to lay up anything against the period of helplessness. We cannot escape the accusing finger which points toward the United States, demanding rec-

[1] Cf. Byington, M. F., *Homestead*, p. 184.

[2] Claghorn, K. H., "Immigration in its Relation to Pauperism," *Annals of the American Academy of Political Science*, 24: 187.

ognition of the fact that we are by no means prepared to accept the tremendous responsibility of admitting unlimited numbers of aliens whose entire future destiny depends upon the soundness of our political, social, and economic fabric.

It may be worth while to note some of the general causes which lead to pauperism among the foreign-born. (1) Lack of intelligence. This is sometimes represented by figures of illiteracy. This is hardly a fair basis of judgment, however, as illiteracy may be often the result of poor opportunity, rather than of low intelligence. Nevertheless it is true that the average immigrant of the present generation is probably inferior to the average native workingman, and hence is handicapped in the competition with him. (2) Lack of industrial training. Most of the immigrants have had no training in their home countries to fit them for higher industrial pursuits, and many of those who have, find that it is not adapted to American conditions. (3) Lack of foresight. This must not be generally asserted of the immigrant class, for undoubtedly a large proportion of them are well equipped with an appreciation of the future. Yet in many cases, the ease with which a comparatively comfortable living may be secured in the first years of residence, and the apparently inexhaustible riches of the United States, combine to make the alien neglectful of a future period of dearth. (4) Large families. The birth rate of the foreign-born is a high one, and a large number of young children is always a predisposing cause of pauperism in a struggling family. In this connection some significant figures are furnished by the investigation of the charity organization cases, made by the Immigration Commission, and already referred to. Of all the foreign-born male persons, aided by these societies, who were twenty years of age or over, 81.5 per cent were married, 5 per cent deserted, separated, or widowed, and only 13.5 per cent single. Of the females, 62.3 per cent were married, 33.9 per cent deserted, separated, or widowed, and only 3.8 per cent single. When we remember how much the single men outnumber the married men in the general population of the foreign-born above twenty years of age, we see that if the time ever comes when immigration becomes more of a family matter than at present — in many ways a condition much to be desired — it must inevitably bring with it a tremendous increase in the amount of foreign-born pauperism. (5) Money sent home. If the situation of the immigrant was such that these large sums could be retained in this country, as a reserve fund against future want, his liability to pauperism would be much diminished. This, of course, cannot be expected, since much of this money is sent back to meet obligations which no one would wish the immigrant to evade. In cases where it is sent back to support a family, it is doubtless a more economical arrangement than if the wife and children were maintained in the United States. (6) Low wages, and the maladjustment between the supply of labor and the demand. Enough has already been said to establish this as a fundamental condition, and it is the proximate cause of pauperism in the majority of cases. The attempt to analyze and classify the causes of pauperism is unsatisfactory at best; yet a certain amount of light may be shed on the subject in this way if carefully done. The Immigration Commission's Report on Immigrants as Charity Seekers assigns the cases studied to certain general causes in the following proportions:

PERCENTAGE OF THE TOTAL NUMBER OF CASES ASSIGNABLE TO THE SPECIFIED CAUSES

Cause	Per Cent
Lack of employment or insufficient earnings	59.0
Death or disability of breadwinner	28.7
Death or disability of another	18.9
Neglect or bad habits of breadwinner	18.7
Old age	6.2
Other causes	10.0[1]

There is no great difference in the proportions of the different causes in the different general groups. It may be significant to note that the per cent of cases due to the neglect or bad habits of the breadwinner is a little larger for the native-born white of native father than for the foreign-born, and larger for the native-born white of foreign father than for either. If we take persons instead of cases, the showing of the native-born of foreign father is even worse. The relatively small number of cases due to this cause — the only one which may be charged directly to the "fault" of the breadwinner — indicates that the difficulty lies rather with the industrial system of the United States than with the culpability of the individual.

That assimilation, in so far as it is represented by ability to speak English, will not remedy the situation is indicated by some suggestive figures given in the report on Charity Seekers above quoted. It is shown (p. 70) that of the total number of persons assisted, six years of age or over, belonging to non-English speaking races, 76.3 per cent were able to speak English. Now in the report on Manufactures and Mining it appears

[1] The total of per cents adds up to more than 100 as more than one cause is often reported for the same case.

that only 53.2 per cent of the foreign-born employees studied, belonging to non-English speaking races, could speak English. That is, the percentage of dependents, who are so far "assimilated" as to be able to speak English, is much greater than the percentage of those who are at work, in spite of the fact that the former class includes younger children than the latter. This harmonizes with the fact already demonstrated, that dependent foreigners have been in this country much longer than the average of their group. It also lends color to the suggestion made by a charity worker, that one reason why the newer immigrants do not appear in larger numbers on the books of philanthropic organizations is that they are not yet "on to the ropes," and that as they become familiarized with American methods, they will seek relief in increasing numbers.

The subject of crime is customarily linked with that of pauperism in the discussions of immigration, and the same claim is frequently made, viz. that immigration has increased the amount of crime in this country. The attempts at proof of this assertion generally follow the same method adopted in the case of pauperism, that is, they consist in an examination of the relative tendency toward criminality of the general groups of native-born and foreign-born. In other words, the line of argument is, if the foreign-born manifest a larger proportion of criminals among their number than do the native-born, all increases in the foreign-born population will mean a more than proportional increase in crime for the country as a whole. There is, however, another way in which immigration might operate to increase crime. That is, by interfering with the natural adjustment of economic relations between different classes, it may so alter the condition of the native-born as to lead to an increase in crime in this class. For instance, it has been claimed that a large proportion of the "hobo" class (who are, to be sure, not necessarily criminal) are native Americans who have been forced out of employment by foreign competition. In a similar way, other individuals may have been driven into active crime. This proposition, whatever the incidental evidence for or against it, is manifestly incapable of statistical proof, and for any semi-mathematical demonstration we must rely on the other method of approach.

In the matter of crime the effort to make generalizations is complicated by the fact that it is necessary to take into account, not only the number of crimes, but the nature and severity of the criminal act. Tests of criminality, to be accurate, should include quality as well as quantity. This is obviously very difficult to do. We are accustomed in everyday phraseology to speak of one crime as being worse than another. Presumably crimes against the person are more serious than crimes against property. In the case of crimes against property, we might naturally consider it "worse" to steal $1000 than $5, but it would not necessarily be so.

These conditions frequently result in an injustice to the immigrant. The police and court records of our great cities show an amazing proportion of crimes chargeable to the foreign population. For instance, out of 71,253 persons held for trial or summarily tried and convicted in the Magistrates' Courts of New York City in 1907, only 30,261, or considerably less than half, were born in the United States. But when these records are studied more closely it becomes apparent that a large share of the offenses of the foreign-born are violations of the city ordinances, — offenses which are comparatively trivial in themselves do not indicate any special tendency toward criminality, and are in many cases intimately associated with a low station in life. The moral character of alien groups may in this way be seriously misrepresented.

Nevertheless, if comparisons are to be made at all, they must rest upon such records as these, and such allowances as are possible be made afterwards. Figures of this kind are available in the publications of the Census Bureau, the Commissioner General of Immigration, and the Immigration Commission. In the census report on Prisoners we find that of the prisoners enumerated in the United States on June 30, 1904, 76.83 per cent were native-born, and 23.7 per cent foreign-born. In the general white population, ten years of age or over, in 1900, 80.5 per cent were native-born and 19.5 per cent foreign-born. If a due allowance is made for a disproportionate growth of the foreign-born population between 1900 and 1904, the relative proportions of prisoners among the two groups would be approximately equal. Of the white prisoners of known nativity committed during 1904 the percentages were as follows:

Nativity	Total	Major Offenders	Minor Offenders
Native-born . .	71.2 per cent	78.3 per cent	69.9 per cent
Foreign-born. .	28.8 per cent	21.7 per cent	30.1 per cent

The somewhat less favorable showing made by the foreign-born in the case of those committed than of those enumerated, is accounted for by the large proportion of minor offenses among the foreign-born. Many minor offenders, serving short sentences, would not be included at all in the enumeration. Over half the major offenders among the foreign-born had been in the United States ten years or more, and about two thirds of the minor offenders.

According to the Report of the Commissioner General of Immigration for 1908 (p. 98), there were in the penal institutions of the United States, including Alaska, Hawaii, and Porto Rico (in which the figures are not large enough to affect the conclusions materially), in 1908, 149,897 inmates, of whom 15,323 were aliens, 8102 naturalized, and 126,562 native-born. Thus the percentage of native-born was 84.4 and of foreign-born 15.6.

The Immigration Commission made a careful study of the matter of crime among the immigrants, reviewing the foregoing data, and collecting some original data of its own, covering 2206 convictions in the New York City Court of General Sessions from October 1, 1908, to June 30,1909. This is, so far as known to the Commission, the first time that any court in the United States had made a record of the race of persons convicted in it. This fact illustrates the utter inadequacy of the data for making any deductions as to the influence of immigration upon crime in the United States. Not only courts, but police departments and penal institutions, are very lax in their keeping of records in this respect.

In response to the questions, "Is the volume of crime in the United States augmented by the presence among us of the immigrant and his offspring?" and "If immigration increases crime, what races are responsible for such increase?" the Commission says that no satisfactory answer has ever been made, or can ever be made, without much more complete data than have ever been collected or are available. Certain general conclusions, however, have been reached by the Commission, which harmonize with those reached by other students, and are worthy of acceptance as far as they go. First, "No satisfactory evidence has yet been produced to show that immigration has resulted in an increase in crime disproportionate to the increase in adult population. Such comparable statistics of crime and population as it has been possible to obtain indicate that the immigrants are less prone to commit crime than are native Americans."[1] Second, "Immigration has, however, made changes in the character of crime in the United States."[2] These changes have been in the direction of an increase in offenses of personal violence, and offenses against public policy (disorderly conduct, drunkenness, violation of corporation ordinances, etc.), some of which are incident to city life, and probably in offenses against chastity. There does not appear to have been any increase in the majority of offenses against property, or, as they may be better called, gainful offenses.[3]

Comparing the different races as regards criminality, it appears that the Irish stand at the head as regards the total number of offenses and the Germans next. In respect to major offenses, however, the Germans stand first, while the Irish again take first place in the minor offenses.[4] The Germans are much addicted to crimes against property, the Irish and Scotch to drunkenness, Greeks and natives of Russia to violations of corporation ordinances, and immigrants from France, Russia, Poland, and Canada to crimes against chastity. The Italians

[1] Rept. Imm. Com., Immigration and Crime, Abs., p. 7. [2] *Ibid.*, p. 8.

[3] Cf. Hourwich, I. A., "Immigration and Crime," *Am. Jour. Soc.*, 17:4, p. 478.

[4] Census Report on Prisoners, 1904, pp. 42, 45.

are preëminent in crimes of violence or crimes against the person.[1]

It is even more difficult to postulate the causes of crime than of pauperism. Until the criminologists have furnished us with a more efficient means of determining the causes of crime in general, there can be no profit in the attempt to classify the causes of crime among a particular group of the population. In respect to the nature of crime committed by different races, there seems to be something in the racial character of some of our immigrants which predisposes them in a certain direction, as exemplified in the preceding paragraph. There is also evidence that among some of the newer immigrants, crime is largely a matter of economic position. This is well illustrated by the case of the Greeks. Among the members of this very recent immigrant group, there has been a noteworthy decline in the average of criminality within the last few years, and the explanation appears to be that the crimes of the Greeks are such as correspond with a low economic situation — violations of corporation ordinances, of the sanitary code, etc. As a larger and larger proportion of the individuals of this nationality rise above this lowly estate, the percentage of crime among them falls off correspondingly.[2] This emphasizes once more the responsibility of the United States for some of the evil conditions for which we habitually blame the immigrants.

There are two particular forms of crime which are closely associated with foreign groups in the United States. These are the Black Hand outrages and the

[1] *Ibid.* Cf. also Bingham, T. A., "Foreign Criminals in New York," *No. Am. Rev.*, September, 1908, p. 381; Rept. Imm. Com., Imm. and Crime, Abs.; *Americans in Process*, pp. 199–207; *The City Wilderness*, p. 172.

[2] Fairchild, H. P., *Greek Immigration to the United States*, p. 203.

white slave traffic. The former of these is confined almost wholly to persons of the Italian race. In some of its features it recalls the Molly Maguire occurrences of a generation earlier. In fact, the resemblance between the Irish societies and the Mafia of southern Italy was noted in a contemporary magazine article at the time of the disturbances in the anthracite region of Pennsylvania.[1] In both cases no organic connection between the societies in the new world and the old is manifest. In fact, the best judgment in regard to the Black Hand appears to be that there is no real organization in existence in America, but that individuals of Italian race use the power of the dreaded name to accomplish their own ends. Like the Molly Maguires, the Black Hand operators utilize warning letters, but they differ from them in that their purpose is often, if not usually, blackmail, which was seldom the case with the Irish society.

The white slave traffic has aroused tremendous public interest during the last few years, and has been thoroughly exploited in the daily and periodical press. Only the essential features, particularly in their bearing on immigration, need to be reviewed in the present connection. Not all of the girls concerned in this business are immigrants, nor are all the persons who draw a revenue from it foreigners; yet the various investigations of the subject have demonstrated that the whole trade is fundamentally an affair of our foreign population.

One surprising thing about this traffic is that essentially it is an economic phenomenon. It is not a perverted sex passion which demands the perpetuation of the inhuman system; it is the desire for large and easy profits, and the life of indolence that goes with them, which

[1] "Molly Maguire in America," *All the Year Round*, New Series, 17: 270.

actuates the promoters of the traffic, while on the part of the alien women it is frequently the desire for larger earnings which brings them to our shores. The demand has to be stimulated.

There are two classes of these alien girls who are brought over. One consists of innocent girls who are brought over under a false understanding. The incentive is usually a false promise of employment or of marriage. Sometimes false marriages, and occasionally actual marriages, are resorted to. With this class of subjects, the male importer is naturally the most successful. All kinds of inducements are offered by the procurer, including an apparently sincere love-making. About the only inducements which female importers can offer to such girls are easier or more lucrative employment. The other class, probably constituting a large majority, are women who have already been leading an immoral life on the other side, and come in the hope of bettering their prospects, although they recognize the power of the importer.

These women and girls are usually brought over second class, and every conceivable artifice is employed to deceive the inspectors. When a girl has been safely introduced into the country, she is completely in the power of the man who controls her. The supposition is that the man furnishes protection and care to the girl in return for her earnings. She is sometimes kept in a disorderly house, sometimes in a hotel or other resort, but always where the man can keep control of her. She is thoroughly frightened, and every device is employed to keep her from communicating with any outside sources of relief, or escaping. She is often deprived of street clothing, so as to make escape impossible. She is kept heavily in debt, so that there may be a legal claim over her. Only a very small part of her earnings is given to her, and she is charged outrageous prices for all the supplies which are furnished her. Her life is one of hopeless and terrible degradation, and she has nothing to look forward to except a wretched and continually descending existence, and an early death.

Alien women are particularly desirable to the promoters of this traffic because their lack of connections in this country, and their ignorance of the language and customs of the country make it more difficult for them to escape or to make trouble for their men than in the case of native girls. In addition to the terrible wrongs wrought upon the women themselves, this practice has resulted in an increase in the number of prostitutes in the United States, in the introduction and dissemination of dangerous diseases, and in the introduction of various forms of unnatural vice, more degrading and terrible than even prostitution itself in its ordinary form.

The great majority of the alien women found by the Immigration Commission engaged in these pursuits, as well as the men who prosecute the traffic, are French and Hebrews. Belgians are largely engaged in it, according to Commissioner Bingham. Germans are numerous, and there are a few Irish and Italians, with of course a scattering of individuals of other races.

A number of these women are detected at the port of entry and returned, and a good many are deported. But it is a practice very difficult of detection, and it is not easy to get at the facts in regard to its extent in this country. It is certain that the class of abandoned women in this country is largely recruited in this way. Commissioner Bingham estimated in 1908 that there were more than 100,000 such women on the Pacific coast and in Mexico, who had come in through New York.

No evidence has been found to justify the suspicion that there was an organization controlling this traffic in this country. But those engaged in the trade naturally are acquainted with each other, and are always ready to help each other against a common enemy. They have various meeting places where they get together for gambling, conference, and divers forms of recreation.

It has been proven that this traffic is slavery in more than name, as girls are sometimes sold directly by one person to another. The new federal law is designed to put a check to all practices of this sort, by making it illegal to transport women or girls from one state to another for immoral purposes. The efforts of the Immigration Commission and other governmental agencies within the last two or three years have accomplished a good deal in breaking up some of the resorts, and deporting or imprisoning the culprits. But while the traffic has received a serious setback, it is by no means killed. This is emphatically one of the things where eternal vigilance is the price of safety. Nothing short of a sweeping change in public opinion and practice will ever put it out of the way beyond the possibility of resurrection.[1]

In respect to juvenile delinquency the most unenviable place is held by the native-born children of immigrants. They not only manifest two or three times as great a tendency toward crime as the native-born children of native parents, but they are much more criminal than foreign-born children. Of the juvenile delinquents com-

[1] Cf. Bingham, T. A., *The Girl that Disappears*, and "Foreign Criminals in New York," *No. Am. Rev.*, September, 1908; and Rept. Imm. Com., Importing Women for Immoral Purposes; *New York Times*, Jan. 17, 1912, p. 1.

mitted during 1904, according to the census report, 76.7 per cent were native white. This percentage was made up as follows: native parentage, 37.6 per cent; foreign parentage, 24.9 per cent; mixed parentage, 9.7 per cent; parentage unknown, 4.5 per cent. An exact comparison of the children of native parents and of foreign parents in this respect would require information as to the total number of the two classes in the country in the year in question, which is not available. But it cannot be supposed that the number of native-born children of foreign parents compared with the number of native-born children of native parents in anything like the ratio shown in the above figures. This high degree of criminality is attributed by Professor Commons and by the Immigration Commission largely to concentration in the cities. Whatever the cause, this tendency toward lawlessness among the second generation of immigrants is indisputable, and is one of the most disturbing elements in the whole situation.[1]

Still another way in which the immigrant becomes a burden upon the American public is through insanity. The laws are very strict in regard to the admission of aliens who are liable to be subject to this misfortune. Yet it is impossible to prevent the entrance of large numbers who ultimately appear in the category of the insane. The maladaptation of the immigrant to his environment shows itself in this way perhaps as clearly as in any other.

In the institutions for the insane, both public and private, in the United States, including Alaska, Hawaii,

[1] Cf. Census Report on Prisoners, 1904, p. 236; Commons, *Races and Immigrants in America*, p. 170; Hall, *Immigration*, p. 150; Bingham, *No. Am. Rev.*, September, 1908; Addams, *Twenty Years at Hull-House*, p. 252; *Americans in Process*, p. 209.

and Porto Rico, in 1908, there were, according to the Report of the Commissioner General of Immigration, 172,185 inmates. Of these 25,066 were aliens, 25,128 naturalized citizens, and 121,451 native-born. Thus the percentages were 70.5 per cent native-born and 29.5 per cent — nearly one third — foreign-born.[1]

An even larger percentage of foreign-born appears among the insane persons enumerated in hospitals in continental United States on December 31, 1903 — 34.3 per cent of the white insane of known nativity[2] — while of the persons received at Bellevue and Allied Hospitals for treatment for insanity during the period of the investigation of the Immigration Commission, 63.4 per cent were foreign-born, and 36.6 per cent native-born. Moreover, among the native-born, more than half (20.6 per cent of the total) were native-born of foreign father.

Summing up the matter of insanity, the Commission speaks as follows: "For the high ratio of insanity among the foreign-born, several causes have been assigned, and while it is difficult to determine the values of the various factors it is probably true that racial traits or tendencies have a more or less important influence. A further cause of mental disease is probably to be found in the total change in climate, occupation, and habits of life which the majority of immigrants experience after arrival in the United States."

The efficiency of the inspection in regard to feeble-mindedness is shown by the very small proportion of foreign-born of that class appearing in the statistics. This is an affliction which can more easily be detected

[1] Rept. Com. Gen. of Imm., 1908, p. 98.

[2] *Insane and Feeble-minded in Hospitals and Institutions*, 1904, p. 20.

than the liability to insanity, of which there may be no observable indication at the time of admission.[1]

[1] Rept. Imm. Com., Immigration and Insanity. Cf. Williams, William, "Immigration and Insanity," address before the Mental Hygiene Conference, New York City, Nov. 14, 1912. Yet the burden of the feeble-minded immigrant is becoming so strongly felt in New York as to lead the Chamber of Commerce of that state to send resolutions to Congress urging better provisions for excluding this class. *The Survey*, March 2, 1912.

CHAPTER XVI

INDUSTRIAL EFFECTS. CRISES. SOCIAL STRATIFICATION. POLITICAL EFFECTS

It has been observed already that the great argument for immigration during the past half century has been the economic one. The main defense for immigration has rested upon the claim that it has decidedly increased the industrial efficiency of the American people, and has facilitated the development of our resources, and the expansion of industry, at a rate which would not have been possible otherwise. The facts in regard to the age, sex, and physical soundness of the immigrants are mustered to establish them as a peculiarly efficient industrial body.

This contention rests upon two assumptions. First, that our alien residents constitute a net addition to the total population of the country; second, that if there had been no immigration, and the population, particularly that part of it which constitutes the labor supply, had been smaller, that there would have been no inventions and improvements in the way of labor-saving machinery which would have permitted the same amount of work to be accomplished with a smaller amount of labor.

In the light of what has been said in regard to the relation between immigration and the growth of population in Chapter XI, the first of these claims, at the very least, is open to serious question. While the proposition, as has already been stated, is absolutely incapable of mathematical proof, there nevertheless is every reason to believe that our immigrants have not meant a gain in the labor supply, but the substitution of one labor element for another. Not only have the immigrants in general displaced the natives, but the newer immigrants have displaced the older ones in a wide variety of industries and occupations. This latter process has gone on before our very eyes; it is manifest and perfectly comprehensible. A careful consideration of it may make it easier to understand how the same result, in a more subtle way, has been accomplished in the case of the native-born.

The displacement of the English, Irish, Welsh, and German miners in the anthracite region of Pennsylvania by Italians and Slavs is a familiar fact.[1] The Italians are being driven out of the bootblacking business, and other of their characteristic trades, by the Greeks. The Irish laborers on the railroads have been largely supplanted by Italians, Slavs, and Greeks. The "Bravas," or black Portuguese, have forced the Poles, Italians, and, in large measure, the Finns from the cranberry bogs of Massachusetts.[2] Granite City and Madison, Illinois, have witnessed a succession of English, Irish, German, Welsh and Polish, Slovak and Magyar, Roumanian, Greek, and Servian, Bulgarian and Armenian laborers in their industries.[3]

In these cases it is plain that while some of the displaced individuals have gone into other, very likely higher, occupations, the real substitution has been the

[1] Roberts, P., *Anthracite Coal Communities*, pp. 19 ff.; Warne, *Slav Invasion.*

[2] Jenks and Lauck, *Immigration Problem*, p. 92.

[3] *Ibid.*, p. 72. For numerous other cases see Rept. Imm. Com., Imms. in Mf. and Min., Abs., pp. 226 ff.; Commons, J. R., *Races and Immigrants in America*, pp. 151, 152.

concomitant of a cessation of immigration from the older sources. The north Europeans, being unwilling to meet the competition of races industrially inferior to them, have either ceased emigrating in large numbers, or else are going elsewhere. At any rate they do not come here. The diminution of the supply of native labor has been brought about in an analogous way, though in this case the restrictive forces operate upon the principles of reproduction instead of immigration.

Even though it be granted that the numerical supply of labor has been somewhat increased, there has been an undeniable decrease in the efficiency of the individual laborer, as is attested by the uniformly superior earnings received by the native-born as compared with the foreign-born, or the old immigrant as compared with the new. As Dr. Peter Roberts has pointed out,[1] there seems to be a sort of Gresham's law which operates in the field of labor. The fittest to survive in an unregulated economic competition of races is the one least advanced in culture, the one whose demands in respect to comforts and decencies are lowest, even the one, it sometimes seems, whose industrial productiveness per individual is lowest. It is this fact which gives so dark an aspect to the industrial future of the United States under unregulated immigration.[2]

In regard to the second assumption — that a smaller

[1] *Anthracite Coal Communities*, p. 20.

[2] For an opposite view of this whole question, see Hourwich, I. A., *Immigration and Labor*. This book, which should be consulted for an elaborate defense of free immigration from the economic point of view, has come to hand too late to be cited at frequent intervals throughout the present work. It is an ingenious production, but so full of inconsistencies, inaccuracies, and misleading statements that to criticize it in detail would require a volume in itself. The refutation of many of Dr. Hourwich's arguments may be found throughout the pages of the present work.

labor supply would not have been offset by an increase in invention — we are again confronted with an impossibility of proof, one way or the other. The economists tell us that one of the great incentives to invention is a scarcity of labor, and also that many of the greatest inventions have been made by men who are working daily with machines, and consequently are in a position to discover improvements that may be made. There is at least some reasonable basis for the belief that if the absence of immigration to this country had resulted in a smaller laboring force, the greater pressure on employers to secure machinery, and the greater intelligence of the machine worker, would together have brought about such a betterment of labor-saving machinery as would have resulted in a total production equal to what we have actually witnessed.

It is inconceivable that in America, of all countries, any needed work should have to be neglected because of the lack of a foreign labor element, or because of a shortage of labor in general.[1] It is hard to see how in a nation the majority of whose citizens are healthy and intelligent there can be any real shortage of labor. What there can be, is a shortage of labor *at a given wage*. In a prosperous community there may be industries into which a sufficient number of laborers will not go, at the wages which the promoters are originally willing to pay. But if there is an actual social need for those industries, wages will rise to a point high enough to attract a sufficient number of workers, however irksome or disagreeable the employment. No self-respecting community

[1] Mr. W. L. Anderson, who is not an extreme advocate of the opinion that immigration has not increased population, nevertheless says, "Certainly the common assertion that without the foreigner the development of the country would have halted disastrously is fallacious." *The Country Town*, p. 154.

ought to expect industries to be carried on within its borders for which it is not willing to pay such a price as will enable the workers to subsist in reasonable comfort and decency. If there are any industries carried on in the United States which, in the absence of a foreign labor supply, would have to be abandoned, because the native-born laborers or their children would refuse to go into them, it simply means that society is not yet ready to pay a fit price for the products of those industries.

This brings us to the question of the effect of immigration on the amount and distribution of wealth in the United States. It is frequently pointed out that we receive yearly a net increase of half a million or so of able-bodied laborers, for whose upbringing and education we, as a nation, have expended nothing. It is stated that it is cheaper to import laborers than to raise them. The truth of this assertion depends first of all on the quality of the laborer. It may be cheaper in the long run to rear laborers of the American type than to import Portuguese, Russians, and East Indians. Furthermore, while we do not pay directly for the laborers, we pay a great deal for their residence in this country. The estimated amount of money sent abroad by aliens in 1907, $275,000,000, is probably higher than the total for an average year. Suppose $200,000,000 be taken as an average amount.[1] These remittances do not represent commercial payments for imports, but are savings actually withdrawn from the wealth of this country and sent abroad to be expended there. So that for each able-bodied alien laborer who enters the country something

[1] Some allowance needs also to be made for the amount of money brought in. See p. 202.

like $400 goes out. In a sense a good deal of this money might be considered as actual payment for the importation of the laborers, since much of it goes for traveling expenses, debts incurred to provide for emigration, etc.[1]

Whether immigration has increased either the total or per capita wealth of the nation may be open to question. One thing, however, is certain — it has profoundly affected the distribution of wealth in the country. It has been sufficiently demonstrated that the successive waves of immigration have represented an ever cheapening labor supply. As the country has grown in wealth and prosperity the employers of labor have found that they could secure their workers at relatively, if not absolutely, lower rates decade after decade. Whenever conditions became such that the native laboring force, if left to themselves, might have successfully demanded better conditions or higher remuneration, there has appeared an inexhaustible supply of foreign laborers, ready and willing to take what was unsatisfactory to the natives, or less. The workman already in the country, whether native or foreign, has been continually robbed of his advantage. Thus the gap between capital and labor, between the rich and the poor, has grown ever wider. Not only have wages been kept from rising, but conditions of labor have persisted and been tolerated which an American laboring force would never have submitted to. The accounts of terrible accidents in mines and foundries arouse sincere feelings of sympathy in our breasts for the poor foreigners who have to suffer so. They would incite a storm of indignant protest which would not be stilled

[1] Speare, Charles F., "What America Pays Europe for Immigrant Labor," *No. Am. Rev.*, 187 : 106.

until remedies were provided, if those who are subjected to such conditions were our own kin brothers.[1]

There is still another characteristic feature of our economic life, between which and the immigration movement a close and peculiar connection can be traced. This is the frequent recurrence of economic depressions, or crises. The causal relation between these events and the variations in the volume of the immigration current has already been mentioned. There is also a causal relation between these conditions and the fluctuations in the outgoing stream of aliens. This fact has received no little attention of late years, and it has been frequently pointed out that a period of depression in this country is followed by a large exodus of the foreign-born.

The popular interpretation of this fact is that this emigration movement serves to mitigate the evils of the crisis by removing a large part of the surplus laborers, until returning prosperity creates a demand for them again. The Italian, who displays the greatest mobility in this regard, has been called the safety valve of our labor market. Thus the movements of our alien population are supposed to be an alleviating force as regards crises.

The question arises, however, in this connection, whether there is not a converse causal relation; in other words, whether the conditions of immigration are not, partly responsible for the recurrence of these periods. Professor Commons takes this view of the matter, and in his book, *Races and Immigrants in America*, demonstrates how immigration, instead of helping matters,

[1] Cf. Balch, *op. cit.*, p. 302. Fred C. Croxton and W. Jett Lauck find the recent immigrants largely responsible for dangerous and unhealthful conditions in mines and factories, and trace a direct causal relation between the extensive employment of recent immigrants and the extraordinary increase of mining accidents in recent years. Spiller, G., *Inter-Racial Problems*, pp. 218–219.

is really one of the causes of crises. His conclusion is that "immigration intensifies this fatal cycle of 'booms' and 'depressions,'" and "instead of increasing the production of wealth by a steady, healthful growth, joins with other causes to stimulate the feverish overproduction, with its inevitable collapse, that has characterized the industry of America more than that of any other country."[1]

The few pages which Professor Commons devotes to this topic are highly suggestive, and show careful study of the subject. The author, however, at the time this book was written, was handicapped by the lack of data regarding the departures of aliens, which, as we have seen, have since become available. The fact that within the period since the collection of these figures began, the United States has experienced, and recovered from, a severe depression, makes the study of this matter at the present time particularly profitable.

First of all, it will be desirable to see just what the facts of immigration and emigration during this period are; then we shall be prepared to attempt their interpretation. The accompanying table (p. 349) gives the number of aliens admitted to and departed from the United States, and the net increase or decrease of population resulting therefrom, by months, from January, 1907, to December, 1910 (with the exception of the figures of departures for the first six months of 1907, which are not available).

The figures for arrivals given in this table include both immigrant and nonimmigrant aliens, a distinction which has been observed with some care since 1906. The column of departures also includes emigrant and nonemigrant aliens.[2]

[1] pp. 155–159. [2] For the distinction between these classes see p. 125.

TABLE SHOWING THE NUMBER OF ALIENS ADMITTED TO AND DEPARTED FROM THE UNITED STATES, AND THE NET GAIN OR LOSS IN POPULATION RESULTING THEREFROM BY MONTHS, FROM 1907 TO 1910

Month	1907			1908		
	Admitted	Departed	Gain (+) or Loss (−)	Admitted	Departed	Gain (+) or Loss (−)
January	54,417			33,058	60,233	− 27,175
February	65,541			30,266	50,688	− 20,422
March	139,118			43,537	43,506	+ 31
April	145,256			55,220	65,721	− 10,501
May	184,886			48,245	61,251	− 13,006
June	154,734			41,094	60,482	− 19,388
July	107,535	46,198	+ 61,337	37,133	51,508	− 14,375
August	111,135	44,317	+ 66,818	39,606	47,569	− 7,963
September	115,287	43,734	+ 71,553	56,635	43,884	+ 12,751
October	129,564	55,826	+ 73,738	60,715	41,916	+ 18,799
November	132,647	94,440	+ 38,207	50,965	38,609	+ 12,356
December	77,107	88,432	− 11,325	61,111	33,416	+ 27,695
	1909			1910		
January	54,975	18,061	+ 36,914	57,472	20,256	+ 37,216
February	81,992	15,100	+ 66,892	66,072	17,672	+ 48,400
March	135,040	22,550	+ 112,490	152,020	30,894	+ 121,126
April	138,382	24,315	+ 114,067	153,915	40,886	+ 113,029
May	127,139	31,190	+ 95,949	148,822	38,740	+ 110,082
June	100,542	32,274	+ 68,268	115,793	36,119	+ 79,674
July	77,944	27,940	+ 50,004	82,191	39,056	+ 43,135
August	71,992	28,450	+ 43,542	91,460	37,206	+ 54,254
September	85,088	29,950	+ 55,138	100,456	43,023	+ 57,433
October	92,372	30,838	+ 61,534	100,334	39,189	+ 61,145
November	98,020	39,134	+ 58,886	86,144	54,700	+ 31,444
December	78,527	39,539	+ 38,988	68,794	61,814	+ 6,980

It is not necessary to take account of these discriminations for the purposes of the present study.

Turning then to the table, we observe that the monthly

average of arrivals during the first six months of 1907 was a high one. Following a large immigration during the last six months of the preceding year, this made the fiscal year ending June 30, 1907, the record year for immigration in the history of the country. For the next four months the stream of immigration continued high, considering the season, and the number of departures was moderate. Early in October, however, there were signs of disturbance in the New York Stock Exchange. On the sixteenth there was a crash in the market, and within a week the panic had become general. It reached its height on October 24, and continued for many weeks after.[1] The response of the alien population to this disturbance was almost immediate, and manifested itself first in the emigration movement. In November the number of departures almost doubled. But the immigrants who were on the way could not be stopped, and in spite of the large exodus, there was a net gain of 38,207 during the month. The next month, December, however, saw a marked decrease in the stream of arrivals, which, accompanied by a departure of aliens almost as great as in November, resulted in a net decrease in population of 11,325 for the month. During the first six months of 1908 the number of arrivals was small, and the departures numerous, so that, with the exception of March, each month shows a net loss in population. During July the number of departures began to approach the normal (compare the months in 1908 with 1907 and 1910), but the arrivals were so few that there was still a decrease for the months of July and August. In September, 1908, the balance swung the other way, and from that time to the present every month with the exception of December,

[1] White, *Money and Banking*, third edition, Ch. XVIII.

1911, has shown a substantial increase in population through the movement of aliens.

Thus we see that the period during which the number of alien laborers in the United States was decreasing was confined to the months December, 1907, to August, 1908, inclusive.[1] By the end of July, 1908, the effects of the crisis were practically over as far as departures are concerned. It is evident, then, that the effects of the crisis on emigration were immediate, but not of very long duration. During the months of November and December, 1907, when the distress was the keenest, there were still large numbers of aliens arriving. But when the stream of immigration was once checked, it remained low for some time, and it was not until about January, 1909, that it returned to what may be considered a normal figure. The reasons for this are obvious. The stream of immigration is a long one, and its sources are remote. It takes a long time for retarding influences in America to be thoroughly felt on the other side. The principal agency in checking immigration at its source is the returning immigrant himself, who brings personal information of the unfortunate conditions in the United States. This takes some time. But when the potential immigrants are once discouraged as to the outlook across the ocean, they require some positive assurance of better times before they will start out again.

Now what catches the public eye in such an epoch as this is the large number of departures. We are accustomed to immense numbers of arrivals and we think little about that side of it. But heavy emigration is a phe-

[1] The fact that in March, 1908, there was a gain of 31 is not a coincidence. The month of March is always a busy one in immigration, as it opens the spring season, and this influence was sufficient to check the prevailing movement temporarily.

nomenon, and accordingly we hear much about how acceptably our alien population serves to accommodate the supply of labor to the demand. But if we stop to add up the monthly figures, we find that for the entire period after the crisis of 1907, when emigration exceeded immigration, the total decrease in alien population was only 124,124 — scarcely equal to the immigration of a single month during a fairly busy season. This figure is almost infinitesimal compared to the total mass of the American working people, or to the amount of unemployment at a normal time, to say nothing of a crisis.[1] It is thus evident that the importance of our alien population as an alleviating force at the time of a crisis has been vastly exaggerated. The most that can be said for it is that it has a very trifling palliative effect.

The really important relation between immigration and crises is much less conspicuous but much more far-reaching. It rests upon the nature and underlying causes of crises in this country. These are fairly well understood at the present time. A typical crisis may be said to be caused by speculative overproduction, or overspeculative production. Some prefer to call the trouble underconsumption, which is much the same thing looked at from another point of view. Professor Irving Fisher has furnished a convenient and logical outline of the ordinary course of affairs.[2] In a normal business period some slight disturbance, such as an increase in the quantity of gold, causes prices to rise. A rise in prices is accompanied by increased profits for business men, because the rate of

[1] Mr. F. H. Streightoff shows that at the time the census of 1900 was taken, 2,634,336 or 11.1 per cent of all males over ten years of age who were engaged in gainful occupation in the United States were unemployed three months or more during the year. See *Standard of Living*, p. 35.

[2] Fisher, Irving, *The Purchasing Power of Money*, pp. 58 *seq.*

interest on the borrowed capital which they use in their business fails to increase at a corresponding ratio. If prices are rising at the rate of two per cent annually, a nominal rate of interest of six per cent is equivalent to an actual rate of only about four per cent. Hence, doing business on borrowed capital becomes very profitable, and there is an increased demand for loans.

This results in an increase of the deposit currency, which is accompanied by a further rise in prices. The nominal rate of interest rises somewhat, but not sufficiently, and prices tend to outstrip it still further. Thus the process is repeated, until the large profits of business lead to a disproportionate production of goods for anticipated future demand, and a vast overextension of credit. But this cycle cannot repeat itself indefinitely. Though the rate of interest rises tardily, it rises progressively, and eventually catches up with the rise in prices, owing to the necessity which banks feel of maintaining a reasonable ratio between loans and reserves. Other causes operate with this to produce the same result. The consequence is that business men find themselves unable to renew their loans at the old rate, and hence some of them are unable to meet their obligations, and fail. The failure of a few firms dispels the atmosphere of public confidence which is essential to extended credit. Creditors begin to demand cash payment for their loans; there is a growing demand for currency; the rate of interest soars; and the old familiar symptoms of a panic appear. In this entire process the blame falls, according to Professor Fisher, primarily upon the failure of the rate of interest to rise promptly in proportion to the rise in prices. If the forces which give inertia to the rate of interest were removed, so that the rate of interest would fluctuate readily with prices, the great temptation to expand business unduly during a period of rising prices would be removed. It may well be conceived that there are other factors, besides the discrepancy between the nominal and real rates of interest, that give to business a temporary or specious profitableness, and tend to encourage speculative overproduction. But the influence of the rate of interest resembles so closely that resulting from immigration, that Professor Fisher's explanation is of especial service in the present discussion.

The rate of interest represents the payment which the entrepreneur makes for one of the great factors of production — capital. The failure of this remuneration to keep pace with the price of commodities in general leads to excessive profits and overproduction. The payment which the entrepreneur makes for one of the other factors of production — labor — is represented by wages. If wages fail to rise along with prices, the effect on business, while not strictly analogous, is very similar to that produced by the slowly rising rate of interest. The entrepreneur is relieved of the necessity of sharing any of his excessive profits with labor, just as in the other case he is relieved from sharing them with capital. It would probably be hard to prove that the increased demand for labor results in further raising prices in general, as an increased demand for capital results in raising prices by increasing the deposit currency. But if the demand for labor results in increasing the number of laborers in the country, thereby increasing the demand for commodities, it may very well result in raising the prices of commodities as distinguished from labor, which is just as satisfactory to the entrepreneur. This is exactly what is accomplished when unlimited immigration is allowed. As soon as the conditions of business produce an increased demand for labor, this demand is met by an increased number of laborers, produced by immigration.

In the preceding paragraph it has been assumed that wages do not rise with prices. The great question is, is this true? This is a question very difficult of answer. There is a very general impression that during the last few years prices have seriously outstripped wages. Thus Professor Ely says, "Wages do not usually rise as rapidly as prices in periods of business expansion."[1] R. B. Brinsmade stated in a discussion at a recent meeting of the American Economic Association that "our recent great rise of prices is acknowledged to be equivalent to a marked reduction in general wages."[2] Whether this idea is correct, and if correct, whether this effect had transpired in the years immediately previous to 1907, cannot be definitely stated. The index numbers of wages and prices given in the *Statistical Abstract of the United States*, for 1909 (p. 249), seem to show that during the years 1895 to 1907 money wages increased about *pari passu* with the retail prices of food, so that the purchasing power of the full-time weekly earnings remained nearly constant.

But whether or not money wages rose as fast as prices in the years from 1900 to 1907, one thing is certain, they did not rise any faster. That is to say, if real wages did not actually fall, they assuredly did not rise. But the welfare of the country requires that, in the years when business is moving toward a crisis, wages should rise; not only money wages, but real wages. What is needed is some check on the unwarranted activity of the entre-

[1] Ely, R. T., *Outlines of Economics*, p. 268.

[2] Bulletin of the American Economic Association, April, 1911, p. 253.

preneurs, which will make them stop and consider whether the apparently bright business outlook rests on sound and permanent conditions, or is illusory and transient. If their large profits are legitimate and enduring, they should be forced to share a part of them with the laborer. If not, the fact should be impressed upon them. We have seen that the rate of interest fails to act as an efficient check. Then the rate of wages should do it. And if the entrepreneurs were compelled to rely on the existing labor supply in their own country, the rate of wages would do it. Business expands by increasing the amount of labor utilized, as well as the amount of capital. If the increased labor supply could be secured only from the people already resident in the country, the increased demand would have to express itself in an increased wage, and the entrepreneur would be forced to pause and reflect. But in the United States we have adopted the opposite policy. In the vast peasant population of Europe there is an inexhaustible reservoir of labor, only waiting a signal from this side to enter the labor market — to enter it, not with a demand for the high wage that the business situation justifies, but ready to take any wage that will be offered, just so it is a little higher than the pittance to which they are accustomed at home. And we allow them to come, without any restrictions whatever as to numbers. Thus wages are kept from rising, and immigration becomes a powerful factor, tending to intensify and augment the unhealthy, oscillatory character of our industrial life. It was not by mere chance that the panic year of 1907 was the record year in immigration.

Against this point of view it may be argued that the legitimate expansion of business in this country requires the presence of the immigrant. But if business expansion is legitimate and permanent, resting on lasting favorable conditions, it will express itself in a high wage scale, persisting over a long period of time. And the demand so expressed will be met by an increase of native offspring, whose parents are reaping the benefit of the high standard of living. A permanent shortage of the labor supply is as abhorrent to nature as a vacuum. Expansion of any other kind than this ought to be hampered, not gratified.

There is one other way in which immigration, as it exists at present, influences crises. In considering this, it will be well to regard the crisis from the other point of view — as a phenomenon of underconsumption. Practically all production at the present day is to supply an anticipated future demand. There can be no overproduction unless the actual demand fails to equal that anticipated. This is underconsumption. Now the great mass of consumers in the United States is composed of wage earners. Their consuming power depends upon their wages. In so far as immigration lowers wages in the United States, or prevents them from rising, it reduces consuming power, and hence is favorable to the recurrence of periods of underconsumption. It is not probable, to be sure, that a high wage scale in itself could prevent crises, as the entrepreneurs would base their calculations on the corresponding consuming power, just as they do at present. But a high wage scale carries with it the possibility of saving, and an increase of accumulations among the common people. It is estimated at the present time that half of the industrial people of the United States are unable to save anything.[1] This in-

[1] Streightoff, *The Standard of Living*, p. 24.

crease in saving would almost inevitably have some effect upon the results of crises, though it must be confessed that it is very difficult to predict just what this effect would be. One result that might naturally be expected to follow would be that the laboring classes would take the opportunity of the period of low prices immediately following the crisis to invest some of their savings in luxuries which hitherto they had not felt able to afford. This would increase the demand for the goods which manufacturers are eager to dispose of at almost any price, and would thereby mitigate the evils of the depressed market. It is probably true that the immigrant, under the same conditions, will save more out of a given wage than the native, so that it might seem that an alien laboring body would have more surplus available for use at the time of a crisis than a native class. But the immigrant sends a very large proportion of his savings to friends and relatives in the old country, or deposits it in foreign institutions, so that it is not available at such a time. Moreover, our laboring class is not as yet wholly foreign, and the native has to share approximately the same wage as the alien. Without the immense body of alien labor, we should have a class of native workers with a considerably higher wage scale, and a large amount of savings accumulated in this country, and available when needed.

On the other hand, it may be argued that if the desire to purchase goods in a depressed market should lead to a large withdrawal of cash from savings banks and similar institutions, it might tend to augment rather than alleviate the evils of a money stringency. There seems to be much force to this argument. Yet Mr. Streightoff tells us that in a period of hard times the tendency is for the poorer classes to increase their deposits, rather than diminish them.[1] On the whole, it seems probable that a large amount of accumulated savings in the hands of the poorer classes would tend to have a steadying influence on conditions at the time of a crisis, and that by preventing this, as well as in other ways, immigration tends to increase the evils of crises.

In closing this discussion, it may be interesting to note what are the elements in our alien population which respond most readily to economic influences in this country, and hence are mainly accountable for the influences we have been considering. As stated above, the annual reports of the Commissioner General of Immigration give very complete data as to the make-up of the incoming and outgoing streams by years. Thus in the fiscal year 1908 there were 782,870 immigrant aliens and 141,825 nonimmigrant aliens admitted. Of the nonimmigrant aliens, 86,570 were individuals whose country of last permanent residence and of intended future residence were both the United States; that is, they were alien residents of this country who had been abroad for a brief visit. These are the birds of passage in the strictest sense, in which we shall use the term hereafter. In the same year there was a total exodus of 714,828 aliens, of whom 395,073 were emigrants and 319,755 nonemigrants. The former class includes those who have made their fortune in this country and are going home to spend it, and those who have failed, and are going home broken and discouraged — a very large number in this panic year. The latter class includes aliens who have had a permanent residence in the United States, but who are going abroad to wait till the storm blows over, with the

[1] Streightoff, *The Standard of Living*, p. 111.

expectation of returning again — true birds of passage outward bound. There were 133,251 of these. The balance were aliens in transit, and aliens who had been in this country on a visit, or only for a short time. In 1909 there were 751,786 immigrant aliens and 192,449 nonimmigrant aliens. Of the nonimmigrants 138,680 were true birds of passage according to the above distinction — a large number and almost exactly equal to the number of departing birds of passage in the previous year. The storm is over, and they have come back. The departures in that year numbered 225,802 emigrant and 174,590 nonemigrant aliens. These numbers are considerably smaller than in the previous year, but are still large, showing that the effects of the crisis were still felt in the early part of this fiscal year. The number of birds of passage among the nonemigrant aliens, 80,151, is much smaller than in the previous year. In 1910 there were 1,041,570 immigrant aliens and 156,467 nonimmigrant aliens. In the latter class, the number of birds of passage, 94,075, again approximated the corresponding class among the departures of the previous year. The departures in 1910 were 202,436 emigrant aliens and 177,982 nonemigrant aliens, of whom 89,754 were birds of passage. This probably comes near to representing the normal number of this class. A careful study of these figures confirms the conclusion reached above. While a crisis in this country does undoubtedly increase the number of departing aliens, both emigrant and nonemigrant, and eventually cuts down the number of arrivals, the total effect is much smaller than is usually supposed, and taken in connection with the fact that the stream of arrivals is never wholly checked, the influence of emigration in easing the labor market is absolutely trifling.

Comparing the different races in regard to their readiness to respond to changes in economic conditions, it appears that the Italians stand easily at the head, and the Slavs come second. In 1908, in the traffic between the United States and Italy, there was a net loss in the population of this country of 79,966; in 1909 a net gain of 94,806. In the traffic between this country and Austria-Hungary there was a loss in 1908 of 5463; in 1909 a gain of 48,763. In the traffic with the Russian Empire and Finland there was a gain of 104,641 in 1908 and a gain of 94,806 in 1909. This shows how unique are the motives and conditions which control the emigration from the two latter countries. The emigrants from there, particularly the Jews, come to this country to escape intolerable conditions on the other side, not merely for the sake of economic betterment. They prefer to endure anything in this country, rather than to return to their old home, even if they could.

Hand in hand with the economic disparity caused by immigration has come an increasing social stratification.[1] This is based partly on wealth, partly on race. Already certain occupations are regarded as the special province of certain nationalities, and native parents recoil from the prospect of having their children enter them to work side by side with the aliens. Only the beginnings of these changes are as yet manifest, and no one can foretell what the outcome will be. But even the beginnings must give us pause. There can be no more pernicious social classification in a nation than one based on race. Distinctions resting on wealth, religion, or education can be overcome, potentially at least. Distinctions of birth affect only a small proportion of a society, and exist only in nations

[1] See quotation from Professor Taussig, footnote, p. 309.

long habituated to them. But distinctions of race affect the entire population are fundamental, and can never be obliterated except as assimilation is so perfect that race is forgotten. No effort of the individual can blot out his racial identification. The most familiar example yet developed in the United States is that of the Hebrews. However sincerely we may admire their fine racial traits, however closely we may associate with individuals of the race, we cannot deny that they constitute a separate body in our population in many respects.[1] Summer hotels are closed to them, or else other people avoid those resorts. Americans move out of the sections of cities where they are moving in. Select clubs are closed to them. It is an indictment against the American people that these things are so. We, who pose as the friends of all races, however downtrodden and despised, should be ready to take them into equality with us when they seek refuge on our shores. Both Hebrews and Americans may resent the bald statement of such facts. Can we deny their truth?

Nor is it only in high society, nor only among Americans, that this friction is felt. In the slums of our cities bitter feeling exists between the Italians and the Jews.[2] Nor is racial antagonism confined to any two or three races.[3] Employers of labor find it wholly expedient to arrange their workers in groups of the same nationality.[4] Austria-Hungary is an example of the conditions that may

[1] Israel Zangwill, in an address before the Universal Races Congress in London, said, "Even in America, with its lip-formula of brotherhood, a gateless Ghetto has been created by the isolation of the Jews from the general social life," Spiller, G., *op. cit.*, p. 270. Cf. also Peters, Madison C., *The Jews in America*, pp. 123–138.

[2] "The Jews associate little with other nationalities, principally from the choice of the other nationalities." Bushee, F. A., *City Wilderness*, p. 42.

[3] Cf. *Americans in Process*, pp. 61–63, 157.

[4] Jenks and Lauck, *Immigration Problem*, p. 172.

result when too many jarring nationalities are included within a national territory. But the racial groups in Austria-Hungary do not compare in diversity with those which are gradually forming in the United States.

In the political aspects of the immigration situation there has been a peculiar reversal of public opinion in the last three quarters of a century. In the days of the Native Americans and the Know-nothings, the uneasiness was mainly due to the fear that too many aliens would acquire the rights of citizenship. Then it was the naturalized foreigner who was the undesirable. Nowadays, the fear is that the foreigners will ignore the priviliges of citizenship, and a high percentage of naturalization is a test of desirability in any foreign group. This change may be attributed to a change in the situation of the United States, and to a difference in the character and causes of immigration. During the first half of the nineteenth century the United States was essentially a new country. Political questions were predominant, and the memory of the men who fell in the fight for freedom was still fresh in the minds of their sons. The immigrants of the period, on the other hand, were actuated to a large extent by the desire for political freedom, and were keen to secure all the power possible in this country. At the present time, the predominating interests are wholly economic, and even the political questions of the day have an economic flavor. At the same time, the motives of the immigrants are almost wholly economic. So the jealousy between native and foreigner now concerns itself mainly with the industrial relations, and anything which indicates an inclination on the part of the alien to ally himself permanently with the interests of the country is welcomed. The temporary immigrant was an almost unknown quantity in the old days.

The naturalization laws of the United States have undergone only slight modifications in the past hundred years.[1] The main provisions of the present laws are as follows: In order to become a citizen of the United States an alien must follow out the following method of procedure: At least two years before he is admitted he must file a preliminary declaration of intention. To do this he must be at least eighteen years old. This declaration shall state that it is his bona-fide intention to become a citizen of the United States, and to renounce all other allegiance to a foreign power, and shall set forth his name, age, occupation, personal description, place of birth, last foreign residence and allegiance, date of arrival in the United States, name of the vessel, if any, by which he came, and present place of residence in the United States. Not less than two years nor more than seven years after he has made application, he shall present a petition in writing, signed in his own handwriting, stating the essential facts about himself, including his declaration of allegiance to the United States, and disclaiming belief in anarchy, or belief in or practice of polygamy.

This petition shall be verified by at least two credible witnesses, who are citizens of the United States, who shall state that they have known the applicant to be a resident of the United States for a period of at least five years continuously, and of the state or territory at least one year immediately preceding, and that they have personal knowledge of his good moral character and general fitness to become a citizen of the United States.

[1] Cf. Franklin, Frank G., *Legislative History of Naturalization in the United States*.

With this petition is filed a certificate from the Department of Commerce and Labor, stating the date, place, and manner of his arrival, and also his declaration of intention. He shall swear in open court his allegiance to the United States and renounce all other allegiance.

In accordance with a recent law, no alien can now be naturalized without an ability to speak the English language, unless he has made entry upon the public lands of the United States. No person may be naturalized within thirty days preceding the holding of a general election in the territorial jurisdiction of the court. Chinese are not admissible to citizenship.

A woman who is married to a citizen of the United States is herself a citizen, provided she herself might be legally naturalized. This provision has been the subject of considerable attention lately on account of the practice of women engaged in the white-slave traffic marrying a citizen in order to avoid deportation. The Commissioner General in his report for 1910 recommended that a more definite statement be made of this clause, admitting of no doubt as to its interpretation.

Children of naturalized citizens who were under the age of twenty-one at the time of the naturalization of their parents, if dwelling in the United States, are considered citizens, as are children of citizens, born outside of the United States.

If any alien who has received a certificate of citizenship shall, within five years thereafter, go to the land of his nativity or to any other foreign country, and take up permanent residence therein, it shall be deemed evidence of his lack of intention to become a permanent citizen of the United States at the time of filing his application, and warrants the canceling of his certificate.

According to the regulations of September 15, 1910, clerks of courts are instructed not to receive declarations of intention or file petitions for naturalization from other aliens than white persons, and persons of African nativity or of African descent.

Jurisdiction to naturalize aliens is conferred on the following courts: United States circuit and district courts in any state, United States district courts for the territories, the supreme court of the District of Columbia, and the United States courts for the Indian territory; also all courts of record in any state or territory, having a seal, a clerk, and jursidiction in actions at law or equity, or law and equity, in which the amount in controversy is unlimited.

Since the establishment of the division of naturalization by the act of June 29, 1906, the business of naturalization has been in the hands of the Bureau of Immigration and Naturalization.

The statistics of naturalization for the five years 1908–1912 are as follows:

Year	Declarations filed	Petitions filed	Certificates granted
1908	137,229	44,029	25,963
1909	145,794	43,161	38,372
1910	167,226	55,038	39,206 [1]
1911	186,157	73,644	55,329
1912	169,142	95,627	69,965

[1] Repts. Comm. Gen. of Imm.

In addition to the certificates granted there were, in 1912, 9635 certificates denied. These were for a variety of causes, the most important of which was failure of the petitioners to prosecute them, so that they were stricken from the docket. Of those which were actually refused the largest single cause was incompetent witnesses.

There has been a large amount of fraud and trickery in connection with naturalization, and presumably it has not wholly ceased. This has been due partly to a lax attitude on the part of some of the court officials, and partly to the physical impossibility of giving proper attention to the number of candidates who apply, with the existing machinery. There is a story of one judge in New York City who issued nearly seven thousand papers in October, 1891, at the rate of two a minute.[1] Many states have been very lax in their requirements for voting. In some states aliens have been allowed to vote in both state and federal elections, sometimes after a residence of only six months.[2]

Even where naturalization is desired by recent immigrants, it is not always for the most commendable reasons. Sometimes the motive is the desire for a better chance of securing employment,[3] sometimes the facilitating of entrance into the United States after a trip abroad. Natives of some foreign countries, particularly Turkey, have come to the United States with the express intention of securing citizenship, in order to return to their native land, and carry on business under the protection of the American flag, which carries with it greater guarantees than their own. A special law, passed to put a stop to such practices as these, provides that when a naturalized alien has resided two years in the foreign

[1] Hall, P. F., *op. cit.*, p. 194.

[2] *Ibid.*, p. 186. For a general discussion of these abuses, see Hall, *op. cit.*, Ch. IX.

[3] *American in Process*, p. 157.

state from which he came, or five years in any other foreign state, he forfeits his citizenship.[1]

Of all foreign races, the Irish have taken by far the largest place in politics in this country. According to Professor Commons, the "ward boss" is the logical product of the mixture of nationalities in the various divisions of a city, and the Irishman is the logical man for the work.[2] "The Irishman has above all races the mixture of ingenuity, firmness, human sympathy, comradeship, and daring that makes him the amalgamator of races."[3] Possibly a sense of humor ought to be added to these qualifications. In the eyes of Professor Commons, such a system makes it the merest chance if the best man is elected, and subverts our whole system of representative government.[4] It seems beyond question that the existence of separate racial groups in a community, each with its own prejudices and group loyalty, must have a very disturbing influence on the course of elections. Measures become of much less import than men in the minds of the voters, and in the choice of men race rather than fitness is often the determining element.

[1] Act of March 2, 1907. [2] Cf. Champernowne, Henry, *The Boss*, Ch. XIII.

[3] Commons, J. R., *Races and Immigrants in America*, p. 182.

[4] Cf. throughout, Commons, *op. cit.*, Ch. VIII.

CHAPTER XVII

THE NEW PROBLEM OF IMMIGRATION

IT was stated on an earlier page that the immigration situation, in most of its important characteristics, presents an entirely new aspect to the men of this generation, and that these changes might be looked for under six general heads, as follows: race, volume, distribution, economic condition of the United States, native birth rate and quality of the immigrants. We are now prepared to consider the truth of this assertion.

In regard to race, nothing further need be said. Sufficient facts are already before the reader to establish the fact that the racial aspect of the situation has undergone a sweeping and significant change in the last thirty years. The change in volume has naturally been one of degree, not of kind. But the change in degree has been a profound one — more so than is often admitted. It has been pointed out occasionally, as a sedative to the fears aroused by the immense immigration of the twentieth century, that while the positive immigration has increased tremendously, it has not increased at so great a rate as the population of the country. The ratio between immigration and total population was higher in the early fifties and early eighties than at any subsequent period. The assumption is that if we could successfully assimilate the immigrants of the earlier period, we certainly ought to be able to take care of those of to-day. But the question of assimilation depends not only upon the ratio of immigrants to total population, but upon the proportion of foreign-born population already in the country. In this connection the following figures are significant. The number of foreign-born to 100,000, native-born in the population of the country at the time of the last seven censuses was as follows:

1850	10,715	1890	17,314
1860	15,157	1900	15,886
1870	16,875	1910	17,227
1880	15,365		

It thus appears that the proportion of foreign-born, even at the time of the census of 1900, after a decade of very slight immigration, was much higher than at the time of the beginning of large immigration, while the last census, after the enormous immigration of the past ten years, shows a proportion of foreign-born higher than at any previous census, except that of 1890. Now it is the proportion of foreign-born to native-born which determines the assimilating power of the nation, so that without this correction the comparison between immigration and total population is inadequate and misleading. It is as if a fireman whose steam boiler lacked a safety valve was warned that his gauge was going up more and more rapidly all the time, and he replied, "Never mind, the pressure is not coming in so fast, compared to what I already have, as it was awhile ago."

Another circumstance which affects the ability of the country to assimilate immigrants, and in which there has been a marked change during the history of immigration, is the ratio of men to land, upon which much emphasis has already been laid. As the amount of unappropriated and unsettled land diminishes in any country, the need of new settlers also diminishes, while the difficulty of assimilation and the possible evils resulting from foreign population proportionally increase. In the case of the United States the first and simplest comparison to make is that between immigration and the total territory of the nation. In this, as in the subsequent comparisons, it will be desirable to leave Alaska out of consideration. The enormous extent of that inhospitable region, to which practically none of our immigrants ever find their way, if included in the reckoning, would simply confuse the issue. The gross area of the United States, exclusive of Alaska and Hawaii, at the time of the different censuses, has been as follows: 1790 and 1800, 827,844 square miles; 1810, 1,999,775 square miles; 1820, 2,059,043 square miles; 1830 and 1840, the same; 1850, 2,980,959 square miles; 1860 down to the present, 3,025,600 square miles.[1]

Estimating the immigration before 1820 at 10,000 per year, and using the official figures after that date, we find that the immigration by decades from 1791 to 1910 was as follows:

1791–1800 . . .	100,000	1851–1860	2,511,060
1801–1810 . . .	100,000	1861–1870	2,377,279
1811–1820 . . .	98,385	1871–1880	2,812,191
1821–1830 . . .	143,439	1881–1890	5,246,613
1831–1840 . . .	599,125	1891–1900	3,687,564
1841–1850 . . .	1,713,251	1900–1910	8,795,386

Combining these two sets of figures, it appears that for each immigrant coming to this country during the decades specified, there was at the close of the decade the following number of square miles of territory in the United States:

[1] Twelfth Census, Vol. I, p. xxxii. Includes land and water. Figures for land area alone are given in *A Century of Population Growth*, p. 54. Taking land in this restricted sense would not materially affect the conclusions.

1800	8.278	1860	1.205
1810	19.998	1870	1.273
1820	20.927	1880	1.076
1830	14.355	1890	.570
1840	3.437	1900	.824
1850	1.739	1910	.347

This table illustrates forcibly the fact that from the point of view of the need of new settlers immigration at the present time is a vastly different matter from what it has ever been before in the history of our country. This impression is strengthened if we make another comparison, which is even more significant for our purposes, viz. the relation of immigration to the public domain, that is, to the land which still remains unclaimed and open to settlement. If there were still large tracts of good land lying unutilized, and available for settlement, as there have been in other periods of our history, we could take comfort in the thought that as soon as the incoming aliens caused too great a congestion in any region, the surplus inhabitants would overflow, by a natural process, into the less thickly settled districts. Let us consider what the facts have to show in this respect.

In 1860 there were, as nearly as can be estimated, 939,173,057 acres of land lying unappropriated and unreserved in the public domain. In 1906 there were 424,-202,732 acres of such land, representing the leavings, after all the best land had been chosen. In other words, for each immigrant entering the country during the decade ending 1860 there were 374 acres in the public domain, at least half of it extremely valuable farm land. In 1906, for each immigrant entering during the previous ten years, there were 68.9 acres, almost wholly arid and worthless.

The fact that the immigrants in this country do not, to any great extent, take up this unclaimed public land does not destroy the significance of this comparison. As long as there was a strong movement of the native population westward, it was not so much a matter of concern, if large numbers of foreigners were entering the Atlantic seaboard. And this was exactly the case during the middle of the nineteenth century. This was the period of the great internal migration to the new lands of the Middle West. In point of fact also, at this time, many of these pioneers were actually immigrants. It is scarcely necessary to say that nothing comparable to this is going on at the present time. The frontier, which has had such a determining influence on our national life, is a thing of the past. Of the 424,202,732 acres remaining in the public domain in 1906, only a very small part consisted of valuable farm lands, such as existed in great abundance when the Homestead Act was passed in 1862. Evidence of this fact is furnished by the act recently passed allowing homesteads of 640 acres to be taken up in certain sections of Nebraska, where it is impossible for a man to make a living from less. Not only are the incoming hordes of aliens not now counterbalanced by an important internal migration, but there is an actual movement, of noteworthy dimensions, of ambitious young farmers from the United States to the new and cheaper wheat lands in Canada.

This set of conditions may be stated in another way by saying that the United States has changed from an agricultural to a manufacturing and commercial nation.[1] In the early nineteenth century the rural family was the

[1] This change has been furthered, according to Professor Taussig, by immigration. *Principles of Economics*, Vol. I, p. 545.

typical one, to-day it is the urban family. Then the simplicity and independence of the farm gave character to the national life; to-day it is the complexity and artificiality of the city which govern. The nineteenth century was a period of expansion. Particularly in the earlier part of it was the subduing of new land the fundamental consideration of national development. This was the period of internal improvements, the building of roads and canals, and later of railroads. It was the adolescence of the American people. At such a period the great demand is for accessions of population, and it is no wonder that many of the writers of that day were frank in their demands for the encouragement of immigration. And even in the thirties and forties, though the miserable shipping conditions and the large number of incoming paupers aroused a countercurrent of opinion, still the immigrants found a logical place on the great construction works of the period, as well as on the vacant arable lands.

This period is past. The labors of the typical alien are not now expended on the railroad, the canal, or the farm, but in the mines and foundries, the sweatshops and factories. The immigrants of to-day are meeting an economic demand radically different from that of a century or half a century, yes, we may say a quarter of a century ago.[1]

This change is further exemplified by the increased concentration of population in cities which the United

[1] The importance of this change is emphasized by noting Professor Guy S. Callender's statement, "Perhaps the most important circumstance affecting American society is the fact that the people have always been in contact with unoccupied lands." *Economic History of the United States*, p. 667. Professor Taussig points out also, in this connection, that unskilled labor is more needed when a plant is being constructed than when it is being utilized. *Principles of Economics*, Vol. II, p. 154, footnote.

States has witnessed in the past century. In 1790 there were only 6 cities in the United States with over 8000 population each, containing 3.4 per cent of the total population. In 1840 the percentage of population in cities of this size was still only 8.4. But in 1900 there were 545 cities of over 8000, counting among their inhabitants 33.1 per cent of the total population. In other words, the ratio between city and country dwellers (taking the city of 8000 as the dividing line) has changed from one to twenty-eight in 1790 to one to two in 1900. At the same time the average density of population of the country as a whole has increased from 3.7 per square mile in 1810 to 10.8 in 1860, 17.3 in 1880, and 25.6 in 1900.

Hand in hand with these changes has come a sweeping change in the scale of production, which must have an important bearing on the immigration situation. The early immigrants, to a very large extent, came into more or less close personal relations with their employers, often working side by side with them on the farm or in the shop. Now foreigners are hired by the thousands by employers whom they perhaps never see, certainly never have any dealings with, the arrangements being made through some underling, very likely a foreigner himself. Working all day side by side with others of their own race, or of other races equally foreign, and going home at night to crowded dwellings, inhabited by aliens, and with a European atmosphere, the modern immigrants have but slight commerce with anything that is calculated to inculcate American ideas or contribute any real Americanizing influence.

Mention of the declining native birth rate in the United States had already been made (Chapter XI), with some consideration of the causes thereof. The fact needs to be called attention to in this connection as another element in the changed aspect of immigration. It is unfortunate that our census figures do not give us positive data as to the respective birth rates of the native-born and foreign-born, so that we have to rely upon estimates. All of these estimates, however, agree that there has been a marked decline in the rate of native increase, though the causes assigned vary. The population of the United States in 1810 was 1.84 times as great as in 1790, and that of 1840, 1.77 times as great as twenty years earlier. Since the immigration during all this period was relatively slight, this increase may be taken as representing a very high native birth rate. In 1900, in spite of the large element of foreign-born with a high birth rate then in the country, and the large immigration of the previous twenty years, the population of the country was only 1.52 times as large as in 1880. This must represent a tremendous fall in the native birth rate. Mr. S. G. Fisher has estimated that the rate of native increase by decades has fallen from 33.76 per cent in the decade ending 1820 to 24.53 in the decade ending 1890. Some eminent authorities, as previously mentioned, are of the opinion that at the present time the native population of parts, if not the whole, of New England is not even maintaining itself. Thus our present immigrants are being received by, and are mingling with, a people, not vigorous and prolific as in the early days, able to match the crowds of aliens with a host of native-born offspring, but weak in reproductive power, and constantly decreasing in the ability to maintain itself. In this connection it is significant that during the last intercensal decade the total foreign-born population increased 30.7

per cent, while the native-born population increased only 19.5 per cent. This fact, in connection with the high birth rate of our now large foreign-born population, puts a new face on the question of the elimination of the native stock.

There yet remains to be considered the matter of the quality of immigrants to-day as compared with those of past generations. In regard to this but little can be said in the way of positive declarations. Quality in an immigrant is a very uncertain matter, and differs according to the individual point of view and prejudices. What may seem to an employer of labor high quality in an immigrant may appear quite the reverse in the eyes of a minister. With the facts of immigration in mind, each student of the question must determine for himself whether the quality of our present immigrants compares favorably with that of earlier groups. There is, however, one consideration to which attention should be directed when examining changes, which has materially altered the character of immigration. This is the selective influence of the act of immigration itself, upon those who are to come. It used to be the prevailing idea that the immigrant represented the better individuals of his race or class, that he was more daring, energetic, or enterprising. Traces of this notion are still very common.[1] There was, moreover, a great amount of truth in this view during earlier periods of immigration. Many of the migrations of two or three centuries ago were inspired by religious or political motives, or very often by a combination of the two. Such was the exodus of the Huguenots from France, of the Palatines from

[1] Thus, "Immigration calls for courage and every other personal quality which makes for social progress." Lincoln, *The City of the Dinner Pail*, p. 141.

Germany, the Puritans from England, the Scotch-Irish from Ireland. In such cases as these, emigration implies strength of character, independence, firmness of conviction, moral courage, bravery, hatred of oppression, etc. Motives such as these played no small part in immigration movements even as late as the middle of the nineteenth century.

More than this, it is doubtless true that the earliest immigration from any region at any time involves a certain degree of ambition, independence, courage, energy, forethought, all of those characteristics which are required in the individual who forsakes the known for the unknown, the familiar for the untried, the stable for the unstable, the certain though hopeless present for the hopeful but uncertain future. Such were the early immigrants to this country from every land — not north European alone, but south European. They possessed something of the intrepidity and daring of pioneers. They had the strength of character to break the shackles of age-long tradition and custom, and, taking their destiny in their hand, seek their fortune in a new and unknown land. In this respect all new immigration differs from all established immigration.

But all this is now a thing of the past. Not only have the religious and political motives almost wholly disappeared in favor of the economic in modern immigration, but the European immigrant of to-day is in no sense going to a new or unknown land, when he embarks for the United States. American life and conditions, particularly economic conditions, are well known in those sections of Europe which furnish our large contingents of immigration. The presidential election, the panic, the state of the crops in the United States, are familiar topics of conversation.[1] Almost every individual in the established currents of immigration has at least one friend in this country. Many of them know exactly where they are going and what they are going to do. To a host of them the change is no greater than to go to the next village in their native land, perhaps less so. For as likely as not, just as many of their friends and relatives are awaiting them in the new country as are lamenting them in the old.

Neither is the voyage to-day, bad as it is, beset with the uncertainties, hardships, and perils which used to characterize it. The way is cleared for the travelers at every step. If their ticket is not actually supplied to them from America, probably all or part of the money with which it is purchased came from America. At least they may now secure a ticket direct from a European center to their ultimate destination in America, and every stage of the journey is facilitated by the ingenuity of financially interested agents. Induced immigration has always existed since the days when the press gangs in the coast towns of England carried inducement to the point of abduction. But probably never in the history of our country has artificially stimulated immigration formed so large a part of the whole as now. There is nothing, therefore, in the modern conditions of immigration which serves as a guaranty of high quality in the immigrants.

One other element which concerns the quality of the immigrant, and therefore should be mentioned in this connection, is the immense increase in what may be designated temporary or seasonal immigration. The prominence of this type of movement in recent years

[1] See page 160.

has radically modified the industrial aspect of the situation.[1]

It is possible that some of the changes reviewed above may be of a beneficial character. However that may be, there can be no question that, taken together, they indicate so complete an alteration in the circumstances surrounding the admission of aliens to this country as to require that the entire immigration situation be considered in the light of present conditions, rather than of past history. The old stock arguments, *pro* and *con*, which seem to have stood the test of time, need to be thoroughly reviewed. The modern immigrant must be viewed in the setting of to-day. Especially must it be borne in mind that the fact — if such it be — that immigration in the past has worked no injury to the nation, and has resulted in good to the immigrants, by no means indicates that a continuance of past policy and practice in the matter will entail no serious evil consequences, nor bring about disaster in the future.

[1] Cf. Bailey, W. B., "The Bird of Passage," *Am. Jour. of Soc.*, 18: 3, p. 391.

CHAPTER XVIII

THE NATURE OF THE PROBLEM

MUCH is said and written in these days about the "immigration problem," yet it is only rarely that there appears a conscious effort to prove that such a problem exists, or to analyze its character. Is there in the United States an immigration problem? If so, in what does it consist? To answer these two questions is the purpose of the present chapter.

When the great new lands of the Western Hemisphere were made available to the inhabitants of Europe by the efforts of Columbus and the later explorers and discoverers, there opened up before humanity tremendous possibilities of advance.[1] The ratio between men and land was changed for the whole civilized world. An enormous area of fertile country was presented to the nations of Europe, by which the operation of the Malthusian principles was checked. Peoples who had reached the saturation point of population in Europe were given the opportunity to utilize their acquired arts in a virgin and practically uninhabited region. On account of the difficulties of transportation, and the consequent slow settlement of the new world, the results of this great alteration were only tardily developed. In many ways the entire progress of civilization during the nineteenth century is the outward expression of the transformation in conditions which then took place.

[1] See Professor Keller's introduction to Fairchild's *Greek Immigration*.

So far as the human mind can anticipate, nothing of a similar nature can ever happen again on this earth.

To the people of the new nation of the United States, as the possessors of the most favored portion of this new territory, was intrusted the responsibility of utilizing its marvelous resources, not only for their own advantage, but for the securing of the greatest and most permanent amelioration of the living conditions of the whole human family. It was not to be expected that our forefathers should have completely recognized the full significance of this responsibility, nor have undertaken the administration of it with a degree of scientific wisdom which they did not possess. Their past experience of bad political systems enabled them to frame a plan of government which has held the admiration of all civilized people down to the very present. In the utilization of the material resources of the country, however, they had no past experience to serve as a guide. No other civilized people within the compass of human history had been intrusted with such a profusion of virgin resources, absolutely open to exploitation. There is no wonder that the possibilities of the country seemed limitless, and that men proceeded to make the most of them to serve present needs, with no thought of what the consequences might be to future generations. Forests were cut down, mines were wastefully worked, rivers were dammed, natural gas was burned day and night, the soil was cultivated year after year without enrichment, and when exhausted, abandoned. In our modern age of conservation we are beginning to realize how ruthlessly these rich treasures have been squandered, and are making eager and earnest efforts to save what is left.

Something of the same sort took place in the more

tangible domain of population. Into the minds of the less than four million people who were enumerated in the United States in 1790, even the thought of a redundant population could hardly enter. The one great thing that seemed to be needed was more people, and while the natural increase of the native stock seemed to many ample to meet the demands, there was nevertheless a hearty welcome to all sturdy and well-intentioned aliens who elected to establish themselves within the territory of the new nation. Especially was there a feeling of sympathy toward those who came seeking refuge from political tyranny or oppression in the nations of Europe. Thus the principle of an open door, and a welcome to the "oppressed and downtrodden of all races," became the established policy of the nation, and as decade succeeded decade acquired all the power and authority of tradition and usage. As a consequence, all efforts to control or regulate the ingress of aliens, which have been incited by the apparent needs of the situation, have been confronted with the necessity of bearing the burden of proof, and of assailing established dogma. This has put the advocates of restriction into the category of "antis," and has laid them open to the charge of narrow-mindedness and bigotry. If it can be conceived that the United States should have been in her present industrial situation when she first began to frame national policies, it is wholly probable that the restrictionists would have been considered the conservatives, and the advocates of free immigration, the radicals.

However this may be, the fact is that in general the open-door policy has prevailed, and only within the last generation have restrictive laws been passed, which have served merely to weed out the manifestly undesirables, scarcely to diminish in any significant measure the great bulk of the current. The resulting transfer of people from Europe to America has been truly phenomenal. In the period of years from 1820 to 1912 a total of 29,611,052 immigrants came to the United States.[1] No population movement of equal social significance, and comparable in volume, has ever taken place within the recorded history of the human race. And never again, so far as the human eye can see, can it be repeated, when the heyday of immigration to the United States is over. It is inconceivable that such a phenomenon should not have important and far-reaching effects upon every country concerned in the movement. There is, then, an immigration problem.

But just what is the problem? The answer to that question depends upon the point of view. In the first place, it must be decided whether it is desirable for nations consciously to interfere with, and try to control, such a natural movement as this; secondly, if interference is to be undertaken, whose welfare is to be held prominently in view — in other words, from what standpoint is the problem to be attacked? If the former of these queries is answered in the negative, the problem remains a purely academic one — the study of causes and effects, and the recording of conclusions and data, without any telic purpose in view. No programs, schemes, or systems of reform can emanate from such a study. If answered in the affirmative, the problem then becomes one in applied sociology — perhaps the most complex and important that any modern nation

[1] A slight element of inaccuracy is given to these figures by the different methods of recording immigration at different periods. Rept. Imm. Com., Stat. Rev., Abs., p. 8.

has ever had to deal with. In regard to the second part of the above query, it is to be noted that there are four possible standpoints open to choice. First, that of the United States; second, that of the countries of source; third, that of the immigrants; fourth, that of humanity in general. There are possibilities of a different aspect of the problem from each of these viewpoints. Let us consider the two parts of this query in turn.

There is a natural and deep-seated reluctance on the part of every careful and scientific student of sociology to advocate the regulation of any great human activity according to any man-made scheme or formula. The laws of nature seem so much safer a guide than any plan which, as Professor Summer says, some one has thought out in bed.[1] The *laissez-faire* doctrine makes a great initial appeal. This probably accounts in large measure for its great vogue. The broad minded and liberal man says, "What can be better or more just than to let each individual work out his own destiny in the way that seems to him best?" Particularly does such a tremendous movement as modern immigration inspire the student with feelings of reverential awe, rather than a desire to intermeddle. It is such a gigantic and complex thing, and cuts straight across all social relations with such an inclusive and unsparing sweep, that one can never know what the unknown factors are, nor what unforeseen and unexpected developments may arise. Certainly this seems one of the things that had better be left alone.

But as we look at the world around us, we realize that the doctrine of *laissez-faire* has proved inadequate to meet the conditions of modern industrial life, and has

[1] *War and Other Essays*, p. 169.

broken down under the strain.[1] We realize that self-interest, even enlightened self-interest, is not the safest guide for the individual or for the race. We recognize the fact that the safety of society demands that men shall not be allowed to do as they please, nor to go where they please. The law places many restrictions upon the free movements of men. I may not trespass upon my neighbor's property; I may not enter public buildings except at specified times. If I wish to visit a fever-stricken and quarantined city, I either am not allowed to go, or I am prevented from coming away when I wish. These are familiar and trivial illustrations, but they emphasize the fact that complete *laissez-faire* is impossible under present conditions — in fact, probably always has been. A host of other instances of social legislation, pure-food laws, trust regulation, etc., might be invoked to establish the point, were it necessary. The whole series of immigration statutes, increasing in severity from 1882 down to the present, are evidence of the acceptance of this principle with special relation to immigration. The question is not, shall we have regulation or not, but how much and what kind of regulation shall we have? The doctrine of *laissez-faire*, *per se*, would have no greater weight as an argument against complete suspension of immigration than it would have against the exclusion of contract laborers.

If the personal inclinations of the individual lead him to prefer to regard the immigration problem in the strictly academic light, no fault can be found; but the denial of the propriety of suggesting plans of control, the demand that the immigrants be let alone, represents

[1] Cf. Kidd, Benjamin, *Social Evolution*, p. 237; Ellis, Havelock, *The Task of Social Hygiene*, pp. 2–4.

an obsolete point of view. Any amount of regulation, which proves necessary to safeguard the interests of society, can be justified in the light of modern opinion and practice.

Furthermore, it is to be observed that immigration will not be let alone. It has already been demonstrated that the immigration of to-day is not in any sense a wholly natural movement. It is stimulated at the outset, partly by disinterested friends and relatives, partly by purely selfish transportation interests. It is subjected to various controls all along the way. After the immigrants reach this country, they are often, for a long time, in almost complete subjection to the padrone, the contractor, or the importer. Once again, the question is not, shall immigration be a natural and uncontrolled movement or not, but shall it be controlled by greedy, selfish, and unscrupulous individuals, or by a well intentioned government? For the rest of this book we shall take the position that the immigration problem is one of applied sociology, and that immigration is a proper subject for government control, by such means and to such an extent as the most careful and scientific study shall warrant.

Most problems in applied sociology have to do with interests; certainly the problem of immigration does. Having answered the first part of our query in the affirmative, the problem now expresses itself thus: how shall the movement of aliens from foreign countries to the United States be so controlled as to further the best interests of somebody? But of whom? This is the second part of our query. It is manifest that the United States, the countries of source, the immigrants, and humanity in general all have interests which may be affected by immigration, that these interests are not always harmonious or correlative, but that they may be, and in some cases must be, in direct opposition to each other. Any one who has opinions on the subject must make it plain, to himself at least, which of these interests he regards as paramount, which of these standpoints he proposes to assume. Many of the popular arguments on the question have been confused by the unconscious effort to take two or more of these viewpoints at once. Each of these viewpoints is legitimate, and has arguments on its own side, and no one should be blamed for choosing any one. Evidently the fourth is a sort of summation and balance of the other three. It will be profitable to consider the first three in turn; we shall then be prepared to take the point of view of the welfare of humanity in general.

What, then, are the arguments for and against immigration from the point of view of the United States? The positive arguments for, and the negative arguments against, immigration center around the question whether the United States needs the immigrants. The positive arguments against, and the negative arguments for, immigration have to do with the claim that immigration injures the United States.

The argument for immigration which, if not the strongest during the first half of the nineteenth century, was probably the most frequently expressed, was the sentimental one which exhibited the United States as the natural haven of refuge for the oppressed and unfortunate of all lands, and extended a hearty welcome to all seekers of liberty who should come. This, as has been mentioned, was natural under the conditions of the time. It found expression in such words as the following, appearing in a magazine in the year 1855:

"If the physiologic principle we have endeavored to establish is correct, it follows that America pre-eminently owes its growth and prosperity to the amalgamation of foreign blood. To cut off, therefore, or to discourage its influx, will be to check the current from which our very life is drawn. The better course is evidently to welcome and provide for this tide of immigration, rather than to oppose and turn it away; to cherish the good influence it brings, and regulate the bad, rather than to trample them both under foot. What, though the population which is annually cast upon American shores is all of the filthiest and most degraded kind! The farmer might as well complain of the black and reeking soil into which his seed is dropped, as the statesman of such materials as these. . . . Let us welcome the houseless and the naked of every land to American shores; in the boundless forests of the north and the south there is room to make a home for them all. Let us invite the ill-fed and the starving of every grade to partake of American abundance; on the fertile fields of the west there grows corn enough to feed them all. Let us urge the oppressed and the down trodden of every name to the blessings of American freedom; the Star Spangled Banner is broad enough to cover, and the eagle that sits over it is strong enough to defend, them all." [1]

Such talk as this is so thoroughly out of date as to sound almost ridiculous in modern ears. In fact, the sentimental argument plays but little part in the present agitation, for the reason that the conditions which justify

[1] *De Bows's Review*, 18: 698, "Sources from which Great Empires Come." Signed L.

it furnish the motive to an insignificant portion of our present immigrants, with the exception of the Russian Jews.

Two other arguments for immigration may be styled the social and the biological. These claim respectively that the national character and the physical stock of the American people may be much improved by the addition of new elements brought in by foreign immigrants. It is pointed out that the German love for music, the artistic temperament of the Italian, the thrift of the Slav, the outdoor sociability of the Greek, might add — perhaps have added already — something of great value to the life of the country. There is much weight to this argument. It is quite conceivable that under proper conditions of social contact on a plane of equality between foreigner and native some such desirable transfusion of character might take place. It is another matter altogether to claim that any such beneficial result is transpiring, under the present conditions of the immigrant in this country.

The biological argument brings up the much-vexed question of the desirability of mixed stocks. There has been a prevalent opinion that the interbreeding of two races, not too far separated in physical stock, resulted in a type superior to either of the parent races. But there is no agreement as to where the line between the favorable and the unfavorable mixing shall be drawn. Some of the papers read at the Universal Races Congress in London would seem to convey the impression that any two races on earth might be mixed to good advantage. But this is by no means the universal opinion of careful anthropologists.

In regard to both of these arguments it may be said

that, whatever their intrinsic worth, they have no great positive weight as respects the present situation in the United States. It seems likely that this country has already within its borders all the alien elements that will be needed for a long time to come — certainly until they are more completely absorbed than they are at present.

There remains by far the greatest and most universal argument for immigration — the economic one. The one plea for the free admission of aliens, that has weight to-day, is that our industrial organization demands it. Not only is it asserted that the rapid development of the country would not have been possible without the immigrant and cannot be prosecuted in the future without him, but that the cessation of immigration would seriously cripple many of the basic industries of this country. The former of these points has already been considered at some length, and the conclusion was reached that it was inconceivable that in such a country as the United States any socially important or necessary work should have had to be foregone in the absence of a foreign labor supply. Such an assertion implies a lack of self-sufficiency on the part of a young and vigorous people which is unthinkable. Whether the exploitation of our resources would have proceeded at such a rapid pace in the past, whether this pace could be kept up in the future, without the immigrant — these are questions more difficult of answer. There is no doubt that at present a large portion of our industry — possibly the greater part — is closely dependent upon a foreign labor supply, and that a sudden cessation of immigration would check the expansion of those industries, though it would not necessarily prevent their continuing on the present basis. It seems wholly probable that the development of the country would be retarded for a time if the immigration current was stopped.

But why this insistent demand for a rapid exploitation of our resources? Wherein are we the gainers if the wonderful natural riches of the country, which, as we have seen, constitute one of the two great elements which have accounted for our past prosperity, are consumed in the shortest possible time? In the words of Prescott F. Hall, "what boots an extended railroad mileage or the fact that all our coal and minerals are dug up or all our trees cut down some years or decades sooner?" Are we so greedy for luxury in the present that we wish to leave as little as possible of this natural advantage to future generations? It seems hardly possible. Rather is this idea another of those traditional survivals from the early life of the country, when conditions were such that the exploitation of resources was really essential to growth in per capita, as well as total, wealth, and prosperity. Our country has, in point of fact, developed so rapidly that the public mind has not adjusted itself to new conditions, and the idea of the value of a rapid exploitation lingers on as an anachronism. Possibly there is a slight element of modern megalomania mingled with it.

If it were true that the United States, having reached its present point of development, was unable to advance along the path of steady and solid growth, depending solely upon its own resources, human as well as material, it would be one of the most serious indictments against our social situation that could possibly be made. It is inconceivable that it should be true. It seems much more reasonable to believe that while the suspension of accessions of population from foreign sources would entail numerous and serious readjustments in social and economic relations, nevertheless the United States still has enough native virility to work out a prosperous and independent destiny of its own. It is hard to see any important respect in which the United States, at the present time, really needs immigrants.

There is still another type of argument for immigration, which might be called the indifference argument, which says, in effect, "Very likely we do not need the immigrants, but they do us no harm. Let them come, anyway." The answer to this throws the burden of proof upon the restrictionist, and makes it incumbent upon him to show that immigration really injures the United States.

The positive arguments against immigration as at present conducted may be grouped under eight main heads, which may be designated as follows: (1) the numbers argument; (2) the distribution argument; (3) the standard of living and wages argument; (4) the pauperism and crime argument; (5) the stimulation argument; (6) the illegal entrance argument; (7) the biological argument; (8) the assimilation argument. In the discussion of these arguments it must be borne in mind that they are considered with reference to immigration as it now exists, not as it might be under other conditions.

(1) The common argument that we have too many immigrants is really no argument at all. There cannot be too many immigrants unless the excessive number manifests itself in some positive evil. What the average person who uses this argument probably means, if he has any definite meaning in mind at all, is that there are

so many aliens coming to this country that their presence results in one or another of the undesirable conditions which are included in the other seven arguments.

(2) In like manner the statement that immigrants are poorly distributed is no real argument. It has been demonstrated that there are certain excessive tendencies toward concentration on the part of our alien population, but unless positive evils emerge from this condition, it is no argument against immigration.

(3) The claim that immigration has lowered the wages and standard of living of the American workman has already been examined, with the conclusion that it would be nearer the truth to say that it has kept them from rising. This, however, amounts to practically the same thing. If somebody prevents me from getting that to which I am entitled, he to all intents and purposes makes me suffer deprivation. The evidence on this point is so strong that it can hardly be gainsaid. As we have seen, practically all careful students admit it. About the only answer that can be made to this argument is that it is not the immigrant's fault.[1] This is undoubtedly true, partly at least. The immigrant has no grudge against the American workman, nor any desire to injure him.

[1] This point is frequently pressed by writers who adopt the standpoint of the immigrant, as for instance, Professor Steiner. Much effort is expended to establish the high character of the immigrant, his noble motives and worthy ambitions. The wealthy American on the promenade deck is contrasted unfavorably with the alien in the steerage. No criticism is to be made of this position. It is beyond doubt that there is a great deal to admire in the very humblest of our immigrants. But a most emphatic exception must be taken to the conclusion which apparently is assumed to follow this premise; namely, that therefore anything in the way of restriction is wrong. Granted that the admirable character of the immigrant is thoroughly established. This fact does not obviate the need for action, if it appears that evils arise. If the welfare of the nation is menaced; if the immigrants are not reaping the benefits for which they have sacrificed all in the old country; if the wonderful patrimony of the United States, fitted to render an enduring service to mankind, is being thought-

Undoubtedly he would be glad to earn as good wages as the native, if he could. Inasmuch as he cannot, he is not to blame if he consents to work for what he can get. And inasmuch as his wages are low, and his family is large, and he is anxious to save, he is not to blame if he lives on a miserably low standard. In the whole procedure the immigrant may display the most admirable qualities. He is simply playing his part in an impersonal struggle for existence. But the result to the American workman is the same. It is a question of causes and effects, not of blame. It must be accepted as a fact that each successive wave of immigration has tended to check the advance of the laboring men already in the country, be they native or foreign. And here is where the numbers argument applies. For it is obvious that the greater the numbers the more aggravated will be the evils of this kind.

(4) The argument that immigration increases the amount of pauperism and crime in the country has already been examined. As far as the past is concerned it appears that pauperism has been immensely increased through our foreign-born population, while the amount of crime has not. But there has been a change in the character of crime, in the direction of an increase in crimes against the person relative to crimes against property. What the future will bring forth, it is impossible to predict. It seems likely that the tendency

lessly squandered; if conditions in foreign countries are not improved; if the most remarkable population movement in history is being left to the machinations of selfishly interested parties — if any of these things are true, the fact that it is not the immigrant's "fault" does not remove the responsibility from those upon whom it naturally rests of taking active measures to secure to humanity the greatest and most enduring benefits which such a tremendous sociological phenomenon may be made to yield. If the first step in such a conservation program is restriction, then that step must be taken.

toward an excess of pauperism on the part of the foreign-born will become greater as the average length of residence of the newer immigrants increases. Here, again, the claim that it is not the immigrant's fault might be advanced, and the answer be made that whether it is the fault of the immigrant, or of our industrial system, or of the individual American, makes no difference in the facts as they exist. It does make a difference, of course, as to where the remedy must be applied.

(5) The extent to which the immigration movement of the present is a stimulated one has already been indicated. It might seem at first that it made no difference to the United States whether the immigrant was induced to come, or whether he came of his own volition. But a closer consideration shows that there is a fundamental difference. A strictly natural immigration would mean that immigrants came in response to some actual economic demand in this country which was strong enough to make itself felt abroad. They would also be the ones best fitted to meet that demand. But when one of the greatest motives back of immigration is the desire of the transportation companies to make money, the mere fact of emigration is no indication of any real need for the immigrant in this country, nor of his fitness to enter into its life.

(6) Owing to the very strict wording of our contract labor law, a very large proportion of our immigrants enter the country under the impression, either false or correct, that they are evading the law. This has a very serious effect upon their character, and upon their attitude toward American institutions. They may readily conceive that a country that has such laws that it is necessary to break them to get in, probably has other

laws that need to be broken after one is in. The whole system engenders a most dangerous attitude of indifference or hostility to law.

(7) The biological argument of the restrictionist is the obverse of the biological argument of the pro-immigrationist, and is equally vague in the present state of our knowledge on the subject of race mixing. Those who urge this argument against immigration are those who believe that only when the mingled races are closely allied is the resulting stock of a superior type, or else those who hold the extreme view that no mixed race is as good as a pure race. At any event, they believe that the racial elements which are now coming to the United States are too diverse to produce anything but an inferior stock through their interbreeding. In this connection it should be observed that there are two possible results of this gathering of races in the United States, each with its own problems. One is that these races will, in the course of time, become so blended through intermarriage as to produce one composite but homogeneous whole — the new American people. The other is that race prejudice and the forces of segregation will result in the growth of a large number of ethnic groups within the nation, each with its own peculiarities, and each distinct from the others. There are some indications which point to the latter as the more probable outcome.[1]

(8) The charge that our immigrants are not completely assimilated, or are not assimilated at all, is one of the most frequent and gravest complaints made against our present immigration situation. It is made to include — as, indeed, it rightfully does in a sense — all the other arguments against immigration. The term

[1] Cf. Hall, P. F., "The Future of American Ideals," *No. Am. Rev.*, Jan., 1912.

assimilation is almost unfailingly suggested by the mere mention of immigration. But assimilation is a big word, and needs to be used with great caution and understanding.

In its general application, assimilation is defined as the "act or process of assimilating, or bringing to a resemblance, conformity, or identity," [1] or "the act or process of making or becoming like or identical; the act or process of bringing into harmony"; [2] or again, "the action of making or becoming like; the state of being like; similarity, resemblance, likeness; . . . the becoming conformed to; conformity with." [3] It is evident from these definitions that the essence of assimilation is likeness or conformity; this of necessity implies a type to which such likeness approaches. It appears that it would not be incorrect to speak of assimilation when there is nothing more than resemblance; it seems equally clear that *complete* assimilation involves identity. This is particularly evident in reference to the special application of the term, which is the one generally in mind when it is used, viz. the assimilation of food in the body. In this sense the process is described as "the reformation of biogen molecules by those already existing, aided by food-stuffs." [4]

It is this physiological analogy which underlies the term assimilation when applied to population, and the whole matter may be best understood by keeping that analogy in view. When nutriment is taken into the system of a living organism, it passes through certain processes by which it ultimately becomes an integral part of the physical body of that organism. It is then

[1] *Webster's Dictionary.*
[2] *Century Dictionary.*
[3] *New English Dictionary.*
[4] *Encyc. Britannica,* article "Physiology."

said to be assimilated. Every suggestion of separate origin disappears, each new constituent entering harmoniously into relation with the others, new and old, and fulfilling its own functions. While it is true that certain food elements contribute particularly to certain portions of the organism, yet the whole is a coördinated unit. Any portion of the food which created disturbance with reference to the body would not be said to be assimilated.

This is only an analogy, and analogies are dangerous if used as arguments. But it may contain a helpful suggestion. Transferred to the field of population, it means that true and complete assimilation of the foreign elements in the United States involves such a complete transformation and unification of the new constituents that all sense of difference between the new and the old completely disappears. The idea of a type, into conformity with which the new elements must be brought, is here present also. In the case in point, this is manifestly the "American type." Just what this is, it might be difficult to say. Some writers appear even to question its existence. But the very idea of assimilation presupposes a type. In general terms, this type in the United States is the "native American." [1]

A foreigner, or the descendant of a foreigner, can be truly said to be assimilated only when the natives around him are conscious of no feeling of alienation on account of his origin, and when the newcomer himself feels no degree of separateness, nor possesses divergent interests or loyalties traceable to the source from which he came. This is not inconsistent with the fact that certain ele-

[1] For an enumeration of important American characteristics, see Mayo-Smith, R., *Emigration and Immigration*, pp. 5–6.

ments contribute more fully to specific characteristics of the body politic than others. The political, religious, or artistic aspects of the national life may, in fact, owe their character more to one element of the population than to another. But if assimilation is complete, there can be no disturbances or friction arising from differences of origin among the members of the nation.

Perhaps the most efficient test of entire assimilation is that of free intermarriage. If marriage might take place between any man and woman in the country, without suggesting differences of race or ethnic origin to either contracting party, or their families, it is a safe evidence of complete assimilation. There may be objections on the grounds of wealth, social station, or religion; there must be none based on race.

This may seem like strong doctrine. It may, indeed, not be necessary for the welfare of the country that assimilation should be so thoroughgoing as this. It is possible that different racial groups within the body politic do not constitute a menace. But if so, the fact should be stated by saying that complete assimilation is not necessary, rather than by saying that the absence of serious difficulties or evils arising from a composite population is a proof of complete assimilation.

It is disheartening to note the frequency with which even careful writers on the subject accept trivial and superficial indications as evidence of the assimilation of our foreign residents. The wearing of American clothes, the laying of carpets on the floors, the abandonment of sleeping in the kitchen and taking large numbers of boarders, the use of better food, and most of all the knowledge of English are taken as proofs of assimilation.

Not all of these improvements, to be sure, are in

themselves trivial. They may indicate a great advance in living conditions, and in so far an approach to Americanization; but they are superficial as proofs of assimilation. Particularly is this true of the knowledge of English, upon which so much emphasis is laid, and which is often accepted as an evidence of essential assimilation. Now the knowledge and use of the English language is of the greatest importance, and is one of the first steps — perhaps the most essential one — toward assimilation. But it is not assimilation itself. Missionaries in China, Turkey, and other foreign lands learn to speak the languages almost perfectly, and sometimes their children speak the language of the country more readily than they do English. But that is no proof that either the missionaries or their children are assimilated into the nations in which they reside. The outlook for foreign missions would indeed be dark, were it so. The importance of the knowledge of English to our foreign residents must not be underemphasized. The lack of it is an almost insuperable bar to assimilation. But the two should not be confused. Even people whose native tongue is English may need to go through a process of assimilation before they become Americans. The following incident may serve as an illustration of this point.

Two young men, one an American and the other an Englishman, both teachers in a foreign city, were discussing the conditions in the armies of their native lands. The Englishman remarked that in his country the officers were chosen from the noble families, and that it was a fine system, as it caused the men to look upon their superiors with great respect. The American replied that in America officers were chosen for bravery, ability, or distinguished conduct, and that made the men respect them much more. "Oh, no," said the Briton, "it is impossible that such a system as that could result in as profound a respect as exists in our army." The point was argued for half an hour, with naturally not the slightest alteration of opinion on either side. It is probable that that young Englishman might have lived all the remainder of his life in the United States, without actually getting the American point of view. But until he did, in this respect as well as others, he could not be said to be truly assimilated, although he might have been a very useful citizen.[1]

Regarding the matter of assimilation from the American point of view, there are two questions to be asked. First, are our immigrants being thoroughly assimilated? Second, is complete assimilation necessary or desirable? As to the first of these queries, it seems that there can be but one answer, as far as the immigrants themseves — those of the first generation — are concerned. We have seen in how large a proportion of this class the first step, the mastery of the English language, has not been taken. In the various other conditions of life, which we have studied, it is apparent that a large part of the foreign-born are very far from American standards. With length of residence, an approach to Americanization is made. Yet it is very doubtful if it is possible for even the most exceptional adult immigrant, from the southeastern European races, at least, to become thoroughly assimilated in his lifetime. The barriers of race, set for the most part by Americans, can hardly be

[1] It is noteworthy that while the English are in many respects more similar to Americans than any other foreign race, yet their complete assimilation to the American type is said to be very difficult, because of their unwillingness to give up their own ideas and character. *City Wilderness*, p. 52; *Americans in Process*, p. 65.

broken down. The immigrant is still an Italian, or a Slav, or a Greek, as long as he lives, and Americans regard him as in a measure a stranger, no matter how cultivated, or wealthy, or broad-minded he may be. The mental habits, also, which are the result of long race inheritance, are very deep-seated, and can hardly be altered even after a long residence in a foreign country.[1] Assimilation for the adult means the abandonment of one set of mores and the adoption of another. But the mores of a race become too thoroughly ingrained into individual character and thought to be subject to complete revision in a changed environment, even under the most favorable circumstances. And when attention is directed to the slums, the question of assimilation becomes almost a mockery. These matters are so obvious as to be almost an axiom, and even the adherents of the "liberal" policy of immigration have come to lay little stress in their arguments upon the assimilation of the first generation. The attention of all is turned to the children of the foreign-born — the immigrants of the second generation.

Judged by the superficial tests upon which reliance is generally placed, the native-born children of foreign parents seem to be very well assimilated. They wear American hats, clothes, and shoes, they speak English, they are as literate as the offspring of native parents of the same social class, they play American games when

[1] Professor Lester F. Ward says, "The assimilation of an alien civilization . . . cannot be accomplished in a single generation, no matter how favorable the conditions may be." *Applied Sociology*, p. 109. Professor Sumner says, "The only way in which, in the course of time, remnants of foreign groups are apparently absorbed and the group becomes homogeneous, is that the foreign element dies out." *Folkways*, p. 115. Mr. Joseph Lee says, "Whether we in this country shall succeed in doing in a few centuries what Europe in fifteen or twenty or more has not been able to accomplish, is a problem of which the present generation of Americans is not in a position to fully judge." *Charities and the Commons*, 19:17.

they are young, and engage in American business when they grow up. In the words of Professors Jenks and Lauck, speaking of the foreign races in the larger cities, "Their children differ little from those of the American-born, unless they are brought up throughout their childhood in the race colonies," — a weighty exception.[1] But are they really assimilated? Are the tests which have been enumerated above fulfilled? This is a matter worthy of the most serious consideration, and very difficult of determination, withal.

It is a very hopeless task to attempt to decide upon the degree of assimilation of any group on a statistical basis. Statistics which might give light are meager and unreliable, and it is not a matter which lends itself well to such treatment at best. In many of the statistics which might be appealed to, the second generation of immigrant is included under the general head of the native-born, and sometimes gives that class a more unfavorable appearance than it would otherwise present. As far as the statistics of criminality and tendency to pauperism are concerned, the native-born of foreign parents appear to be the most troublesome class in the population. They seem to have earned an unfortunate reputation for lawlessness, although their crimes, as the Immigration Commission has pointed out, tend to resemble those of the native element in character. But these things alone are not sufficient tests of assimilation. We need to know whether in their mental processes, in their attitude toward life, and in their position in regard to political or moral questions, there linger peculiarities traceable to their foreign origin. We need to know whether their neighbors, of the old American stock,

[1] *The Immigration Problem*, p. 209.

think of them as different from themselves, because of race. We need to know whether, in respect to international questions, their views are colored by inherited affiliations or prejudices. In regard to such considerations as these it is impossible to make any positive and sweeping statements. It seems wholly probable that there are large numbers of the descendants of immigrants, particularly of the earlier races, who would measure up to the full standard of assimilation even by these tests. But it seems also beyond question that there are great bodies of immigrants of the second generation who are prevented from complete absorption into the body politic, if not by their own lack of adaptation, at least by the attitude of the representatives of the old American stock.

It would be foolhardy to deny that, at the present time, there are immense unassimilated elements in our population, — immigrants of the first or second generation, possibly even of the third. Every foreign-American society, be it Irish, German, Italian, Slovak, or any other, whatever its aims and purposes, is a standing evidence of a group of people who recognize certain affiliations or loyalties which are foreign to the out-and-out American. The number of such organizations is legion, and the membership, if it could be reckoned, would reach an imposing total. The recent protests by Irish-American societies against the production of certain plays by the Irish Players, the German-American demonstration which broke up the peace meeting in Carnegie Hall on December 12, 1911, as well as the German-American meetings held four years previously to protest against the enforcement in New York of what was styled a Puritan Sunday, the discrimination of the Russian government against certain of our citizens — these and a host of similar events occurring from time to time emphasize the existence within this country of racial contingents which have not become indistinguishably blended into the American people. If, for any conceivable reason, the United States should be drawn into any European international complication, she would find that hosts of her citizens, as well as mere residents, displayed a divided allegiance, of which the preponderance might easily be on the side of some foreign nation. As long as such conditions as these prevail, it is idle to claim that assimilation is complete.

Assimilation is a matter of the force of environment pitted against that of heredity. The protracted discussion as to the relative influence of these two factors continues unsettled. But the claim that the second generation of immigrants are thoroughly assimilated seems to deny the importance of either. To assert that the children of foreign parents, brought up in a home made by foreigners though located in the United States, are in the end equally American with children born of native parents, and reared in a home upon which the American type is indelibly stamped, is to claim that heredity is of no account whatever, and that the only environment which has weight is that rather vague environment of "country." It is to say that a man's character is solely the result of the region in which he lives, without reference to either birth or breeding. It seems hardly credible that such an assertion should be seriously made. It is more likely that those who say that the children of the foreign-born are assimilated really mean that they are nearly enough assimilated for all practical purposes.

Professor Franz Boas, in his study of "Changes in the Bodily Form of Descendants of Immigrants," which forms a part of the report of the Immigration Commission, and has attracted wide attention, lays much stress on the change in environment which follows immigration. He reaches the conclusion that there is a tendency manifest in the American-born children of immigrants to approach a common physical type in this country, and that this tendency becomes more marked as the mother's length of residence in the United States, previous to the birth of the child, increases. His main investigations are concerned with the head form, and have to do particularly with Sicilians and east European Hebrews. The cephalic index has always been considered one of the most permanent of race characters, but Professor Boas's figures seem to show that the naturally long-headed Sicilians tend to become less so in this country, while the relative length of head of the naturally brachycephalic Hebrews increases. The results reached by Professor Boas are somewhat startling, and challenge attention. It is to be hoped that they will be subjected to the most careful scrutiny by anthropologists qualified either to verify or to correct them. Until they have been thus tested they can be accepted only tentatively. On the face of them they suggest certain weaknesses or limitations. In the first place, they are concerned with too few races, and too few individuals in each race, to justify general conclusions. Again, they are concerned almost wholly with persons under twenty years of age, who are naturally still in a plastic state. It would be much more significant if it could be shown that this tendency still persisted after the individuals were fully matured. Furthermore, the curves show a decided tendency to lose their regularity, and go to pieces, in the upper ages tabulated, either because there were too few individuals in those age groups to afford regularity, or because the tendencies actually diminish as age advances. Finally, it must be said that if the mere change of residence from eastern Europe or southern Italy to America is sufficient to produce a complete change of head form in the offspring, it can only mean that after all the head form is not such a permanent race character as has been supposed, and really has little significance. Certainly we should avoid such sweeping deductions from this study as Professors Jenks and Lauck make in the statement, "If these physical changes are so great, we may well conclude that the whole mental and even the moral constitution of the people may also rapidly change under the new conditions."[1]

It will not do to assume, as is sometimes done apparently, that mere residence in the United States is enough to make Americans of foreign immigrants or their children. America is something more than merely a section of the earth's surface. It is a set of standards, customs, ideals, institutions, mores, embodied and personified in a group of people. Like many other of the deepest things in life they would be very hard to enumerate or describe, yet their existence is none the less sure. They are exemplified more completely in some persons than in others, and he who most thoroughly personifies them is the truest American. Historically, they have been associated with a certain physical strain, with which many of them appear to be inherently connected. Real assimilation means adoption into this spiritual inheritance. The only way it can be brought about is through

[1] *The Immigration Problem*, p. 267.

close, intimate, constant association with those in whom it is embodied.

The agencies of assimilation then, in addition to the physical one of race blending, are those things which further contact and association between the newcomer and those who are truly Americans. Professors Jenk and Lauck give a list of such causes or influences.[1] The list might perhaps be amplified, but as it stands it is an enumeration of forces which contribute to interrace association. It is not essential that the influence of the American upon the immigrant be an intentional, or even a conscious, one. Many of the most powerful forces are unobserved. The foreigner is very much aware of the differences between himself and his American neighbors, and the laws of imitation work strongly. But to have these forces work, there must be contact.

Under the modern conditions which surround the immigrant this contact or association is all too often wholly lacking, or very meager. The entire life of many of our foreign-born and the youth of their children is spent in compact colonies, where, except for a few externals, the atmosphere is much more suggestive of the old world than of the new. The conditions of the old home are reproduced with the utmost possible fidelity, though often with a loss of much of the charm. So far as there is any social life, it is almost wholly confined within the boundaries of race. Even in the industrial life of to-day, as has been pointed out, there is practically no contact with Americanizing influences. It is really a wonder that the aliens are Americanized at all. When we stop to consider that in Massachusetts and New Jersey there are only two natives for every foreigner, and that many

[1] *Ibid.*, p. 293.

of these natives are of foreign parentage, we realize how slight are the chances for assimilation. It would be almost the task of a lifetime for two Americans to thoroughly Americanize a native peasant from a backward district of southeastern Europe, if they gave their whole time to it.

The one great assimilative agency, which is continually cited as the hope of the coming generation of the foreign-born, is the American public school. It certainly is a tremendous force in the right direction, and its possibilities are immeasurable. Yet even the public school is not a panacea for all ills. It cannot take the place of both birth and home training. During the hours that the pupils are in school, a wise and tactful teacher can instill many of the principles of Americanism into their minds. But the means, good as it is, is not adequate to the end. And it is to be feared that under recent conditions even the public schools are losing some of the power in this direction that they once had. With the growth of localized colonies of a single race, or of several foreign races, the schools in many of our large cities are losing their American character, as far as the pupils are concerned, so that the immigrant child finds himself associating with others equally foreign with himself, instead of with children from American families. There is a story that in a certain New England city, of high scholastic traditions, an American lady determined to place her son in the public school, and on taking him down found that he was the only American child in that school. A Russian Jewess edged up to her and remarked confidentially, "Ain't it a shame, the way the Dagoes are crowding in everywhere these days?" Furthermore, a very large proportion of the children of the foreign-born do not receive even such Americanizing influence as the public school exerts, because of the religious prejudices which compel them to attend parochial schools.

Aside from the characteristics of the immigrants themselves, the positive forces which prevent or retard assimilation may be considered under three heads, viz. the indifference, love of wealth, and race prejudice of the older residents of the United States. As to the first of these, no elaboration is required. The attitude of those who are perfectly content to let things drift along as they will, without any care on their part, is too familiar and too well understood to need comment. The love of wealth manifests itself as a barrier to assimilation, in two principal ways. First, the greed for economic gain results in bringing in continually cheaper supplies of labor, represented by ever lower and more backward races, and paying them such wages as of necessity keep them on the lowest scale of living. Secondly, the well-developed distinctions between the rich and the poor prevent Americans from associating on friendly terms with these same foreigners for whose presence and condition they are at least indirectly responsible. The growing tendency for certain occupations of the lower type to become the especial province of certain foreign races, as has been observed above, is continually accentuating these distinctions.

There can be little doubt that race prejudice is the greatest single barrier to assimilation. It is a disgraceful anomaly that the people of the United States, who preach and profess to believe in the doctrine of universal brotherhood, who have given political equality to the negroes, who proclaim all men born equal, should in their lives exemplify the narrowest race prejudice. The very currency of the terms, "Dago," "Sheeny," "Griner," "Hunkie," "Bohunk," "Guinea," "Wop," etc., however insulting to the people addressed, is more of a shame to those who use them. Many of the sincerest efforts toward a better understanding between races are thwarted by this feeling. Ministers who try to attract the foreigners to their churches find that their old parishioners do not wish to associate with them — though quite willing to foot the bills — and do not wish their children to mingle with them in Sunday school. The fact that a certain perfectly natural fastidiousness contributes to this result does not in the least lessen the problem. All praise is due to such broad-minded persons as Professor Steiner and Miss Addams, who are doing all in their power to break down this barrier. But their task is a hard one.

In addition to the race prejudice existing between Americans and foreigners, there is an even more bitter prejudice existing between various foreign groups, as has been mentioned already. This is also a most serious obstacle in the way of assimilation. One of the first to cry, "Down with the foreigners," is the Irishman.[1] In this connection it has been pertinently pointed out that it is possible for foreign races to become so far assimilated as to be in practical harmony with Americans, and yet to be seriously at variance among themselves.[2]

It must be confessed that, under present conditions, the outlook for the complete assimilation of our foreign population, even in the second generation, is far from bright. Even Miss Balch's thoughtful and sympathetic

[1] Cf. Coolidge, Mary R., *Chinese Immigration*, p. 267; and Fairchild, H. P., *Greek Immigration*, footnote, p. 242.

[2] *Americans in Process*, p. 50.

chapter on assimilation, though written in an optimistic spirit, makes it plain that there are many and grievous difficulties, and leaves one with a somewhat gloomy feeling at the close. Professor Sumner used to say that the United States had no claim to the name of nation, because of the diverse population elements — foremost among them the negro — which it contains. Exception may be taken to so narrow a conception of the term "nation." But there can be no question as to the fact that the problem of maintaining national solidarity is immeasurably complicated by the great variety of ethnic constituents with which the United States has to deal.

There are, of course, countless institutions and agencies, of a benevolent or philanthropic nature, which are consciously working to assimilate the immigrant. Such are the night schools, the social settlements, the religious missions, the boys' clubs, etc. Conscientious efforts of this kind, when wisely directed, are worthy of the fullest commendation and support. But the extensive and valuable work they are doing must not be allowed to obscure the fact that such agencies, at best, can only touch the border of the problem. Just as philanthropy is inadequate to abolish poverty or to do away with the evils of factory employment, so it is inadequate to secure the assimilation of the immigrants in this country. Such immense problems can be met, if at all, only by profound and sweeping changes in the conditions of life. The whole aim of social legislation is to remedy the conditions of employment, and to regulate the relations between workman and employer, so as to reduce the need of philanthropy to a minimum. So it is vain to hope for the assimilation of the alien as a result of conscious, benevolent effort. The only possibility of accomplishing such assimilation is through such a change in the conditions of life of the immigrant, that Americanization will inevitably and naturally result from the unconscious and normal influences which surround him in the daily routine of his existence.

In the event of failure of assimilation to the American type, there seem to be two possibilities, as mentioned above. One, the development of a new, composite race, with a character all its own; the other, the growth of a number of separate racial groups in the same territory. There are some who regard the latter outcome as the more desirable of the two.[1]

As to the question whether complete assimilation is desirable or necessary from the point of view of the United States, there is little ground for argument. If a person sincerely holds the opinion that neither of the two eventualities mentioned in the foregoing paragraph is unfortunate or undesirable, his opinion could hardly be changed by any amount of argument. Another individual, who believes that such an outlook, on the face of it, is ominous, is likely to remain of the same opinion still, no matter how much logic is brought up on the other side. The appeal to history is not fruitful, for two main reasons. First, it can be used equally by the adherents of either side. Montesquieu is often quoted as saying that the fall of Rome was due to the heterogeneity of its population, while on the other hand it has been asserted that the strength of Rome, as well as of all other great empires, was due to the mixture of population elements, even from the very lowest sources.[2] The

[1] Hall, P. F., "The Future of American Ideals," *No. Am. Rev.*, Jan., 1912.

[2] *De Bow's Review*, "Sources from which Great Empires Come," 18:698 (1855).

opposing camps in the mixed race controversy are evidently ranged on opposite sides of this question. Secondly, as has been pointed out, immigration is distinctly a modern movement, and history furnishes no parallels, but only more or less remote analogies.

The opinion of the average American citizen, based perhaps upon prejudice or conviction, rather than reasoning or investigation, is probably that a certain degree of assimilation is essential to the welfare of the American nation, and that the nearer the approach to complete assimilation, the better. Any plan for regulating immigration, devised to meet the wishes of the American people, would probably have to proceed on this assumption.

It is now necessary to take the opposite point of view, and examine this whole matter from the standpoint of the countries of source. What have been, what are likely to be, the effects of emigration upon those nations, and accordingly what is desirable, from their point of view, as respects the regulation of this great movement?

CHAPTER XIX

OTHER POINTS OF VIEW

THE effects of the immigration movement upon the countries of source are in a way much more simple than the effects upon the United States. None of the problems of race mixture, assimilation, varying racial inheritances, etc., are involved. They are confined principally to the three questions of the effect of the removal of parts of the population, the effect of the remittances from America, and the effect of the returned immigrant. But while simpler, these effects are perhaps none the less subtle than those in the United States, nor any less difficult of prediction — for in Europe, as in America, the effects of this great movement must be largely in the future.

It is one of the corollaries of the Malthusian theory of population that a steady, regular emigration from a country has no power to check the rate of increase of population in that country. This opinion has been accepted by many leading students of social subjects from Malthus' day down to the present. In fact, the general idea was expressed as early as 1790 by an anonymous writer in that quaint old magazine, the *American Museum*. He says: "When a country is so much crowded with people that the price of the means of subsistence is beyond the ratio of their industry, marriages are restrained: but when emigration to a certain degree takes place, the balance between the means of subsistence and industry is restored, and population thereby revived. Of the truth of this principle there are many proofs in the old counties of all the American states. Population has constantly been advanced in them by the migration of their inhabitants to new or distant settlements." [1] John Stuart Mill believed that a steady emigration was powerless to cure the ills of overpopulation.[2] Roscher and Jannasch maintain that not only will emigration not decrease population, but may actually make the increase of population greater than it would otherwise be.[3] Réné Gonnard, the French writer, says that the fact of emigration gives a stimulus to the birth rate, and cites Adam Smith, Malthus, Garnier, Roscher, and De Molinari in support of the view.[4] Robert Hunter also expresses his adherence to this opinion.[5]

With the laws of population in mind we can easily understand how this condition may result — in fact, how it must result theoretically. Every society, in the course of its development, reaches a balance between the means of subsistence and the desire for reproduction. This balance is represented by the standard of living. In a society where the desire for reproduction greatly overbalances the desire for comforts and luxuries, the standard of living will be low, and the rate of increase of population high. In a society where the appetite for material welfare is strong, the opposite conditions will prevail. changing conditions present the possibility of change either in the rate of reproduction or in the standard of living. As we have already observed, the former is the more flexible of the two. Particularly in static societies, such as exist in European countries, where social positions

[1] *American Museum*, 7 : 240. [2] *Political Economy*, Vol. II, 13 : 265.
[3] *Kolonien, Kolonialpolitik, und Auswanderung*, pp. 333 ff.
[4] *Op. cit.*, p. 135. Cf. also Bonar, J., *Malthus and His Work*, p. 144.
[5] *The Commons*, April, 1904.

have become thoroughly stratified, any gradual amelioration in circumstances is much more likely to result in an increased rate of population growth than in an improved standard of living.

Emigration, by *temporarily* relieving congestion to a certain extent, offers a chance of betterment. But in general, if the emigration is moderate, this chance is seized by the reproductive power rather than by the standard of living. The rate of increase of population rises until the drain of emigration is offset, while the standard of living remains unaltered, and the total population continues virtually the same. The very fact of emigration gives a sense of hopefulness to the people, and the knowledge that there is an ever ready outlet for redundant inhabitants causes the population of the country to multiply more rapidly than it otherwise would. This is the result which must reasonably be expected to follow all regular and gradual emigration movements.

On the other hand, while the withdrawal of a more or less uniform number of inhabitants, year by year, has no power to reduce population, and may actually tend to increase it, the opposite result may be achieved where there is such a sudden and extensive removal of people from a country, that those who remain feel a definite and profound lightening of pressure. This must be sufficiently immediate and widespread to produce a sudden and significant rise in wages or fall in prices. In such a case it may occur that, before the forces of population have had time to fill the breach, the people may have become accustomed to a somewhat higher standard of living, which thereafter they may be able and inclined to maintain.

The peculiar sex distribution of modern emigration probably has the effect of increasing the possibility of reducing the population in the countries of source, out of proportion to the actual number of emigrants, just as it lessens the likelihood of increasing population in the country of destination.

Such is the theoretic argument as regards the effect of emigration upon the population of a country. It may be summed up in the words of John Stuart Mill, "When the object is to raise the permanent condition of a people, small means do not merely produce small effects, they produce no effects at all."

There is no lack of authoritative opinions to support this view. In addition to those already cited, the following may be noted. Douglas, Earl of Selkirk, in his pamphlet on "Emigration" dated 1806, expresses his belief that emigration does not reduce population, and cites the Isle of Skye as a case in point. The population of this island in 1772 was about 12,000. Between this date and 1791, 4000 people emigrated, and at least 8000 more moved in a more gradual and less conspicuous way to the Low Country of Scotland. Yet the population more than kept even.[1]

Mr. Whelpley says, "There is no hope of an exhaustion of supply, for the most prolific races are now contributing their millions, and yet increasing the population of their own countries. There is no hope of an improvement in quality, for the best come first and the dregs follow."[2] Professor Mayo-Smith says, "Emigration does not threaten to depopulate the countries of Europe. Had there been no emigration during this century (the nineteenth) it is not probable that the population of

[1] Douglas, *Emigration*, pp. 117–118. [2] *The Problem of the Immigrant*, p. 15.

Europe would have been any greater than it is. The probabilities are all the other way." [1]

Professor Taussig, while not stating this opinion in so many words, appears to adhere to it when he says that without emigration Sweden and Italy would have had — not a larger population — but either a higher death rate or a lower birth rate.[2]

If we seek for a statistical demonstration of the foregoing argument we are confronted with the same impossibility of securing it which has become so familiar in the course of this work. These matters do not adjust themselves with clocklike regularity, but operate over long periods, and are complicated by innumerable other factors. Even though two phenomena are shown to operate harmoniously, it is not always possible to prove which is cause and which effect. The declining birth rate has been a common phenomenon in almost all European countries during the last forty years, and particularly during the last twenty years of the nineteenth century.[3] An opponent of the view we are considering could point to this fact as a contradiction of the claim, while one on the opposite side could assert that the decline would have been equally rapid and perhaps more so without any emigration at all. Neither could prove his case. Even if it could be demonstrated that the countries which experience the largest emigration also manifest the highest rate of increase in population, it might be easily maintained that it was the extreme growth of population that accounted for the large emigration, rather than the reverse. About all that

[1] *Op. cit.*, p. 23.

[2] *Principles of Economics*, Vol. II, p. 217. For a statement of the opposite opinion, see Bourne, S., *Trade, Population, and Food.*

[3] Bailey, *Mod. Soc. Cond.*, 101, and Gonnard, *L'Emig. Eur.*, 120.

can be shown is that a large emigration and a high rate of increase of population may go together. Examples of this state of affairs are numerous.[1]

Of the opposite case, where a sudden and extensive emigration has cut down population, there have been a few historical examples, notably that of Ireland. The population of Ireland diminished from 8,100,000 in 1841 to 6,500,000 in 1851, and 5,700,000 in 1861. Since then it has steadily declined to 4,456,000 in 1901.[2] The fact that the beginning of this decline was coincident with the great exodus to America has made it customary to explain the decreasing population by emigration. But even in this case, it is a question whether it would not be more accurate to assign the decrease in population in Ireland in the middle of the nineteenth century to the famine, rather than to emigration. The famine was the primary fact, and had passed the death sentence upon a large proportion of the people; emigration — to carry out the figure — merely commuted that sentence to exile. It furnished an outlet to thousands who were otherwise doomed to die. It has been claimed that Norway has lost a greater part of her population by emigration to America than any other European country except Ireland.[3]

The obvious effect of the remittances from America is a beneficial one, inasmuch as it increases the purchasing power of those of the peasant class who remain at home. The immigrant in the United States who sends money

[1] In spite of the enormous emigration from Italy, and the almost entire depopulation of certain districts, the population of the country as a whole increased 6.81 per cent during the period from Feb. 10, 1901, to June 10, 1911, without regard to those subjects temporarily residing abroad. Daily Consular and Trade Reports, Jan. 20, 1911, p. 1440.

[2] Gonnard, *op. cit.*, p. 22. [3] Flom, George T., *Norwegian Immigration*, p. 27.

back to Europe is earning in a country where the price level is high and spending in a country where it is low, which is a manifest advantage. Even though his real wages are the same as he might command at home, as long as there is a margin of saving his family benefits financially by the arrangement. But in so far as this money sent home results in an increase of the monetary circulation in the European country, its desirability is more questionable. The Immigration Commission notes an increase in wages in some immigrant-furnishing sections of southern and eastern Europe. If this were accompanied by a corresponding rise in prices, there would of course be no real gain. Something of this sort has actually occurred in Greece. Several forces, among which the remittances from America stand prominent, have within the last few years brought the exchange between paper and gold down nearly to par. The result has been to diminish seriously the purchasing power of the income of the ordinary workingman. For while large payments are made in gold, ordinary purchases are made in paper, so that while both money incomes and prices have remained approximately the same, the workman who gets his gold piece changed finds that he now has only 108 paper drachmas or so to make his purchases with, where ten years ago he had 160 or so.[1]

Even where no such disadvantageous effects can be observed, it is a question whether it is a healthy state of affairs for any nation to be largely supported by money earned in another land, and sent back in a form which gives it the nature of a gift in the eyes of the common people.

As to the effect of the returned immigrant upon his

[1] Fairchild, *Greek Immigration*, p. 71.

native country, opinions again differ. Some observers see a great advantage accruing to European countries from the better habits of life, the more advanced knowledge of agricultural and other industrial methods, and the more independent and self-reliant spirit, which the returned immigrants bring back with them. To them, the returned emigrant appears as a disseminator of new ideas and higher culture, and a constant inspiration to more effective living. There are others in whose opinion the evil influences exerted by the returned immigrant largely outweigh the good. While they build better houses, and wear better clothes, they are idle and egoistical. They take no active interest in the life of those around them, and make no effort to spread among their fellows the advantages of what they have learned in America. Their example arouses feelings of discontent and restlessness among their neighbors, and leads to further emigration, rather than to the betterment of conditions at home. They are misfits in the old environment.

There is undoubtedly much of truth in both of these opinions, and numerous cases might be found to illustrate either. A very helpful idea of the two-sided aspect of this matter may be gained by studying a concrete case, furnished by a single country. For this purpose, excellent material is furnished by the careful study of "The Effect of Emigration upon Italy" made by Mr. Antonio Mangano,[1] who has gone into all the divisions of his subject in an admirable way.

This author finds that emigration, great as it has been, has not decreased the population of Italy, which, on

[1] Mangano, Antonio, "The Effect of Emigration upon Italy," *Charities and the Commons*, Jan. 4, 1908, Feb. 1, 1908, April 4, 1908, May 2, 1908, June 6, 1908.

the contrary, is larger than ever. He does not say that the rate of increase has been as great as it would have been without emigration, nor could this be proved. It is certain that some sections of Italy have been seriously depopulated, though the population of the country as a whole has increased. It is quite possible that emigration from Italy at the present time approaches the sudden and sweeping type sufficiently so that it may actually check the rate of increase of population.

As to the effects of the money sent home, and the returned immigrants, he finds contrary opinions, and facts on both sides of the case. Among the beneficial results of emigration he finds that wages have increased fifty per cent, so that the peasants who remain have benefited by the departure of others. Farm machinery has been introduced, usury has almost disappeared, and the percentage of violent crimes has been reduced. The returned immigrant carries himself better, dresses better, and has a greater spirit of independence, which he communicates to others. There has arisen a growing demand for rudimentary education. Many peasants have been enabled to buy land.

But on the other side there are many evil results to be reckoned with. The ignorant peasant has been cheated in the quality and price of the land he has bought, and after two or three years of unsuccessful effort learns that he cannot make even a living from it, and sells it at a great loss, sometimes to the very landlord from whom he purchased it. The southern provinces are losing their working population, so that the production, which was inadequate before, has become even more insufficient. Carefully cultivated and terraced land is being laid waste through neglect. As a result there has been a notable increase in prices and in the cost of living, which nearly or entirely offsets the higher wages of the peasants, and brings a disproportionately heavy burden on the salaried and clerical classes. Women have been driven to take up hard labor in the fields, to the extent that a physical injury to the rising generation is already observable. As a consequence of the breaking up of families, there has been a tendency toward moral degeneracy, not only on the part of the men who have emigrated, but of the women who are left. Prostitution, illegitimacy, and infanticide have increased. Children are growing up without salutary restraint. Tuberculosis, almost unknown in Italy before emigration, is spreading rapidly. Only a few of the returned emigrants are willing to settle down permanently in the old country, and work for its uplift, and there is no assurance that the money which has been sent to Italy for safe-keeping will be ultimately spent there. Many of the young men who return, bring back vices with them, and serve as a demoralizing example while they remain.[1] From the governmental point of view, there is an alarming deficiency of recruits for the army. Even the new houses, built with American money, are not always an improvement on the old, as no new ideas come in with the remittances.

A comparison of these two categories emphasizes the fact that the favorable effects are, in general, the more obvious and immediate ones. They are the ones which catch the eye of the traveler or the superficial observer. They are the ones which appear to have particularly impressed the Immigration Commission, as evidenced

[1] For a corroboration of these facts, see Borosini, Victor von, "Home-Going Italians," *The Survey*, Sept. 28, 1912.

by their seemingly hasty review of conditions on the other side.[1] It is upon these that Professor Steiner, with his warm fellow-feeling for the immigrant lays special stress. Even Miss Balch gives prominence to this class of effects. The injurious results of such a movement as emigration are likely to be of such a nature as makes them slow of development, and difficult to observe and calculate. Physical and moral degeneracy are slower to appear than high wages and new houses, but at the same time they are more important. Taking everything into account, it seems probable that, for Italy at least, emigration under the present conditions will prove at least as much of a curse as a blessing.

Conditions in Greece resemble in many respects those in Italy, though the depopulation of the country seems even more imminent. Not only has the emigration been very sudden, but it is almost exclusively male, so that there seems a real danger of a serious diminution of population in the kingdom. Although the emigration movement is so recent in Greece that effects can hardly yet be looked for, yet here, as in Italy, the immediate favorable results of better houses, a reduction of the rate of interest, mortgages cleared from the land, higher wages and lower rates of interest are already manifest. The darker side, too, is beginning to show in the assumption of hard labor by the women, the lack of laborers in certain sections, the increase of immorality among the women, and the introduction of a demoralizing example by returned young men. Prices and the cost of living have increased. The returned immigrant, instead of serving as an uplifting example of intelligent industry, is likely so to conduct himself as to add to the

[1] Rept. Imm. Com., Emig. Cond. in Eur., Abs., pp. 10, 11.

already prevalent scorn for hard work, and increase the prevailing unrest and discontent which leads to further emigration.[1]

The general conclusion in regard to the effects of emigration upon European countries, which the facts appear to justify, is that the movement is at least of doubtful benefit to the countries of source.[2] The obvious beneficial results are partially if not wholly offset by certain undesirable consequences, insidious and persistent in their nature, and likely to make themselves more manifest with the passage of years. The attitude of European governments serves as a verification of this conclusion. It is certain that the advantages of emigration do not sufficiently outweigh its drawbacks in the eyes of most of these governments to lead them to regard it otherwise than with disfavor, although none of them now practically forbid it.[3] Nor is that attitude due to the military interest alone.

The question of the effects of immigration upon the immigrants is perhaps the most difficult of all to determine. It is manifest that it must affect all of their life interests, in their own generation and for many generations to come. And particularly, if it is desired to ascertain whether the immigrant gains or loses in the long run by his undertaking, the effort involves the attempt at evaluation of almost every human activity, in order that a balance may be struck between the good and the bad.

[1] Fairchild, H. P., *Greek Immigration*, pp. 220–235, Ch. XI.

[2] Gonnard, while he has little to say of the effects of emigration, other than those on population, in his book on *European Emigration*, nevertheless gives the general impression that these effects are injurious as far as Austria-Hungary is concerned, quoting Count Mailath to that effect (p. 280). The so-called emigration from Russia to Siberia, which Gonnard regards as advantageous, does not fall within the strict definition of emigration adopted in this book.

[3] Rept. Imm. Com., Emig. Cond. in Eur., Abs., p. 10.

On the face of it, it seems that there must be some gain to the immigrants from immigration. It is inconceivable that such a movement should continue year after year unless those directly concerned in it were profiting thereby. It is true, to be sure, that there is a vast deal of misinformation, and false hope, on the part of the immigrants. Those who are interested in their coming strive to paint the future in the brightest possible colors, and to minimize the drawbacks. The example of one or two eminently successful acquaintances is likely to wholly outweigh that of many who only scrape along or fail altogether. Nevertheless, making all allowances, it seems necessary to believe that there is a net margin of advantage in the long run. It is perhaps possible that this advantage may often be more specious than real, and that the immigrant may believe himself the gainer when, if he could balance true values, he would find himself in a more pitiable case than before.

The great gain of the immigrant is to be looked for in the field of wealth, or material prosperity. There can be little doubt that on the average the immigrant is able to earn and save more, not only of money, but of wealth in the broader sense, than he could at home. This is the great underlying motive of modern immigration, and if it were illusory, the movement must soon fail. A comparison of economic conditions in Europe and America, as far as this can be made, seems to bear this out. Both wages and prices are lower, on the whole, in the countries which send us most of our immigrants than they are in the United States. But wages appear to be proportionally lower than prices. The money sent from America is a very real and tangible thing, and represents a great economic advance on the part of a large proportion of the immigrants.

Doubtless, there is also somewhat of gain in independence and freedom for many of the immigrants. The growth of class distinctions in the United States has not yet proceeded so far that the immigrant from Austria-Hungary or Italy does not feel an improvement in his social status. To be sure, the classes of population with which the immigrant establishes this social equality in the United States are not such as to do him the greatest conceivable good, but a sense of heightened self-respect and self-reliance does undoubtedly develop, nevertheless.[1]

Many of the immigrants, of course, forge ahead, either because of unusual ability or exceptional good fortune, and attain a position of advancement in every way which would have been utterly inconceivable in their old home. There are countless instances of prosperous business men, eminent and respected citizens, invaluable servants of society in this country, who could never have been anything but humble peasants in their home land. These shining examples attract much attention here and abroad, and serve as valuable illustrations of what may be accomplished under favorable circumstances.[2]

But for the bulk of the ordinary immigrants the economic and other advantages are offset by terrible hardships and losses. As one thinks of the broken and separated families, often never reunited; of the depressing, and degrading group life of men in this country;

[1] Miss Balch gives a pathetic and significant instance of a Ruthenian woman, returned to her native land, whose highest ideas of American social life were based on her acquaintance with negroes. *Our Slavic Fellow-Citizens*, p. 144.

[2] See the series of articles on foreigners in the United States in *Munsey's Magazine* for 1906.

of religious ideals shattered and new vices acquired in the unwonted and untempered atmosphere of American liberty; of the frequent industrial accidents and unceasing overstrain of the Slavs in mine and factory, upon which they reckon as one of the concomitants of life in America, and which sends them back to Europe in a few years, broken and prematurely aged, but with an accumulation of dollars;[1] of the tuberculosis contracted by Italians in the confined life to which they are unaccustomed, and by Greek boot-blacks in their squalid quarters and their long day's labors;[2] of the sad conditions of labor in the sweatshops and tenement workrooms;[3] of the child-labor in the cranberry bogs of Massachusetts and New Jersey;[4] of the destruction of family life by the taking of boarders, and the heartbreaking toil of the boarding-boss's wife;[5] of the unremitting toil and scant recreation, of the low wages and insufficient standard of living, of the unsparing and niggardly thrift by which the savings are made possible — as one thinks of these things, which are all too common to be considered exceptional, and compares them with the conditions which characterize peasant life in Europe, where many æsthetic and neighborly circumstances tend to offset the poverty, one cannot help wondering how large a proportion of our immigrants finally reap a net gain in the things that are really worth while.

It is useless for any individual to undertake to answer

[1] Balch, E. G., *op. cit.*, pp. 154–155, pp. 300–303; Steiner, E. A., *The Immigrant Tide*, Ch. II.

[2] Mangano, A., *The Survey*, April 4, 1908, p. 23; Rept. Imm. Com., Greek Bootblacks, Abs., pp. 12 ff.

[3] Adams and Sumner, *Labor Problem*, pp. 130–138.

[4] Chute, Charles L., "The Cost of the Cranberry Sauce," *The Survey*, Dec. 2, 1911, and Lovejoy, Owen R., *The Survey*, Jan. 7, 1911.

[5] Page 246.

this question categorically for immigrants in general. The answer rests too much upon personal opinion and estimation of relative values. The point that needs to be emphasized in this connection is that against the evident and unquestioned economic gain of most, and the general social and intellectual gain of many, there must be set off a long list of serious, though not always obvious, evils which result for a large proportion of the immigrants under present conditions.

The question of the desirability of immigration from the point of view of humanity as a whole, as previously stated, is a summation of the aspects of the problem from the point of view of the United States, the countries of source, and the immigrants. This balance must be struck by every student for himself. The effort has been made in the foregoing pages to set forth the facts which condition this great movement at the present time, as a groundwork upon which reasonable conclusions may be based. It has appeared that for the United States there is at present no real need of further immigrants, and that the most that can be said is that they do no harm. On the other hand, it seems likely that the evil effects from the movement as at present conducted — effects to be developed mainly in the future rather than existent at the present time — will overbalance any good that may result. From the point of view of European countries, while the advantages are obvious, it appears that there are also fundamental drawbacks which may in the end more than offset the gain. For the immigrant there is an undoubted net margin of advantage on the average; but this advantage is less general and real than is often supposed, and is qualified by many weighty considerations. In striking this balance it is important to bear in mind the influence of emigration and immigration upon total population. If it is true that immigrants in a large measure are supplanters of native population, rather than additions to population, it then becomes a question whether the immigrants as a body are happier than the native population would have been, which would otherwise have filled their places.

In regard to national prosperity and welfare, moreover, it must ever be remembered that the effects of immigration upon all countries concerned, particularly upon the receiving country, are scarcely more than in the embryo. Such a tremendous movement as this must inevitably have significant and far-reaching results. But only a prophetic vision could state with assurance what those results will be.

One thing, however, seems certain — that the movement is not accomplishing all the good that it might. Many of the foregoing statements in regard to immigration have been qualified by the phrase "as at present conducted." The peculiar circumstances which have given rise to the immigration movement certainly contain possibilities of great advantage to the human race. It ought to be possible so to utilize them as to bring about a great and permanent uplift for the whole of mankind. There is no assurance that our present policy, adopted in its main features at a time when conditions were radically different,[1] guarantees this uplift in its maximum degree. What, then, ought to be done about it? This is the real kernel of the immigration problem for the statesman and the practical sociologist.

One of the great difficulties with which sincere social workers have to contend in almost every field of their

[1] See page 383.

efforts is that practical economics has advanced so much more rapidly than practical sociology. Our knowledge of the technique of production and transportation, and of the industrial arts, has made phenomenal strides in the past century. The growth of cities, the development of the factory system, easy means of communication between all countries, the growth of the world market, advances in agricultural methods which have made the soil much more productive per unit of labor, have coöperated to introduce a new set of social conditions and problems with which we have not yet learned to grapple. Our knowledge of how to produce satisfactory social relations is far behind our knowledge of how to produce wealth. This is strikingly evident in the matter of immigration. If transportation conditions and means of communication had remained as they were at the time of the Revolution, our present immigration situation could never have arisen. There would have been a natural barrier which would have prevented too large increments of European population from entering the new country while it was working out its problems and gradually finding itself. The problems of immigration which presented themselves would have been of sufficiently moderate dimensions so that they could have been dealt with as they arose. As it is, the recent rapid development of communication has made the ease of immigration so great that we have been overwhelmed by the resulting problems. The movement of millions of people from one region to another is a phenomenon of prodigious sociological import. Modern mechanical progress has made this movement possible, before the nations or the individuals concerned have advanced far enough in social science to know how to make the most of it.

Granting that there is an immigration problem, and granting that there is a desire to grapple with it, there are two methods of attack. The first is, to pick out the obvious evils, and apply a specific to them one by one. The other is to endeavor to determine the underlying principles and to devise a consistent and comprehensive plan which will go to the root of the matter, relying upon established sociological laws. The first method is much the simpler. It is the one which has hitherto been followed out in our immigration legislation. One by one certain crying evils have been met by definite measures. After half a century of protest, paupers and criminals were refused admission. A little later contract laborers were debarred. Certain diseased classes, growing more comprehensive with the years, have been excluded. The principle of deportation has been introduced and gradually enlarged. Steamship companies have been made responsible for the return of nonadmissible aliens. The net result of these measures has unquestionably been beneficial. This type of remedy, if wisely administered, is always valuable, and should be adopted, in the absence or delay of the other kind of solution.

Certain other improvements of this general type readily suggest themselves. The steerage should be abolished, and United States inspectors placed on all immigrant-carrying vessels. If possible, better provisions should be adopted for turning back inadmissibles early on their journey. Immigrant banks and lodging-houses should receive stricter supervision. The padrone system and the unrestricted contract labor system should be abolished. Tenement houses should be supervised in the strictest way possible. Every remedial agency designed to better the lot of the alien in this country should be encouraged.

It appears that many of the ills of immigration are due to faulty distribution and the lack of efficient contact between aliens and the better classes of Americans. Consequently, the need of better distribution, and various schemes for securing it, are constantly urged in the press, and in other writings on the subject. Yet we are warned to be on our guard against pinning too much faith to this solution of the problem. There are many evils which distribution alone cannot remedy, and there is competent authority for the statement that much of the agitation for better distribution emanates from interests which profit by a large immigration, and which hope in this way to blind the eyes of the American people to the more deep-seated evils, and to hush the cry for some restrictive measures. Some think, also, that if there ever was a time when any scheme of distribution would have been effective, it is now long since past.[1]

In such ways as the foregoing, great good may be accomplished, and many of the more obvious evils avoided or mitigated. It does not seem possible, however, that in such a manner can the greatest possible good be derived from the immigration movement. This can be achieved only through the operation of some far-reaching, inclusive plan of regulation, based on the broadest and soundest principles, in which all countries concerned will concur. The formulation of such a plan requires the greatest wisdom of which man is capable. It is possible that we have not yet advanced far enough in social science to make the construction of such a plan

[1] Cf. Rept. Com. Gen. of Imm., 1911, pp. 4–7.

feasible. In such a case, it might be the part of wisdom and honor to radically restrict the numbers of immigrants until such a plan can be devised and put into operation. Otherwise, the peculiar situation of the United States among nations may disappear, and the possibilities of gain to the race be lost forever, before the maximum advantage has been secured. One of the strongest arguments for restriction at the present time is that the United States is not yet qualified to accept the responsibility of admitting unlimited numbers of eager seekers for advantages, and giving them in fullest measure those things which they desire, and which their earnest efforts merit.

One thing, meanwhile, must be remembered — the problem will not solve itself. If there are evils connected with immigration, there is no prospect that in the natural course of events they will disappear of themselves. The history of immigration has been a history of successive waves of population, from sources ever lower in the economic, if not in the social, scale. If it has seemed at any time that the country was about to adjust itself to a certain racial admixture, a new and more difficult element has presented itself. And the process will go on. As General Walker pointed out long ago, immigration of the lowest class "will not be permanently stopped so long as any difference of *economic level* exists between our population and that of the most degraded communities abroad."[1] Under present conditions a diminution in the immigration stream should not be interpreted as a cause of congratulation, but rather deep consternation. For, except to the extent that restriction is actually accomplished by our

[1] Quoted by Hall, P. F., *Immigration*, p. 128.

laws, a cessation of the stream of immigration to the United States can only mean that economic conditions in this country have fallen to so low a pitch that it is no longer worth while for the citizens of the meanest and most backward foreign country to make the moderate effort to get here.

BIBLIOGRAPHY

NOTE. A bibliography on Immigration might be extended almost indefinitely. Nearly every book written on any social question, particularly in America, contains material on immigration. The magazine articles on the subject are legion. By no means all the works which may profitably be consulted, nor all those cited in the foregoing pages, are included in the following list.

GENERAL AND MISCELLANEOUS

Books

ADDAMS, JANE: Newer Ideals of Peace, 1907; Twenty Years at Hull-House, 1910.

ANDERSON, W. L.: The Country Town, 1906.

BLODGET, SAMUEL: Economics: A Statistical Manual for the United States of America, 1806.

BRANDENBURG, BROUGHTON: Imported Americans, 1904.

BROMWELL, WILLIAM J.: History of Immigration into the United States, 1856.

BUSHEE, F. A.: Ethnic Factors in the Population of Boston, American Economic Association, 3d Series, 4: 2, 1903.

BYINGTON, MARGARET F.: Homestead: The Households of a Mill Town, 1910.

CHICKERING, JESSE: Immigration into the United States, 1848.

COMMONS, JOHN R.: Races and Immigrants in America, 1908.

DONALDSON, THOMAS: The Public Domain, 1881.

EDWARDS, RICHARD H.: Immigration, 1909.

ELLWOOD, CHARLES A.: Sociology and Modern Social Problems, 1910.

ENDICOTT, WILLIAM C., JR.: Immigration Laws, State and National, in Commercial Relations of the United States, 1885–1886. Appendix III, 1887.

EVANS-GORDON, W.: The Alien Immigrant, 1903.

GONNARD, RÉNÉ: L'Émigration européenne au XIX Siècle, 1906.

GROSE, HOWARD B.: Aliens or Americans? 1906.

HALL, PRESCOTT F.: Immigration, 1906.

HENDERSON, C. R.: An Introduction to the Study of the Dependent, Defective, and Delinquent Classes, 1893.

HUNTER, ROBERT: Poverty, 1904.

Immigration Commission: Report, Authorized, 1907.

JENKS, JEREMIAH, and LAUCK, W. JETT: The Immigration Problem, 1911.

KAPP, FRIEDRICH: Immigration and the Commissioners of Emigration of the State of New York, 1870.

KENNGOTT, GEORGE F.: The Record of a City, 1912.

LINCOLN, JONATHAN T.: The City of the Dinner Pail, 1909.

MACLEAN, ANNIE M.: Wage-Earning Women, 1910.

MARTINEAU, HARRIET: Society in America, 1837.

MAYO-SMITH, RICHMOND: Emigration and Immigration, 1890.

New York Bureau of Industries and Immigration: First Annual Report, 1911.

New York Commission of Immigration: Report, 1909.

VON RAUMER, F. L.: America and the American People, 1846.

RAUSCHENBUSCH, WALTER: Christianity and the Social Crisis, 1910.

RIIS, JACOB: How the Other Half Lives, 1890; The Making of an American, 1901.

ROBERTS, PETER: Anthracite Coal Communities, 1904; The New Immigration, 1912.

ROSCHER, WILHELM, and JANNASCH, ROBERT: Kolonien, Kolonial politik, und Auswanderung, 1885.

SEYBERT, ADAM: Statistical Annals of the United States, 1789-1818, 1818.

SPILLER, G.: Interracial Problems, 1911.

STEINER, EDWARD A.: On the Trail of the Immigrant, 1906; The Immigrant Tide, 1909.

STELZLE, CHARLES: The Working Man and Social Problems, 1903.

SUMNER, WILLIAM G.: Folkways, 1907; War and Other Essays, 1911.

TAUSSIG, F. W.: Principles of Economics, 1911.

TROLLOPE, MRS. T. A.: Domestic Manners of the Americans, 1832.

United States Bureau of the Census: Census Reports; A Century of Population Growth, 1909.

United States Bureau of Immigration and Naturalization: Commissioner General of Immigration, Annual Reports; Immigration Laws (Pamphlets).

United States Bureau of Statistics: Immigration into the United States from 1820 to 1903, 1903; Special Report on Immigration, by Young, Edward, 1871.

United States Congress: Documents, Reports, etc.

United States Library of Congress: A List of Books (with references to periodicals) on Immigration, 1907.

WALKER, F. A.: Discussions in Economics and Statistics, 1899.

WATSON, JOHN F.: Annals of Philadelphia, 1830.

WHELPLEY, JAMES D.: The Problem of the Immigrant, 1905.

WILKINS, WILLIAM H.: The Alien Invasion, 1892.

WOODS, ROBERT A., and others: Americans in Process, 1902; The City Wilderness, 1898.

Magazine Articles, etc.

AINSWORTH, F. H.: Are We Shouldering Europe's Burden? Charities, 12: 134, 1904.

American Museum: 1: 13; 2: 213; 5: 109; 7: 87, 233, 240; 8: 124; 10: 114, 221; 12: 112; 13: 196, 263, 268, 1787–98.

BARROWS, W.: Immigration; Its Evils and their Remedies. New Englander, 13: 262, 1855.

BRANDENBURG, BROUGHTON: The Tragedy of the Rejected Immigrant, Outlook, 84: 361, 1906.

Chambers' Journal: Warning to Emigrants, 50: 644, 1873.

CHAMBERS, W.: Emigrant Entrappers, Chambers' Journal, 23: 141, 1855.

COMMONS, JOHN R.: Social and Industrial Problems of Immigration, Chautauquan, 39: 13, 1904.

De Bow's Review: Sources from which Great Empires Come, 18: 698, 1855.

DEVINE, EDWARD T.: The Selection of Immigrants, The Survey, Feb. 4, 1911.

EVERETT, A. H.: Immigration to the United States, North American Review, 40: 457, 1835.

GOLDENWEISER, E. A.: Immigrants in Cities, The Survey, Jan. 7, 1911.

HALL, PRESCOTT F.: The Future of American Ideals, North American Review, 195: 94, 1912.

HART, A. B.: The Disposition of Our Public Lands, Quarterly Journal of Economics, 1: 169, 251, 1887.

HAZARD, SAMUEL: Register of Pennsylvania, 1: 25; 6: 266; 8: 31, 27, 33, 54, 88, 108, 116; 11: 361, 416; 15: 157, 1828–35.

LEE, JOSEPH: Conservation of Yankees, The Survey, Oct. 28, 1911.

Monthly Anthology: Letter from a French Emigrant, 6: 383, 1809.

Niles' Register: 11: 359; 13: 35, 378; 17: 38, 63,; 20: 193; 22: 155, 310; 23: 305; 24: 113, 411; 25: 232; 34: 411; 40: 74, 130, 273; 41: 356; 43: 40, 391; 44: 131, 233; 45: 2; 46: 1, 218, 244, 398; 49: 62, 69; 52: 250, 1816–38.

North American Review: Review of von Fürstenwärther, M., Der Deutsche in Nord-Amerika, 11: 1, 1820; Figures of Immigration, 1812–21, 15: 301, 304, 1822; Review of Schmidt and Gall on America, 17: 91, 1823; Quotations from Hodgson's Remarks on America, 18: 222, 1824.

RIPLEY, William Z.: Races in the United States, Atlantic Monthly, 102: 745, 1908.

ROSSITER, W. S.: A Common-Sense View of the Immigration Problem, North American Review, 188: 360, 1908.

SATO, S.: History of the Land Question in the United States, Johns Hopkins Studies, 4: 259, 1886.

SHALER, N. S.: European Peasants as Immigrants, Atlantic Monthly, 71: 646, 1893.

TOBENKIN, ELIAS: Immigrant Girl in Chicago, The Survey, Nov. 6, 1909.

WILLIS, H. PARKER: Review of Findings of the Immigration Commission, The Survey, Jan. 7, 1911.

GENERAL MIGRATION

Books

BRADLEY, HENRY: The Story of the Goths, 1888.

HODGKIN, THOMAS: Theodoric the Goth, 1891.

JORDANES: The Origin and Deeds of the Goths, English version by Mierow, Charles C., 1908.

KELLER, ALBERT G.: Colonization, 1908.

Leroy-Beaulieu, Paul: De la Colonisation chez les Peuples Modernes, 1908.
Merivale, Herman: Lectures on Colonization, 1861.
von Pflugk-Harttung, Julius: The Great Migrations, translated by Wright, John Henry, 1905.

Magazine Articles, etc.

Bryce, James: Migrations of the Races of Men Considered Historically, Contemporary Review, 62: 128, 1892.
Mason, Otis T.: Migration and the Food Quest, American Anthropologist, 7: 275, 1894.

COLONIAL PERIOD

Books

Archives of Maryland.
Armstrong, Edward: Correspondence between William Penn and James Logan and Others, 1870–72.
Bittinger, Lucy F.: The Germans in Colonial Times, 1901.
Cobb, S. H.: The Story of the Palatines, 1897.
Dexter, F. B.: Estimates of Population in the American Colonies, 1887.
Diffenderffer, F. R.: The German Immigration into Pennsylvania through the Port of Philadelphia, 1700–75, 1900.
Documents relating to the Colonial History of New York.
Fiske, John: Old Virginia and Her Neighbors, 1897.
Geiser, K. F.: Redemptioners and Indentured Servants in the Colony and Commonwealth of Pennsylvania, 1901.
Massachusetts Election Sermons, 1754.
Mittelberger, Gottlieb: Journey to Pennsylvania in 1750, translated by Eben, C. T., 1898.
New Jersey Archives.
North Carolina Colonial Documents.
Pennsylvania Colonial Records.
Proper, E. E.: Colonial Immigration Laws, Columbia College Studies, 12: 2, 1900.
Rhode Island Colonial Records.

RACIAL STUDIES

Books

ANTIN, MARY: The Promised Land, 1912.
BALCH, EMILY G.: Our Slavic Fellow-Citizens, 1910.
BENJAMIN, G. G.: The Germans in Texas, 1909.
BERNHEIMER, CHARLES S.: The Russian Jew in the United States, 1905.
CARO, L.: Auswanderung und Auswanderungspolitik in Österreich, 1909.
COOLIDGE, MARY R.: Chinese Immigration, 1909.
FAIRCHILD, H. P.: Greek Immigration to the United States, 1911.
FAUST, A. B.: The German Element in the United States, 1909.
FLOM, GEORGE T.: Norwegian Immigration into the United States, 1909.
GREEN, S. S.: The Scotch-Irish in America, 1895.
HALE, E. E.: Letters on Irish Immigration, 1852.
HANNA, CHARLES A.: The Scotch-Irish, 1902.
KING, BOLTON, and OKEY, THOMAS: Italy To-day, 1901.
LORD, ELIOT, TRENOR, J. D., and BARROWS, S. J.: The Italian in America, 1905.
MACLEAN, J. P.: Settlements of Scotch Highlanders in America, 1900.
MAGUIRE, J. F.: The Irish in America, 1868.
NELSON, O. N.: History of Scandinavians and Successful Scandinavians in the United States, 1900.
PETERS, MADISON C.: The Jews in America, 1905.
RUBINOW, I. M.: Economic Condition of the Jews in Russia, United States Bureau of Labor, Bulletin No. 72, 1907.
SEWARD, GEORGE F.: Chinese Immigration, 1881.
SPARKS, E. E.: The Chinese Question, in National Development, 1877–85, p. 229, 1907.

Magazine Articles, etc.

ABBOTT, GRACE: The Bulgarians of Chicago, Charities, 21: 653, 1909.
BODIO, L.: Dell' Emigrazione Italiana,Nuova Antologia, 183: 529, 1902.

EVERETT, E.: German Immigration to the United States, North American Review, 11: 1, 1820.

HOUGHTON, LOUISE S.: Syrians in the United States, The Survey, July 1, Aug. 5, Sept. 2, Oct. 7, 1911; The above criticised, The Survey, Oct. 28, 1911.

MANGANO, ANTONIO: The Effect of Emigration Upon Italy, Charities and the Commons, Jan. 4, Feb. 1, April 4, May 2, June 6, 1908.

MILLIS, H. A.: East Indian Immigration to British Columbia and the Pacific Coast States, American Economic Review, 1: 72, 1911.

North American Review: The Irish in America, 52: 191, 1841.

RUBINOW, I. M.: The Jews in Russia, Yale Review, 15: 147, 1906.

INDUSTRIAL RELATIONS

Books

ADAMS, T. S., and SUMNER, H. L.: Labor Problems, 1905.

DEWEES, F. P.: The Molly Maguires, 1877.

HOURWICH, ISAAC A.: Immigration and Labor, 1912.

STEWART, ETHELBERT: Influence of Trade Unions on Immigrants, In LaFollette, R. M., The Making of America, Vol. 8, p. 226, 1906.

WARNE, F. J.: The Slav Invasion and the Mine Workers, 1904.

Magazine Articles, etc.

All the Year Round: Molly Maguire in America, New Series, 17: 270, 1876.

BAILEY, W. B.: The Bird of Passage, American Journal of Sociology, 18: 391, 1912.

CANCE, ALEXANDER E.: Immigrant Rural Communities, The Survey, Jan. 7, 1911; Jewish Immigrants as Tobacco Growers and Dairymen, The Survey, Nov. 4, 1911; Piedmontese on the Mississippi, The Survey, Sept. 2, 1911; Slav Farmers on the "Abandoned-Farm" Area of Connecticut, The Survey, Oct. 7, 1911.

CHUTE, CHARLES L.: The Cost of the Cranberry Sauce, The Survey, Dec. 2, 1911.

DARLINGTON, THOMAS: Medico-Economic Aspect of the Immigration Problem, North American Review, 183: 1262, 1906.

HOLCOMBE, A. N.: Minimum Wage Boards, The Survey, April 1, 1911.

KELLOGG, PAUL U.: An Immigrant Labor Tariff, The Survey, Jan. 7, 1911; The above criticised, The Survey, Feb. 4, 1911.

LAUCK, W. JETT: Industrial Communities, The Survey, Jan. 1, 1911.

LOVEJOY, OWEN R.: Cost of the Cranberry Sauce, The Survey, Jan. 1, 1911.

Political Science Quarterly: Levasseur's American Workman, 13: 321, 1898.

RHODES, J. F.: The Molly Maguires in the Anthracite Region of Pennsylvania, American Historical Review, 15: 547, 1910.

RIPLEY, WILLIAM Z.: Race Factors in Labor Unions, Atlantic Monthly, 93: 299, 1904.

ROBERTS, PETER: The Foreigner and His Savings, Charities, 21: 757, 1909.

SPEARE, CHARLES F.: What America Pays Europe for Immigrant Labor, North American Review, 187: 106, 1908.

POLITICAL RELATIONS

Books

FRANKLIN, FRANK G.: The Legislative History of Naturalization in the United States, 1906.

United States Bureau of Immigration and Naturalization: Naturalization Laws, 1911.

Magazine Articles, etc.

MCMASTER, J. B.: The Riotous Career of the Know-Nothings, Forum, 17: 524, 1894.

RELIGIOUS RELATIONS

Books

United States Bureau of the Census: Religious Bodies, 1906.

Magazine Articles, etc.

COUDERT, FREDERIC R.: The American Protective Association, Forum, 17: 513, 1894.

GLADDEN, W.: The Anti-Catholic Crusade, Century, 25: 789, 1894.

WHITE, GAYLORD S.: The Protestant Church and the Immigrant, The Survey, Sept. 25, 1909.

WINSTON, E. M.: The Threatening Conflict with Romanism, Forum, 17:425, 1894.

SOCIAL RELATIONS

Books

ARONOVICI, CAROL: Some Nativity and Race Factors in Rhode Island, 1910.

BINGHAM, T. A.: The Girl that Disappears, 1911.

BONAR, J.: Malthus and His Work, 1885.

BOURNE, S.: Trade, Population, and Food, 1880.

United States Bureau of the Census; Insane and Feeble-Minded in Hospitals and Institutions, 1906; Paupers in Almshouses, 1904; Prisoners and Juvenile Delinquents in Institutions, 1907.

WHITE, ARNOLD: The Destitute Alien in Great Britain, 1892.

Magazine Articles, etc.

BINGHAM, T. A.: Foreign Criminals in New York, North American Review, 188:383, 1908.

BUSHEE, F. A.: The Declining Birth Rate and Its Cause, Popular Science Monthly, 63:355, 1903.

CLAGHORN, K. H.: Immigration and Dependence, Charities, 12:151, 1904; Immigration in its Relation to Pauperism, Annals American Academy of Political Science, 24:187, 1904.

COMMONS, JOHN R.: City Life, Crime, and Poverty, Chautauquan, 38:118, 1903.

DAVENPORT, CHARLES B.: The Origin and Control of Mental Defectiveness, Popular Science Monthly, 80:87, 1912.

DUNRAVEN, EARL OF: The Invasion of Destitute Aliens, Nineteenth Century, 31:985, 1892.

FAIRCHILD, H. P.: Distribution of Immigrants, Yale Review, 16:296, 1907.

FISHER, S. G.: Alien Degradation of American Character, Forum, 14:608, 1893; Has Immigration Increased the Population? Popular Science Monthly, 48:244, 1895.

HART, H. H.: Immigration and Crime, American Journal of Sociology, 2:369, 1896.

HUNTER, ROBERT: Immigration the Annihilator of our Native Stock, The Commons, 9: 114, 1904.

Monthly Chronicle: Pauperism in Massachusetts, 3: 564, 1842.

PATTEN, S. N.: A New Statement of the Law of Population, Political Science Quarterly, 10: 44, 1895.

ROSS, E. A.: Western Civilization and the Birth Rate, American Journal of Sociology, 12: 607, 1907.

ROSSITER, W. S.: The Diminishing Increase of Population, Atlantic Monthly, 102: 212, 1908.

ROUND, WILLIAM M. F.: Immigration and Crime, Forum, 8: 428, 1889.

TUKE, J. W.: State Aid to Immigrants, Nineteenth Century, 17: 280, 1885.

WHITE, ARNOLD: The Invasion of Pauper Foreigners, Nineteenth Century, 23: 414, 1888.

WILLCOX, W. F.: The Distribution of Immigrants in the United States, Quarterly Journal of Economics, 20: 523, 1906.

STANDARD OF LIVING

Books

CHAPIN, ROBERT C.: The Standard of Living Among Workingmen's Families in New York City, 1909.

STREIGHTOFF, FRANK H.: The Standard of Living Among the Industrial People of America, 1911.

Magazine Articles, etc.

ALMY, FREDERIC: The Huddled Poles of Buffalo, The Survey, Feb. 4, 1911.

BRECKENRIDGE, SOPHONISBA, and ABBOTT, EDITH: Housing Conditions in Chicago, American Journal of Sociology, 16: 289, 433; 17: 1, 145, 1910–11.

CHAPIN, ROBERT C.: Living Costs: A World Problem, The Survey, Feb. 3, 1912.

HUNT, MILTON B.: The Housing of Nonfamily Groups of Men in Chicago, American Journal of Sociology, 16: 145, 1910.

MARK, MARY L.: The Upper East Side: A Study in Living Conditions and Migration, American Statistical Association, 10: 345, 1907.

THOMPSON, CARL D.: Socialists and Slums, Milwaukee, The Survey, Dec. 3, 1910.

WARD, ROBERT DE C.: Congestion and Immigration, The Survey, Sept. 9, 1911.

SHIPPING CONDITIONS

Magazine Articles, etc.

All the Year Round: Aboard an Emigrant Ship, 7: 111, 1862.

Chambers' Journal: Emigrant Ship *Washington*, 16: 27, 1851; Trip in an Emigrant Ship, etc., 1: 228, 262, 302, 1844.

Living Age: Scenes in Emigrant Ships, 26: 492, 1850.

United States Senate Reports: Sickness and Mortality on Board Emigrant Ships, 33d Congress, 1st Session, Committee Report No. 386, 1853–54.

INDEX

www.ingramcontent.com/pod-product-compliance
Lightning Source LLC
LaVergne TN
LVHW010527100826
845148LV00001B/114

9781425573553